José M uñoz

D1565855

The Complete Correspondence
1928–1940

THEODOR W. ADORNO AND
WALTER BENJAMIN

The Complete
Correspondence
1928–1940

Edited by Henri Lonitz
Translated by Nicholas Walker

Harvard University Press

Cambridge, Massachusetts

Second printing, 2000

Library of Congress Cataloging-in-Publication Data
Adorno, Theodor W., 1903–1969.
[Correspondence. English. Selections]
The complete correspondence, 1928–1940 / Theodor W. Adorno and
Walter Benjamin.
p. cm.
Includes bibliographical references and index.
ISBN 0-674-15427-4 (c1 : alk. paper)
1. Adorno, Theodor W., 1903–1969—Correspondence. 2. Benjamin,
Walter, 1892–1940—Correspondence. 3. Philosophers, Modern—
Germany—Correspondence. 4. Authors, German—20th century—
Correspondence. I. Lonitz, Henri. II. Benjamin, Walter, 1892–1940.
Correspondence. English. Selections. III. Title.
B3199.A34A4213   1999
193—dc21
[B]   99-10988

Contents

Abbreviations

~∞~

Principal works referred to in the annotations of the main text and repeated in the Textual Notes and Source References at the end of the book are abbreviated as follows:

GS [1–20]: Theodor W. Adorno, *Gesammelte Schriften*, edited by Rolf Tiedemann with the assistance of Gretel Adorno, Susan Buck-Morss and Klaus Schultz. 20 volumes. Frankfurt a.M. 1970–86.

GS [I–VII]: Walter Benjamin, *Gesammelte Schriften*, edited by Rolf Tiedemann and Hermann Schweppenhäuser with the assistance of Theodor W. Adorno and Gershom Scholem. 7 volumes. Frankfurt a.M. 1972–89.

Adorno, *Über Walter Benjamin*: Theodor W. Adorno, *Über Walter Benjamin. Aufsätze. Artikel. Briefe*, annotated by Rolf Tiedemann (revised and expanded edition). Frankfurt a.M. 1990.

Briefwechsel Adorno/Krenek: Theodor W. Adorno and Ernst Krenek, *Briefwechsel*, edited by Wolfgang Rogge. Frankfurt a.M. 1974.

Briefwechsel Adorno/Sohn-Rethel: Theodor W. Adorno and Alfred Sohn-Rethel, *Briefwechsel 1936–1969*, edited by Christoph Gödde. München 1991 (Dialektische Studien).

Briefe: Walter Benjamin, *Briefe*, edited and annotated by Gershom Scholem and Theodor W. Adorno. 2 volumes. 2nd. ed. Frankfurt a.M. 1978.

Briefwechsel Scholem: Walter Benjamin–Gerhsom Scholem, *Briefwechsel 1933–1940*, edited by Gershom Scholem. Frankfurt a.M. 1980.

Benjamin-Katalog: *Walter Benjamin 1892–1940*. Eine Ausstellung des Theodor W. Adorno Archivs Frankfurt a.M. in Verbindung mit dem Deutschen Literaturarchiv Marbach am Neckar. Bearbeitet von Rolf Tiedemann, Christoph Gödde und Henri Lonitz. Marbacher Magazin Nr. 55.3. Marbach a.N. 1991.

The Correspondence
1928–1940

Dear Herr Wiesengrund,
    Your cordial lines[1] have encouraged me in the pleasant anticipa-
tion of receiving your 'Schubert' manuscript.[2] For that is surely what
you allude to. I can only hope that in the meantime you have brought
the piece to a successful conclusion. Might I request in advance your
permission to communicate the manuscript to Bloch[3] as well? It would
be a great advantage for me if I could read the text with him.
    You showed so much friendliness and support for my friend Alfred
Cohn[4] that time in Berlin that I feel I really have to inform you about
how matters have turned out, or more unfortunately and more precisely, about the liquidation of the business in which he is employed
and the consequent loss of his position there. None of this is as yet
official – the liquidation of the business is still a commercial secret.
But by October his situation will certainly have become extremely
difficult, unless his friends are able to intervene on his behalf. In this
connection I must and shall now do my best: but that can only succeed if I speak to you again concerning my friend. Naturally I understand that the suggested Berlin arrangement is impossible. Do you
not feel there may now be certain possibilities for him in Frankfurt?
    I know I have said enough for you to express your friendship and
influence once again, if you think there is any prospect of success in
the matter.
    Here I am, commencing with a request, and then it strikes me that
I may seem to have forgotten my intention of inviting Fräulein Karplus[5]
to drop in on me. But this is not a case of forgetfulness on my part. It
is simply that during the last few weeks I have felt so preoccupied
with various tasks and predicaments, which have all become dreadfully
entangled with one another,[6] that I have not had the opportunity to
approach her.
    As soon as things are better here, very shortly I hope, you will hear
from me through her.
    With warmest regards for the present,
                                        Yours,
                                            Walter Benjamin
2 July 1928
Berlin-Grunewald
Delbrückstr. 23

1 *Your cordial lines*: Adorno and Benjamin had first got to know each other
in Frankfurt in 1923 and had subsequently met up once again in Frankfurt,
and possibly – in September 1925 – in Naples, to continue their discussions.

However, the correspondence between them apparently only began to lead to greater intimacy and communication in the summer of 1928, after Adorno had spent some weeks in Berlin in February of that year – The letters Adorno wrote to Benjamin prior to 1933 were left behind in Benjamin's last apartment in Berlin when he was finally forced to leave Germany in March 1933 and have all disappeared.

2 *your 'Schubert' manuscript:* cf. Adorno, 'Schubert', in *Die Musik* 21, Issue 1 (October 1928), pp. 1–12; now in GS 17, pp. 18–33. – No manuscript of the essay has survived.

3 *your permission to communicate the manuscript to Bloch:* Ernst Bloch, whom Benjamin had known since 1919, had been shown a draft and sketches for the Schubert piece by Adorno and had strongly encouraged the author to complete the essay. (cf. *Briefwechsel Adorno/Krenek*, p. 70.)

4 *my friend Alfred Cohn:* for Alfred Cohn (1892–1954), a very close school friend of Benjamin, cf. *Briefe*, p. 866. – Since the beginning of 1928 Benjamin had been attempting to help Cohn, a businessman by profession, to find a new position: 'He [sc. Benjamin] is also pursuing his aim of getting one of his friends employed in the same business as Gretel [Karplus], and it seems to be working out.' (Unpublished letter from Adorno to Siegfried Kracauer of 28.2.1928.) The attempts which Adorno made in Frankfurt and Gretel in Berlin – *the suggested Berlin arrangement* – came to nothing in the end.

5 *my intention of inviting Fräulein Karplus:* Margarete Karplus (1902–1993), later Adorno's wife, had got to know Benjamin at the beginning of 1928.

6 *various tasks and predicaments . . . dreadfully entangled with one another:* Benjamin is probably referring here to the resumption of work on the 'Goethe' article for the *Great Soviet Encyclopaedia* (cf. GS II [2], pp. 705–39.) – The heart attack suffered by Benjamin's mother in July also contributed substantially to the increasing difficulties of Benjamin's personal situation, largely determined by the conflict between his planned journey to Palestine (cf. Gershom Scholem, *Walter Benjamin – die Geschichte einer Freundschaft*, 2nd ed. (Frankfurt a.M. 1976), pp. 185–90) and his renewed intimacy with Asja Lacis (cf. ibid., p. 187).

2 BENJAMIN TO WIESENGRUND-ADORNO
   BERLIN, 1.9.1928

Dear Herr Wiesengrund,
   It would prove truly difficult to find an excuse for my long silence. Therefore please take these few lines as a word of explanation. But first I must properly thank you for your manuscript.[1]
   As it happened, I was with Bloch when it arrived and he was so impatient to take the material home with him that, *contre cœur*, I let

4

him have it. And then, owing to circumstances which suddenly took him away from Berlin, he was unable to find an opportunity to study it or, unfortunately, to return it to me.

And that is why it is only in the last few days that I have managed to reclaim it. But since I should not like to compound this misfortune with another, namely that of reading your 'Schubert' all too hastily, I have decided simply to let you know in brief that you may expect a substantive response in a week, together with what I hope will be a rather less formal thank you.

But to deal with the whole humiliating business all at once: the editorial board of 'The Literary World' had responded immediately and enthusiastically to my suggestion that they should approach you for the planned contribution to the journal's George issue.[2] They assured me that they would be in contact with you directly. I was foolish enough to believe the whole matter was settled, without reckoning with the infinite incompetence of such organizations. In this regard too I must tender my apologies.

Anticipating more fortunate auspices for the future,
and with cordial regards for now,
Yours,
Walter Benjamin

1 September 1928
Berlin-Grunewald
Delbrückstr. 23

Many thanks for everything you have done for my friend.[3] Since the matter is still in progress I shall come back to it if the opportunity arises.

1 *your manuscript*: the manuscript of the 'Schubert' essay and the series of aphorisms 'Motive III' (cf. *Musikblätter des Anbruchs* 10, issue 7 (August/September 1928), pp. 237–40; now in GS 16, pp. 263–5 and GS 18, pp. 15–18. The version which Benjamin probably had before him was entitled 'Neue Aphorismen'.

2 *the editorial board of 'The Literary World'* . . . *contribution to the journal's George issue*: on the occasion of Stefan George's 60th birthday the weekly journal 'Die literarische Welt', edited by Willi Haas for the Rowohlt publishing house, had commissioned a survey, the results of which were published in the issue of 13.7.1928. Benjamin had obviously attempted to get Adorno accepted as one of the respondents to whom the survey was directed. – On the George issue and Benjamin's contribution to it, cf. GS II [2], pp. 622–4 and GS II [3], pp. 1429f.

3 *everything you have done for my friend*: nothing further is known about the steps taken by Adorno to assist Alfred Cohn.

Dear Herr Wiesengrund,
Please forgive me for disturbing you, but I was careless enough to forget the name of one of the authors you mentioned[1] amongst those who had written about Kraus. I think I was even somewhat amazed by the name when you mentioned it. I remember Liegler,[2] Haecker,[3] Viertel[4] – but there was also another one. If I am not mistaken, you referred to him as a student of Kraus.

Would you be so kind as to let me know by postcard as soon as possible?
With sincere thanks!

Yours,
Walter Benjamin

29 March 1930
Berlin W
Friedrich Wilhelm Str. 15[III]

1 *one of the authors you mentioned*: apart from the authors mentioned in the letter, Benjamin also cites works by Robert Scheu and Otto Stoessel in his 'Kraus' essay (cf. GS II [1], pp. 334–67), on which he was working around this time; whether one of these two was the author whose name Benjamin had forgotten – and if so, which one – can no longer be determined.

2 *Liegler*: Leopold Liegler (1882–1949), Secretary of the Austrian Academy of Sciences, was also secretary to Karl Kraus until 1924; Benjamin is quoting from the book *Karl Kraus und sein Werk* (Vienna 1920).

3 *Theodor Haecker*: Haecker (1879–1945) was a principal contributor to the journal 'Brenner'; there is a passage about Kraus in his book *Kierkegaard und die Philosophie der Innerlichkeit* (Munich 1913). – In his letter Benjamin had spelt the author's name as Hecker, presumably confusing it with that of the famous philologist Max Hecker.

4 *Berthold Viertel*: Kraus had published poems by Berthold Viertel (1885– 1953), poet, writer, dramatist and director, in the journal 'Fackel'; Viertel's book *Karl Kraus. Ein Charakter und seine Zeit* had been published in Dresden in 1921.

Dear Herr Wiesengrund,
My mother passed away a few days ago,[1] which is why I have delayed in writing. I regret that I shall have to be briefer than I would

have wished. Your letter touched upon so much that is important to me that I would dearly like to respond in detail, but I have so much urgent work to do.[2] Your thoughts upon the subject I proposed for Frankfurt[3] correspond closely to my own reservations. I am therefore particularly happy to adopt your formulation: 'On the Philosophy of Literary Criticism'. I am writing about it to Horkheimer[4] in the next few days. But it would be very nice if you could communicate this new formulation to him right away, and suggest further in the same connection that, in view of the recent bereavement I have mentioned, I would be particularly grateful if my address could be postponed to some time after Christmas – like the middle of January perhaps.

You should be very pleased to learn that your gently insistent remarks about 'The Old Curiosity Shop'[5] have finally defeated my external inhibitions on the subject, and that I have been absorbed in the book for some days now; awareness of the way in which you have already read it makes me feel as though someone with a lamp were guiding me along these dark passageways. I have seen the most astonishing veins of silver light up before me.

How much I would like to communicate my thoughts to you in something written of my own, since the resounding echo of the extended and extremely stimulating conversations I am currently enjoying – in my meetings with Brecht[6] – has yet to reach you. I was rather relying on the *Frankfurter Zeitung* – I am thinking especially of my Kästner article[7] here – but things are proving extremely difficult with them. It is obvious that they are busy considering every option.

I have read Korsch's *Marxism and Philosophy*.[8] Rather faltering steps – so it seems to me – in the right direction.

Please let me know the fate of your own work[9] as soon as possible. I will also ask Fräulein Karplus about this when Brecht next comes to visit.

With cordial regards,

Yours,

Walter Benjamin

10 November 1930
Berlin-Wilmersdorf
Prinzregentenstrasse 66

1 *My mother passed away a few days ago*: Benjamin's mother had died on 2 November 1930.

2 *so much urgent work to do*: in connection with the journal 'Krisis und Kritik', which Benjamin planned to edit in collaboration with Brecht and Herbert Ihering and publish with Rowohlt Verlag; Benjamin's 'Memorandum' for the journal contains a list of prospective contributors, including Adorno; cf. GS VI, pp. 619–21.

3 *the subject I proposed for Frankfurt*: the projected lecture for the Institute of Social Research, which Benjamin was probably invited to give by Max Horkheimer, Director of the Institute since October 1930, seems never to have materialized.

4 *I am writing about it to Horkheimer*: no letter from Benjamin to Horkheimer at this period seems to have survived.

5 *'The Old Curiosity Shop'*: the novel by Charles Dickens; cf. the German translation: Charles Dickens, *Ausgewählte Romane und Novellen. Zweiter Band: Der Raritätenladen. Unter Benutzung älterer Übertragungen neu gestaltet von Leo Feld,* (Leipzig, undated); sometime towards the end of September 1930 Adorno had read the novel 'with enormous emotion' and described it as 'a book of the very first rank – full of mysteries compared with which the Blochian kind reveal themselves as the toilet stench of eternity which they are' (unpublished letter from Adorno to Kracauer of 27.9.1930). – Towards the end of the year Adorno composed 'A Discussion concerning The Old Curiosity Shop of Charles Dickens' which was first broadcast on Frankfurt radio and subsequently appeared in the *Frankfurter Zeitung* on 18.4.1931. (cf. GS 11, pp. 515–22).

6 *in my meetings with Brecht*: in connection with the project for the new journal mentioned above; Benjamin had got to know Brecht in May 1929.

7 *my Kästner article*: cf. Erich Kästner, *Ein Mann gibt Auskunft* (Stuttgart, Berlin 1930); Benjamin's review, entitled 'Linke Melancholie. Zu Erich Kästners neuem Gedichtbuch', was rejected by the *Frankfurter Zeitung* and appeared in 'Die Gesellschaft' 8, vol. 1 (1931), pp. 181–4; now in GS III, pp. 279–83.

8 *Korsch's Marxism and Philosophy*: cf. Karl Korsch, *Marxismus und Philosophie* (Leipzig 1930).

9 *the fate of your own work*: Adorno had just submitted his work 'The Construction of the Aesthetic in Kierkegaard's Philosophy' under Paul Tillich as his *Habilitationsschrift* (Post-Doctoral Dissertation), which was formally accepted in February 1931.

5   BENJAMIN TO WIESENGRUND-ADORNO
    BERLIN, 17.7.1931

Dear Herr Wiesengrund,

Now that my initial Berlin arrangements[1] have been settled, *tant bien que mal*, I am in a position to respond. A prior condition was my having read your inaugural lecture[2] in its entirety and having studied it in detail. I have spoken also to Ernst Bloch about it and he also gave me your letter[3] to read. To come directly to my own view: there is no doubt that the piece as a whole succeeds in its aim, that in its very concision it presents an extremely penetrating articulation of the most essential ideas which we share, and that it possesses every quality 'pour faire date', as Apollinaire put it. I think Bloch is right to claim that the connection between materialism and the ideas in question seems forced in places, but this is fully justified by the spiritual climate and can probably be defended wherever it is a question not simply of 'applying' Marxism like a coat of fresh paint, but rather of working with it, and that means, for all of us, struggling with it. He seems to have a stronger point in his remarks about your critique of the Vienna Circle.[4] I believe I understand the appropriate diplomatic considerations you have brought to your formulation in this respect. It is almost impossible to discern clearly how far one can go in this direction. But there is no question about your critique of the development taken by phenomenology;[5] what you claim about the role of death in Heidegger is decisive. What strikes me as particularly congenial generally is not so much the diplomatic attitude itself as the extremely subtle and persistent manner in which your address combines this attitude with such, so to speak, authoritative claims, in short the masterly fashion in which at certain places you avoid the traditional polemics so beloved of philosophical 'Schools'.

And now a word concerning the question Bloch raised about the possible mention or otherwise of my name. Without the slightest offence on my side – and hopefully without causing the slightest offence on yours – and after close study of the piece, the very importance of which seems in part to justify such otherwise undignified questions concerning original authorship, I must now take back the remarks I made in Frankfurt.[6] The sentence which decisively articulates the positions you have taken up over against the philosophy of the 'Schools' runs as follows:

'The task of systematic enquiry[7] [Wissenschaft] is not to explore the concealed or manifest intentional structures of reality, but to interpret the intentionless character of reality, insofar as, by constructing figures and images out of the isolated elements of reality, it extracts the questions which it is the further task of enquiry to formulate in the most pregnant fashion possible'.

I can subscribe to this proposition. Yet I could not have written it without thereby referring to the introduction of my book on Baroque Drama,[8] where this entirely unique and, in the relative and modest sense in which such a thing can be claimed, new idea was first expressed. For my part I would have been unable to omit some reference to the book at this point. I do not need to add that if I were in your position this would be even more the case.

I hope you will also perceive from this the great sympathy which I feel for this, as it seems to me, extraordinarily important lecture, as

9

well as the desire to maintain our philosophical friendship in the same alert and pristine form as before.

Perhaps I may express the wish that you would discuss the matter with me, if the lecture should be published and you did want to mention my name in it as you suggested.

I read your 'Words without Songs'[9] with the greatest pleasure, and most especially with regard to the fourth and the resounding conclusion of the final two pieces.

Many thanks for the tobacco pouch.[10]

As always, cordially yours,

Walter Benjamin

17 July 1931
Berlin-Wilmersdorf
Prinzregentenstr. 66

PS Dear Herr Wiesengrund,

Schoen[11] is here again and asking all kinds of things of me with which only you can help. Would you be so kind as to respond to his two, rather urgent, questions? Could you 'please send' the following to his address, Eschersheimer Landstrasse 33:

1) The melody and the text of your favourite setting of 'To the gate the beggar flees'.[12]
2) The melody of 'At the mountain there I stood'.[13]

Many thanks,
WB

1 *my initial Berlin arrangements*: i.e. after Benjamin's return from the south of France.

2 *your inaugural lecture*: Adorno presented his academic inaugural lecture under the title 'The Actuality of Philosophy' on 2 May 1931; the manuscript is dated 7 May (first published in GS 1, pp. 325–44). – Benjamin, Kracauer and Bloch had all received typescript copies of the piece.

3 *your letter*: Adorno's letter to Kracauer of 8 June gives some idea of Bloch's criticisms as outlined in his letter to Adorno (now lost) and addressed in Adorno's letter in response (also lost): 'Dear Friedel, and in great haste: yesterday I received a rather substantial letter from Bloch concerning my inaugural lecture, and which I have also answered in some detail. Since the drift of his letter very much coincides with your own (the introduction of materialism; I assume that shared discussions lie behind all this), the answer I gave him is also effectively my answer to you. I have already asked him to show you the letter, and would ask you to read it as soon as possible since I believe I have defended fairly carefully the things which you attacked. Above

10

all, why the transition to materialism is made in the way it is, and not from the perspective of the 'totality'. The whole question is addressed less tactically than perhaps you imagine. What is essentially at issue is an attempt to attain a new approach to materialism, one which I believe is pointing in the right direction, although I am fully aware of the problems attached to the project. – The question about the essay must be put into its concrete context. It is a response to the objections raised against the Kierkegaard book by [Max] Wertheimer and [Kurt] Riezler and which I have literally reproduced in the essay. It must also be understood in the light of a quite specific situation. It goes without saying that I would not wish arbitrarily to reduce philosophy to the essay form. I simply believe that the essay genre harbours a principle which could be very fruitfully exploited with regard to philosophy at large.

I would be delighted if you could take up the discussion as I have elaborated it in my letter to Bloch. – In so far as your objections concern university *tactics*, then I am more than ready to agree with you. On the other hand, the theme demanded of me did not really permit me to produce anything very different from the lecture as it was. I am not entirely clear about what it was that so upset people about it. Everyone expressed a different opinion. Mannheim's was the most foolish of all: he thought that I had defected to the Vienna positivists!!!!' (Unpublished letter from Adorno to Siegfried Kracauer of 8.6.1931)

4 *your critique of the Vienna Circle*: cf. GS 1, pp. 331f.

5 *your critique of the development taken by phenomenology*: cf. ibid., pp. 327–31; the passage concerning *the role of death in Heidegger* is found on p. 330.

6 *the remarks I made in Frankfurt*: the remarks in question, which Benjamin probably made during a meeting with Adorno at the end of June or the beginning of July at Frankfurt station on the way back from Paris to Berlin, and which he now wished *to take back*, may have concerned the question whether his name and 'The Origin of German Tragic Drama' should be expressly mentioned and cited as sources. On his first reading of the lecture, or parts of it, in Frankfurt he still seems to have thought not. As Benjamin's letter suggests, a close reading of the text and the influence of Bloch caused him to think differently about the issue.

7 *'The task of systematic enquiry'*: cf. GS 1, p. 335; in the inaugural lecture Adorno actually says 'the task of philosophy'; otherwise Benjamin reproduces the original correctly.

8 *the introduction of my book on Baroque Drama*: cf. Benjamin, *Ursprung des deutschen Trauerspiels* [The Origin of German Tragic Drama] (Berlin 1928); now in GS I [1], pp. 203–430; for the 'Erkenntniskritische Vorrede' [Epistemo-critical Preface], cf. ibid., pp. 207–37.

9 *your 'Words without Songs'*: cf. Adorno, 'Worte ohne Lieder', in the *Frankfurter Zeitung*, 14.7.1931; now in GS 20 (2), pp. 537–43.

10 *the tobacco pouch*: probably a present from Adorno to Benjamin on his birthday on 15 July.

11 *Schoen*: Ernst Schoen (1894–1960), musician and writer, was one of Benjamin's closest friends since his school days, and from May 1929 was employed as director of artistic programmes with South-West German Radio in Frankfurt; in 1933 he emigrated to London (cf. *Benjamin-Katalog*, pp. 77–81).

12 *'To the gate the beggar flees'*: on the significance of this verse from Wilhelm Taubert's 'Wiegenlied' [Lullaby] for Adorno, cf. Adorno, *Minima Moralia*, nr. 128 (GS 4, p. 227); see also letters 94, 96 and 105 below.

13 *'At the mountain there I stood'*: it has not proved possible to identify the song in question.

6 BENJAMIN TO WIESENGRUND-ADORNO
[BERLIN,] 25.7.1931

Dear Herr Wiesengrund,
   Thank you for your last letter.
   I think we can now see land at last. It is my sincere, even urgent wish that your piece[1] should appear. How could I possibly be a hindrance to the programmatic announcement of a view which I so strongly share myself.
   I hope you will be quite happy if I express a preference for a dedication over a motto.[2] We can surely postpone mutual discussion about your precise formulation until the time comes for publication. On the other hand I have already started looking around for the quotations and discover that you can choose between pages 21 and 33;[3] perhaps the second one is the more significant.
   I would send you a new copy of the book immediately, were it not for the fact that with the collapse of Rowohlt[4] I have been unable to lay my hands on any copies for the moment.
   You should now pursue the question of finding a publisher[5] even more intensively. What do you think of Cohen in Bonn?
   And do you ever write to Grab? If you do, please tell him that I have responded to his request,[6] but that because of many similar undertakings to send off my writings the warehouse is short of copies and it is no easy matter to get hold of them now. But I shall not forget about it.
   Since I have now touched upon the subject of my own affairs, I have to report the monstrous circumstance that – because of some printing error – in my essay[7] for the last issue of 'The Literary World' a cancelled part of the manuscript actually appeared as the conclusion.

The essay now ends with the word 'fair'. A correction will appear in the next issue.

And now the only thing I still have to tell you is that I harbour no resentment whatsoever, or anything remotely like that which you may have feared, and that in a personal and substantive sense matters have been perfectly clarified by your last letter.

With the most cordial greetings,

Yours,

Walter Benjamin

25 July 1931

1 *your piece*: Benjamin is referring to the Inaugural Lecture 'The Actuality of Philosophy' mentioned in his previous letter.

2 *dedication . . . motto*: The typescripts amongst Adorno's literary remains contain neither a dedication to Benjamin nor a motto by him.

3 *quotations . . . you can choose between pages 21 and 33*: cf. GS I, p. 335.

4 *the collapse of Rowohlt*: as the result of a financial crisis the publisher Ullstein acquired two-thirds of the share in Rowohlt publishing company.

5 *the question of finding a publisher*: Adorno's inaugural lecture was not in fact published during his lifetime.

6 *Grab . . . his request*: since the mid 1920s Adorno had been on friendly terms with Hermann Grab (1903–49), born in Prague, who originally graduated in philosophy and jurisprudence, spent a short time in chambers, and then pursued a career as a writer and musician. Grab also got to know Benjamin through Adorno. – Grab had attempted to make contact with the Prague Germanist and Baroque specialist Herbert Cysarz, who later became a Nazi sympathizer, in order to help Benjamin to obtain a university teaching post. To this end Grab had obviously asked Benjamin, in a letter which has not survived, to send him some of his publications, which Grab was clearly intending to pass on to Cysarz, as an undated and unpublished letter from Grab to Adorno written in April or the beginning of May reveals: 'First of all I must report the following in haste: I have just come from Cysarz, to whom I have spoken in enthusiastic terms concerning Benjamin; I found him very interested and reliable, and realized once again that, of all the people with an academic position, he is probably the only one whom one can really seriously consider in this connection. Benjamin's approach will initially have to reckon with a superabundance of prospective lecturers in the field of German studies, but they are all so second-rate (in Cysarz's eyes as well) that competition for academic advancement from that quarter should not be too much of a problem. I simply wanted to mention this fact, but do not ascribe that much importance to it. Without wishing to raise too much 'hope', I can honestly say that success is certainly a possibility. Cysarz is *not* acquainted with Benjamin's literary-historical writings and will obviously have to express an opinion after consulting them. I would ask you to ensure that

13

Benjamin sends the following to *my* address: 'The Origin of German Tragic Drama', his work on Goethe's 'Elective Affinities', and any of his other publications which he considers important. Cysarz particularly asked . . . to see *reviews* (not reviews *of* Benjamin's work but reviews by Benjamin on the works of other authors). Cysarz will not be able to read the material before the second half of July, but would like them to be sent as soon as possible. The essay on Kraus need not be included since I have rather illegitimately kept a copy of Dr Benjamin's and will pass this on to Cysarz with his permission. That is everything which I have to relate at the moment, but it would be wonderful if things turn out successfully. The strictest discretion must be maintained concerning the fact that I have instigated the business.' Grab's intervention proved unsuccessful; cf. also letter 8.

7 *my essay*: cf. Benjamin, 'Ich packe meine Bibliothek aus. Eine Rede über das Sammeln' ['Unpacking my library'], in 'Die Literarische Welt', 17.7.1931 (year 7, nr. 29), pp. 3–5, and ibid., 24.7.1931 (year 7, nr. 30), pp. 7f (now in GS IV [1], pp. 388–96); for the cancelled conclusion, cf. GS IV [2], pp. 997f.

7   BENJAMIN TO WIESENGRUND-ADORNO
    BERLIN, 31.3.1932

Dear Herr Wiesengrund,
   It is a real delight to read how you weave your invitation to me[1] with the description of the country and climate down there where you are, and I feel somewhat embarrassed to see our shared hopes of reliving in intensified form those former wonderful days in Königstein[2] gradually evaporating. But the reason is just that I cannot for the simplest of reasons[3] manage to get away as yet. This might prove possible by the beginning of May – but by then time might well be very short for both of you. My route[4] may therefore turn out to be rather more meandering than it would have been in different circumstances. I have asked after some brochures according to which one can make the fourteen-day sea trip via Holland and Portugal in a relatively human fashion for 160 Marks – albeit in third class, naturally. Accordingly, I shall most likely depart Hamburg for the Balearic Islands on 9 April. Whether all this works out or not, you will soon receive information about my whereabouts in any case. Hopefully I shall still be able to contact you on the Côte d'Azur. All friendly and affectionate regards to you and Gretel,
                                        Yours,
                                        Walter Benjamin
31 March 1932
Berlin-Wilmersdorf
Prinzregentenstr. 6

1 *your invitation to me*: Adorno had obviously sent a postcard from Ort le Trayas, located between St Raphäel and Cannes, inviting Benjamin to visit him and Gretel Karplus, with whom Adorno had been staying there for ten days since around the middle of March.

2 *those former wonderful days in Königstein*: in order to work undisturbed, Adorno frequently stayed in Königstein im Taunus or in nearby Kronberg, where Benjamin occasionally visited him between 1928 and 1930. Benjamin is probably referring here to the days in September or October 1929 when he read out passages from the early drafts of the Arcades project to Adorno and Horkheimer (cf. GS V [2], p. 1082).

3 *for the simplest of reasons*: in order to earn some money, Benjamin had compiled a 'Bibliographie raisonnée' of literature on Goethe for the literary section of the *Frankfurter Zeitung* – 'A Hundred Years of Literature on Goethe' – which appeared anonymously in the edition of 20.3.1932 (now in GS III, pp. 326–40).

4 *My route*: Benjamin actually sailed from Hamburg to Barcelona on the merchant steamer 'Catania' on 7 April, not 9 April as suggested in his letter, and then crossed over to Ibiza.

8   BENJAMIN TO WIESENGRUND-ADORNO
    POVEROMO[1] (MARINA DI MASSA), 3.9.1932

Dear Herr Wiesengrund,

I have had to wait such a long time for your letter that it has proved a great pleasure for me now it has arrived. Especially because of how closely certain passages in it coincide with the design of the properly culminating and conclusive final section of 'The Natural History of the Theatre'.[2] I must sincerely thank you for your dedication. The entire sequence arises from a highly original and truly baroque perspective on the stage and its world. Indeed, I would even like to claim that it contains something like a series of 'Prolegomena to any Future History of the Baroque Stage', and I am particularly gratified to see how you have illuminated these subterranean thematic connections through the dedication.[3] It is hardly necessary for me to say that this piece has turned out to be a complete success. There are, however, also some very fine things in the 'Foyer' section,[4] such as the image of the two clock faces[5] and the extremely perceptive remarks about fasting[6] during the interval. I hope to be able to consult your essay for the Horkheimer Archive[7] very soon – and, if I might be allowed to express a further variation on this wish, along with the essay I hope to receive the first issue of the Archive, in which I am naturally extremely interested. We have a good deal of time for

15

reading here. I have already worked my way through the small library[8] which I brought with me when I left five months ago. You will be interested to learn that once again it includes four volumes of Proust which I frequently peruse. But now to a new book which came into my hands here and which I would like to draw to your attention – Rowohlt has published a history of Bolshevism[9] by Arthur Rosenberg, which I have just finished reading. It seems to me a book that cannot under any circumstances be ignored. For my own part, at least, I have to say that it has really opened my eyes to many things, including those areas in which political destiny bears upon individual destiny. Various circumstances, along with your own recent references to Cysarz, give me cause to think about the latter. I would be quite interested in establishing some contact with him. But I still do not understand why he hasn't taken any steps to approach me himself, either directly or by letter from Grab, if he is interested in the same thing. I have no doubt that, in a comparable situation, I would do so in his place. Otherwise, it is naturally not for reasons of prestige that I hesitate, but because I am well aware that mistakes made at the beginning of such a relationship tend to be magnified proportionately in what follows. I imagine that Cysarz's influence, for example, would be sufficient to procure me an invitation to lecture from an appropriate body or institute in Prague. You might be able to inform Grab about this if an opportunity arises. In the meantime, however, I must express my sincere gratitude for the invitation which you append[10] to the report on the meetings of your seminar. I know there is no need to assure you either of how pleased I would be to attend or of the great value which I attach to the opportunity of consulting the documents of the proceedings so far.[11] It would, of course, be highly desirable if we could do this together. At the moment, however – and this touches upon my chances of getting to Frankfurt – I am even less than ever master of my own decisions. I know neither when I shall be able to return to Berlin nor how things will work out there. I shall almost certainly be here for the next few weeks. After that I shall probably have to return to Berlin, partly to deal with the problem of accommodation,[12] partly because Rowohlt seems to be insisting on publishing my essays[13] after all. In itself, however, the temptation to remain in Germany for any length of time is certainly not very great. There will be difficulties everywhere and those arising in the field of broadcasting[14] will probably ensure that my appearances in Frankfurt are even rarer. If you happen to know how things are going for Schoen, please let me know. I have heard nothing from him. That is all for today. The only other thing I wanted to mention is that I am now working on a series of sketches[15]

16

concerning memories of my early life. I hope I shall be able to show some of them to you very soon.

With the most cordial greetings,

Yours,

Walter Benjamin

3 September 1932
Poveromo (Marina di Massa)
Villa Irene

PS To my great delight I have discovered your piece on 'Distortion'.[16] – The remark by Wolfskehl cited in my review[17] goes like this: 'Should we not say of the spiritualists that they are fishing in the *Beyond*?'

1 *Poveromo*: following an invitation from Wilhelm Speyer (1887–1952), Benjamin had left Ibiza in the middle of July and travelled to Italy via Marseilles and Nice. He advised Speyer while the latter was working on his play *Ein Hut, ein Mantel, ein Handschuh* [A Hat, A Coat, A Glove], and was to receive 10 per cent of the theatre takings for his assistance; cf. *Benjamin-Katalog*, p. 178. – His principal literary concern at this time however was *A Berlin Childhood Around 1900*.

2 *the design ... conclusive final section of 'The Natural History of the Theatre'*: cf. Adorno, 'Naturgeschichte des Theaters', in 'Blätter des Hessischen Landestheaters Darmstadt' 1931/32, nr. 9, pp. 101–8 and nr. 13, pp. 153–6; Adorno had sent Benjamin a typescript of the section 'Cupola as Culmination' which was never published (now in GS 16, pp. 319f); for the entire text see GS 16, pp. 309–20.

3 *the dedication*: the typescript with the dedication of the final part has not survived; cf. Adorno's note on the first publication of this letter: 'The unpublished final part was dedicated to Benjamin in the manuscript' (*Briefe*, p. 559).

4 *the 'Foyer' section*: the penultimate section of 'The Natural History of the Theatre'; cf. GS 16, pp. 317–19.

5 *the image of the two clock faces*: cf. ibid., p. 317.

6 *perceptive remarks about fasting*: cf. ibid., p. 318.

7 *your essay for the Horkheimer Archive*: Benjamin is referring to 'The Journal for Social Research', the first issue of which appeared in 1932. – The first issue (actually a double issue) contained the first part of Adorno's essay 'On the Social Situation of Music' and the third issue contained the second part. For the complete essay, cf. GS 18, pp. 729–77.

8 *the small library*: cf. Benjamin's 'List of Writings Read' in which he entered all the books he had read while he was in Poveromo between August and November (GS VII [1], pp. 465f.

9 *a history of Bolshevism*: a book by Arthur Rosenberg (1889–1943) which appeared in 1932 under the title: *Geschichte des Bolschewismus von Marx bis zur Gegenwart*.

10 *an invitation to lecture ... the invitation which you append*: such an invitation to Benjamin to deliver a lecture in Prague never materialized; for his part Adorno had obviously invited Benjamin to visit him in connection with his two-semester seminar on recent contributions to aesthetics, in the course of which Benjamin's book on Baroque Drama in particular was discussed.

11 *documents of the proceedings so far*: Benjamin is referring to the as yet unpublished protocol reports of Adorno's seminar.

12 *Berlin ... the problem of accommodation*: cf. *Briefwechsel Scholem*, p. 30.

13 *my essays*: since 1928 Benjamin had been planning a volume of his own 'Collected Essays on Literature' to be published by Rowohlt (cf. *Briefwechsel Scholem*, p. 23); the contract drawn up in 1930 in this connection names the already published essays on Gottfried Keller, Johann Peter Hebel, Karl Kraus, Julien Green, Marcel Proust, on Surrealism, together with 'The Task of the Translator', and mentions pieces still to be written on André Gide, Franz Hessel, Robert Walser, 'The Novelist and the Writer', 'On Art Nouveau' and 'The Task of the Critic'.

14 *difficulties ... arising in the field of broadcasting*: Benjamin's financial position in these years had been alleviated by radio lectures on literary subjects that he was invited to present by Ernst Schoen and which Benjamin composed between 1929 and 1932 for South-West German Radio in Frankfurt; as a result of the increasing political pressure exerted on the radio broadcasts, first by von Papen's government and subsequently by the Nazi authorities, it was no longer possible for Schoen to facilitate similar broadcast opportunities for Benjamin. (cf. GS II [3], p. 1505).

15 *a series of sketches*: i.e. A Berlin Childhood Around 1900; for the genesis, gestation and publishing history of the piece, cf. GS IV [2], pp. 964–70 and GS VI, pp. 797–9.

16 *your piece on 'Distortion'*: cf. Adorno, 'Zerrbild' [Distortion], in the *Frankfurter Zeitung*, 31.8.1932 (year 76, nr. 648/649); now in GS 20 [2], pp. 565f.

17 *The remark by Wolfskehl cited in my review*: Benjamin had written a review of Hans Liebstoekel's book *Die Geheimwissenschaft im Lichte unserer Zeit* [Secret Knowledge in the Light of the Present Age] (Zürich, Leipzig, Wien 1932), which appeared in the literary section of the *Frankfurter Zeitung* on 21.8.1932 under the title 'Erleuchtung durch Dunkelmänner' [Illumination at the hands of Obscurantists]; the text was distorted because of a misprint and read 'im Trüben' [in the dark] instead of 'im Drüben' [in the beyond]. The review is now in GS III, pp. 356–60.

18

Dear Herr Wiesengrund,
I hear that you are back from Berlin.
I am now on the way there myself, and since this time I shall probably only be able to spend a very short time in Frankfurt, I would really like to arrange a proper rendezvous with you here and now.
I shall be arriving on Sunday midday, at around one o'clock. I shall probably be staying with Schoen. For me that Sunday evening would be an ideal time to meet. Perhaps you will be able to manage this. Any further details could best be arranged with Schoen.
Shall I already be able to see the galley proofs of the Kierkegaard book?
This time I am also extraordinarily keen to see Horkheimer. And indeed for a quite particular reason. If the Institute ever can and will give some support to my work, now is certainly the time to do so, since it is currently being sabotaged[1] on all sides. (You understand what I mean; and you will also understand if I ask you here and now to deal with my arrival in the most confidential manner.)
I should like to make some relevant proposals to Horkheimer concerning a major essay for the Archive, very much comparable to your own.[2] Please inform him urgently of the necessity for a discussion in this regard.
I am bringing with me a new manuscript[3] – a tiny book in fact – which will amaze you.
Cordially as ever,

Yours,

Walter Benjamin

10 November 1932

[Benjamin's letter of Thursday, 10.11.1932, carries no indication of where it was written; since the precise date of Benjamin's departure from Poveromo is unknown, and he writes in the letter that he is already *on the way* to Berlin himself and expects to arrive in Frankfurt on Sunday, 13 November, it seems likely that the letter was written after he had left Poveromo. Because of shortage of money, Benjamin was obliged to make the return trip to Germany in Speyer's car with Speyer at the wheel.]

1 *some support to my work . . . since it is currently being sabotaged*: Benjamin was complaining at this time that the radio as well as the newspapers were closed off to him. – He seems to have agreed with Horkheimer to produce the essay 'Zum gegenwärtigen gesellschaftlichen Standort des französischen

Schriftstellers' [On the Present Social Situation of the Writer in France]; cf. the 'Journal of Social Research' 3, Issue 1 (1934), pp. 54–77; now in GS II (2), pp. 776–803.

2 *a major essay . . . very much comparable to your own*: see the preceding note; Benjamin was thinking of Adorno's essay 'On the Social Situation of Music' mentioned in the previous letter.

3 *a new manuscript*: i.e. *A Berlin Childhood Around 1900*, first mentioned in letter 8. – Adorno related the impression made upon him by Benjamin's readings of the piece in a letter to Kracauer: 'Benjamin has been here. He read me a large part of his new piece, *A Berlin Childhood Around 1900*. I think it is wonderful and entirely original; it even marks a great advance over *One-Way Street* in so far as all archaic mythology is thoroughly liquidated here and the mythical is sought only in what is most contemporary – in the 'modern' in each case. I am convinced that it will also make a great impression on you.' (Unpublished letter from Adorno to Kracauer of 21.11.1932.)

10   BENJAMIN TO WIESENGRUND-ADORNO
     BERLIN, 1.12.1932

Dear Herr Wiesengrund,
     I am interrupting my reading of the Kierkegaard book[1] for a moment simply in order at last to give you some (still provisional) idea of the impression which this extremely interesting and most significant piece of work is making upon me. It is truly, as I would say, a reading *in* Kierkegaard. I do not yet feel competent to speak at this stage about the overall argument and structure of the text. And the conclusion is still missing. I am expecting decisive clarification from the completed copy-text. Merely possessing the proofs produces an enormous temptation to immerse oneself in the loose pages, a temptation which is truly rewarded. Whether I turn to your presentation of the baroque motif in Kierkegaard, to the ground-breaking analysis of the 'intérieure', to the marvellous quotations which you supply from the philosopher's technical treasure trove of allegories, to the exposition of Kierkegaard's economic circumstances, to the interpretation of inwardness as citadel or of spiritualism as the ultimate defining limit of spiritism – I am constantly struck in all of this by the wealth of insight, as well as by the penetrating character of your evaluation. Not since reading Breton's latest verse[2] (in the 'Union libre') have I felt myself so drawn into my own domain as I have through your exploration of that land of inwardness from whose bourn your hero never returned. Thus it is true that there is still

20

something like a shared work after all; that there are still sentences which allow one individual to stand in for and represent another. Moreover, although I cannot know this for sure, I presume that your book owes an enormous amount to the total re-working to which you subjected it even when you originally felt it was complete. Such a readiness harbours a mysterious prerequisite for success, something which is well worth pondering upon.

That is enough for today. But I should also just like to add that amongst your shorter works there are few which I value as greatly as the piece on 'The Tales of Hoffmann'.[3] Bloch, too, with whom I spoke yesterday, is also particularly fond of it. The second part of your sociological critique of music[4] is the very next thing I shall be looking at.

Every free minute I have is dedicated to my 'Berlin Childhood'. How far I shall be successful in adding more new pieces to the old[5] I do not really know. But I have done some serious re-working on some of the sketches. It was very gratifying to see how G K[6] responded to some of the material which I read out to her. This meeting with her provided me with an opportunity to discover that she enjoys very friendly relations with the 'Parca'.[7] Certain difficulties with the authorities here over accommodation[8] might make it advisable for me to get in touch with some local artists' association or other on account of my studio. Thus this has to remain a rather confidential matter and it would have to involve an appropriate position for me. Would you be able to gain me any access to such an association? – Have you heard anything from Prague?

With cordial regards,

Yours,

Walter Benjamin

1 December 1932
Berlin-Wilmersdorf
Prinzregentenstr. 66

1 *my reading of the Kierkegaard book*: at this time Benjamin was busy reading the greater part of the proofs for Adorno's study of Kierkegaard. Between September and November Adorno completely re-worked the text which appeared under the title *Kierkegaard. The Construction of the Aesthetic* in January 1933 with the publishers J. C. B. Mohr (Siebeck) in Tübingen; now in GS 2, pp. 7–203.

2 *Breton's latest verse*: the publication *Union libre*, which appeared anonymously in Paris in 1931.

3 *'The Tales of Hoffmann'*: cf. Adorno, 'The Tales of Hoffmann and Offenbach's Motifs', in 'Theaterwelt. Programmschrift der städtischen Bühnen Düsseldorf', 8, issue 2 (1932/33), pp. 17–20; now in GS 17, pp. 42–6.

4 *the second part of your sociological critique of music*: Benjamin is referring to the second part of Adorno's essay 'On the Social Situation of Music';
see the relevant note to letter 8.

5 *'Berlin Childhood'* ... *adding more new pieces to the old*: cf. the editor's
note in GS IV [2], p. 965.

6 *G K*: i.e. Gretel Karplus.

7 *the 'Parca'*: identity unknown.

8 *Certain difficulties with the authorities here over accommodation*: on
7 August Benjamin had already written to Scholem from Poveromo: 'The
authorities want me to move out of my Berlin apartment, something which
on the one hand fits in absolutely perfectly with my difficult financial circumstances, and on the other hand fits in with my disinclination to keep on
pursuing the hopeless struggle for any opening with either the radio or the
press here in Berlin.' (*Briefwechsel Scholem*, p. 25.)

11   BENJAMIN TO WIESENGRUND-ADORNO
     BERLIN, 14.1.1933

Dr. Walter Benjamin   Berlin-Wilmersdorf,
                                                 Prinzregentenstr. 66
                                                 14 January 1933.

Dear Herr Wiesengrund,
    I just wish to inform you in brief that I have succeeded in getting
the 'Vossische Zeitung' to allow me to review your Kierkegaard book.[1]
    This has been no simple matter, for I have never published any
reviews with them before. But since for the time being I do not have
anything to do for 'The Literary World', and I will certainly get to
review it for them anyway (for if I do not mention the book there, it
won't get reviewed at all), I thought it far more important to take up
the task which might well otherwise fall to some incompetent. I have
agreed to the condition of restricting myself to two-and-a-half typed
pages: they have actually never given more than this to any reviewer.
    Unfortunately I was unlucky enough to give the manuscript proofs
you sent me to my friend Gustav Glück,[2] who has now gone off on
holiday. Since the newspaper has not yet sent me the book, could I
ask you to supply me with a copy as soon as possible. I should like to
undertake the task without further delay.
    Thus we shall soon strike with united forces and mutually rejoice
in the fact.
    With the most cordial regards,
                                    Yours,
                                        Walter Benjamin

1 *to review your Kierkegaard book*: Benjamin's review (shortened by one paragraph – cf. *Briefe*, p. 581) appeared under the title 'Kierkegaard. The End of Philosophical Idealism' in the *Vossische Zeitung*, Literarische Umschau (Beilage) on 2.4.1933 (nr. 14); now in GS III, pp. 380–3.

2 *Gustav Glück*: Gustav Glück (1902–1973) from Vienna was employed until 1938 as the Director of the External Division of the bank *Reichskreditgesellschaft* in Berlin; he emigrated to Argentina in 1938, became a member of the board of the the the *Dresdner Bank* in Frankfurt a.M., and spent his remaining years once again in Vienna. Benjamin had got to know Gustav Glück in 1930.

12 BENJAMIN TO WIESENGRUND-ADORNO
    PARIS, 29.1.1934

Dear Herr Wiesengrund,
    There are certain circumstances which only add weight to the difficulties and dangers attendant upon any long period of separation. This is exactly what has happened with regard to 'The Treasure of Indian Joe'.[1] In the relationship in which we have stood to one another for some years, it has been a rare thing for a major piece by one of us to reach the other simply and directly in its final form. On reading the piece I have occasionally wished that we could have discussed the project in detail with one another earlier. A rather selfish wish, perhaps; but how it would have relieved me in my present predicament, had it been fulfilled. You would soon have realized that this range of material itself – quite apart from the musical question about which I cannot venture any opinion whatsoever – appears to me to be an unpromising one. I am not even sure whether or not you mentioned it to me, at least by title. But if so, this Mark Twain simply remained a title and nothing more to me. But we have had no real contact during the period in which the plan progressed, and the circumstances which occasioned this fact[2] perhaps led you to withdraw even further into your work. However that may be – my protracted silence will certainly have alerted you to the unusual difficulties which have obstructed the expression of my reaction in this case. If I have nonetheless decided to express it now, you will also recognize here – inasmuch as you weigh *that* rather than *how* I do so – an untarnished image of our relationship. I should have much preferred to have congratulated you in detail upon your sketch of children in 'Four-Handed Once Again'[3] – the most recent thing of yours which I have read. This piece is closer to me than the atmosphere in which your opera has surrounded childhood. I believe I can imagine what you were attempting here. And unless my suspicion is quite wrong, it

23

is difficult to see, after Cocteau, how such a thing could properly succeed. For in his 'Enfants terribles'[4] everything unfolds *more dangerously*. And it is indeed this danger which constitutes the measure for working out what you seem to me – in the very highest sense – to have been intending. You can be sure that I have not overlooked certain very fine things in the piece. Especially the cave scenes, for example. But it is essentially the reduction to the idyllic, as expressed both by the songs and the course of the action itself, which is incompatible, in my opinion, with the substantive issues with which you are here concerned. For in fact, childhood could only be invoked so immediately with the spilling of sacrificial blood. And in Cocteau that flows freely enough. But in your case the straightforward, rustic tone of the dialogue only impedes this.

Without seeing in these lines any other claim than that contained in my *most personal* judgement, I would ask you to recognize in them the same solidarity which for my part I shall soon express in my *public* judgement on your Kierkegaard book.

With the most heartfelt regards,

Yours,

Walter Benjamin

29 January 1934
Paris VI
1 Rue Du Four
Palace Hotel

1 *'The Treasure of Indian Joe'*: cf. Adorno, *Der Schatz des Indianer-Joe. Singspiel nach Mark Twain*, edited with an afterword by Rolf Tiedemann (Frankfurt a.M. 1979). – Adorno wrote the libretto between November 1932 and August 1933. Of the music for his planned opera, Adorno only completed 'Two Orchestral Songs' (cf. Adorno, *The Musical Compositions*, ed. Heinz-Klaus Metzger and Rainer Riehn, vol. 2: The Chamber Music, Choral Music and Orchestrations (Munich 1984), pp. 63–72. – Adorno had already sent the manuscript of the libretto to Benjamin in the summer of 1933 and had received no response. Gretel Karplus had repeatedly asked Benjamin for his reactions to the piece, for the last time in her (unpublished) letter of 20.1.1934: 'Teddie sent you the Tom manuscript in the summer and has been longing to receive your judgement and a letter ever since.'

2 *the circumstances which occasioned this fact*: an allusion to Hitler's seizure of power which led to Benjamin's emigration in March 1933, whereas Adorno remained in Germany until early 1934.

3 *your sketch of children in 'Four-Handed Once Again'*: cf. Adorno, 'Vierhändig, noch einmal', in the *Vossische Zeitung*, 19 December 1933; now in GS 17, pp. 303–6.

4 *in his 'Enfants terribles'*: the novel by Jean Cocteau which appeared in Paris in 1929.

Berlin N 20, Prinzenallee 60, chez Karplus
4 March 1934

Dear Herr Benjamin,

For weeks now I have been carrying around a detailed letter concerned with the question of Tom Sawyer, since your lines are naturally the only thing of substance on the matter which I have received. But in the meantime I have heard from Felicitas[1] about your own highly critical predicament,[2] and under these circumstances I can well imagine that any extended aesthetic discussion would only seem rather insulting in the context.

I have preferred therefore to do something for you, and indeed through Frau Herzberger,[3] whom you met once in Frankfurt in my company, and through my aunt,[4] who broached the issue with Frau Herzberger when the latter happened to be staying in Frankfurt (she actually lives in Neunkirchen where she owns a business). My aunt has written to inform me that her intervention has met with some success. At the moment I cannot say anything about the amount of assistance,[5] and one should assume that it will prove rather modest, but it will still meet the acute and imminent danger of your situation. I have endeavoured to explain everything in the most urgent fashion and requested that something be done without delay; I think I can assume that this will duly happen. In any event I should be very grateful for speedy information from you concerning your entire situation, so that I am in a position, if necessary, to exert further pressure in the matter on your behalf.

A further plan[6] has not yet come to fruition, since the man in question, who lives in Paris, is not resident there at present. Here too I shall do whatever I can to help.

About 'Tom' I will say only this: I believe that the stars which preside over 'les enfants terribles' are not particularly favourable to this piece. What is at issue here is something very different, and something which, I hope, is not merely personal to me. The hearty language is not the heartiness of real children, so much as that encountered in the literature written for children; nor does the course of the action, the focal point of which is of course the cave scene, strike me as that harmless either; if it doesn't sound too arrogant, I would perhaps suggest that I have smuggled a great deal into the piece, that nothing is quite intended in the sense in which it immediately appears, and that I am using the childlike imagery to present some extremely serious things: in this connection I am far more concerned

25

with presenting this image of childhood than I am with invoking childhood as such. The process in which the piece has evolved also possesses something of those perilous moments which you found lacking in it. It is certainly not to be measured in comparison with Cocteau, nor with anything in 'epic theatre'; if anything, it is most closely related to my Kierkegaard book. The central issue is the violation of the oath and the whole thing represents a projected flight: the expression of fear. Perhaps it will show a different and more congenial face to you if you take another look at it; for I can hardly believe with regard to this work above all that you, its ideal reader, should have failed to appreciate it. – Incidentally, you were familiar not only with the general plan, but also with two scenes (the cemetery and the haunted house) which I read out at Schoen's place, on the very same evening[7] when you read us the first instalments of the Ar (I nearly wrote: the Arcades![8] What a telling lapse!), no, of the Berlin Childhood. So much simply in defence against the charge of launching something wholly unexpected upon you. As far as the music is concerned,[9] that is well underway.

But how are things actually going with the Arcades? The thought has occurred to me that we could pursue one of our two courses of action (the second, still outstanding one) in the old-fashioned way and arrange for a formal dedication through our friend. I do not know whether I shall be able to get him to do this, but I should at least like to know in advance how you would feel about the idea. Naturally I hardly have to tell you just how much my own downright egotistical interest in really immersing myself in your work on the Arcades is involved! And perhaps the support of such a precise commission would not prove unfavourable to the work.

I have a lot of work to do at present, and some very curious things too. At the moment I am writing a substantial essay on the crisis of musical criticism[10] for the journal 'Music'. It is closely connected with my musico-sociological piece.[11]

Faithfully and sincerely,

Yours,

Teddie Wiesengrund

1 *Felicitas*: Benjamin's name for Gretel Karplus, after the principal female character in Wilhelm Speyer's play 'Ein Mantel, ein Hut, ein Handschuh', on which Benjamin had collaborated and in which he had a share in the takings (see letter 8 and the relevant note). The inconsistent spelling – Adorno and Gretel Karplus usually write *Felicitas*, while Benjamin generally has *Felizitas* – has been retained in the text. – For her part Gretel Karplus often addressed Benjamin with the Christian name of his pseudonym, *Detlef Holz*.

2 *your own highly critical predicament*: Benjamin described his situation in an undated letter to Gretel Karplus (probably towards the end of February 1934): 'What is actually going to become of me. [. . .] In the meantime the situation is getting worse and worse. The last fourteen days – after the room had been paid for – have been a series of disappointments. [. . .] But I shall not say any more about it. Without you I could only face the next few weeks with despair or apathy. I am no longer a dilettante in either of these moods.

In my current predicament I hardly have the power to address such questions. I have been lying here for days – simply in order not to need anything or to see anyone – and working as well as I possibly can.

Do consider what you can do to help. I need 1,000 francs to meet essentials and to see me through March.' (GS V [2], p. 1099; the first line previously unpublished). – Gretel Karplus replied to Benjamin on 3 March: 'It was a very good thing your last letter but one managed to reach Teddie while he was still here – you will surely forgive me for reading it to him, since it has produced some result. I shall merely mention the matter briefly here and Teddie will give more details later. It concerns the H[erzberger] family of my former *compagnon*; they have been on extremely friendly terms with the Wiesengrunds for decades, and I think you once actually met Else in Fr[ankfurt]. With the help of Teddie's aunt Agathe we have tried to engage her and possibly her brother Alfons in your cause, and we have been *reliably* promised some assistance.' (Unpublished letter from Gretel Karplus to Benjamin on 3.3.1934). – Benjamin had been receiving financial support from Gretel Karplus since the beginning of 1933 as his earnings from literary journalism became increasingly meagre; from April 1934 he began to receive the initial monthly sum of 100 Swiss francs from the Geneva office of the Institute of Social Research.

3 *Frau Herzberger*: the businesswoman Else Herzberger (1877? –1962) was a long-standing friend of Adorno's parents, and particularly of his aunt and mother. – For an image of Else Herzberger, see the piece 'Heliotrope' in Adorno's *Minima Moralia* (GS 4, pp. 199–201).

4 *my aunt*: the pianist Agathe Calvelli-Adorno (1868–1935), a sister of Adorno's mother, also lived in his parents' home. – Adorno's father Oscar Wiesengrund (1870–1946), a wealthy Frankfurt business man, had spent many years in England during his youth, before he married the singer Maria Calvelli-Adorno (1864–1952). Adorno's parents left Germany early in 1939 and went first to Cuba; from the middle of 1940 onwards they lived in New York.

5 *the amount of assistance*: the contribution actually came to 450 French francs; see letter 19.

6 *A further plan*: Adorno had considered trying to interest Else Herzberger's brother, Alfons Herzberger, in becoming the dedicatee of the Arcades project (see the letter below); the idea is further elaborated in letter 15.

7 *at Schoen's place, on the very same evening*: in November 1932, when Benjamin stopped off in Frankfurt on the way back from Poveromo.

8 *the Arcades!*: for the fragments of the uncompleted Arcades project which Benjamin had been working on between 1927 and the year of his death, cf. GS V. – Adorno formulated his own attitude to the Arcades project in his letter to Horkheimer of 8 June 1935: 'It is about Walter Benjamin. Pollock told me that Benjamin had explained to him in Paris the plan for his work 'Paris. Capital of the Nineteenth Century', the work we know as the Arcades project and which has stood at the centre of my discussions with Benjamin over the last ten years. I told Pollock that I regard this piece as Benjamin's genuine *chef d'œuvre*, something which will prove to be of the greatest imaginable theoretical significance, and indeed as – if such a word is appropriate for us here – as brilliant in conception.' (GS VII [2], p. 860).

9 *As far as the music is concerned*: cf. the relevant note to letter 12.

10 *a substantial essay on the crisis of musical criticism*: Adorno's essay 'On the Crisis of Music Criticism' did not actually appear in the journal 'Die Musik', but was not published until 1935 in the Vienna music journal '23', edited by Ernst Krenek and Willi Reich (nr. 20/21, 25.3.1935, pp. 5–15); now in GS 20 [2], pp. 746–55.

11 *my musico-sociological piece*: Adorno is referring to the essay 'On the Social Situation of Music', first mentioned in letter 8 above.

14   BENJAMIN TO WIESENGRUND-ADORNO
      PARIS, 9.3.1934

Dear Herr Wiesengrund,
    For all the protracted silence between us over the past year, you have brought it to an end in a memorable and decisive fashion on your own side. Believe me when I say that I am most profoundly touched by, and shall always remember, the attitude you express with regard to everything discussed in your letter.
    Also, please tell your aunt how much I am deeply obligated to her for her successful intervention on my behalf. I cherish the hope of one day being able to thank her in person.
    I also hope that we shall no longer have to put off a meeting between ourselves[1] in the near future either. This seems to me all the more urgent since we really do have to discuss 'Tom' in some detail with one another. It was quite obvious to me from the first that, as the old Bedouin proverb has it, death is hiding within the folds of Tom's cloak. And the reservations expressed in my letter concerned the execution rather than your central intentions. But everything does indeed depend upon the concept of the 'children's approach' itself, and in order to discuss and develop all that I would need you to be here in person.
    If you do manage to come, it would be one of my greatest desires to reveal various aspects of the *Bibliothèque Nationale*, things which can appeal to no one more than yourself.

In fact the library contains one of the most remarkable reading rooms in the world,[2] and working there is like being surrounded by an operatic set. The only disadvantage is that the place closes as early as six – an arrangement that derives from the time when the theatres still opened at that time. My work on the Arcades has begun to revive, and it is you yourself who have breathed life into the embers – which could never be livelier than I felt myself to be. Since I have started going out again, I actually spend the entire day in the library reading room and have finally even come to feel quite at home with the rather officious *règlement* of the place.

One of my most interesting discoveries, remarkably enough, is a German book[3] which you may not have come across, but which you should be able to obtain fairly easily in a library near you: Engländer's four-volume history of the French workers' associations.

My nights are short. I go to sleep late and wake up early. These lines are the first ambassador of a new day which has been cheered by the bells of Saint-Germain and lulled asleep again by the sound of falling rain.

With heartfelt regards,

Yours,

Walter Benjamin

9 March 1934
Paris VI
1 Rue Du Four

1 *a meeting between ourselves*: a reference to a remark in an unpublished letter from Gretel Karplus to Benjamin of 3 March 1934: 'Teddie is still in Berlin, but will be leaving for London via Frankfurt during the coming week since he wants to get his bearings there and there is no urgent business to be taken care of here – and he may be able to travel back via Paris.' No such meeting transpired.

2 *one of the most remarkable reading rooms in the world*: cf. illustration Nr. 80 in the *Benjamin-Katalog*, p. 226.

3 *a German book*: cf. Sigmund Engländer, *Geschichte der französischen Arbeiter-Associationen*, 1–4 (Hamburg 1864).

15   WIESENGRUND-ADORNO TO BENJAMIN
      BERLIN, 13.3.1934

Berlin, 13 March 1934

Dear Herr Benjamin,
    Many heartfelt thanks for your last letter, which was forwarded on to me here – I shall be staying here over the Easter period, then I

29

shall be off to Frankfurt for a week and then over to England, where at last an opportunity for a university opening[1] seems gradually to be shaping up for me. – I am very pleased that my efforts on your behalf have met with some success. There are one or two other things I need to ask you in order to ensure the continuance of this assistance: above all, whether what we have achieved already[2] will prove sufficient as a financial basis for you, granted that we can procure a certain regularity in the matter, or whether you feel that I should exert some further pressure with the same people; if the assistance really is too modest, then this would certainly be quite appropriate and indeed necessary, but otherwise it might merely make matters worse. – You will understand that I really wish to see clearly ahead in order to act in your interest and the interest of the plan to be embarked upon. Further, I should like to know how you feel about my suggestion for a dedication with regard to the Arcades. In this case it would be a matter of interesting the brother (resident in Paris) of the lady who would herself be principally involved this time. He is a rather difficult man who will not be easy for you to get on with (no more than he is for me too: something of a frustrated intellectual who has become a businessman and now in all his practical successes and the resulting consequences still likes to express his resentment about everything else he has failed to do). But if one knows how to approach him properly he is a man of extraordinary generosity, and in dire straits would prove a friend like very few others, one capable of responding to your predicament in more than one respect. At the moment he is not actually in Paris, but he has written to tell me that he will soon be returning there, and I have good reason to believe that this would be a relatively opportune moment to get him involved. And in this regard, for the reasons I have already mentioned to you, something like the suggested dedication would be extraordinarily suitable, though naturally only if he can really offer some significant assistance – in any case I am sure you will understand my insistence in this matter. Please give me an answer right away.

Incidentally, there has also been another development: I have been able to interest the nephew of the lady I mentioned[3] in your case; he is living here at the moment and, although he is not wealthy himself, he does have numerous connections, and he is making a great effort on your behalf. He has approached a Paris friend of his, one Herr Schwartz[4] (with the business name of Martin), who is keen to do something to help and has repeatedly attempted to contact you at the hotel in vain, whether in person or by telephone I do not know. This Schwartz is supposed to be a highly active and circumspect character. If you generally spend the whole day working in the *Bibliothèque Nationale*, it might well be advisable for you to leave him notice at the hotel of some specific time when he could contact you, and further to make sure that no one overlooks him if he does appear at the hotel. My friend here certainly expects some practical result to come of this connection. Furthermore, this same friend (the nephew I mentioned), who used to be a bookseller, has also undertaken to promote your interests with the Rowohlt publishing house. (Although I must say he did so without asking me about it in advance; I would not have given him the go-ahead without asking you first.) He has obtained some modest success already: Rowohlt have twenty copies of your book on the Baroque and twenty of 'One-Way Street' at their disposal which ought really to be dispatched to people we know etc.; the entire profit should go to you. Since all the relevant people I know here already naturally possess both books, Gretel and I are not sure who else we should approach – perhaps it is possible for you to find recipients for at least some of the books amongst your Paris circle. If so, I shall ensure that a consignment is sent off to you immediately. It goes without saying that I myself am also doing everything I can here.

Did you actually attempt to interest them in the Berlin Childhood at the Erich Reiss[5] publishing house? I know someone who was once a reader for them,[6] who also knows your work very well and holds you in very high regard; it is true that he is no longer actively employed there, but I can imagine that he might still have some influence with them. In any case, it would be an advantage if we had a copy at our disposal here. In general, however, opportunities with publishers don't seem promising at all. Bote and Bock, for instance, have rejected the publication[7] of my musical compositions, even though they were extremely highly recommended to them by a very prominent representative in the field of contemporary music. One must therefore neither overestimate nor underestimate the options here. Incidentally, the current director at Erich Reiss[8] is a mighty Zionist before the Lord. Perhaps your friend Gerhard[9] could be of assistance here.

Since I have played the role of a constructive Cato in this matter, I do not need to inform you how pleased I am about your returning to work upon the Arcades project. I have also been writing a great deal myself: a good number of musical things,[10] all of them accepted by the *Vossische Zeitung*, but very slow in appearing there; also an essay on the recently published volume of George's prose writings[11] for the same organ, something which I hope will not fail to interest you. There are some extraordinary things in the George volume, above all the dream narration and the translation of an unparalleled piece by Mallarmé[12] with which I was not familiar. – I have also written numerous philosophical pieces,[13] although none has been

31

published as yet. On the other hand, the substantial essay on the crisis of musical criticism, which I recently completed, does seem to be about to appear.

I am not yet in a position to see how everything will work out with my journey to London, but I most urgently hope that the return trip will take me via Paris.[14] – Unless, that is, I have to stay over there right at the beginning of the academic term and give some lectures (with Cassirer[15] in Oxford, for example): a possibility that strikes me as too rosy for me seriously even to worry about. In any case, they will soon get to see me make an appearance there, although I hardly flatter myself with the hope that they are really as enthusiastic to receive me as, to my greatest delight, you yourself would be for the sake of your Arcades project and further discussion of my 'Tom'.

I am spending a great deal of time learning English. Learning a foreign language when you are an adult must count amongst the strangest of experiences.

Please respond to my letter very quickly. Have you heard anything from Friedel[16] and can you tell me his address? And how are things going with Schoen?

With heartfelt regards,

Yours,

Teddie

---

1 *an opportunity for a university opening*: in 1935 Adorno provided Kracauer with a résumé of what he had accomplished in England: 'About my own affairs just this: I am attached to Merton College in Oxford as an Advanced Student (and not as a Fellow or Professor) and am currently writing a book on epistemological issues which is fairly substantial, in the external and perhaps also the inner sense of the word; at the moment it bears the title "The Phenomenological Antinomies", and the subtitle "Prolegomena towards a Dialectical Logic". I hope to be able to present one of the sections, the analysis of categorial intuition, as a dissertation in English. One success I can report is that they have made me a member of the highly exclusive "Oxford Philosophical Society". The prospects for the future may not be all that bad. But I am still only temporarily resident in Oxford and my proper address remains Frankfurt just as before.' (Unpublished letter from Adorno to Kracauer of 5.7.1935). – Adorno had originally hoped to acquire a teaching position in Oxford or London. (cf. *Briefwechsel Adorno/Krenek*, pp. 43f).

2 *what we have achieved already*: the financial support received by Benjamin amounted to 450 French francs (cf. letter 13). Adorno, his aunt Agathe and Else Herzberger each contributed a third, as Gretel Karplus informed Benjamin on 19.4.1934 (cf. letter 19).

3 *the nephew of the lady I mentioned*: Arnold Levy (also known as Levy-Ginsburg), a qualified art historian who later turned his interests to the

32

antiquarian book trade. In France, where he lived after the Second World War, he changed his name to Armand Levilliers. – The Levy-Ginsburg family belonged amongst Benjamin's closest acquaintances during the last years of his life.

4 *a Paris friend of his, one Herr Schwartz*: nothing further known.

5 *Erich Reiss*: the publisher Erich Reiss (1887–1951), heir to a considerable fortune, had owned his own publishing house since 1908; as a Jew he was forbidden in 1935 to publish any non-Jewish literature; he was interned in a concentration camp in 1938, but Karin Michaëlis and Selma Lagerlöf succeeded in getting him released and he made his way to New York via Sweden.

6 *someone who was once a reader for them*: the writer Hans Hennecke (born 1897); see letter 17.

7 *Bote and Bock ... have rejected the publication*: nothing more has been discovered concerning Adorno's relationship with the Berlin music publishers 'Bote und Bock'; it is also impossible to identify the *very prominent representative in the field of contemporary music*.

8 *the current director at Erich Reiss*: nothing further known.

9 *your friend Gerhard*: i.e. Gershom Scholem (1897–1982); in a letter to Scholem of 8 April 1934, Benjamin had asked Scholem if he could intervene with Reiss on his behalf; for Scholem's reply, see *Briefwechsel Scholem*, p. 135.

10 *a good number of musical things*: for the essays on music which Adorno wrote for the *Vossische Zeitung*, with which he made contact through the offices of Friedrich T. Grubler, see letter 17 and the relevant note.

11 *the recently published volume of George's prose writings*: cf. Stefan George, *Tage und Taten. Aufzeichnungen und Skizzen, Gesamt-Ausgabe der Werke* (Berlin 1933), vol. 17; Adorno's essay on George has not survived.

12 *an unparalleled piece by Mallarmé*: Adorno is referring to Mallarmé's prose poem 'Frisson d'hiver', translated by George under the German title 'Winter-Schauer'; cf. George, *Tage und Taten*, pp. 94f.

13 *numerous philosophical pieces*: it is impossible to identify precisely which pieces are being referred to here.

14 *the return trip will take me via Paris*: in fact Adorno did not travel back to Germany via Paris.

15 *Cassirer*: at this time Adorno had turned to Ernst Cassirer (1874–1945), who was then teaching in Oxford, in order to find out more about the academic possibilities there.

16 *Friedel*: i.e. Siegfried Kracauer (1889–1966), who had been a close friend of Adorno since the latter's youth; cf. Adorno, 'Der wunderliche Realist. Über Siegfried Kracauer' (GS 11, pp. 388–408).

Dear Herr Wiesengrund,

My sincere thanks for your judicious letter, so circumspect in every regard. It has allowed me to take a deep breath of hope – and in my predicament that in itself is something of infinite value. This same hope also harbours the prospect that we shall finally be able to discuss so many things of mutual concern to us in the near future. I am very pleased about your opportunities in England which have indeed facilitated this prospect.

London is still the gateway to the world, as someone returning from there only recently assured me. And if one can also get by in English, then there are probably much greater openings there than for someone in Paris, however familiar he may be with the place. You will be able to see Schoen, from whom, incidentally, I hardly hear anything. The fact that he has still kept his family together is no bad testimony to the reliability of English ground.

I thanked you in my last letter for the speedy and helpful intervention of your friends, but I would also add – in response to your particular enquiry – that a certain regularity in their assistance would be more valuable than these unknown benefactors could probably imagine. For this would enable me at least to try and plan ahead and anticipate matters. And in the kind of life which I have been leading over the last few months, there is perhaps nothing that has a more destructive effect than the total impossibility of seeing beyond even the most modest of time spans.

The hope which has been opened up for me at the hands of your friends, and then through your own letter, has led me back to my work – and indeed to the very heart of it – with an intensity which has now first revealed to me the full extent of my previous feelings of dejection. But I am all the more relieved from the task of confiding all this now by the thought of seeing you in the near future. One day soon I hope to be able to show you the spot where I like to work in the library. As far as the question of the dedication is concerned, I think that the following suggestions correspond very closely with your own: the accomplishment of this work would indeed be wrested from the 'Now-Time' – that which belongs to me and to the one who has made it possible for me to finish it. The accomplishment of the work would represent an anachronism in the better sense of the word. In the better sense, because it will hopefully do less to galvanize the past than to anticipate a worthier human future. This is what I would like to be expressed in the dedication of this work to which I myself am providing a future.

For the rest, I assume that the precise articulation of this sentiment and of the contribution [of the dedicatee] will be further determined on the basis of a personal meeting to be arranged in the future, if you feel that this is the proper approach.

In the meantime I have actually met Herr Schwartz who is, as you say, an active and circumspect individual, and my short conversation with him turned out very cordially. He left me with the distinct impression that I would be hearing more from him again.

I am particularly gratified to learn from what you tell me that you have remained so constantly productive. I do not have to expatiate in any detail upon the eager interest with which I await your essay on George. Please send it on to me as soon as it is ready; and I would also ask you to do the same with your essay on music criticism.[1] I shall be getting my own back here with the manuscript of an extended review of Kommerell's 'Jean Paul',[2] though it does not seem very likely to find a publisher.

The fate of your compositions with Bote and Bock only supplies me with one more unwelcome and superfluous demonstration of the difficulties which continue to face anything that we produce. But then are we not destined to an apocryphal influence? It is in this sense – as you know – that I always like to interpret the public fate of my own writings; whether it is a question of the burnt edition of my dissertation[3] or Rowohlt's proposals as mentioned in your letter: I recognize the same law at work and would be only too glad in this sense to take on half of the twenty copies of each text here.

You also mention Erich Reiss; I cannot really judge what the possibilities are like there. But I could certainly provide a manuscript copy of the 'Berlin Childhood' if required. Hermann Hesse[4] has written to me about the book in a very nice and perceptive – but also quite melancholy – fashion. His own sphere of influence has certainly shrunk, and the problems with his eyes do not seem to have improved at all.

You will write to me again before you leave for Frankfurt? And you will also be able to tell me the precise date of your arrival in Paris as soon as it is arranged?

With heartfelt regards,

Yours,

Walter Benjamin

18 March 1934
Paris VI
1 Rue Du Four
Palace Hotel

1 *your essay on music criticism*: the essay 'On the Crisis of Music Criticism', first mentioned in letter 13.

2 *an extended review of Kommerell's 'Jean Paul'*: cf. Max Kommerell, *Jean Paul* (Frankfurt a.M. 1933); Benjamin's review, entitled 'Der eingetunkte Zauberstab. Zu Max Kommerell's "Jean-Paul"' ['Dunking the Magic Wand. On Kommerell's "Jean Paul"'], appeared under the pseudonym K. A. Stempflinger in the *Frankfurter Zeitung* of 29.3.1934 (now in GS III, pp. 409–17).

3 *the burnt edition of my dissertation*: Benjamin's dissertation *The Concept of Art Criticism in the German Romantics* had appeared in 1925 with the Bern publisher A. Francke, as the fifth number of 'New Bern Essays on Philosophy and its History', a series edited by Benjamin's doctoral supervisor Richard Herbertz; in 1924 a fire in the publisher's depot destroyed 'the entire existing edition of my dissertation' (*Briefe*, p. 341); for the dissertation, see GS I [1], pp. 7–122).

4 *Hermann Hesse has written to me about the book*: cf. Hermann Hesse, *Gesammelte Briefe*, vol. 2: 1922–1935, edited in collaboration with Heiner Hesse by Ursula and Volker Michels (Frankfurt a.M. 1979), pp. 412f.

17 WIESENGRUND-ADORNO TO BENJAMIN
    BERLIN, 5.4.1934

Berlin, 5. April 1934.

Dear Herr Benjamin,

Once again my Berlin stay has turned out much longer than anticipated – but I am now expecting to go back home for eight days, and then immediately on to London, so I just wanted to write you a few words beforehand.

At home I am hoping to meet the lady who is actually organizing the financial intervention, and I shall of course do all within my power to ensure a certain regularity in the matter is observed. I shall also be able to discover exactly what course of action she was contemplating; but given the urgency of my original request, I cannot imagine that she is not planning for a regular arrangement to be put in hand. And if I am wrong about this, I shall certainly still be in a position to press for that; it goes without saying that I shall do my utmost. So I am definitely hoping that we will manage to see you through the critical months.

In the meantime I have not been idle with respect to the 'Berlin Childhood'. Tau[1] has expressed some interest to my contact in the name of the Cassirer publishing house, but I would not entertain too much hope here for several reasons, above all because of Tau himself, who strikes me at least as the very last person who could be expected to represent our interests here in the appropriate manner.

The matter concerning Erich Reiss is much more important. He has clearly shown serious interest and the man who is mediating here, his former reader Hans Hennecke, is a real connoisseur and genuine admirer of your work; he has made, and continues to make, the greatest efforts on your behalf. It seems a highly favourable sign that Reiss felt he could recognize his own childhood in your 'Childhood'. (Hennecke spoke to him about the concept of the work and also showed him some of the newspaper extracts.)[2] The problem which arises here is a quite peculiar one. For the publishing house has become orthodoxly Zionist, so to speak – that is also precisely why Hennecke, as a Christian, is no longer in charge of the readers there. And there are certain doubts about whether your work is really suitable for them. I do hope that things do work out; but anyway it would be of the *greatest* imaginable importance, if you could mobilize your friend Scholem in the whole business, and if he would testify, for example, that all your work is profoundly connected with the Jewish theological tradition (even if this is not immediately obvious from your subject matter). And the sooner something like this could be arranged the better. And then, without delay, please send Gretel a manuscript copy of the 'Childhood' immediately ready for printing (she telegraphed you today in this regard), so that she can give it to Hennecke. Finally, it is very important for you to belong to the Literary Writers' Association,[3] which has no special regulations concerning Aryan descent. At any rate you must be officially registered there or possess confirmation of impending *registration* if you are to avoid difficulties in getting your work published – for the admissions procedure itself is a tedious and involved affair. Believe me when I say that I would not insist so strongly on this point if it were not really of crucial importance for your publishing prospects here. I think that the book on Baroque Drama and the essay on the Elective Affinities[4] (and these two *alone*) would provide sufficient justification for you, and one which no one should be able to undermine. If you know Benn[5] at all, that would certainly ease matters along.

Felizitas is feeling much better than she was. On her two-week 'cure' she has put on eight pounds and is now hardly recognizable. She has a healthy appetite and has managed to get rid of the headaches. The new doctor is the first sensible one she has had. I am now considerably relieved in this matter at least, and can leave Berlin in a much happier mood than I have experienced in the last seven lean days.

As far as my own affairs are concerned, I have been deeply affected by the death of the *Vossische Zeitung*.[6] That means that eleven of my manuscripts already accepted, all of them weighty and serious pieces, have gone unpublished and as yet I have no idea where I could possibly place them; what is more, four further essays, including the one on 'Loan Words',[7] have been returned to me because of the collapse of Haas' journal.[8] The most recent piece which I wrote for the 'Vossische Zeitung' was an analysis of Beethoven,[9] together with a note on the late style[10] (my *very first* works on Beethoven), and things I had some faith in. This material, along with the essay on George,[11] a piece on Brahms,[12] and a new article on Ravel,[13] now has to wait. Nonetheless, I have been truly 'writing myself in' during the last three months, and am now quite determined to start on my new book as soon as possible and whatever the circumstances. This will be a theory of musical reproduction,[14] a work I have been mulling over for almost ten years and of which various fragments ('Night Music', 'New Tempi'[15] etc.) have already appeared, although the whole will certainly now assume much greater proportions. Perhaps this material will all seem rather remote to you at first. But I believe I am also one with you in the conviction that the more remote matters are not necessarily the least significant ones, and the work (– a thoroughly philosophical one and not a work of practical aesthetic criticism) is therefore much more closely connected with your own interests than the title alone might suggest. I will simply express the following thought to you for now: the question concerning the muteness of works of art has led me in the most remarkable fashion right into our central question, that of the coincidence of the modern with the archaic. And indeed from the other end of the spectrum: from the archaic itself. For I have come to realize that just as the modern is the most ancient, so too the archaic itself is a function of the new: it is thus first produced historically as the archaic, and to that extent it is dialectical in character and not 'pre-historical', but rather the exact opposite. For it is precisely nothing but the site of everything whose voice has fallen silent because of history: something which can only be measured in terms of that historical rhythm which alone 'produces' it as a kind of primal history. I think I only have to suggest this much to you in order to arouse your interest in my project, which will contain a critique of 'primal form' at its very centre. And perhaps it will represent not such a remote counterpart to your Arcades as initially appears to you as you complete them: at least as a counterpart: a counterpart to the primal history of the nineteenth century as a presentment of the essential and categorial historicity of the archaic: which is not historically the most ancient, but rather something which first emerges from the innermost law of time itself. And thereby I would hopefully arrive at the *ceterum censeo*, at your Arcades, that is, a work which must at all costs be written, completed and accomplished in all possible rigour and precise articulation, with all those astonishing pages about the gambler,[16] which I already know,

38

the ring of Saturn,[17] the dialectic at a standstill and the 'self same'. Let me close therefore with the yearning mythological desire to conjure up the conjurer!

Yours ever,
Teddie

I would ask you to write back to me at home. – Would it be possible for you to let me see the *manuscript* of your review of the Kierkegaard book?

1 *Tau*: the philologist Max Tau (1897–1976) was a reader in Bruno Cassirer's publishing house at this time; he emigrated to Norway in 1938, and then to Sweden in 1942.

2 *your 'Childhood' ... the newspaper extracts*: for details concerning Benjamin's previously published pieces cf. GS IV [2], pp. 970f.

3 *the Literary Writers Association*: Benjamin never applied to become a member of the National Socialist *Reichsschrifttumskammer* [The State Literary Writers Association]; Adorno's application to the same was rejected in an official communication of 20 February 1935.

4 *the essay on the Elective Affinities*: Benjamin's essay on 'Goethe's Elective Affinities' had appeared in two issues (April 1924 and January 1925) of the *Neue Deutsche Beiträge*, edited by Hugo von Hofmannsthal with the publishers Bremer Presse; now in GS I, pp. 123–201.

5 *Benn*: Benjamin subsequently asked Gretel Karplus to send him Gottfried Benn's speech 'Der neue Staat und die Intellektuellen' [The New State and the Role of the Intellectuals].

6 *the death of the Vossische Zeitung*: the newspaper *Vossische Zeitung* ceased publication on 31 March 1934.

7 *including the one on 'Loan Words'*: Adorno's essay 'On the Use of Loan Words' (cf. GS 18, pp. 185–8) was never published during the author's lifetime.

8 *the collapse of Haas' journal*: Adorno is referring to 'Die literarische Welt' [The Literary World], formerly edited by Willi Haas, and since the middle of 1933 by Karl Rauch; the journal had been brought under direct political control by the authorities in September 1933.

9 *an analysis of Beethoven*: cf. Adorno, 'Ludwig van Beethoven: Sechs Bagatellen für Klavier, op. 126'; first published in GS 18, pp. 185–8.

10 *a note on the late style*: cf. Adorno, 'Beethovens Spätstil', in the journal *Der Auftakt. Blätter für die tschechoslowakische Republik* XVII, issue 5/6 (1937), pp. 65–7; now in GS 17, pp. 13–17.

11 *the essay on George*: the lost essay mentioned above in letter 15.

12 *a piece on Brahms*: cf. Adorno, 'Brahms aktuell' [Brahms Our Contemporary], first published in *Adorno-Noten*, edited by Rolf Tiedemann (Berlin 1984), pp. 34–9; now in GS 18, pp. 200–3.

13 *a new article on Ravel*: probably the piece published from Adorno's literary remains under the editor's title as 'Ravel', 'circa 1928', (cf. GS 18, p. 273f); Adorno seems to have sent Benjamin a revised version of the piece in 1936 (see letter 58 and the relevant note).

14 *a theory of musical reproduction*: no materials for the work, which remained a fragment, have survived from this period; cf. letter 47 and the relevant note.

15 *'Night Music', 'New Tempi'*: cf. Adorno, 'Nachtmusik', in the journal *Anbruch* 11, issue 1 (January 1929), pp. 216–23; now in GS 17, pp. 52–9, and Adorno, 'Neue Tempi', in the journal *Pult und Taktstock* 7, issue 1 (1930), pp. 1–7; now in GS 17, pp. 66–73.

16 *all those astonishing pages about the gambler*: cf. GS V [2], pp. 1056f.

17 *the ring of Saturn*: cf. GS V [2], p. 1060.

18 BENJAMIN TO WIESENGRUND-ADORNO
    PARIS, 9.4.1934

Dear Herr Wiesengrund,
   Many thanks for your substantial letter.
   What I immediately had to do on receiving it was write to Scholem,[1] and I did that yesterday. To see just how you have handled the matter was as important for me as to learn that you have done so. And I must take this opportunity to tell you how much I share your reservations about Tau. If he can be useful after all, so much the better. The manuscript is going off to Felizitas with the same post in any case.
   I am very happy to learn of the improvement in her health. It was high time she found a doctor who knows what he is doing. In the meantime I have recommended her to seek the advice of one Dr Wissing,[2] in whose medical judgement I have a great deal of faith and who will shortly be in Berlin.
   I must not forget to tell you that Hermann Hesse is familiar with the 'Berlin Childhood', that he has expressed extremely favourable comments about it, and would perhaps express the same sentiments to Reiss if asked to do so. – The business with the Writers' Association is more difficult since the final date for application, as far as I

40

know, has long since passed. Do you have any more information about all this?

But now I turn to the extremely significant suggestions you made in your letter concerning the concept of the archaic and the modern in connection with your investigation of musical reproduction. It is not as if I could do anything else at the moment but confirm your judgement that you have indeed touched here upon a central question in the Arcades. But won't your return trip from England give the opportunity of finally arranging a meeting between us in Paris? You can imagine what it would mean to me to have you here in person and reveal the latest stages of the work to you.

I shall have all the more time to dedicate myself unreservedly to the work since a substantial task to which I had given priority over my other work during the past few weeks has, to my great consternation, just begun to evaporate. You will perhaps have heard from Felizitas that I had been offered the prospect of delivering a lecture on the German literature[3] of the last decade at the home of a gynaecologist who is rather well-known here. The importance of the venture would have consisted in being introduced to certain prominent circles. But one week before the appointed date – the invitation cards had already been sent out – the doctor fell ill with serious pulmonary inflammation, and even now it is still an open question whether he will survive or not. It now seems highly unlikely that I shall be able to present the lecture this season, and the prospect of delivering any further lectures has also disappeared.

The planned series of lectures was intended to vouchsafe me some respite for the summer. There is no longer any question of that now. Even more than ever therefore I will now depend upon the intervention which you have set in motion. I am also rather concerned not to have heard anything further from Herr Schwartz-Martin. After our first meeting, which went very well, I telephoned at the end of March to let him know my change of address. He strongly suggested that he would be in touch after Easter. As yet I have heard nothing from him. That is why your intervention has now become the ardent focus of my hopes.

Reading page proofs now seems set to become an unusual, even festive event for us both. After learning about the publishing conditions which you would have to meet in order to participate in the professional musical press, I hardly dare to put myself forward. It says enough that eleven of your contributions went off to Berlin at all. But since you mention fifteen pieces in all, I can just imagine the amount of work you must have been doing over the last year. I would love to get to know this work more closely. And this is yet another reason why I am looking forward to your visiting.

41

That is all for the present. I hope to hear from you very soon. With warmest regards,

Yours,

Walter Benjamin

9 April 1934
Paris XVI
25bis Rue Jasmin

1 *write to Scholem*: cf. *Briefwechsel Scholem*, pp. 129–31.

2 *Dr Wissing*: Egon Wissing (1900–1984) was a nephew of Benjamin's on his mother's side and very friendly with Benjamin. 'Before the Nazi period Benjamin lived in the same house as Wissing in the Prinzregentenstrasse in Berlin, and when Benjamin was contemplating suicide in July 1932 he named Dr Wissing as his legal executor in a letter to Wissing accompanying the last will and testament that still survives in East Berlin.' (Gershom Scholem, *Walter Benjamin und sein Engel. Vierzehn Aufsätze und kleine Beiträge*, edited by Rolf Tiedemann (Frankfurt a.M. 1983), p. 149.) – After spending some time in the Soviet Union, Wissing went to the USA and soon afterwards found employment at the Massachusetts Memorial Hospital in Boston; he married the dentist Liselotte Karplus (born 1900), the sister of Gretel Karplus.

3 *a lecture on the German literature*: Benjamin had written to Brecht on 5 March 1934: 'In the French circles I am familiar with, and in one or two other ones, I have announced a series of lectures entitled "L'avantgarde allemand". It will consist of five lectures – and one must subscribe to the entire series to receive admission tickets. From the various areas concerned I have in each case selected a single figure who expresses the current scene in an exemplary manner.

1) le roman (Kafka)
2) l'essay (Bloch)
3) théâtre (Brecht)
4) journalisme (Kraus)

These will be preceded by an introductory lecture "Le public allemand"' (*Briefe*, pp. 602f).

19 WIESENGRUND-ADORNO TO BENJAMIN
    FRANKFURT A.M., 13.4.1934

Frankfurt, 13 April 1934.

Dear Herr Benjamin,

I must respond in haste, in the turbulent midst of imminent departure, to your letter which I found waiting for me yesterday on my return from Amorbach.[1]

It is a good thing that you mentioned the sum[2] to Felizitas. I find it less than expected since two-thirds of it represent the contributions of my aunt and myself. As it happened the lady in question dined with us the other evening and I made some very precise suggestions – with some success, I hope. In any case the relevant contribution can now certainly be relied upon as a minimum.

I spoke with Benno[3] today to the same effect and he informed me that we can definitely expect monthly payments amounting to two-thirds of the sum[4] in question from that quarter. With the other contributions, that will produce a minimum at least, and I think I can assume after my – extremely drastic – intervention that it will actually be increased somewhat. I would like to hope therefore that you no longer have reason to feel seriously threatened at present. In any case make sure to inform the firm[5] – and Benno as well if you have not already done so – about your change of address as soon as possible.

About the Writers' Association: as far as the closing date for applications is concerned things are not so bad. You must tell them that because of your stay in the Balearic Islands you were not aware of the deadline (which is of course quite true!). It would be a good idea to point out to them that you used to spend months there in your early years, lest they are tempted to regard you as an emigrant. You can easily prove all this if necessary. But I would certainly pursue the matter with the *utmost* urgency, given its extreme importance as far as getting things published is concerned – you can believe me that I would not be plaguing you about it otherwise. The point that you have already spent years travelling about in this way is particularly important.

I travel to England on Sunday and will be in London by Monday evening. My address[6] is: T.W-A, c/o Dr Bernard Wingfield, Brooklyn-House, *West-Drayton*, Middlesex. – I continue to harbour the wish for a detour via Paris on my return journey; now, at the beginning of the term,[7] I have to be in London. The precise date and opportunity for my special Paris detour[8] are still in the dark: for it is still quite possible that I shall have to spend the whole semester here, and there is still a financial problem about transferring funds.[9] I would have really loved to meet Felizitas in Paris. 'Let us hope the best.'

Yesterday I spotted a proper wild otter leaping into the lake in the Amorbach Gardens, and even in this factual letter I cannot resist sending you greetings from the pampered creature.[10] Please write soon!

With warmest regards,

Yours,

Teddie

I think you ought *unreservedly* to follow up Hesse's recommendation!

1 *Amorbach*: Adorno and his parents frequently stayed in Amorbach during the summer months, a little town in the Odenwald region.

2 *the sum*: for the size of the financial contribution, cf. letter 15 and the relevant note.

3 *Benno*: Benno Reifenberg (1892–1970) edited the features and cultural section of the *Frankfurter Zeitung* from 1924–1929, acted as the Paris correspondent for the newspaper from 1930–1932, and became its political editor in 1932.

4 *monthly payments amounting to two-thirds of the sum*: i.e. approximately 300 francs.

5 *the firm*: Adorno is probably referring to the address of Else Herzberger's department store in Neunkirchen in the Saarland region.

6 *My address*: the address given by Adorno was that of his cousin on his father's side.

7 *at the beginning of the term*: the Oxford term began in the middle of April.

8 *my special Paris detour*: Adorno's idea of visiting Paris to meet Gretel Karplus did not materialize.

9 *problem about transferring funds*: since the Nazi seizure of power, the restrictions governing the transfer of capital already in force since 1931 were transformed into an almost total ban on transferring money abroad. Even the regulations for certain exceptions, allowing the transfer of funds for foreign travel unconnected with business affairs (for studying abroad or for reasons of health), were almost entirely abolished in the autumn of 1934. After that the transfer of funds was only permitted if a crucial cultural-political interest in studying abroad could be demonstrated.

10 *a proper wild otter / the pampered creature*: Adorno is alluding to the section 'The Wild Otter' in Benjamin's *Berlin Childhood Around 1900*, a passage that had already been published, along with two other sections, in the *Frankfurter Zeitung* of 2.3.1933 under the title 'Berliner Kindheit um 1900. III' (now in GS IV [1], pp. 255–7 and GS VII [1], pp. 406–8).

20 WIESENGRUND-ADORNO TO BENJAMIN
    BROOKLYN (WEST DRAYTON), 21.4.1934

Telegrams: Wingfield   Brooklyn
           West Drayton   West Drayton
Telephone: West Drayton 58   MDX
                                        21 April 1934

Dear Herr Benjamin,

Many thanks for your letter[1] and for the 'Shorter Pieces'[2] which I received early this morning. It is certainly a great pity that we did not have the opportunity to discuss the question of the Writers

Association earlier. For I am afraid that you have actually – if I may put it that way – rather neglected matters in this respect because of your absence from Germany. Even your nomination as librarian, as the author of a work pertaining to the Germanistic field, does not seem to me particularly hopeful now; especially since you failed to fill out the application after you had been approached to that effect. I think it is extremely doubtful that anyone knows anything about the business in Switzerland;[3] if any enquiries are made in this regard, you could explain things by referring to pulmonary disease, something that would now be just as difficult to check up upon as your racial credentials. But even that would not yet settle everything. Rather, the situation is such that, generally speaking and amongst non-Aryan authors (myself included), one first merely receives confirmation of the official application, and that usually without difficulty, while the definite approval for admission is postponed until much later. I put in my own application last November and have still not received formal notice of the accepted application. Nonetheless, this is not actually required, since according to the official regulations this confirmation is sufficient documentation for editors as well as publishers even before the final decision on admission has been agreed. If I were in your position, therefore, despite the fact that matters may have suffered from your delay, I would fill out the application even now and try to provide *some suitable excuse for this delay*. Of the two citizens whose names you have to supply, it would perhaps be best to choose Rudolph Alexander Schröder as one of them, for he could certainly be contacted by you through the Bremer Press; the other one should be selected from people on the political right; apart from Benn, the name of Fechter[4] – do not be too horrified! – comes to mind. The fact that you left Germany in March 1933 will certainly weigh more heavily against you than the business in Switzerland. In this regard you must definitely emphasize, with documentary proof if possible, that you always did spend considerable time abroad for financial reasons before, and the first spell in Ibiza[5] will certainly be useful confirmation in this connection. I do not think that relinquishing your authorial rights[6] is very advisable: partly because even now you do not need to take this step, and partly because such things always lead to misunderstandings later (à propos: have you attempted to get 'Coat, Hat and Glove'[7] staged in London? My own fleeting impressions of the theatre here suggest that it might stand a good chance of success – perhaps Schoen could do something and translate it for you, if you are indeed still interested in it); finally, also because I feel the whole procedure is rather risky now that so many excerpts have been published. The declaration of loyalty required has absolutely no significance – from our point of view it is no more significant than

45

the official declarations of obligation which all state employees used to make under the Republic. I cannot conceal from you that I am now beginning to doubt whether the Nazi state will continue much longer to draw any conclusions from such declarations. For although I am certainly not optimistic, and expect the future to bring a kind of right-wing anarchy along with the fulfilment of Bronnen-style fantasies,[8] if not a downright military dictatorship or something like the Dollfuss regime, the signs of collapse are nevertheless starting to accumulate so much that one no longer needs to ignore them for fear of the wish proving father to the thought.

And with this turn of phrase I come to find myself within the horizon of your 'Smaller Pieces', which pleased me enormously. In large measure I was already familiar with them as *parerga* to 'One-Way Street',[9] like the threefold dream and the beautiful piece on 'Festivities and Panic' which, if I am not mistaken, has been changed somewhat: before it was not as strongly concentrated around 14 July, the fireworks of which Debussy glorified so much with a roaring Marseillaise in the middle, – that is, not so carefully organized with respect to hour and time of day, and it has now certainly gained as a result. It was the piece on the newspaper which made by far the greatest impression upon me, and I can subscribe to everything you say there without reservations. It corresponds so closely with my own intentions – though you will understand this as a clarification of our mutual agreement rather than as an expression of arrogance. For I once tried years ago to defend the chaotic language of journalism against the charges of Kraus.[10] As some small recompense I hope very soon to be able to send you my piece on loan words,[11] somewhat lengthier than yours, which undertakes a defence of such words in a rather analogical fashion, namely there where they are most inappropriately used. I have sent the piece to 'Muttersprache', the journal of the General Language Association, but I have not actually heard anything back from them as yet. That would indeed be a snobbish place of publication from which I could even look down on you. It is the very organ of the feeblest kind of purism.

My own affairs are still very much in the air; but I feel extremely pessimistic about things. The task of living here, especially at the University, almost compares with the Brechtian problem of 'Mann ist Mann' (isn't the title itself best translated as 'A Man's a Man'?). There is no question of my acquiring an official post-doctoral degree here. In addition, everything has been further and seriously complicated by the new regulations governing the transfer of funds, and it is now difficult to get even the most modest sums out of Germany. I hope to see my way ahead more clearly by the middle of next week.

– In Germany I regard the dismissal of Diels[12] as an incalculably significant blow to Göring. It is the first time that the internal party conflicts have outwardly revealed themselves, and it might well lead to an open power struggle.

Horkheimer had invited me to join him for a few days in Paris, where he is going next week before beginning a rather extended trip. But I had to decline because I have some extremely urgent and definite appointments for tomorrow and Wednesday, arrangements which as a newcomer here I can hardly cancel in the name of a trip to Paris: a meeting with Plant from the School of Economics, and following that a shared discussion with Cassirer and Adams, the General Secretary of the Assistance Council.[13] If you see Horkheimer, I would ask you to emphasize to him the impossibility of my postponing these engagements. I do not need to add how sorry I am about this.

For the sake of clarification I would just like to say that my aunt and I are also involved in about two-thirds of Frau Herzberger's transfer. We find ourselves in a kind of 'clearing' arrangement: we deal with the contributions for your purposes in Germany, while she transfers funds from the Saargebiet. Arnold Levy is not indeed in Paris.

I did inform you that Reifenberg would be pleased to receive an essay by you on the Kierkegaard book, but I will, sans phrases, leave the entire matter up to you to decide whether you want to consider doing so. My own impression of Reifenberg this time was a very positive one from the personal point of view, and I think we can expect a certain solidarity from him.

May I also repeat my request for the addresses of Schoen and Kracauer?[14] I would ask you to let us hear from you soon. In any case I shall no longer be living out here after the middle of next week, but will be off to Oxford – or somewhere in the proximity of the library in the British Museum. I would also ask you to destroy this letter. – Gretel is really feeling better. At the moment that is the only ray of light I can see.

With all heartfelt regards,

Yours,
Teddie.

1 *your letter*: this has not survived and was possibly destroyed on Benjamin's instructions (see this letter below).

2 *the 'Shorter Pieces'*: cf. the 'Denkbilder' [Thoughtful Images]: 'Der Wissende' [The Knowing One] (GS IV [1], pp. 422f); 'Schönes Entsetzen' [Beautiful Horror] (GS IV [1], pp. 434f); 'Die Zeitung' [The Newspaper] (GS II [2], pp. 628f); further see this letter below.

3 *the business in Switzerland*: early in 1917 Benjamin succeeded in avoiding the imminent call-up for military duty on the medically attested health grounds of suffering sciatica, and thereupon took up residence in Bern with his wife Dora in the middle of the year.

4 *Fechter*: the journalist and historian of literature Paul Fechter (1880–1958) was co-editor of the weekly journal 'Deutsche Zukunft' [The German Future] between 1933 and 1942.

5 *the first spell in Ibiza*: a reference to Benjamin's first stay in Ibiza in 1932.

6 *relinquishing your authorial rights*: the publication of all books in Germany was dependent upon the author's membership of the State Writers' Association.

7 *'Coat, Hat and Glove'*: see letters 8 and 13 and the relevant notes.

8 *Bronnen-style fantasies*: The writer Arnolt Bronnen (1895–1959) had been friendly with Brecht in the 1920s but later became a Nazi sympathizer. Adorno is probably thinking here of Bronnen's enthusiasm for the military volunteer corps; cf. Bronnen's novel 'O. S.' (1929).

9 *parerga to 'One-Way Street'*: cf. GS IV [2], pp. 911f.

10 *to defend the chaotic language of journalism against Kraus*: nothing further is known about Adorno's attempted defence.

11 *my piece on loan words*: see letter 17 and the relevant note; the essay did not in fact appear in the journal 'Muttersprache'.

12 *the dismissal of Diels*: the founder and first head of the Gestapo, Rudolf Diels (1900–1957), a close associate of Göring's, was dismissed from his post on 1 April 1934 and replaced by Himmler.

13 *the Assistance Council*: the 'Academic Assistance Council' mediated between Adorno and the British educational authorities, and officially acted as the institution which 'invited' Adorno to continue his philosophical studies in England. Adorno met Walter Adams and Ernst Cassirer on the afternoon of 3 May.

14 *the addresses of Schoen and Kracauer*: see letter 21 following.

21 BENJAMIN TO WIESENGRUND-ADORNO
    PARIS, 28.4.1934

Dr Walter Benjamin   Paris (14ᵉ), 28 April 1934
                                      28, place Denfert-Rochereau
                                      Hôtel Floridor

Dear Herr Wiesengrund,
    I take advantage of the élan which I feel at just having finished dictating the text of a substantial lecture[1] to activate the typewriter

48

for your sake. This is all the more fortunate in that there are so many important matters to discuss.

But first of all I must thank you for your letter from London. The issue concerning my relationship to the Writers' Association is naturally not so fundamental, and merely represents a question of opportunity. I would therefore only enter into contact with these people once all our other enquiries with the Reiss publishing house have been clarified. Unfortunately that does not yet seem to be the case at present. For I have still heard nothing direct from them, nor received any further relevant news from Felizitas. But I have taken the step of informing Scholem[2] about the matter, in the event of any favourable developments, and he is ready to express his opinion about the book to the publishers if asked to do so.

In the meantime Arnold Levy has been here. I think I have made the acquaintance in him of an uncommonly intelligent and – thanks to you – extremely benevolent human being. We have discussed my current situation at length. It thereby transpired that he had indeed already envisaged the sort of assistance which would go further than the Neunkirchen arrangement, but has not yet been able to organize everything. But I don't know whether he feels the prospects of success for such an organization are really favourable or not.

Since he was only able to speak very briefly with Frau Herzberger before his departure, he was not particularly clear about her position in the matter. Thus it came about that he asked *me* whether the assistance coming from Neunkirchen is also expected to continue. On the basis of your penultimate letter I felt justified in giving him an affirmative answer to this question, and indeed I would hardly dare to look the future in the face if this were not the case.

Thanks to you we have almost become used to discussing these things in this way. It is by no means an easy matter for me to express in a letter just how I feel, for all the objectivity in question, when I reflect upon this new kind of involvement between us. And this is yet another reason why I am so desirous of the prospect of seeing you alight in Paris.

If you could be here now, I think that the lecture I mentioned at the beginning would give us abundant material for discussion. The lecture is entitled 'The Author as Producer' and will be presented here at the 'Institute for Research into Fascism'[3] before an extremely small but highly qualified audience; it represents an attempt to supply a companion piece on literary writing to the analysis which I undertook for the stage in the piece on 'Epic Theatre'.[4]

You shall now become the first person to learn my new pseudonym, intended for use abroad: O. E. Tal = an anagram of the Latin *lateo* – 'I conceal myself'.

49

I wrote immediately to the Frankfurt paper about your Kierkegaard book, asking them for confirmation of the commission,[5] for which I naturally strongly urged on my own part. I do not need to tell you how much I would like to write this review.

Kracauer's address is: Paris (6e), Madison Hotel, Boulevard St Germain. Schoen's address may well be out of date, for I have not heard anything from him for months now. Ernst Schoen c/o Lea Steps, Vale of Health, Hampstead (Hampstead 3410).

I hope to hear something good from you very soon, also concerning the progress of your academic affairs. Do keep me as closely informed as you can all the time.

Cordially yours,

[Walter Benjamin]

1 *a substantial lecture*: i.e. the essay 'The Author as Producer' mentioned in this letter below, not published during Benjamin's lifetime; cf. GS II [2], pp. 683–701, and the relevant remarks in GS II [3], pp. 1460–3.

2 *the step of informing Scholem*: in a letter of April 8; see letter 18 and the relevant note.

3 *the 'Institute for Research into Fascism'*: for information concerning this institute, cf. GS II [3], p. 142.

4 *the piece on 'Epic Theatre'*: Benjamin's essay, probably written at the beginning of 1931: 'What is Epic Theatre? A Study on Brecht', which was only published from the literary remains in 1966; now in GS II [2], pp. 519–31.

5 *confirmation of the commission*: Benjamin's prospective review of Adorno's book on Kierkegaard for the *Frankfurter Zeitung* never materialized.

Dear Herr Wiesengrund,

These few lines are simply intended to remind you about the concluding request of my last letter: to keep me constantly informed about your English travels as far as you can. For I have not heard anything from you for a good while, and have only received mention of you in one brief card from Schoen, who only communicates at truly meteorological intervals himself.

I do not know whether your next news will now reach me here or in Denmark.[1] The date of my departure is not yet firmly fixed, but will be as soon as I can possibly make it. If you could write to me here beforehand – I shall not be leaving before 4 June at any rate

– I would be delighted. If you write later, then you will have to await further communication from Denmark; for one has to consider that mail sent on to Denmark from here can sometimes pass via Germany.

As far as Germany is concerned, there is no lack of reliable and recent information. The better informed the observers are, the less they are naturally inclined to express any prognoses. It seems highly probable that a crisis is imminent – but the outcome is uncertain.

I am no longer sure whether I already wrote to you about my most recent work. It is called: 'The Author as Producer' and is a kind of companion piece to my earlier one on Epic Theatre. At the moment I am negotiating to have it published in the journal 'Sammlung',[2] something which certainly requires a great deal of persistence.

You will have heard that Reiss have turned down the 'Berlin Childhood'. That cannot prevent me from thanking you once again for all the efforts you gave to the matter.

Before my departure I intend to see some important people here: Paulhan,[3] Pierre-Quint,[4] Du Bos.[5] And Kracauer too, who, so it seems to me, is increasingly retreating from view. He seems to be withdrawing completely to finish work on his novel.[6] I really hope for him that the aspirations which he links with its translation are fulfilled, although I cannot conceal my own literary reservations about the work.

Did I enquire of you in my last letter after one Paul Binswanger, who has just brought out a scandalous book[7] on 'The Aesthetic Question of Flaubert' with Klostermann?

And now one concluding request: could you yourself possibly remind Geck[8] or Reifenberg once again about the Kierkegaard review? I have already made enquiries twice, without receiving any further response.

But enough for today. Please write to me here if you can. Very cordial greetings,

Yours,

Walter Benjamin

24 May 1934 Paris XIV
28 place Denfert-
Rochereau
Hôtel Floridor

1 *Denmark*: Benjamin travelled to Denmark in the middle of July as a guest of Brecht.

2 *the journal 'Sammlung'*: a journal edited by Klaus Mann.

3 *Paulhan*: Jean Paulhan (1884–1968) was the extraordinarily influential principal editor of the 'Nouvelle Revue Française'; see further letter 28 and the relevant note.

4 *Pierre-Quint*: the novelist and essayist Léon Pierre-Quint (1895–1956) who made his name with major studies of Marcel Proust (1926) and André Gide (1933).

5 *Du Bos*: Charles Du Bos (1882–1939), a French essayist and literary critic.

6 *Kracauer / his novel*: at this time Kracauer was working on his second novel, entitled 'Georg', which was only published posthumously (cf. Siegfried Kracauer, *Schriften*, edited by Karsten Witte, vol. 7 (Frankfurt a.M. 1973), pp. 243–490).

7 *Paul Binswanger / a scandalous book*: cf. Paul Binswanger, *Die ästhetische Problematik Flauberts. Untersuchungen zum Problem von Sprache und Stil in der Literatur* [The Aesthetic Problematic in Flaubert. Investigations into the Problem of Language and Style in Literature] (Frankfurt a.M. 1934); Benjamin's critique of the book – which originally formed part of a review of several other books – also appeared separately under the pseudonym Detlev Holz in the literary section of the *Frankfurter Zeitung* of 12.8.1934; now in GS II, pp. 423–5.

8 *Geck*: Rudolf Geck (1863–1936) had been employed in the features and cultural section of the *Frankfurter Zeitung* from 1896; soon after 1933 he was replaced by Benno Reifenberg.

23 WIESENGRUND-ADORNO TO BENJAMIN
OXFORD, 6.11.1934

Oxford, Merton College
6 November 1934.

Dear Herr Benjamin,

Thank you very much indeed for your last letter.[1] My long silence is quite unconnected with problems of assimilation, which I have certainly encountered here in a rather unrelenting fashion, and no state of silence between us can ever endure for that long in any case. Thus I hasten to answer you right away. Since Gretel's visit[2] you will have learnt why I have been silent for as long as I have; her visit, together with the intimations in your letter, have served to remove the difficulties in question. They were all entirely connected with the sphere of our shared work; I was unable to conceal the most profound reservations concerning some of your publications (and this for the very first time since we have properly known each other); namely, your work on the French novel[3] and your essay on Kommerell – which also caused me some considerable distress in a personal sense,[4] given that this writer once openly expressed the wish that people like me should be stood up against a wall etc. – thus my attitude in this matter hardly requires any further explanation. Yet

52

the really controversial issues were far too fundamental and involved in every sense to permit adequate clarification in a letter, especially during your stay in Copenhagen;[5] and on the other hand, during the last three months in London I have felt deprived of just that sense of freedom and security which such a discussion would require. That is why I remained silent in the expectation that another letter would come and rouse me to action, and then your letter duly arrived. And indeed your communication has exerted this influence all the more effectively precisely because you have now distanced yourself some-what from certain other positions. I hope I will not be suspected of any unreasonable desire to interfere if I confess that the whole diffi-cult problem is connected with the figure of Brecht and with the credence you are willing to give him; for this also touches upon fundamental questions of principle with regard to materialist dialec-tics, like that concerning the concept of use-value, the central role of which I can no more accept today than I could previously. Unless I am much mistaken, you have also renounced such ideas, and the most important thing it seems I can do now is to assure you of my fullest support in taking this step, without any fear that you will interpret this either as an expression of conformism or of any ten-dency to reserve my own rights in the matter. What you say about concluding the period of essay writing and finally resuming work on the Arcades is in fact the brightest piece of news that I have heard from you in many years. You are well aware that I really regard this work as part of our destined contribution to *prima philosophia*, and that there is nothing I desire more than to see you finally capable, after all the long and painful hesitations involved, of bringing this work to a conclusion which does justice to the momentous subject matter. And if I can contribute any aspirations of my own to this work, without you taking this as an immodest suggestion, it would be this: that the work should proceed without qualms to realize every part of the theological content and all the literalness of its most extreme claims, everything that was originally harboured within it (without qualms, that is, concerning any objections stemming from that Brechtian atheism which we should perhaps one day attempt to salvage as a kind of inverse theology, but which we should certainly not duplicate!); further, that for the sake of your own approach you should strongly refrain from associating your thought with social theory in an external manner. For it really seems to me that here, where the most absolutely decisive and fundamental issues are con-cerned, one has to speak out loudly and clearly, and thereby reveal the undiminished categorial depth of the question, without neglect-ing theology here; and then, at this decisive level, I believe that we can all the more easily avail ourselves of the Marxian theory precisely because we have not been forced to appropriate it externally in a subservient fashion: that here the 'aesthetic' dimension will be capable of intervening in reality in an incomparably more profound and revolutionary manner than a class theory conceived as some 'deus ex machina' is capable of doing. It therefore seems indispensable to me that precisely the most remote themes: that of the 'ever-same' and of the infernal, should be expressed with undiminished force, and that the concept of the 'dialectical image' should also be expounded with the greatest possible clarity. No one is more aware than I am that every single sentence here is and must be laden with political dynamite; but the further down such dynamite is buried, the greater its explosive force when detonated. I would not dare to offer you 'advice' in these matters – what I am attempting to do is simply to stand before you almost like a representative of your own intentions against a certain tyranny, which, as you yourself once did with Kraus, only needs to be named as such in order to be banished. – What is more, another important external impulse for the Arcades seems to have arisen just now. In an English film magazine I found a review of Breton's new book (*Les vases communicants*),[6] which, unless I am much mistaken, appears to converge very closely with many of our own intentions. It too counters the psychological interpretation of dreaming and defends an approach in terms of objective images; and it also seems to ascribe a crucial historical character to such images. The entire piece is so closely related to your own thematic concerns that it will probably necessitate a fairly radical revision precisely with regard to the most central issue (although from the review I cannot tell exactly where); but if the piece does indeed produce such a revision it may prove to be of great significance for you, comparable perhaps – what a parallel – to the significance of Saxl and Panofsky for your book on the Baroque! As far as the Arcades is concerned I must also add that it would surely be a misfortune if this work, which will have to represent the integration of all your own experience of language, were to be written in French, namely in a medium which, even with the most fluent knowledge of the language, cannot be used to effect that level of integration which presupposes the dialectic of your own living mother tongue! If this should produce problems in getting the work published, then the right path would seem to be that of *translation* – for the loss of a German original version would strike me, sans phrase, as nothing less than the most grievous loss our language has suffered since Uhland burnt his share of Hölderlin's literary remains.[7] – It goes without saying that I would do the utmost in my power to help facilitate publication of the work; the most favourable prospects seem to me to be in Austria, where Krenek[8] currently occupies a number of important positions, and there is no question that he would do absolutely everything conceivable for this work.

As far as my work on Husserl[9] is concerned, I have simply marched on with my eyes bound as if to the place of execution, something which is perhaps not so utterly inappropriate for a logical contribution of this kind. My original idea was to attempt a kind of retranslation of an eminently 'philosophical' language back into a language of images; whether I shall be successful in that here and now unfortunately no longer depends simply on me; but I shall certainly not fail to demonstrate the immanent contradictions of such a formal ontology and its grounding – one which is attempted from the most advanced position of his class, admittedly something that can only appear here, where 'philosophy' is the object in question, in a somewhat unmediated fashion. As yet, however, I am still too deeply involved in the beginning to be able to say anything about it without talking nonsense, and I would ask you to be patient for another three months, when I shall be able to see things more clearly. The external chances of my writings enabling me to acquire the rare and difficult Oxford D Phil[10] do not seem too bad; and the personal relations involved are extremely agreeable; I cannot really say the same for the life of a mediaeval scholar 'in Cap and Gown' which I find myself forced to lead.

I have neither seen Brecht, nor heard anything from him. On the other hand I did meet Eisler[11] one day in the street in London, and he took the opportunity to express such shameless arrogance that I lost any desire on my part to enter a realm of thinking which is certainly a 'style of comportment', but hardly a proper way of behaving. Eisler subsequently felt it advisable to tender his apologies to me via Schoen, but *sunt certi denique fines*.[12] – I actually saw Schoen twice, and since I was craftily successful in keeping Hansi[13] away, our meeting was an extremely agreeable one – much more so than his own situation, which looks rather dire to me, although I am quite incapable of helping him out in any way. And now I have not heard from him either, except for a single card. It may well be that things are so desperate at his end that we should not continue to count on him. His address is London NW, 32 Belsize Park.

Could I have a copy of the essay on Kafka?[14] I don't have to tell you how crucially significant it would be for me. – I have just written a substantial critique of Mannheim's bourgeois sociologism,[15] the most explicitly Marxist piece I have ever undertaken; however, he has asked me to postpone the completion of the essay until his book has appeared in print, and in all loyalty I could hardly deny him that; so the matter will rest for a few weeks as a result. As soon as the fair copy is ready you will receive one (it is already growing into a little book, and also contains elements towards a theory of fascism).

I hope that your decision to visit San Remo[16] will prove more fruitful to you than it may appear right now, and all my best wishes, in every regard, go with you on your journey. Do you know that I once spent some months living there?[17] For your friendly delight I can recommend the Café Morgana, right out over the sea, as a suitable place to work. And on no account must you miss the opportunity of going out to visit the dead village of Bussana Vecchia[18] high up in the mountains, a place that can compare with the most remarkable environs of Positano. And if the prospect of enjoying bouille à baisse attracts you, the proprietor of the Hôtel de l'Europe, one Signor Coddoni – to whom you must give my greetings – knows everything there is to know about it and will be happy to share his knowledge with you. He will also be able to initiate you into the mysteries of *uòva all' òstrica*.[19]

I have a very bad conscience about Kracauer,[20] although I cannot regard my reservations as accidental. I have not yet seen the Threepenny Novel.[21] I am currently reading Richard Hughes[22] and Norman Douglas[23] with enormous profit.

I have also received and examined the Rundschau pieces from Sternberger.[24] I cannot think they are as poor as Felizitas finds them, and in the essay on photography in particular there are some excellent things, in criticism of the 'New Objectivity' for example; his piece on 'Art Nouveau', of course, is nothing but a list. But I would be very pleased if one could simply alight on such places and put up a sign there saying 'For Adults Only'. I have written to him cautiously suggesting that essays against Heidegger, Jaspers and Philosophy as Form are certainly appropriate, but that precisely here it is only the dearest and most difficult philosophical categories that will suffice. This will be settled once and for all through the mere existence of your Arcades book.

With the most cordial greetings as ever,

Yours,

Teddie Wiesengrund.

Else Herzberger was supposed to have arrived in England, but has remained as invisible to me as your English friends[25] have to you. If I do get to see her, I shall not forget the practicalities. Please send my regards to Dora Sophie![26]

1 *your last letter*: the letter has not survived.

2 *since Gretel's visit*: Gretel Karplus had met Benjamin in the Gedser region of Denmark on 22–3 September.

3 *your work on the French novel*: cf. Benjamin, 'Zum gegenwärtigen gesellschaftlichen Standort des französischen Romans' [On the Present Social

Perspective of the French Novel], in the *Zeitschrift für Sozialforschung* 3, issue 1 (1934), pp. 54–78; now in GS II [2], pp. 776–803.

4 *your essay on Kommerell – which also caused me considerable distress*: see the note to letter 16. – Adorno touched upon the reasons for his irreconcilable hostility to Kommerell in a letter to Francis Golffing as late as 1968: 'I actually knew Kommerell personally, we received our post-doctoral degrees in Frankfurt at almost exactly the same time. Our acquaintance was a fairly superficial one – at that time the political differences overshadowed everything to such a degree that no real communication between myself and such a decidedly right-wing individual could possibly be established; at the time I regarded him as a highly gifted fascist certainly, and I am sure he could not stand me either. It all looks rather strange today, but things were very different before 1933. [. . .] He certainly was a highly gifted man, but he was not particularly appealing to me in a personal sense, and I have never really been able to understand Benjamin's tendency to admire his enemies.' (Unpublished letter from Adorno to Francis Golffing of 4.1.1968.)

5 *your stay in Copenhagen*: Adorno is referring to Benjamin's stay as Brecht's guest in Denmark.

6 *Breton's new book (Les vases communicants)*: this book by André Breton had appeared in Paris in 1932; it has been impossible to identify the review of the book in an English film magazine.

7 *since Uhland burnt his share of Hölderlin's literary remains*: Adorno was mistaken here.

8 *Krenek*: the composer Ernst Krenek (1900–91), who had been corresponding with Adorno since early in 1929, was also no stranger to Benjamin. In the first half of 1930 there were plans for some kind of collaboration between them, although nothing further is known about the details. In April 1931 Krenek visited Benjamin in Berlin to discuss the latter's essay 'Karl Kraus'; for Krenek's account, cf. *Der hoffnungloser Radikalismus der Mitte. Der Briefwechsel Ernst Krenek-Friedrich T. Gubler 1928–1939*, edited by Claudia Maurer Zenck (Wien, Köln 1989), pp. 122f.

9 *my work on Husserl*: the work mentioned in the first note to letter 15, from which Adorno developed his book of 1956: *Zur Metakritik der Erkenntnistheorie. Studien über Husserl und die phänomenologischen Antinomien* [The Metacritique of Epistemology]; now in GS 5, pp. 7–245.

10 *the rare and difficult Oxford D Phil*: on account of his moving to New York in 1938 Adorno never received the degree.

11 *Eisler*: the composer Hanns Eisler (1898–1962), a pupil of Arnold Schönberg, was acquainted with Adorno since the latter's period of study with Berg in Vienna in 1925; Adorno and Eisler later met in New York, and then again in California where they began collaborating at the end of 1942 on the book *Komposition für den Film* [Composing for Films]. (cf. GS 15, pp. 17–155.)

12 *sunt certi denique fines*: cf. Horace, *Satires*, I, 106: 'Est modus in rebus, sunt certi denique fines, / quos ultra citraque nequit consistere rectum' [Keep the measure in everything, for in all things there is a mean which defines the right – a little either way and all is lost].

13 *Hansi*: i.e. Johanna, Countess Rogendorf, the wife of Ernst Schoen.

14 *the essay on Kafka*: in Benjamin's lifetime only two sections of his essay 'Franz Kafka' were published, namely 'Potemkin' and 'The Little Hunchback', which appeared under the title 'Franz Kafka. Eine Würdigung' in the journal 'Jüdische Rundschau' on 21.12.1934 and 28.12.1934; for the complete essay, cf. GS II [2], pp. 409–38.

15 *a substantial critique of Mannheim's bourgeois sociologism*: Adorno originally conceived his piece as a 'running critical commentary on the unspeakable lecture [by Mannheim] on "Cultural Crisis and Mass Democracy" [. . .] with a long introductory analysis'. (Unpublished letter from Adorno to Horkheimer of 24.11.1934.) It actually became a commentary, actively encouraged by Mannheim who was in contact with Adorno in England, upon the latter's book *Mensch und Gesellschaft im Zeitalter des Umbaus* [Man and Society in an Era of Transformation] (Leiden 1935). Adorno's resulting essay 'New Value-Free Sociology' was only posthumously published from his literary remains; cf. GS 20 [1], pp. 13–45. – After the war Adorno revised and published the piece under the new title 'Consciousness and the Sociology of Knowledge' in his essay collection *Prismen*; cf. GS 10 [1], pp. 31–46.

16 *your decision to visit San Remo*: in the letter which has not survived, Benjamin had obviously told Adorno of his intention to leave for San Remo, where his former wife ran a guest house first called 'Villa Emily' and subsequently 'Villa Verde'.

17 *I once spent some months living there*: Adorno had spent considerable time in San Remo during the late summer and autumn of 1927; cf. letter 25.

18 *the dead village of Bussana Vecchia*: the site had been largely destroyed by an earthquake in 1887.

19 *uòva all' òstrica*: raw egg yolks seasoned with some salt and a little lemon juice slurped directly from the spoon like an oyster (*all' òstrica*).

20 *I have a very bad conscience about Kracauer*: written communication between Adorno and Kracauer, who had fled to Paris on 28 February 1933, came to a temporary end in April 1933. Correspondence between them was not resumed until the summer of 1935.

21 *the Threepenny Novel*: the first edition of Brecht's *Dreigroschenroman* [Threepenny Novel] had appeared in October.

22 *Richard Hughes*: cf. Richard Hughes, *Ein Sturmwind nach Jamaica* [A High Wind in Jamaica] (Berlin 1931).

23 *Norman Douglas*: a copy of a later edition of the novel *South Wind* (first published in 1917) was found in Adorno's personal library. cf. Norman Douglas, *South Wind* (London 1934).

24 *Sternberger*: Dolf Sternberger (1907–1989) enjoyed close contact with Adorno between 1930 and 1933 and took part in the latter's teaching seminars; Adorno encouraged Sternberger to work on his dissertation, *Der verstandene Tod. Eine Untersuchung zu Martin Heideggers Existential-Ontologie* [Conceptualizing Death: An Investigation of Heidegger's Existential Ontology] (Leipzig 1934), and wrote an official academic report on the work. *The Rundschau pieces from Sternberger*: cf. Dolf Sternberger, 'On the Art of Photography', in the journal 'Die neue Rundschau' 45, issue 2 (1934), pp. 412–35; and the piece 'Art Nouveau. Concept and Characterization', also in 'Die neue Rundschau' 45, issue 9 (1934), pp. 255–71.

25 *your English friends*: it is impossible to identify the *English friends* who were probably mentioned in Benjamin's letter that has not survived.

26 *Dora Sophie*: i.e. Dora Sophie Benjamin (1890–1964), née Kellner, Benjamin's divorced wife.

24 BENJAMIN TO WIESENGRUND-ADORNO
    SAN REMO, 30.11.1934

[The beginning of the letter is lost]

and if this should transpire, then it would only be fragmentary, and in that case the whole thing would naturally be at your immediate disposal in manuscript.[1]

I am extremely eager to see your piece against Mannheim; hopefully I shall receive it very soon.

Ernst Bloch, of whom incidentally I know almost next to nothing and from whom I have heard nothing, has announced a new book.[2] But the publishers Oprecht and Helbling have not yet brought it out. – A few days ago I also finally heard some news from Schoen, none of which unfortunately contradicts what you had written to me. – It already struck me last summer that Eisler[3] gets on with film music much better than anyone ever gets on with him.

Your recommendation of the Café Morgana has only filled me with sadness. For indeed it would certainly appear by virtue of its location to be an incomparably suitable place in which to work. From this perspective the other cafés here about are even worse than those in the smallest Italian eeries. But, to be brief, it has gone bankrupt, fallite, and is now closed down. – I shall shortly be going up to Bussana Vecchia. In the same general direction I recently went as far as Taggia. That is a mountain town in a splendid setting where I discovered 'the fairest stairway in the world'. – When was it you were here?

59

My former wife sends you the friendliest greetings in return.
I would be delighted to hear more from you and remain with the
most cordial greetings,

Yours,

Walter Benjamin

30 November 1934
San Remo
Villa Emily

1 *the whole thing . . . in manuscript*: Benjamin is clearly responding to
Adorno's request in letter 23 for a copy of his essay 'Franz Kafka' and
discussing the possibility of getting it published.

2 *Ernst Bloch . . . a new book*: cf. Ernst Bloch, *Erbschaft dieser Zeit* [Herit-
age of our Age] (Zürich 1935) [actually published: 1934].

3 *Eisler*: Benjamin had met Hanns Eisler during his summer stay in Denmark
with Brecht.

25 WIESENGRUND-ADORNO TO BENJAMIN
    OXFORD, 5.12.1934

5 December 1934.   MERTON COLLEGE,
                                                   OXFORD.

Dear Herr Benjamin,

It was a great pleasure to receive your letter, and I respond at once
in order to be able to write from England: for in the middle of next
week I am going to Berlin to see Felizitas. Until then my address is
Albemarle Court Hotel, Leinster Gardens, London W2, and if you
are quick you could certainly reach me there – otherwise I fear a real
interruption of our correspondence, at least in open terms, until the
beginning of January.

First, as far as plans for a meeting are concerned, there is no one
who could possibly desire this more than I do, and it goes without
saying that we cannot allow next year to pass without talking to one
another at length. However, this will be very difficult to arrange
during the next few months, unless your travels bring you to London. From the middle of January to the middle of March, and then
again from the end of April to the middle of June, I am tied down in
Oxford, and in the intervening period it is extremely likely that I
shall have to go to America, since I cannot really refuse Horkheimer's
urgent invitations[1] without endangering a number of interests, not to
mention the personal obligation involved. However, given that the
vacations here are exceptionally extended – from the middle of June

to at least the middle of October – we should certainly be able to arrange something at that time, and I am already giving careful consideration to how and where it can be accomplished.

Else Herzberger: my hopes of speaking to her directly have been dashed since she didn't come to England after all. There is a chance that I may get to see her in Frankfurt at Christmas – although this seems unlikely – and I do not feel that intervention by correspondence is advisable. In principle it seems to me that we should really only pursue this possibility (limited as it unfortunately is) in the most urgent and extreme circumstances – precisely so that we should then be in a position to rely on it. I would therefore be very grateful if you could indicate your present situation – whether such an *ultima ratio* is actually required or whether you are more or less managing at the moment – and in the latter case, I would advise you to let matters stand as they are (precisely, and indeed *only*, for the reasons I have already suggested). And especially in the light of the Saarland decision,[2] which of course weighs very heavily upon Else. May I therefore request you to let me know how to proceed?

And now a few words about the Arcades again. The question of a relationship between your 'dream of the collective' and the collective unconscious of Jung (and I have actually seen none of his more recent publications apart from a not insignificant essay on Joyce)[3] is certainly not something to be dismissed out of hand. But I must say how much it has always amazed me that you have been able to distance yourself most emphatically and resolutely from what might initially have seemed to lie closest of all to you: from Gundolf in the essay on Elective Affinities,[4] and likewise from those interpretations of the Baroque[5] from the Expressionist quarter and up to Hausenstein and Cysarz, whose book on Schiller[6] indeed exceeds our darkest fears. Indeed I would even ascribe a certain systematic dignity to your intentions in this regard, connected as they are with the category of the 'extreme', something which is of singular importance to me at the moment. I am still well aware of how profoundly impressed I was, a good ten years ago now, when you so sharply opposed the Scheler[7] of that time, even though you were then far less reticent about expressing theological, that is theocratic-ontological, propositions yourself. And it is indeed only in this sense that I can imagine any relationship to Jung, or Klages for example (whose doctrine of 'phantoms'[8] in the section 'The Actuality of Images' from his 'Spirit as Antagonist of the Soul' lies closest of all, relatively speaking, to our own concerns). Or to put it more precisely still: it is exactly here that the decisive distinction between archaic and dialectical images really lies, or, as I once formulated the issue against Brecht, this is the place for a materialist doctrine of ideas. But it seems highly probable to me

61

that you might find *Freud's* debate with Jung an appropriate vehicle in this regard, for although Freud himself is quite unconcerned with our own question, he does confront Jung with the serious nominalistic challenge that is certainly required for any genuine access to the primal history of the nineteenth century *itself*. But it is equally intimately connected with this question, that is with the dialectical character of these images, so it seems to me, that the latter must be interpreted objectively rather than merely 'psychologically' in an immanent sense. If I understand the constellation of concepts correctly here, then Freud's individualistic but dialectical critique can actually help to break the archaicizing tendency of the others, and then itself be used, dialectically, to overcome Freud's own immanentist standpoint. Please forgive these vague and topological suggestions – to elaborate them in concrete detail would mean nothing less than anticipating your own theory, and that is the last thing I would dare to do. But it seems to me beyond question that Freud's writings on the interpretation of analysis[9] are extremely important to this complex of issues. In your book on Baroque Drama you succeeded in salvaging induction:[10] here it is the nominalist and psychologistic thinker who must be salvaged in order to destroy and transcend all bourgeois ontologism. In this connection I would also be very interested to learn whether or not you came into contact with Reich and his circle[11] while you were in Copenhagen. There is much of real value here, but naturally combined with a lot of romantic Feuerbach, anarchistic regression, and a dubious glorification of 'genital', and to that extent ahistorical, sexuality.

I am very keen, ardently keen indeed, to read your new pieces for the *Childhood*[12] and, above all, the piece on Kafka:[13] for we have all surely owed a redeeming word to Kafka, and Kracauer[14] most of all – and how urgent the task of liberating him from the shackles of an existentialistic theology and freeing him for a different theology. And since we must still reckon with a not inconsiderable period of time before our reunion, would it not perhaps be possible for me to have a look at these pieces now?

I happened to mention Krenek because at the moment he is trying to find a publisher for a prospective collection of my musical writings[15] (which Felizitas has entitled 'Great Pan is Dead', and for which I have now discovered a truly extraordinary motto from George).[16] His development has followed a very favourable course, and in our current correspondence he has revealed a knowledge concerning the most remote aspects of music such as I have hardly ever encountered in anyone before. It is quite impossible to understand the man, thank goodness, from the perspective of his politics.[17]

Have you seen *Dämmerung*[18] [*Twilight*] yet?

I wish you all the best with your work – from my work I simply offer this proposition from Bolzano,[19] one which I defend, and hopefully have not already sent you before: according to him logic is 'that science which teaches us how to present systematic knowledge in useful manual form'.

I have known San Remo since 1927, the first time I spent a short while there with Gretel, and then later some months on my own; my study of Freud belongs to this period. The picture of the Alps and the lake is quite incomparable – especially up in the mountains themselves which boast the most beautiful paths along the top.

I would ask you most warmly to return the greetings of your former wife with my own. Sincerely yours as ever,

Teddie Wiesengrund

1 *Horkheimer's urgent invitations*: Adorno is referring to Horkheimer's letter of 16 October in which the latter describes the prospects in America for Adorno and then continues: 'this perspective upon our current situation, together with the conviction that you too must regard the continuing existence and increasing influence of the Institute in this ever darkening world of ours as a positive duty, support my suggestion that you should seriously consider making a trip to America. If I can manage to get to Europe in the early months of next year, we would have an opportunity of discussing such a trip with one another. But since under certain circumstances my own trip may prove further off than that, the idea of your coming over this winter does not seem so odd. I do not exclude the possibility that after seeing and experiencing the place first hand you will feel that your chances here, and that quite independently of the purely material assistance offered by the Institute, are much more promising than those in England. With the reservation that disappointments are always of course possible, the extremely encouraging attitude of certain crucial circles at Columbia University, and a number of important people at other universities towards everything our Institute represents, give me good grounds to entertain a very favourable prognosis. At any rate, your current situation in relation to the constellation of interests here at present seems to provide more than good enough reason for you to come and look around for yourself. We could share the return travel costs in such a way that the matter would not inconvenience you more than you feel is justified in the light of your own vital interests. Please give serious consideration to my proposal! It naturally goes without saying that my own desire to see and speak to you once again also plays a role in my suggestion.' (Unpublished letter from Horkheimer to Adorno of 16.11.1934). – Adorno's trip to America did not actually transpire until 1937.

2 *the Saarland decision*: the plebiscite of the Saar region, in which 90.36 per cent of the population voted for reunification with the rest of Germany, took place on 13 January 1935.

3 *Jung . . . essay on Joyce*: Adorno probably knew Carl Gustav Jung's essay ' "Ulysses". A Monologue', which first appeared in the September issue of

the 'European Review', from consulting Jung's book *Wirklichkeit der Seele* [The Actuality of the Soul] (Zürich 1934).

4 *Gundolf in the essay on Elective Affinities*: cf. GS I, pp. 158–67.

5 *those interpretations of the Baroque*: cf. the sections entitled 'Appreciation' and 'Baroque and Expressionism' in the 'Epistemo-Critical Prologue' to Benjamin's *Origins of German Tragic Drama* (cf. GS I, pp. 232–6); in the first of these sections Benjamin cites Wilhelm Hausenstein's *Vom Geist des Barock* [The Spirit of Baroque] and Herbert Cysarz's *Deutsche Barockdichtung. Renaissance, Barock, Rokoko* [German Poetry of the Baroque].

6 *Cysarz, whose book on Schiller*: cf. Herbert Cysarz, *Schiller* (Halle 1934).

7 *Scheler*: it is no longer possible to discover the context of Benjamin's remarks on Scheler.

8 *Klages ... doctrine of 'phantoms'*: cf. Ludwig Klages, *Der Geist als Widersacher der Seele* [The Spirit as Antagonist of the Soul], vol. 3, part I: *Die Lehre von der Wirklichkeit der Bilder* [On the Actuality of Images] (Leipzig 1932), pp. 1223–37 ('Primal Images and Phantoms').

9 *Freud's writings on the interpretation of analysis*: Adorno is probably thinking of the following writings of Freud: *Self-Presentation* (1925), *The History of the Psychoanalytic Movement* (1915), *A Short Outline of Psychoanalysis* (1924/28) and *Resistances to Psychoanalysis* (1925).

10 *you succeeded in salvaging induction*: cf. GS I [1], pp. 223–7.

11 *Reich and his circle*: the psychoanalyst Wilhelm Reich (1897–1957) had emigrated to Denmark and was now director of 'Der Verlag für Sexualpolitik' in Copenhagen.

12 *your new pieces for the Childhood*: Adorno learned of these *new pieces* from an undated letter (but probably written around the end of November 1934) from Benjamin to Gretel Karplus: 'As far as work is concerned – and this indefatigable interest may well astonish you – the first thing I have done is to take up the "Berlin Childhood" once again. There are still a few pieces which I have been thinking about for years. But I think I have now finally accomplished one thing in this regard; the title of the piece tells you just how central it is for me. It is called "Colours". If I can possibly get hold of someone to transcribe it for me, I shall send you a copy. In addition there are now pieces on "The Gate at Halle" and "A Christmas Carol"' (cf. GS IV [2], p. 967).

13 *Kafka*: see letter 23 and the relevant note.

14 *Kracauer*: Kracauer's writings on Kafka included reviews of his novels and the collection entitled 'Building the Great Wall of China', as well as two substantial essays on the writer; cf. the three-volume collection of essays: Siegfried Kracauer, *Schriften*, vol. 5, edited by Inka Mülder-Bach (Frankfurt a.M. 1990).

15 *a prospective collection of my musical writings*: the collection which was to be entitled 'Great Pan is Dead' never came to fruition; cf. *Briefwechsel Adorno/Krenek*, p. 73.

16 *a truly extraordinary motto from George*: the verses from Stefan George's *Der Siebente Ring* [The Seventh Ring], cited by Adorno in his letter to Krenek of 5 November 1934: 'Und wenn die grosse Nährerin im zorne / Nicht mehr sich mischend neigt am untern borne / In einer weltnacht starr und müde pocht: / So kann nur einer der sie stets befocht / Und zwang und nie verfuhr nach ihrem rechte / Die hand ihr pressen, packen ihre flechte / Dass sie ihr werk willfährig wieder treibt: / Den leib vergottet und den gott verleiblicht.' [And when the mighty Nurturing One in wrath / No longer willingly betakes herself unto the nether spring / And knocks with lifeless weariness in this world's night: / So only one who long has fought her / Forced her and never once submitted to her law / Can press her hand and grasp her hair / That she might once again perform her wonted work with joy: / to deify the body and to body forth the god.] (cf. *Briefwechsel Adorno/Krenek*, pp. 59 and 73.) – Benjamin could already be found quoting these lines in 1933 (cf. GS III, p. 397).

17 *Krenek . . . from the perspective of his politics*: at that time Krenek still supported the Habsburgs' claims to legitimacy.

18 *Dämmerung*: cf. Heinrich Regius [pseudonym of Max Horkheimer], *Dämmerung. Notizen in Deutschland* [Twilight] (Zürich 1934); now in Max Horkheimer, *Schriften*, edited by Alfred Schmidt and Gunzelin Schmid Noerr, vol. 2: *Philosophische Frühschriften 1922 bis 1932*, edited by Gunzelin Schmid Noerr (Frankfurt a.M. 1987), pp. 309–452.

19 *this proposition from Bolzano*: Adorno is quoting from Edmund Husserl's *Logische Untersuchungen* [Logical Investigations], vol. 1: *Prolegomena to a Pure Logic*, 3rd unchanged edition (Halle 1922), p. 29; Husserl refers to 'B. Bolzano, *Wissenschaftslehre* (Sulzbach 1837), I, p. 7'.

26 WIESENGRUND-ADORNO TO BENJAMIN
    BERLIN, 16.12.1934

Berlin, 16 December 1934

Dear Herr Benjamin, thanks to Wissing* I have been able to have a look at your Kafka essay, and would merely like to tell you right away that the intentions behind the work have made a most extraordinary impression upon me – the greatest impression anything of

* *Adorno was mistaken*: a remark added by Egon Wissing in order to tell Benjamin that Adorno had not in fact received the manuscript of the essay on Kafka from him.

yours has made on me since the completion of the Kraus essay.[1] I hope I shall find time during the next few days to express my response more thoroughly, and you should simply take it as an advance payment on that if I emphasise here the tremendous definition of attentiveness as a historical figure of prayer[2] at the end of the third chapter. As for the rest, our agreement on the fundamental philosophical issues has never seemed clearer to me than it does in this work! – I am having a lovely time here.

Yours ever,
Teddie W.

1 *the Kraus essay*: i.e. Benjamin's essay of 1931, which had appeared in four numbers of the *Frankfurter Zeitung* (10.3; 14.3; 17.3 and 18.3.1931); cf. GS II [1], pp. 334–67.

2 *definition of attentiveness as a historical figure of prayer*: cf. GS II [2], p. 432.

27   WIESENGRUND-ADORNO TO BENJAMIN
     BERLIN 17.12.1934

Berlin, 17 December 1934.

Dear Herr Benjamin, please allow me in the greatest of haste – for Felizitas is about to take away my copy of your Kafka essay, which I have only managed to read through a couple of times – to redeem my earlier promise and say a few words about it. And indeed more in order to express the immediate, indeed overwhelming, sense of gratitude which seized hold of me because of it, than because I could even imagine having properly fathomed this astonishing torso, or being in the slightest position to pass 'judgement' upon it. Do not take it for immodesty if I begin by confessing that our agreement in philosophical fundamentals has never impressed itself upon my mind more perfectly than it does here. Let me only mention my own earliest attempt to interpret Kafka,[1] nine years ago now – I claimed he represents a photograph of our earthly life from the perspective of a redeemed life, one which merely reveals the latter as an edge of black cloth, whereas the terrifyingly distanced optics of the photographic image is none other than that of the obliquely angled camera itself – no further words seem necessary to demonstrate our agreement, however much your analyses also point beyond this conception. And this also, and indeed in a quite principled sense, touches upon one's position with regard to 'theology'. Since I always insisted on such a position, before entering into your Arcades, it seems to me doubly important that the image of theology, into which I would gladly see our thoughts dissolve, is none other than the very one which sustains your thoughts here – it could indeed be called an 'inverse' theology. This position, directed against natural and supernatural interpretation alike, first formulated here as it is with total precision, strikes me as utterly identical with my own – indeed my Kierkegaard study[2] was concerned with nothing else, and when you pour scorn upon the connection between Pascal and Kierkegaard,[3] I might well remind you that I express the same scorn about the connection between Kierkegaard and Pascal and Augustine[4] in my own study. But if I nonetheless still insist upon a relationship between Kafka and Kierkegaard, then it is decidedly not that espoused by dialectical theology, the representative example of which is Schöps[5] as far as Kafka is concerned. This relationship is to be found rather precisely with respect to the position of 'scripture',[6] and here you claim so decisively that what Kafka regarded as a relic of scripture can be understood much better, namely in social terms, as the prolegomenon of scripture. And this is indeed the secret coded character of our theology, no more, and indeed without loss of a single iota, no less. The fact that this should emerge here with such enormous force strikes me as the finest proof of your philosophical success I have witnessed since I became acquainted with the first fragments of your Arcades.[7] – I would also like especially to count your remarks about music, and about the gramophone and photography, as further evidence of our agreement – in a few weeks you should hopefully be receiving something which I wrote about a year ago concerning the nature of phonographic records,[8] a piece which takes a specific passage in your book on Baroque drama[9] as its point of departure and simultaneously employs the category of ambiguous and alienated thinghood in almost exactly the sense in which I now see you are construing it in the piece on Kafka; and above all the same is true of your remarks on beauty and hopelessness.[10] I must say I almost regret that although you explicitly note the vacuousness of the standardly theological interpretations[11] of Kafka, you do not explicate this so fully as you did with Gundolf's interpretations in your essay[12] on the Elective Affinities (and incidentally, Kaiser's psychoanalytical platitudes[13] actually distort the truth far less than the bourgeois profundities of the former). In Freud the uniform and the paternal imago belong together.

If you yourself describe the work as 'incomplete', it would be very foolish and indeed utterly conventional of me to contradict you. You are only too well aware how intimately the significance of the work is bound up with its fragmentary character. But that does not mean that the place where it is incomplete cannot be identified – and indeed precisely because the work precedes the Arcades. For this is its incompleteness. The relationship between primal history and modernity has yet to be conceptualized, and the success of an interpretation of Kafka must depend in the last analysis upon the former. There is a first empty gap at the beginning with the quotation from Lukács[14] and the antithesis between the concept of 'Historical Age' [Zeitalter] and epochal 'Age of the World' [Weltalter].[15] This antithesis cannot be exploited fruitfully simply as a contrast, but only in a dialectical manner. I would put it this way: that *for us* the concept of the historical age is simply non-existent (just as we cannot know decadence or progress in the obvious sense which you yourself dismantle in this connection), and we can only grasp an epochal age of the world as an extrapolation from the literally petrified present. And I know that no one would theoretically concede me that more readily than you. But in the piece on Kafka the concept of the age of the world still remains abstract in the Hegelian sense (incidentally, though you are probably unaware of it, there are some astonishingly close connections between Hegel and this work. I would simply point out that the passage on 'nothing' and 'something'[16] corresponds very sharply indeed to the opening dialectical movement of the Hegelian concept: being – nothing – becoming, and further that Cohen certainly took over the theme[17] concerning the inversion of mythical law and guilt from Hegel's philosophy of right, as well as from the Judaic tradition). But that simply means that the anamnesis – or the 'forgetting' – of primal history in Kafka gets interpreted in your work in an essentially archaic rather than thoroughly dialectical sense; and this brings the work right back to the beginning of the Arcades. I am certainly the last person to pass judgement here, for I am only too aware that I can be accused of falling back in the same way, of failing adequately to articulate the concept of myth in the same way in my own Kierkegaard book, where this concept was dealt with as a logical construction rather than in a concrete manner. But that is precisely why I am in a position to point this out to you. It is no accident that, amongst all the other interpreted anecdotes, one in particular, namely Kafka's image of children,[18] passes *without* interpretation. But the interpretation of the latter would be tantamount to the neutralization of the age of the world in the glare of a lightning flash. And this touches all of the potential difficulties *in concreto* – the symptoms of archaic enthralment, the unexplicated character of the mythical dialectic here too. The most important difficulty seems to me to be that of Odradek.[19] For it is merely archaic to have him spring forth from the 'immemorial world and guilt', rather than re-reading him precisely as that prolegomenon which you so penetratingly identified in the problem of scripture. If his origin lies with the father of the house, does he not then precisely represent the anxious *concern* and

68

danger for the latter, does he not anticipate precisely the overcoming of the creaturely state of guilt, and is not this concern – truly a case of Heidegger put right side up – the secret key, indeed the most indubitable promise of *hope*, precisely through the overcoming of the house itself? Certainly, as the other face of the world of things, Odradek is a sign of distortion – but precisely as such he is also a motif of transcendence, namely of the ultimate limit and of the reconciliation of the organic and the inorganic, or of the overcoming of death: Odradek 'lives on'. Expressed in another way, it is only to a life that is perverted in thingly form that an escape from the overall context of nature is promised.* There is more than merely 'cloud' here,[20] for the dialectic and the imagery of the cloud are certainly not to be 'explained away', but they are to be rendered dialectical through and through – and the parables will come falling thick and fast – for this must remain the innermost intention of any interpretation of Kafka; the same intention as the thorough theoretical articulation of the 'dialectical image'. No, Odradek is indeed so dialectical that it can also properly be said of him that 'almost nothing has made everything well again'.[21] – The passage about myth and fairy-tale[22] belongs to this same complex, and one could at least pragmatically defend the suggestion that the fairy-tale appears as the foxing of myth, or as its dissolution – as if the Attic tragedians were really story-tellers, which is precisely what they are in the final analysis, as if the key image of the fairy-tale were not the pre-mythical, no, the sinless world, as it appears to us under a thingly cipher. It is extremely strange that the substantive 'errors' of which the work might well be accused find their source here. Unless I am most cruelly deceived, the machine inscribes not merely the backs of the delinquent inhabitants of the penal colony,[23] but their entire bodies, and indeed the process in which the machine turns them around is even described (this turning round is the heart of the story, and is also immediately obvious to the understanding; what is more, in this story in particular, the principal section of which betrays a certain idealist abstraction, as do the aphorisms you rightly ignore,[24] we should not forget about the detached conclusion and the old Governor's grave beneath the café table). The interpretation of natural theatre expressed in terms of 'the country fair or children's party'[25] also strikes me as archaic – the image of a song-festival in a large town during the 1880s would certainly be a truer one, and Morgenstern's 'Dorfluft' [Village Air][26] has always seemed highly suspect to me anyway. If Kafka is not to be regarded as the founder of a religion[27] – and how

* and this is also the deepest reason why I am against establishing an immediate relationship to 'use-value' in other contexts as well.

69

right you are there! for nothing is further from the truth! – then there is also absolutely no way he can be regarded as a poet of the Judaic homeland either! And here I feel that your remarks about the inner involvement of the German and the Jewish element[28] are quite decisive. The tied-back wings of the angel[29] represent no real loss, but constitute the angel's very 'movement' – these wings, in all their obsolete appearance, are hope itself, and there is no other hope but this.

It is this perspective, the dialectic of appearance as a premature modernity, it seems to me, which first properly illuminates the very function of theatre and gesture[30] to which you were the first person to ascribe the central importance which it deserved. The whole tenor of the process is of this kind. If one were to seek out the origin of such gesture, one would look for it less in the Chinese theatre, so it seems to me, than in modernity itself, that is, in the extinction of language. What we see in Kafka's gestures is the self-liberation of the creature which has been deprived of the language of things. That is certainly why, as you say, it discloses itself on deeper reflection and study as prayer – I do not think it can really be understood as an 'experimental attempt',[31] and the only thing about the work that strikes me as alien to the material is the adoption of categories drawn from epic theatre. For this world-theatre, since indeed it is only played out before God himself, tolerates no standpoint external to itself, in relation to which it would simply contract to the dimensions of the stage; and, as you say, we can no more identify a stage context for the scene itself (other than precisely the heavens[32] above and beyond the earthly course of events) than we can hang the sky upon the wall surrounding the stage; and that is why it belongs constitutively to the conception of the world as the 'theatre' of salvation, in the mute acceptance of language, that the very form of Kafka's art (and there can certainly be *no* question of ignoring this artistic form once the idea of an unmediated presentation of doctrine has been abandoned) stands in the most extreme antithesis to the form of theatrical art in so far as it is a novel. Thus it seems to me that with his banal allusion to film, Brod has here hit upon something far more precisely than he could have imagined. Kafka's novels are not screenplays for experimental theatre, since they lack in principle the very spectator who might intervene in such experiments. They represent rather the last and disappearing connecting texts of the silent film (and it is no accident that the latter disappeared at almost exactly the same time as Kafka's death); the ambiguity of gesture lies somewhere between sinking into speechlessness (the destruction of language) and the emergence from the latter in music – thus the most important contribution to the constellation gesture-animal-music is certainly the depiction of the group of dogs and their silent music-making in the 'Observations of a Dog',[33] something I would not hesitate to compare with Sancho Panza.[34] Perhaps it would clarify the issue considerably if this could be taken up. As far as the fragmentary character of the piece is concerned, let me simply say that the relationship between forgetting and remembering,[35] certainly central, has not yet become entirely clear to me, and could perhaps be articulated even more unambiguously and emphatically; about the passage on 'characterlessness'[36] let me also say, just for the sake of curiosity, that I wrote a short piece last year on the process of 'levelling',[37] in which I also interpreted the elimination of individual character in a similarly positive sense; and allow me to tell you, as a further curiosity, that I wrote a piece early this year about the countless colourful ticket designs[38] in use on the London buses, something which also touches in the strangest way upon your piece on colours in the 'Berlin Childhood',[39] which Felizitas had shown me. But above all, let me underline once again the significance of the passage on attentiveness as prayer.[40] I cannot think of anything more important from your hand than this – nor of anything which could better and more precisely communicate your innermost intentions.

– And it almost looks to me as though the blasphemy of our mutual friend Ernst[41] has found atonement in your Kafka. I have still had no reply from him to my substantial letter, and I am particularly keen to learn whether one will ever arrive. – We are off to Frankfurt on Saturday. I found Felizitas to be in good health and I myself am very well.

I shall be writing to Levy in clear terms. In friendship,

Yours,

Teddie W.

1 *my own earliest attempt to interpret Kafka*: nothing more is known about this *earliest attempt*; but cf. the beginning of the essay 'Remarks on Kafka' (GS 10 [1], p. 254).

2 *my Kierkegaard study*: see letter 10 and the relevant note.

3 *the connection between Pascal and Kierkegaard*: cf. GS II [2], p. 426.

4 *the connection between Kierkegaard and Pascal and Augustine*: cf. GS 2, p. 91.

5 *Schöps*: Hans Joachim Schöps, together with Max Brod, published Kafka's posthumous volume *The Building of the Great Wall of China* in 1931; Adorno is referring to the afterword composed by the editors which also announced the forthcoming publication of a monograph by Schöps which was 'to present a detailed interpretation of Franz Kafka's entire work as ultimately expressing a *negative actualization of Judaic understanding of*

revelation, and one conditioned by the advancing process of secularization in western history' (p. 258).

6 *the position of 'scripture'*: cf. GS II [2], p. 437.

7 *the first fragments of your Arcades*: see letter 7 and the relevant note.

8 *the nature of phonographic records*: cf. Adorno, 'Die Form der Schallplatte' [The Phonographic Record as Medium], first published in the Viennese music journal '23' (5.12.1934, nrs. 17–19, pp. 35–9); now in GS 19, pp. 530–4.

9 *a specific passage in your book on Baroque drama*: Adorno is referring to Benjamin's characterization of 'music as the last universal language after Babel' (GS I [1], p. 388), which Adorno had mentioned in his essay on the 'The Phonographic Record as Medium' without citing its source (cf. GS 19, p. 533).

10 *your remarks on beauty and hopelessness*: cf. GS II [2], pp. 413f.

11 *the standardly theological interpretations*: cf. ibid., pp. 425f.

12 *Gundolf's interpretations in your essay*: cf. GS I [1], pp. 158–67.

13 *Kaiser's psychoanalytical platitudes*: Adorno is referring to Hellmut Kaiser's book *Kafkas Inferno* (Wien 1931), also mentioned in Benjamin's essay (cf. GS II [2], p. 425).

14 *the quotation from Lukács*: cf. GS II [2], p. 410.

15 *the antithesis between the concept of 'Historical Age' and epochal 'Age of the World'*: cf. ibid.

16 *the passage on 'nothing' and 'something'*: cf. ibid., p. 435.

17 *Cohen certainly took over the theme*: cf. ibid., p. 412.

18 *Kafka's image of children*: cf. ibid., p. 416; the photograph in Benjamin's possession is reproduced in the *Benjamin-Katalog*, p. 247.

19 *Odradek*: see Kafka's prose piece 'The House-Father's Concern' in the volume entitled *A Country Doctor*; for Benjamin's interpretation in terms of *immemorial world and guilt*, cf. GS II [2], p. 431.

20 *more than merely 'cloud' here*: cf. ibid., p. 420.

21 *'almost nothing has made everything well again'*: a line in Adorno's opera, *Der Schatz des Indianer-Joe*, ed. Rolf Tiedemann (Frankfurt a.M. 1979), p. 95.

22 *the passage about myth and fairy-tale*: cf. GS II [2], p. 415.

23 *the delinquent inhabitants of the penal colony*: cf. ibid., p. 432.

24 *the aphorisms you rightly ignore*: see Kafka's *Betrachtungen über Sünde, Leid, Hoffnung und den wahren Weg* [Reflections on Sin, Suffering, Hope and the True Path] in the 1931 collection entitled *The Building of the Great Wall of China*; for Benjamin's rejection see GS II [2], pp. 425f.

25 *'the country fair or children's party'*: cf. ibid., p. 423.

26 *Morgenstern's 'Dorfluft'*: cf. ibid.; for the remark of Soma Morgenstern which arose during a conversation between him and Benjamin, cf. GS II [3], p. 1231.

27 *the founder of a religion*: cf. GS II [2], p. 424.

28 *the inner involvement of the German and Jewish element*: cf. ibid., p. 432.

29 *the tied-back wings of the angel*: cf. ibid., p. 423.

30 *the function of theatre and gesture*: cf. ibid., pp. 418–20.

31 *an 'experimental attempt'*: Benjamin is referring to a concept belonging to Brecht's style of Epic Theatre; cf. GS II [2], p. 418.

32 *world-theatre . . . the stage . . . the heavens*: cf. ibid., p. 419.

33 *'Observations of a Dog'*: cf. Kafka's eponymous story in the collection *Beschreibung eines Kampfs* [Description of a Struggle].

34 *Sancho Panza*: cf. Kafka's story 'The Truth About Sancho Panza' in the collection *Hochzeitsvorbereitungen auf dem Land* [Preparations for a Country Wedding]; Benjamin refers to this story in GS II [2], p. 438.

35 *the relationship between forgetting and remembering*: cf. ibid., pp. 429–32.

36 *the passage on 'characterlessness'*: cf. ibid., p. 418.

37 *a short piece . . . on the process of 'levelling'*: this untitled little piece of 18.1.1934 will be published in 'Frankfurter Adorno-Blätter III'.

38 *a piece . . . about ticket designs*: this piece of Adorno's dates from 22.4.1934; cf. 'Frankfurter Adorno-Blätter II' (Munich 1993), p. 7.

39 *your piece on colours in the Berlin Childhood*: cf. GS IV [1], p. 263 and GS VII [1], p. 424.

40 *the passage on attentiveness as prayer*: cf. GS II [2], p. 432.

41 *the blasphemy of our mutual friend Ernst*: certainly a reference to Ernst Bloch; the relevant passage on Kafka can be found in Bloch's *Erbschaft dieser Zeit* [Heritage of our Age] (Zürich 1934), p. 182.

28 BENJAMIN TO WIESENGRUND-ADORNO
    SAN REMO, 7.1.1935

Dear Herr Wiesengrund,
    Presuming you are back by now, I come to answer your long letter of 17 December. And not without some trepidation – it is so weighty

73

and goes so directly to the heart of the matter that I cannot begin to do it justice in the form of correspondence. It is thus all the more important that before all else I assure you once again of the enormous pleasure which your vigorous interest in my work has given me. I have not only read your letter, I have studied it; for it demands to be pondered on sentence by sentence. Since you have grasped my intentions so accurately, your suggestions about where I have gone astray are of the greatest significance. This is particularly true of the remarks you make about my insufficient grasp of the archaic; and is therefore also especially true of your reservations about the question of the epochal world-age and the process of forgetting. As for the rest, I will concede your objections to the expression 'experimental attempt' without further ado, and will also bear in mind your very significant observations on silent film. The fact that you refer with such particular emphasis to the 'Investigations of a Dog' has proved a useful hint. For it is precisely this piece of Kafka's – and probably the only one – which has continued to remain foreign to me as I worked on the essay. I also realize – and have said as much to Felizitas – that I was still unsure what it really had to say to me. Your remarks have clarified this expectation.

Now that two parts – the first and third – have been published, the way is clear for revision;[1] of course it is still in question whether this will finally lead to publication, and whether Schocken[2] will publish the expanded version in book form. As far as I can tell at the moment, the revision will principally affect the fourth part[3] which, in spite of the great – and perhaps because of the all too great – stress I have placed upon it, has not really allowed readers even like Scholem and yourself to take up a position. Otherwise, Brecht is also amongst those who have openly expressed a view so far;[4] and thus, all in all, a kind of musical image has come to surround it, and from which I still hope to learn something. I have provisionally planned a collection of reflections and have not yet concerned myself about how they will eventually be projected upon the original text. These reflections centre on the relationship 'Image=Symbol', in which I believe I have captured the antinomy which defines Kafka's works in a manner which does greater justice to his mode of thinking than the opposition 'Parable=Novel'.[5] A more precise definition of the novel form in Kafka, which I agree with you in thinking essential, does not as yet exist and can only be accomplished along an indirect path.

I would hope – and this is not at all so unlikely – that some of these questions might remain open until the next time we see one another. That is to say, if I may really draw some hope from a suggestion from Felizitas that you might be considering a trip to San Remo over Easter.[6] I would be delighted if this is the case – more so, indeed, than you could surmise without being able to appreciate my current state of isolation. At the moment, however, a short break from this isolation is promised; I am expecting Wissing and thus I may yet become an indirect witness to his last months in Berlin, the coda of which you experienced directly. And this also makes me desire to see you.

I am not thinking beyond Easter. Brecht has asked me again to come to Denmark, and indeed right away. But I shall probably not leave San Remo before May in any case. On the other hand, I shall not allow my stay here to be extended indefinitely, though it has proved a valuable refuge, for in the long run my isolation from friends and from the necessary means for working will transform it into a dangerous trial of endurance for me. Another consideration, of course, is the constant and crippling feeling of being severely restricted to the bare necessities of life. In response to the kind suggestion you made in December, for which my sincere thanks – under present conditions the 100 Swiss francs[7] from the Institute means that I can at least meet these necessities, so there is actually no need to approach outsiders in my regard. It is still true that a minimum amount of freedom of movement and thus a great amount of initiative could be procured at this particular moment with the slenderest of means, but how precisely?

On the other hand, you know from your own experience that an enormous amount of initiative must be summoned up to compose one's first pieces in a foreign language. I am aware of this with regard to the essay on Bachofen[8] which I am currently writing for the *Nouvelle Revue Française*. This project could well provide an opportunity for saying a great deal concerning our own most fundamental concerns. Since Bachofen is entirely unknown in France – not one of his works has been translated – I am forced to present a lot of general information in the foreground. In saying this, however, I must not omit to register my unreserved agreement with your remarks on Jung and Klages[9] in your letter of 5 December. Precisely in the sense you indicated I feel I need to acquire much more knowledge about Jung. Do you happen to have his study on Joyce at your disposal?

Can you please tell me the source of the following line: 'Almost nothing has made everything well again'?[10] And could you possibly send me the piece on the London bus tickets to which you allude? In any case, I expect as soon as possible to be able to read your piece on the phonograph, which touches directly upon so many areas of important interest.

The first copy of Bloch's book[11] that was sent to me must have gone astray; the publishers have promised that a second copy is on the way. What I really regret is that Bloch, who surely needs the

75

advice of those of his friends who are experts, just as much as we all do, stakes out his capacious territory without regard to them, and is quite satisfied with his own papers for company.

Have you read *The Threepenny Novel* [Dreigroschenroman]?[12] I feel that it is a consummate success. Do write and tell me what you think of it. Be sure to give me detailed news about everything and do not forget to keep me informed about the state of your own work.

Yours,

Walter Benjamin

7 January 1935
San Remo
Villa Verde

1 *the way is clear for revision*: on Benjamin's plan for an *expanded version in book form*, cf. GS II [2], pp. 1179–88.

2 *Schocken*: Salman Schocken (1877–1959) founded the Schocken publishing house in 1931; he left for Palestine in 1933. – Benjamin's attempt to interest Schocken in a book on Kafka came to nothing.

3 *the fourth part*: i.e. the section entitled 'Sancho Panza' (cf. GS II [2], pp. 433–8).

4 *Brecht . . . those who have expressed a view so far*: cf. Benjamin's 'Notes from Svendborg 1934' (GS VI, pp. 526–30) in which he records Brecht's remarks concerning his essay on Kafka.

5 *a collection of reflections . . . 'Image=Symbol' . . . 'Parable=Novel'*: cf. GS II [3], pp. 1253f.; pp. 1255f; pp. 1258f and pp. 1260f.

6 *a suggestion from Felizitas . . . a trip to San Remo over Easter*: in her (unpublished) letter of 26 December 1934, Gretel Karplus mentioned a planned trip to San Remo which never materialized.

7 *the 100 Swiss francs*: the amount which Benjamin received monthly from the Institute of Social Research.

8 *the essay on Bachofen*: Benjamin was invited to write an essay in French on 'Johann Jakob Bachofen' (GS II [1], pp. 219–33) for the *Nouvelle Revue Française* by its principal editor Jean Paulhan; the piece was eventually rejected by Paulhan (cf. the *Benjamin-Katalog*, pp. 235f) and was never published during Benjamin's lifetime.

9 *your remarks on Jung and Klages*: see letter 25.

10 *'Almost nothing has made everything well again'*: see letter 27 and the relevant note.

11 *Bloch's book*: a reference to *The Heritage of our Age*.

12 *The Threepenny Novel*: see letter 23 and the relevant note.

Dear Herr Wiesengrund,

I would very much like to have responded much earlier to your last letter.[1] But as it is, this will arrive – so I hope – while you are on your German vacation. For the rest, there has been ample reason for my silence: on thinking over your letter I felt like the captain of a sailing vessel who has to take out his log book when he finds himself totally becalmed. But what shall he write in it?

The pieces I am working on here[2] have the same curiosity value which sometimes attach to those still photographs of a fighter in picturesque positions. You may already have had the opportunity to look at one of these pieces through Felizitas; another one is in the process of being written. It is not worth saying anything about either of them. And as far as matters on a different level are concerned, just as important as this self-assertion in immediate affairs, I cannot summon up any energy for them at present.

I am thinking above all about the clarification of our relationship with Ernst B.[3] It is certainly true that the necessity for such clarification has lost some of its weight since I heard that he has married Karola.[4] The connection between them is certainly nothing new, but the position which the young lady may henceforth officially assume does not bode particularly well, it seems to me, even under the most auspicious circumstances, for the future of our friendship. And it is not as if I had to appeal to specific circumstances in this connection either. No, it is essentially a question of atmosphere: just as there are certain women who understand how to give ample scope to the role of friendship in their husbands' lives – and of no one is this truer than of Else von Stritzky[5] – so there are also others in whose presence such things easily wither. Linda[6] was already half-way to becoming one of these, and Karola seems to belong among them completely.

I am naturally profoundly sorry – and not merely on account of this matter – that nothing actually came of our intended meeting. And when can we now hope for one? Even if your return trip takes you through Paris, you will be very unlikely to find me there. My immediate circumstances have become too precarious for me simply to take the chance of leaving here. And it strikes me as increasingly difficult for me to gain a proper foothold there anyway. The latest depiction of conditions there comes from a letter of Siegfried's[7] and he paints the city life in fairly grim colours. The profound transformations which have transpired there are even more clearly perceptible to much better prepared and comfortable observers than myself, and in a French journal I recently discovered a letter from an Englishman[8]

77

– certainly an intellectual as well – which explains why he now avoids Paris. His account supported my own experiences.

Of course, this cannot possibly alter the fact that the Bibliothèque Nationale would still be the most utterly desirable place for me to work. And the piece on Fuchs,[9] which the Institute is urging me so strongly to submit, can really only properly be completed there. But one must bring everything along oneself to this working place, and can only expect to be dealt with *à la longue*.

You have certainly done the most intelligent thing in your new environment by reckoning with very long perspectives – the only ones which will perhaps turn out to be unclouded in the long run. I would dearly love to have heard more about your work on Husserl. What you hinted at with regard to expressionlessness struck me as particularly interesting. And your reference to the myth of the Gorgon seems to me to be especially significant. When you are in Frankfurt, do try and consult the archaeological monograph on the Gorgon myth[10] which, if I am not mistaken, was published by a certain von Levezow in the forties or fifties of the last century.

Perhaps you will be able to drop me a line from Oxford? And when will you be back in Oxford again? – I received a friendly letter from Else H. quite a few weeks back. When I responded to her things still looked a little brighter for me: I thought I would be able to take refuge in San Remo till Easter and to conclude my stay there by meeting you. I shall not now be contacting her – especially not from here – before Easter.

Hopefully you will see something of the spring in Frankfurt. And indeed much more easily than here, where the last forty or fifty financial fortunes in the world present themselves to one another in their yachts and Rolls Royces, the whole place shrouded in those dark storm clouds which are the only things I share with them.

With heartfelt greetings to Felizitas and yourself,

Yours,

WB

Monaco-Condamine
Hotel de Marseille

[Dating of letter 29: the letter was written sometime between 24 March – the date when the 'Conversation Concerning the Corso' was published (see below), and which Benjamin had made available to Gretel Karplus as a newspaper cutting – and his return to Paris on 10 April.]

1 *your last letter*: the letter has not survived.

2 *The pieces I am working on here*: Benjamin is probably referring on the one hand to the 'Conversation Concerning the Corso. Echoes of the Carnival

at Nice' (cf. GS IV [2], pp. 763–71), which was written under the pseudonym Detlev Holz and appeared in the *Frankfurter Zeitung* of 24.3.1935, and on the other hand to the story 'Die glückliche Hand. Eine Unterhaltung über dem Spiel' [The Knack. An Investigation of Play] (cf. GS IV [2], pp. 771–7), which was never published in Benjamin's lifetime.

3 *the clarification of our relationship with Ernst B.*: on the rather tense relationship between Benjamin and Bloch, see the *Benjamin-Katalog*, pp. 95–7.

4 *Karola*: Karola Piotrkowska and Ernst Bloch had got to know each other in 1927; they had married in November 1934.

5 *Else von Stritzky*: Ernst Bloch's first wife, who had died in 1921.

6 *Linda*: i.e. Linda Oppenheimer, whom Bloch had married in 1921.

7 *a letter of Siegfried's*: Kracauer's letter to Benjamin of 24.2.1935; cf. Walter Benjamin, *Briefe an Siegfried Kracauer. Mit vier Briefen von Siegfried Kracauer an Benjamin*, edited by the Th. W. Adorno-Archiv (Marbach a.N. 1987) (Marbacher Schriften 27), pp. 82–5.

8 *a letter from an Englishman*: nothing further known.

9 *the piece on Fuchs*: cf. Benjamin's essay 'Eduard Fuchs. Collector and Historian', written at Horkheimer's behest and published in the *Zeitschrift für Sozialforschung* 6, issue 2 (1937), pp. 346–80; now in GS II [2], pp. 465–505.

10 *monograph on the Gorgon myth*: cf. Konrad Levezow, *Über die Entwicklung des Gorgonen-Ideals in der Poesie und bildenden Kunst der Alten. Eine archäologische Abhandlung*, gelesen in der königlichen Akademie der Wissenschaften in Berlin am 12 April, 15 November, 6 December 1832 und 25 April 1833 (Berlin 1833) [On the Development of the Gorgon-Ideal in the Poetry and Art of the Ancients]. – Jakob Andreas Levezow (1770–1835) studied first theology, and then philology under F. A. Wolf in Halle; he subsequently taught at the Friedrich Wilhelm Gymnasium in Berlin, and from 1828 was Head of Antiquities at the Berlin Museum.

30   BENJAMIN TO WIESENGRUND-ADORNO
     PARIS, 1.5.1935

Dear Herr Wiesengrund,

I was extremely pleased to receive confirmation from Felizitas that you have spent an enjoyable time in Königstein,[1] and that you have indeed, as I already surmised from your postcard,[2] been proceeding in your work with the utmost vigour and concentration.

In the meantime I have been in Paris for a short while and am now preparing, for the first time in years, to resume work on the Arcades, no longer relying merely upon my studies, but rather on the basis of a general plan.[3] Of course, there is still much to be done before such a plan can be finalized. But once I have properly fixed upon it, in this particular case and in view of the extensive documentation I now have at my disposal, a considerable part of the necessary work will already have been accomplished.

It is not merely these circumstances alone, although they are certainly relevant, which once again prompt the hope of arranging a meeting between us this year. In addition to that, it looks highly unlikely that I shall get to Denmark this year. Have you already made any arrangements for the summer holidays? Do you think it might prove possible perhaps for us to meet in France during this time?

It would give me great joy to see you again. The possibility of meeting up with Bloch, on the other hand, something which could indeed transpire under certain circumstances here, rather weighs upon me. Since he rebuked me a couple of months ago for my written comments on his book,[4] in a manner reminiscent of the way a teacher might demand to see his pupil's homework, I have abandoned the already painful attempt to express in letter form an opinion concerning the *Erbschaft dieser Zeit* [Heritage of the Present Age].

In the meantime I have heard talk of something which is confirmed not merely by my own private fears but also by the impression made upon me by many passages of the book itself: he is supposed to have written something for the 'Young Generation', as this is represented by someone like Alfred Kantorowicz,[5] arguing that he would like to point the way forward for contemporary youth (a literary path which Karola must already have marked out for him).

After arriving back here I wrote a letter to Else Herzberger at her Paris address – 38 Quai d'Auteuil c/o Alfons Herzberger – but I have received no reply as yet. I assume that she is not here at the moment. On the other hand, of course, I was particularly keen to make some personal contact with her. Do you think you could do something to facilitate the possibility? And perhaps discover on her side whether she is expected to come here, and if so when? If you could, you would be doing me a very great service.

In the last few days I have laid hands upon a book which I have been tracking down for years and which has fully redeemed all the expectations I had placed in it. Courting the danger that you already know the work, I cannot resist the pleasure of sending you here three, almost arbitrarily selected, maxims from it in my own translation.

XL

The ideas which are important to an individual should be coordinated with his ten fingers and their individual joints.

XLI

What someone presently most has to become, must be associated with those things and those people he loves, but especially with those he hates.

XLII

If one intends to concern oneself with things, or to deal with people, then those ideas which are important to one should be coordinated with a series of objects which lie constantly before our eyes as we pass.

Hérault de Séchelles:[6] Théorie de l'ambition. A precursor not merely of Stendhal, but of Georg Büchner's anthropological materialism as well.

Krenek has sent me his 'Charles V' and the essay on the representation of history.[7] I shall be thanking him for this over the next few days.

I hope to hear from you very soon!

Heartfelt greetings from

Your

Walter Benjamin

1 May 1935
Paris XIV
28 place Denfert-Rochereau
Hotel Floridor

1 *Königstein*: Benjamin knew where Adorno was staying roughly between 7 and 21 April from an unpublished letter from Gretel Karplus of 2.4.1935.

2 *your postcard*: this has not survived.

3 *the Arcades ... on the basis of a general plan*: Benjamin is referring to the *exposé* 'Paris, die Hauptstadt des XIX. Jahrhunderts'; cf. GS V [1], pp. 45–59.

4 *Bloch ... rebuked me ... for my written comments on his book*: see Bloch's letter of 18.12.1934; Ernst Bloch, *Briefe 1903–1975*, vol. 2, edited by Karola Bloch and others (Frankfurt a.M. 1985), pp. 658f.

5 *Alfred Kantorowicz*: the publicist and writer Alfred Kantorowicz (1899–1979) was the Paris cultural correspondent of the *Frankfurter Zeitung* between 1927 and 1929; in 1931 he joined the KPD, the German Communist Party, and fled to Paris in March 1933.

6 *Hérault de Séchelles*: Marie-Jean Hérault de Séchelles (1759–1794) was originally 'advocate general' in the Parliament of Paris; he subsequently participated actively in the French Revolution, was associated with the Jacobin party and became a member of the 'Commission of Public Prosperity', and was guillotined in 1794 on charges of having collaborated with the Royalists.

– For the three maxims, cf. Hérault de Séchelles, *Théorie de l'ambition*. **Introduction par Jean Prévost** (Paris 1927), p. 57.

7 *Krenek . . . his 'Charles V' and the essay on the representation of history*: Benjamin is referring to the libretto, written by the composer, for his opera 'Karl V'. – The essay 'The Artistic and the Scientific Approaches to History' appeared in the journal 'Wiener Politische Blätter' of 24.3.1935; in the essay Krenek frequently cites Benjamin's study on Baroque Drama.

31   WIESENGRUND-ADORNO TO BENJAMIN
     OXFORD, 20.5.1935

Oxford, 20 May 1935
Merton College.

Dear Herr Benjamin,
Many thanks indeed for both of your letters.[1] My response to the first one has been inordinately delayed because I have had to spend a few days in London, which rather set back my own work plans, and this in turn cost me some time catching up on various things; I therefore hasten all the more to reply to your second letter now.

Indeed your elaboration of the schema is the most important and pleasing news I could possibly have heard from you, and I do not have to tell you how extraordinarily keen I should be to see this schema – if a typed copy of it is available; that you will not want to let go of the original and entrust it to the English Channel, problematic as that has once again become, is obvious. But it is not merely my theoretical sympathy – which in the case of this particular work more than any other should be interpreted in terms of the utmost solidarity – that prompts me to ask for your *exposé*, but certain practical considerations as well.

I have been spending a great deal of time with Pollock[2] in London, and it goes without saying that a good part of our discussions has been dedicated to your concerns. Pollock has explicitly assured me that the Institute will continue to support you financially, in spite of all the cutbacks (the last of which led to the closing of the Institute's London branch) – although I was of course unable to hold him to a specific sum. But without excess of optimism, I am inclined to regard this assurance very positively, and this not merely because I know just how much Horkheimer values you, but also on account of my own relationship to the Institute. As you know, the Institute has done practically nothing for me, despite the closest conceivable collaboration on my part[3] over many years. I think the point has now come where this fact is seriously beginning to weigh heavily upon

82

Horkheimer and Pollock, and Pollock's principal concern was to clear up difficulties in the past. We are agreed that I shall continue to live in Oxford next year and finish my work there; the arrangements à la longue are still quite undefined as yet. With regard to the Institute I therefore find myself, now as before, in the not unfavourable position of someone who belongs to it without actually claiming anything for himself at the moment. And the only thing upon which I insisted was the Institute's solidarity with regard to yourself, and rebus sic stantibus it seems to me inconceivable that they could relinquish this obligation.

Pollock defended the view that the Institute could also expect certain contributions from you in return, and I was all the more unable to contradict him here since I am well aware of the hopelessly small number of those productive enough for the Institute to rely on. He discussed three plans with me: concerning the essay on Fuchs, an essay on social-democratic cultural politics[4] in the pre-war period, and finally, to my great amazement, the 'Arcades'.

I have therefore – hopefully with your agreement – come to the view that it is definitely advisable for you to write up the two longer essays; both on account of the incomparable advantage this would procure for the Journal itself and also, to be honest with you, in the hope that these pieces are already so far advanced that writing them up – even while working on the 'Arcades' – should not cost you too much effort.

Matters were not nearly so straightforward with the 'Arcades', especially since I have not seen the *exposé*, although you had clearly already given some indications to Pollock. What Pollock had to tell me about it quite thoroughly suggested a historical-sociological work, for which he proposed the excellent title of 'Paris, capitale du XIXième siècle'. Now I am well aware that the Institute, and especially a journal in which Löwenthal[5] is still heavily involved, will find it hard to accept anything other than such a historical-sociological work. But you will hardly take it amiss if I openly confess to regarding the 'Arcades' not as a historical-sociological investigation but rather as *prima philosophia* in your own particular sense. We certainly have no need to quarrel with one another concerning the decisive significance of the material character of the work, and there is no one who understands better than I do precisely how the interpretation of the piece must be sought in this material character alone. But there is also no one less tempted than I am to try and forgo its interpretation and total articulation in the medium of the concept; and I think I possess a sufficient idea of the project to realize quite clearly that this is also part of your intention. For you have already justified certain uninterpreted preliminary materials, like the essay on surrealism[6] and

83

the essay on photography[7] from the 'Literary World', precisely with reference to the final interpretation to be supplied in the 'Arcades'. The primal history of the nineteenth century, the thesis of the ever-same, of the newest as the most ancient, the gambler, the theme of plushness – all of this belongs in the domain of philosophical theory. But there is also absolutely no question for me that such a theory can only find its own dialectic in the polarity between social and theological categories, and that because of this, as well as through the interpretative procedure involved, it is in principle remote from the a priori approach of a work destined for the Institute – just as my book on Kierkegaard was – and indeed, a thousand times more so.

Now of course I realize that there is the possibility of responding as follows: that it is your concern at the moment to avoid all interpretation; that the assembled material speaks for itself; that the demands of the Institute cannot be avoided and that the procedure must therefore be adapted to the latter. Although I fully understand the need which prompts such a line of argument, I cannot possibly endorse it. You must allow me to speak quite openly in the justified name of a friendship which, in this one case at least, can properly claim the right of total candour. I regard your work on the 'Arcades' as the centre not merely of your own philosophy, but as the decisive philosophical word which must find utterance today; as a chef d'œuvre like no other, and as so decisive in every sense, whether in the private sense or equally in that of public success, that any weakening of the innermost claims of this work, and any consequent repudiation of its own peculiar categories, would strike me as catastrophic and quite irreparably damaging. It really seems to me that, quite irrespective of how your affairs are to be managed, there is no conceivable institution which has the right to exercise any power over this work. Just as I believe it would be a real misfortune if Brecht were to acquire any influence upon this work (I say this without prejudice to Brecht – but here, and precisely here, there is a limit), so too I would regard it as a misfortune if any concessions were to be made to the Institute in this regard – and indeed, the fact that the Institute is extremely unlikely to accept the work as originally conceived, makes me all the happier.

But without knowing the exposé I could not really say anything about all this. Thus, although I left Pollock in absolutely no doubt as to what I think about the 'Arcades', I rather emphasized the other pieces as possible contributions for the Institute. Now it would be extremely important for me to know your own position – and the current status of your negotiations with the Institute – and of course, if possible, to be able to speak on the basis of the exposé itself, especially since I shall be seeing Pollock again in the near future.

– But if, disregarding all practical problems, my words significantly mean something to you, then I would insistently ask you to compose the 'Arcades' in a way faithful to their original history. It is my most profound conviction that the work will thereby turn out for the best even, and indeed especially, from a Marxist perspective; that for us (forgive me if I include myself with you here) the access to social phenomena is grounded more effectively in the inner consistency of our own categories than it could possibly be through the adoption of other pre-given categories – for indeed, in the issues we are concerned with, the essential ones, the Marxian concepts all too often prove too abstract and isolated from one another, merely function as *dei ex machina* and thereby revert to the spuriously aesthetic dimension. This at least is what I have found in my own experience and am very inclined to believe that we hold on all the more effectively to the real, the more thoroughly and consistently we remain true to the aesthetic origins, and that we only become merely aesthetic when we deny the latter. That such remarks, coming from my mouth, are not intended to offer succour to decaying conditions, surely goes without saying – for I myself believe that the liquidation of art can only adequately be attempted from within the aesthetic. In saying this I know that with you I am free from all suspicion of being a reactionary – and the shock which will proceed from the completed work on the 'Arcades', like that of the surrealists, strikes me as more revolutionary than any bare insight into the unclarified social character of urban structures.

I will, of course, write to Else Herzberger, although a letter to her will bring me no joy. If she insists on allowing herself the same kind of illusions about your existence as she does about mine, she will certainly feel better about things than you do. [Added in English:] Let us try and see.

My work is making calm and steady progress. I am currently dwelling on the decisive issue, namely the critical analysis of categorial intuition, which has completely dissolved as a problem for me. I hope to be able to write up the final version of the text by September at the very latest. Given the kind of preliminary studies already made, this work will be essentially editorial in nature. Many thanks indeed for the reference to the Levezow book. I shall get hold of it in the Bodleian, one of the finest libraries with which I am acquainted.

Do you know Max Ernst personally? I have never seen him, but it would be a simple matter for me to arrange a meeting between the two of you through Lotte Lenya,[8] who is an extremely close friend of his. And I can imagine that at the current stage of your 'Arcades' a meeting with the surrealist who, so it seems to me, has really accomplished most, would appear rather à propos. In fact Max Ernst is in a desperately bad way. I have spent a lot of time with Lenya, and she was able to recount lots of lovely stories, amongst other things, about our friends' wives, Carola and Lily.[9] I have worked a little with her and gained a great deal from it. I have now got to know Weill's music for 'Marie galante',[10] but apart from one beautiful and one remarkable piece, the rest is hopeless – quite impossible to distinguish from straightforward Music Hall. Perhaps his English operetta[11] is better stuff. The Hungarian librettist, however, certainly gives grounds for the direst expectations.

I have seen Schoen fairly frequently; he will probably come and visit me this Sunday along with Hansi. He is still very anxious about things but he is not too bad; he has succeeded in transferring that truly great gift he had for obtaining credit in former times into our fascistic era, which in turn seems to show itself grateful to him for the fact. I feel rather relieved with regard to him now that I have been able to do something practical for him at last. And Hansi also seems to have weakened the Jewish boycott that was hanging over me.

Bloch has been complaining[12] that he has heard nothing from you concerning his 'Heritage'; but since in the same letter he also speaks of his own unconstrained pride, which is certainly no mythical invention, and is quite ready to let his nose turn blue, I can easily understand why you are as unwilling to expose yourself bodily to such tribulations as I am to try it a second time. And in fact I still owe him a reply myself. – Gretel was rather ill for eight whole days, but she seems to have recovered somewhat now. Our lengthy separation from one another is proving unbearable.

My plans for the summer are still wholly unclear – especially since it is uncertain whether I can return to Germany at all, or whether I shall have to come back here immediately. But we should certainly already try and plan a meeting now. What do you think about a meeting in San Remo during September?

Sincerely yours as ever,

Teddie Wiesengrund

1 *for both of your letters*: letter 30 and another letter which has not survived.

2 *Pollock*: Friedrich Pollock (1894–1970), an economist and sociologist by academic training, was the Assistant Director of the Institute of Social Research and administered the funds of the Institute.

3 *the closest conceivable collaboration on my part*: Horkheimer had made Adorno's acquaintance in Frankfurt in 1921, when the latter was still pursuing his academic studies there; Adorno's remarks about the closest conceivable collaboration refers not to any official membership in the Institute, but rather to their shared discussions and their collaboration on the Institute journal, the *Zeitschrift für Sozialforschung*.

4 *an essay on social-democratic cultural politics*: the projected essay, to be based upon analysis of the cultural politics expressed in the *Neue Zeit*, never materialized.

5 *Löwenthal*: Leo Löwenthal (1900–93) studied literature, history, philosophy and sociology, and worked as a teacher before he became firmly associated with the Institute of Social Research in 1930; he was the principal editor of the Institute's journal.

6 *the essay on surrealism*: cf. Benjamin, 'Der Surrealismus. Die letzte Momentaufnahme der europäischen Intelligenz' [Surrealism. Final Snapshot of the European Mind], first published in the journal 'Die literarische Welt', on 1.2.1929 (year 5, nr. 5), pp. 3f; 8.2.1929 (year 5, nr. 6), p. 4; and 15.2.1929 (year 5, nr. 7), pp. 7f; now in GS II [1], pp. 295–310.

7 *the essay on photography*: Benjamin's 'Small History of Photography' had appeared in three instalments – on 18.9, 25.9 and 2.10.1931 – in the journal 'Die literarische Welt'; cf. now GS II [1], pp. 368–85.

8 *Lenya*: the actress, singer and dancer Lotte Lenya (1898–1981), married to Kurt Weill since 1926, emigrated in 1933 first to Paris and then to New York.

9 *Carola and Lily*: Benjamin is referring to Karola Bloch and Lily Kracauer.

10 *Weill's music for 'Marie galante'*: Kurt Weill had written the music to Jacques Duval's play 'Marie galante' in 1931.

11 *his English operetta*: i.e. Weill's 'A Kingdom for a Cow', with a libretto by Robert Vambery, was premiered at the London Savoy Theatre on 28 June 1935.

12 *Bloch has been complaining*: see the letter to Adorno of 18 March 1932; cf. Ernst Bloch, *Briefe 1903–1975*, vol. 2, pp. 434–6.

32   BENJAMIN TO WIESENGRUND-ADORNO
     PARIS, 31.5.1935

Dear Herr Wiesengrund,

If you have had to wait some time for these lines, they will now bring, together with the accompanying material, the most thorough account of my work, my own inner and external situation.

Before briefly discussing the content of my *exposé*,[1] let me touch upon the role it plays in my relationship to the Institute. This can be disposed of very quickly. In the first place this role is limited entirely to the circumstance that a conversation I had with Pollock at the end of April provided the incentive for its composition. It is obvious enough that this incentive was a rather disparate and external one. But precisely because of that it proved capable of communicating a

87

shock to the great mass of material which I have carefully preserved for so many years from any external influence, a shock which has now enabled the matter to crystallize. I would strongly emphasize that this circumstance, which is itself a fruitful and legitimate one within the overall economy of the work, exhausts the significance of all external and heterogeneous factors. I am driven to emphasize this by the anxious concerns expressed in your letter, concerns which are quite intelligible to me and must also be regarded as the inevitable result of a friendly participation – after such a long interruption of a dialogue between us that has developed over years. Early this very morning these concerns found a faithful echo in a letter which has just arrived from Felizitas.[2] She writes:

'I am amazed that Fritz (Pollock) has taken interest in your sketches; are you really thinking then of contributing work to the journal? I would certainly regard this as an enormous danger, for the parameters are relatively narrow ones, and you will never be able to write what your true friends have been waiting for all these years, the great philosophical work which exists entirely for its own sake, which has made no concessions and the significance of which will make up for much of the last few years.'

I realize that this is the language of the truest friendship, no less than that which moved you to your claim that you would regard it as a real misfortune if Brecht should come to exercise influence upon the work. Allow me to say the following in response:

If I have ever succeeded in actually realizing my favourite saying of Gracian: 'Seek in all things to bring the time round to your own view', then I believe I have done so through the way in which I have insistently gone about this work. There stands Aragon at the very beginning – *Le Paysan de Paris*,[3] of which I could never read more than two or three pages in bed at night before my heart started to beat so strongly that I had to lay the book aside. What a warning! What an indication of the many years which had to be spent between myself and such a reading. And yet my first sketches for the 'Arcades'[4] date from that time. – Then came the Berlin years, during which the best part of my friendship with Hessel[5] was nourished on myriad conversations concerning the Arcades project. It was at this time that the subtitle 'A Dialectical Fairy-Tale'[6] first emerged – which no longer passes muster now. This subtitle suggests the rhapsodic character of the presentation as I then conceived it, and the relics of which, as I now recognize, contained absolutely no sufficient guarantees either formally or linguistically speaking. But this epoch was also one of a quite unconcerned and archaic form of philosophizing naively caught up in nature. It was my conversations with you in Frankfurt, and particularly that concerning 'historical' matters in the little Swiss hut,

88

and afterwards the certainly historical one at table with you, Asja,[7] Felizitas and Horkheimer, which brought that epoch to an end. There would henceforth be no more rhapsodic naivité. This romantic form had been overtaken in a raccourci of development, but at that time, and for some years to come, I still had no idea of any other possible form. What is more, these years also saw the beginning of those external difficulties which have almost providentially revealed to me that my own inner difficulties had already strongly encouraged a rather hesitant, dilatory manner of working. Then followed the decisive encounter with Brecht, and with it the culmination of every aporia connected with this work, which even then I still refused to relinquish. The significant experience which I was able to gain for my work from this recent period – and it was by no means insubstantial – could not properly take shape before the limits of that significance had become indubitably clear to me, and all 'directives' from that quarter as well had thereby become quite superfluous.

Everything that I am suggesting here will be very clearly expressed, and especially for you in particular, in the *exposé*, to which I would also like to add a few words. The *exposé*, which in no way repudiates my ideas, is naturally not a perfect equivalent for these ideas in every respect either. Just as the self-contained exposition of the epistemological foundations of my book on the Baroque Drama only followed after they had proved their value in the material itself, that will also be the case here. I do not thereby necessarily wish to commit myself to providing such an exposition in the form of a separate chapter, whether at the end or at the beginning. The whole question remains open. But the *exposé* contains certain decisive pointers to these foundations themselves, pointers which can hardly escape your attention and in which you will recognize the themes invoked in your last letter. Furthermore: analogies between this book and my study of Baroque Drama now emerge much more clearly than was the case with any of the earlier stages of the plan (so much so that I am even surprised myself). You must allow me to regard this circumstance as a particularly striking confirmation of that general process of fusion which has led the entire conceptual mass of this material, originally motivated as it was by metaphysical concerns, towards a final shape in which the world of dialectical images is immune to all objections that can be raised by metaphysics.

At this stage of the matter (and now indeed for the very first time) I can prepare myself with some equanimity for everything which could possibly be mobilized against my working methods from orthodox Marxist quarters. And on the contrary, I now believe that *à la longue* I have actually reached solid ground through the Marxist discussion of my work, if only because the decisive question concerning the historical image has been treated in all its range for the first time here. And since the philosophy behind a work is connected more directly to its particular site in the debate than to its terminology, I do believe that my *exposé* belongs to that 'major philosophical work' of which Felizitas speaks, although this formulation does not exactly strike me as the most appropriate. As you know, what I am essentially concerned with is 'the primal history of the nineteenth century'.

And in this endeavour I see the principal, if not indeed the only, reason not to abandon hope in the everyday struggle for existence. I can only write the work from beginning to end here in Paris – that is entirely clear to me now, in spite of the very large amount of fundamental preparatory studies I have already made. Of course, in the first instance, it can only be written in German. My minimum financial requirements in Paris amount to 1,000 francs a month; Pollock put this much at my disposal in May, and I am supposed to be receiving the same for June. But I will need a similar amount for some time if I am to continue my work. There are already plenty of difficulties as it is; frequent attacks of migraine only serve to underline the precariousness of my way of life here. Whether it is possible to interest the Institute in my work and if so under what title, whether under certain circumstances it will be necessary for me to encourage such an interest by submitting other pieces first – this is all something which you could perhaps clarify in conversation with Pollock more easily than I can. I am prepared to undertake any work; but anything of substance, and in particular the piece on Fuchs, would certainly mean postponing work on the Arcades in the meantime. (At the moment I do not feel particularly drawn to the work on 'The New Age', but I will say more about that again.)

I certainly did not assume that the Institute would be able to publish the work 'as originally conceived', and indeed said as much directly to Pollock myself only this April. Another question, however, concerns how far these new and penetrating sociological perspectives, which will supply the firm framework for the interpretative elements, can justify the Institute's support for this work, and without which it will never be realized in this or any other form. For any real distance introduced at the present stage between the original project and its realization now would probably only cause decisive problems for any later attempted presentation. The projected framework, on the other hand, already contains, not indeed at all places, but certainly at the ones which I believe are decisive, those philosophical conceptual determinations which ground them. And if you feel you miss the presence of several themes – plushness, boredom, the development of the 'phantasmagoria' – these are precisely the motifs which I only have to insert in the appropriate place. The fuller

90

development of these motifs, which in some cases has already advanced a long way, did not really belong in the *exposé* itself. And this less because of external technical considerations than for internal reasons: the task of the *exposé* was to help me unite the earlier, and to my mind more secure, materials with the new elements which I have acquired over the years since then.

I would ask you not to show the *exposé* I sent you to anyone else at all and to return it to me as soon as possible. It is only designed to assist my own private studies. Another *exposé* will be ready very shortly, and in several copies, so I shall be sending one off to you in due course.

San Remo does not even seem worth considering as a good place for us to meet this year. Could you not arrange to travel from Oxford to Berlin via Paris? Please do give this thought some serious consideration!

I would love to see Lotte Lenya and Max Ernst. If you could possibly facilitate something, you can be sure I will be cooperative. I am delighted to learn that you have almost finished work on your own text . Will I have to wait until our next meeting before I learn more about it?

I still have not decided whether to write to Else Herzberger myself, but I don't know if I can really put it off for much longer.

My heartfelt greetings!

Yours,
Walter

31 May 1935
Paris XIV
28 place Denfert-Rochereau

1 *the content of my exposé*: cf. GS V [2], pp. 1237–49 for the version of the *exposé* which Benjamin had sent to Adorno.

2 *a letter which has just arrived from Felizitas*: the letter from Gretel Karplus dated 28 May 1935; cf. the excerpt in GS V [2], pp. 1115f.

3 *Aragon . . . Le Paysan de Paris*: in 1928 Benjamin had translated parts of *Le Paysan de Paris* by Louis Aragon (1897–1982); they appeared under the titles 'Don Juan and the Shoe-Shiner', 'Stamps', 'Lady's Boudoir' and 'Café Certa' in *Die literarische Welt* on 8 and 15 June 1928.

4 *my first sketches for the 'Arcades'*: these date back to the middle of 1927; cf. GS V [2], pp. 1041–3 and 1341–7.

5 *Hessel*: Franz Hessel (1881–1941), writer and translator, was a reader for the Rowohlt publishing house between 1924 and 1933; he emigrated to France in 1938; on Benjamin's friendship with Franz Hessel, cf. GS VI, pp. 469f.

6 *the subtitle 'A Dialectical Fairy-Tale'*: cf. GS V [2], pp. 1044–59.

7 *Asja*: Benjamin is referring to Asja Lacis (1891–1979) whom Benjamin had met in 1924 (cf. the *Benjamin-Katalog*, pp. 161–70).

33 WIESENGRUND-ADORNO TO BENJAMIN
    OXFORD, 5.6.1935

5 June 1935   MERTON COLLEGE,
                                               OXFORD.

Dear Herr Benjamin,
   I wonder if I could bother you with a request. With regard to my response to your *exposé* of the 'Arcades' (I cannot bring myself to abandon the old title), it would greatly facilitate the task, both with respect to the time involved and the substantive issues, if you would allow me to pencil in my relevant notes in the temptingly large margins provided. Although you could very easily remove them if you so wish, I would not dream of doing so without receiving your permission first.
   As for the rest, and after an extremely careful reading of the material, I believe that I can now say that my former reservations about the Institute's attitude have been entirely dispelled. I think that the entire work could be, or rather should be, accepted by the Institute; that you certainly have a greater right to have your work appear there than Franz von Borkenau[1] does, for example; and that neither you nor the Institute itself will have to make any concessions in the matter. If Horkheimer should urge some social concretization at certain points, that would actually be in both our interests. In the first place I am thinking about the category of the commodity,[2] which is rather too generally expressed in the *exposé* (as indeed it also was in my Kierkegaard book) if it is supposed to disclose something *specific* about the character of the nineteenth century; and it is not really enough to define the category in purely technological terms – in terms of 'fabrication' say – since it is necessary above all to enquire into the economic function of the same, that is, into the laws of the market within early high capitalism precisely as the 'modern' age in the strict sense. The other concept in question is, of course, that of the collective consciousness.[3] But an examination of this would already lead directly into the central discussion which, given the enormous difficulty of the subject matter itself and the carefully considered response which it properly demands, is certainly not something I would like to undertake in a rather casual manner at this point. For now let me merely risk the following suggestion: that the Marxist objection to

92

the constitution of an intrinsically undialectical conception of collective consciousness, i.e. one that failed fully to integrate the moment of
class itself, probably coincides with an objection that I myself would
raise in a quite different manner: namely with the demand that the
dialectical image should in no way be located in the field of *consciousness*, or indeed of unconsciousness. But however things stand
in this regard, it seems to me beyond question that, here as always,
the empirical specification of the problem itself also involves the specification of interpretation. I shall write to Horkheimer at once[4]
to urge acceptance of the work en bloc and thereby, of course, the
appropriate financial support.

Considering the crucial importance which I ascribe to this work, it
would be blasphemy to express any particular praise for it. But I
cannot resist the temptation here of singling out some of the things in
it which have affected me most profoundly. In the first place there is
your theory of *nouveauté*[5] and your insight into the enormous significance of this category which you quite rightly compare with that of
allegory (we shall have to talk more precisely about the relation between the seventeenth and the eighteenth centuries, the relation which
in truth grounds the connection between your book on the Baroque
and the Arcades). And then there is the passage on fetishism[6] which
served once again to remind me just how closely our thoughts on this
matter still correspond in spite of our two year separation. Indeed,
only about three months ago, in a substantial letter to Horkheimer,[7]
and even more recently in conversation with Pollock, and in opposition to Fromm[8] and, in particular, to Reich, I defended the position
that the true 'mediation' between society and psychology was to be
found not in the family, but rather in the commodity and fetish
character itself, that the phenomenon of fetishism is the authentic
correlate of reification. You find yourself here, perhaps without being
aware of the fact, in the most profound agreement with Freud; there
is certainly much to be thought about in this connection. In any case
you should definitely read everything you can find by Freud or the
extremely important Ferenczi[9] concerning the anal personality and
the anal problematic itself. I also discovered a similar coincidence of
thought in your theory, quite new to me, concerning the transformation of the town into the country:[10] for this was precisely the principal thesis of my uncompleted piece on Maupassant,[11] which again
is unknown to you (if I can find this material now I shall compare it
for you *in extenso* with the appropriate passages in question). I was
concerned there with the town as hunting ground, and the concept of
the huntsman as such played a major role in the discussion (with
regard to the theory of the uniform, for example: all huntsmen look
precisely the same). Incidentally, there is a short story by M which

does not indeed treat of the Sunday hunter but of the closely related phenomenon of the Sunday rider[12] in Bois, which certainly also provides a real 'dialectical image'. Once again I would most emphatically draw your attention to Maupassant. His astonishing story 'La nuit, un cauchemar'[13] constitutes a perfect dialectical counterpart to Poe's 'Man of the Crowd'[14] and really cries out for your kind of interpretation.

Let me also venture the thought that it is the invention of the aeroplane which signifies the end of the nineteenth century. Perhaps I shall soon be able to show you something in this connection. – That the abolition of the opposition between town and country[15] is something demanded by Marx and Engels will of course be quite familiar to you.

And in conclusion for today – the conclusion of a prelude but certainly no fugue – a remark from the past:[16] 'What has recently happened always presents itself as if it were something destroyed by a series of catastrophes.'

In cordial friendship and gratitude,

Your Teddie Wiesengrund

1 *Franz von Borkenau*: Austrian historian and publicist Franz Borkenau (1900–1957), member of the German Communist Party between 1921 and 1929, had already published a book in the series sponsored by the Institute of Social Research, *Der Übergang vom feudalen zum bürgerlichen Weltbild* [The Transition from the Feudal to the Bourgeois Picture of the World] (Paris 1934).

2 *category of the commodity*: cf. GS V [2], pp. 1242ff.

3 *the collective consciousness*: cf. ibid., pp. 1239 and 1246.

4 *I shall write to Horkheimer at once*: This was accomplished with Adorno's letter to Horkheimer of 11 June 1935 in which he strongly urged the immediate acceptance of Benjamin's book for future publication by the Institute (cf. Adorno, *Über Walter Benjamin*, pp. 123–6).

5 *your theory of nouveauté*: See GS V [2], pp. 1246ff.

6 *the passage on fetishism*: cf. ibid., p. 1243.

7 *a substantial letter to Horkheimer*: The question concerning the 'mediation between society and psychology' is a major theme of the aforementioned letter of 8 June 1935.

8 *Fromm*: Erich Fromm (1900–1980), psychoanalyst and participant in the Institute of Social Research, was the founder of analytical social psychology.

9 *Ferenczi*: The Hungarian born Sandor Ferenczi (1873–1933) originally studied medicine in Vienna and practised as a doctor in Budapest before

making the acquaintance of Freud in 1908 and undergoing analysis with him. He subsequently practised as a psychoanalyst in Budapest.

10 *theory concerning the transformation of the town into the country*: See GS V [20], p. 1245.

11 *my uncompleted piece on Maupassant*: The fragment of a book on Maupassant seems to have been lost; but it is also possible that Adorno regarded his marginalia in two collections – 'Das Haus Teller und andere Novellen' [The Teller Household and other Stories] (Berlin, undated) and 'Mondschein. Novellen' [Moonshine. Short Stories] (Munich 1922) – as elements of this projected piece on Maupassant.

12 *a short story . . . the Sunday rider*: see Maupassant's short story 'A cheval' in the collection 'Mademoiselle Fifi'.

13 *the astonishing story La nuit, un cauchemar*: cf. Maupassant's story 'La Nuit-Cauchemar' published in 1887.

14 *Poe's 'Man of the Crowd'*: cf. GS V [2], p. 1245.

15 *the abolition of the opposition between town and country*: See Karl Marx/Friedrich Engels, *Werke* (MEW), vol. 3: *Die deutsche Ideologie* [The German Ideology] (Berlin 1969), p. 50.

16 *a remark from the past*: The remark in question is dated '16 August 1932' (cf. the 'Grünes Buch', p. 10); Adorno later incorporated it into *Minima Moralia* (cf. GS 4, p. 55). Benjamin also preserved it in his 'Aufzeichnungen und Materialien' [Notes and Materials] to the Arcades project (cf. GS V [1], p. 501).

34 WIESENGRUND-ADORNO TO BENJAMIN
    OXFORD, 8.6.1935

8 June 1935   MERTON COLLEGE
                                               OXFORD.

Dear Herr Benjamin,
   I have still to write you the letter about the *exposé*, which is far too important a matter to permit a quickly improvized response; however, I have a few things to report all the same.
   I have received a letter from Else Herzberger in Zürich (Hotel Baur au Lac). She has now been informed by my parents about Agathe's illness,[1] so I was able to write to her directly and without any further reservations. I took the opportunity to ask her in the most urgent and earnest manner imaginable if she could secure the completion of the Arcades project with financial assistance – and indeed I have placed her under a certain moral pressure in this regard. And for all our pessimism before, I am not entirely lacking in hope this time. I think

this is a favourable psychological moment, given the fact that Agathe's illness has clearly affected Else very deeply; and my request was made in such a way that would make refusal extremely difficult for her. If Agathe's predicament could therefore lead to a certain reconcilement in this regard, there would at least be some consolation. What is more, the news from Frankfurt is not entirely unfavourable either – recovery seems a possibility even if it would be a long and difficult process.

I have written to Else saying that if she is seriously interested in the idea, you would be able to make the *exposé* available to her (– naturally I was thinking of the new one you are currently preparing). I assume that you will have no objection to this. From the psychological point of view it would certainly be an advisable thing to do given Else's narcissism. Please be sure at all events to give me your telegram address and telephone number.

In addition, Pollock has informed me that he no longer intends to come to London; I imagine he is already en route to America. My plans in his regard have therefore had to be dropped (one of which was to get him to invite you to London for a meeting between us). And without hesitating overlong, I have just dispatched a very substantial letter to Horkheimer[2] and pressed him – as urgently as I did Else – to accept your work without more ado for the Institute (I was thinking of a partial publication in the Institute's journal and full publication in their book series),[3] to provide financial assistance for its completion, as well as to postpone publication of your other pieces ('Fuchs' and 'Neue Zeit'), when the time comes to submit the manuscript, given the amount of work involved. I have strongly emphasized and justified my belief that the work in its present shape can be fully 'endorsed' by the Institute, that I have no intellectual reservations about it, and that I regard the publication of this work as an obligation. In this matter also I am more optimistic than not. Perhaps it would be advisable from the practical point of view to send Horkheimer the *exposé* I have already seen, for I think I can foresee his reactions very precisely.

One further initiative – with regard to Gabi Oppenheim[4] – has come to nothing, as I very much expected it would. She replied once again by telling me her 'maison' was 'louée' rather than 'achetée'.

I have learned from an acquaintance in London[5] that there is another possible project for you, and of which I am giving you unofficial advance notice. It was instigated by the Palestinian Ernst Simon[6] and is being directed by Mannheim. In the publishing house in question there is an Indian of radical left sympathies who is currently publishing a small series of pieces – I believe the man rejoices in the most peculiar name of Krishna Menon[7] – and the idea was to

96

invite you to write (please don't faint at the thought) a very accessible
account, of about 150–200 pages, of the history of European ideas[8]
in the nineteenth and twentieth centuries. Intrinsically absurd though
this project sounds, and especially in relation to you of all people, I
could nevertheless imagine that its absurdity, together with an honorary payment of £40 and a share in the eventual copies sold, might
exercise a certain appeal. The piece would have to be translated into
English. One advantage would be that one could say absolutely whatever one wanted to say politically. The biggest drawback, apart from
the terrifying magnitude of the subject itself, would be the entirely
popular style of presentation required in an account of this kind.
Both these aims could only be properly accomplished by developing
a quite new approach altogether, one which would be capable of
abruptly grasping and simultaneously shattering the totality and
the intellectual history involved. The problem of finding such a form,
which would truly require a 'left hand'[9] and could only properly be
accomplished beyond *all* the available categories of bourgeois conformism, is nonetheless something which *only* you could really achieve.
(The thought suddenly occurs to me: a catalogue of wares from intellectual history is up for sale; it would not have to be quite as cynical
as that of course, but something of the kind.) Still I do not want to
influence your decision in the matter. Please do not let anyone else
know that you have already learnt anything about the project, and
especially through me.

I hope you will enjoy the vacation. Mine will be an extremely quiet
one.

With the most cordial greetings in friendship,

Yours,

Teddie Wiesengrund

1 *Agathe's illness*: Adorno's aunt Agathe Calvelli-Adorno had suffered a
minor heart attack in May.

2 *letter to Horkheimer*: see Letter 33 and accompanying note.

3 *book series*: published by the Institute of Social Research.

4 *Gabi Oppenheim*: Gabrielle Oppenheim, a good acquaintance of Adorno
from his time in Frankfurt, and wife of the chemist Paul Oppenheim (1885–
1977), who occupied important positions in the chemical industry until 1933.
The Oppenheims emigrated to Belgium in 1933, and later to the USA where
Paul Oppenheim worked as a theorist and philosopher of science.

5 *an acquaintance in London*: identity unknown.

6 *Ernst Simon*: Ernst Simon (1899–1988) was an educationalist from
Berlin. After working at the Jewish Learning Institute in Frankfurt a.M. he

moved to Palestine, where from 1935 he occupied the Chair of Pedagogy at the Hebrew University in Jerusalem.

7 *Krishna Menon*: The Indian lawyer and politician Vengali Krishna Krishnan Menon (1896–1974) was the Secretary of 'The India League' from 1929 to 1947 and a member of the Labour Party in the London County Council between 1934 and 1947.

8 *an accessible account of the history of ideas*: The plan never came to fruition.

9 *a 'left hand'*: an allusion to Benjamin's aphorism in 'One-Way Street': 'These days no one must stubbornly insist on what they are "able" to do. Strength lies rather in improvization. All the decisive strokes are accomplished with the left hand.' (GS IV [1], p. 89.)

35 BENJAMIN TO WIESENGRUND-ADORNO
PARIS, 10.6.1935

Dear Herr Wiesengrund,
I would have written to you earlier and thanked you for your important letter if my health were not so terrible and I was not in such a state of total exhaustion. This was precipitated amongst other things by recent developments in relation to Wissing,[1] for whom these weeks in Paris have been truly fateful, and I am even more concerned for the immediate future since they are saying here that, from the side of the German government, travel to Russia for German citizens is soon to be prohibited. For it was in Russia that I imagined his last permanent chance of building a new life for himself to lie.

Then there were further matters touching directly on myself. In the first place, Pollock's sudden return to America. He had offered me the possibility of writing a review, which was to appear after he had had a look at my manuscript. He has not even had a chance to do so since he left Europe two days after I had sent a manuscript of the *exposé* to Geneva[2] to be transcribed. And it is weighing even more heavily upon my mind that, quite independently, he has indeed agreed to continue supporting me until 31 July, thereby vouchsafing me two whole undisturbed months of work, but has only raised once more the ever more discouraging question of how I am going to survive after this date, once the old monthly rate[3] of 500 French francs comes into force again. – As I said before, this arrangement has not been affected by problems involved in the major work itself. Everything now depends on whether this work will be able to find its place within the intellectual and material economy of the Institute. You can appreciate just how crucial your endorsement is for me.

In order to make matters a little easier, at least strategically, I thought it was advisable to write a letter to Pollock, which he received shortly before his departure, informing him that from August on I shall lay the major work aside and compose the essay on Fuchs.

I am uncommonly eager to read your marginalia, and I can't think of anyone to whom margins make such an urgent appeal as they do to you. You will be providing me with a certain opportunity, given the impossibility at the moment – and I hope it is only temporary – of talking with you directly about the abundance of questions which are raised by the *exposé*. It is quite clear to me that, amongst this host of questions, the two you mention are methodologically of the utmost importance: that concerning the differential definition of the commodity at the beginning of high capitalism, and that concerning class-specific differentiation or indifference of collective unconsciousness. I am particularly pleased, reading between the lines of your letter, that you understand and endorse the care with which I have approached these questions, and the fact that I have hitherto postponed the decisive issue as far as they are concerned. The extraordinary significance of these questions is quite beyond doubt. Although they will have, on the one hand, to be strengthened against legitimate Marxist objections, it will nevertheless be quite impossible to deny in the ensuing discussion the novel approach which the effective abandonment of the idealist picture of history and its harmonizing perspective will produce even, and indeed especially, with regard to Marxist historiography. In this connection I have incorporated your excellent remark[4] concerning the apparently catastrophic destruction of the recent past into my own notes.

A copy of these notes is currently being made, indeed on Pollock's express suggestion, who provided me with the necessary financial assistance. It would surely be a nightmare to have to travel around with this pile of manuscripts.

The opportunity of enriching the latter with your own reflections on Maupassant now and then would certainly mean a *great deal* to me, to judge even from the few remarks you made. The material you quote on the town as hunting ground is excellent. Amongst all the things in your letter, none struck me more forcibly than the position you seem to take up with regard to the question of the 'mediation' between society and psychology. Here we are both pulling at the *same* rope, although I was unaware of the fact in this particular form – though it is hardly an ideal situation to find Fromm and Reich are both pulling hard at the other end. I shall be looking at Freud soon. Incidentally, can you recall whether there is any psychoanalytic study of waking, or studies to that effect, in Freud or his school?

Once the greatest periphery of my studies has been properly traversed – and I can already see this time coming – I shall be approaching the centre in concentric circles, and then, after Freud, I shall take up Baudelaire.

In the meantime I am much looking forward to receiving more information from you sometime concerning your critical destruction of the 'intuition of essences'. Would not Husserl himself welcome such a destruction now that he has been able to see what has become of this instrument at the hands of someone like Heidegger?

Now that my situation has been alleviated for a few weeks, I would find it very difficult to approach Else H at this juncture. If the situation with you, and the sad cause of the same, has not changed in any way by the end of the month, I will certainly have to take some action myself. But I am sure I will be hearing from you before then anyway. I know how close you have always been to your aunt. Please accept my heartfelt wishes for her recovery, and which I should also like you to pass on to your mother in her regard as well.

Cordially yours,
Walter Benjamin

10 June 1935
Paris XIV
28 place Denfert-
Rochereau

PS These lines were written at Easter and I was about to send them off when your last letter arrived. It hardly required what I have already written to express the great significance which your letter possesses for me. If your steps in this regard – even if only one of them – were to meet with success, then I should be able to breathe freely in a way I have not known for years. That I shall do everything I can, for my own part, goes without saying. I would – and indeed should – neglect nothing that needs to be done. Indeed, the very manner in which you introduced the still unofficial project of a 'history of ideas' lends a certain challenging allure to something otherwise eminently resistible to me, as you are well aware.

Any day now I am expecting the copies of the *exposé* to arrive from Geneva, one of which would then be at the disposal of E. H. whenever required. I had originally intended to expand somewhat the *exposé* which you are already familiar with before sending it off to Geneva. But in the end I decided not to do so in order to avoid further delays, so the version which I shall be sending to Horkheimer in the next few days, once I receive the copies from Geneva, corresponds almost exactly with the one you know. It would nonetheless prove extremely valuable to me if you could possibly give me a few hints about the accompanying letter[5] I shall be sending to him, since it is highly desirable that what I write to him should correspond to the way you put things in your own report. Given that the copies from Geneva have not arrived yet, perhaps this will give you the necessary time to do so, although for my own part I am fully aware that this would draw you away from your own work, which is obviously at a quite crucial stage right now. I would also like to thank you for the expression of your friendship contained in your last few communications.

I have now begun to explore the first volume of 'Capital' and, in order to enjoy myself in the humble lowlands as well as the mighty Alpine heights, I have also started looking at Friedell's rather slipshod history of culture.[6]

My address for telegrams is: 28 place Denfert-Rochereau, telephone: Danton 9073.

Once again my best wishes for your well-being and for your work!

1 *recent developments in relation to Wissing*: Egon Wissing had been temporarily addicted to drugs.

2 *to Geneva*: i.e. the Geneva office of the Institute of Social Research.

3 *the old monthly rate*: see letter 28 and the relevant note.

4 *your excellent remark*: cf. Benjamin, GS V [1], p. 501.

5 *the accompanying letter*: Benjamin's letter to Horkheimer of 10 July; cf. *Briefe*, pp. 666f.

6 *Friedell's rather slipshod history of culture*: Benjamin consulted the third volume of the four-volume work 'Kulturgeschichte der Moderne' [Cultural History of the Modern Age] by Egon Friedell (1878–1938); cf. the source references to the Arcades project (GS V [2], p. 1295).

36 BENJAMIN TO WIESENGRUND-ADORNO
    PARIS, 19.6.1935

Dear Herr Wiesengrund,

I am responding with immediate return of post to say that I have received your lines from Frankfurt[1] and to communicate my sincere sympathy concerning the very unfortunate occasion for your sudden trip. I am well aware how close you are to the ailing Agathe and had already expressed heartfelt wishes for her recovery in the letter I sent to you in Oxford.

As far as that rather detailed letter is concerned, I would merely like briefly to repeat the most important matters mentioned there, given that you may not get to see it for some time to come. Your own card from Frankfurt touches upon one of them. I really cannot tell you how much I *must* strive, in spite of everything, to inspire and sustain within me the hope which your card seems to discourage. I surely do not have to tell you in so many words that I am more than ready to put together anything that might help to procure financial support from Else H. Naturally, I can always provide an *exposé* for this purpose as required. I hardly dare to intimate to you – for you know it yourself – how easily this hope could turn out to be my last.

I also wrote to you about sending the *exposé* to Horkheimer. The copies from Geneva have still not arrived and I haven't anything else I can send him. But these copies will hardly constitute a 'second version', as I had originally planned, and will hardly differ from the text you already know. I couldn't help but realize that any such detailed revision as planned would only delay the dispatching of the manuscript to Geneva. But then I was certainly expecting Pollock to receive the material there in person. The news about his sudden departure for America was the most painful blow because this circumstance has put paid to the meeting we were going to have in June to discuss matters on the basis of the *exposé*.

You yourself will certainly be able to judge how impressed I was to read the formerly unknown and highly significant lines of Heine[2] which you sent me. You would not have communicated them to me otherwise, and perhaps, without your assistance, I should never have come across them.

My letter also expressed a favourable expectation concerning the 'Intellectual History' project which you so boldly and enigmatically disclosed to me. A coup like this, which could liberate me from my fetters for a few months, would certainly be welcome news.

What are your arrangements for the holidays? Is there really no prospect of a meeting? You would find me here until about the end of July and, if I can manage it, maybe longer.

I assume that you will not be resting from your labours even in the holidays. The remarks made in your last letter concerning your critique of the idea of phenomenological 'intuiting' have aroused the greatest expectations in me.

Do write to me soon and in detail.

With cordial greetings,

Yours,

Walter Benjamin

19 June 1935
Paris XIV
28 place Denfert-Rochereau
Hotel Floridor

1 *your lines from Frankfurt*: The communication in which Adorno presumably informed Benjamin that his aunt had suffered a second heart attack on 11 June has not survived.

2 *lines of Heine*: Probably the lines from Heine's poem 'Jehuda ben Halevy 4' from Book 3 of 'Romanzero' (cf. GS V [1], p. 99) which Benjamin incorporated into the 'Notes and Materials' of the Arcades project.

37 BENJAMIN TO WIESENGRUND-ADORNO
    PARIS, 5.7.1935

Dear Herr Wiesengrund,
    It is with the greatest sadness that I received your news.[1]
    I know how much this must have affected you, and I have some idea what it has meant to you to encounter so much understanding and such unconditional faith within the intimacy of your immediate and natural domestic environment.
    There have been times when you have known how to extend such faith to me and my work, and thereby brought me closer to the deceased in such a way that I feel your loss as if it were my own.
    I hope you will communicate the sentiment of these lines to your parents and close with particularly heartfelt greetings for today.
                                    Your
                                        Walter Benjamin
5 July 1935
Paris XIV

1 *your news*: Adorno's communication regarding the death of Agathe Calvelli-Adorno on 26 June 1935 has not survived.

38 WIESENGRUND-ADORNO TO BENJAMIN
    [FRANKFURT A.M., 12.7.1935]

Dear Herr Benjamin,
    Thank you very much indeed for your kind words, on behalf of myself and the rest of the family. At the moment I have lost all initiative and capacity for work. Hence the continued delay in responding to the Arcades by letter – once again I must ask you to forgive me. My commitment to your work has not diminished in the slightest. On Friday I shall be going to the Black Forest for three weeks with Felizitas and my mother (our address is: Hotel Bären, Hornberg i. Schwarzwald, Schwarzwaldbahn). After that I hope finally to get round to the letter I still owe you.

I am particularly pleased to hear about Else's suggestion.[1] Here too – as with so many things, and certainly the most important, in my life – I can detect the influence of my dead aunt Agathe. Nor could I imagine a more consoling one than this.

Heartfelt regards,

Yours,

Teddie Wiesengrund

[Dated in accordance with the stamped thank-you card.]

1 *Else's suggestion*: It is not possible to identify the latter since Adorno was probably informed about the matter in Frankfurt by Else Herzberger in person.

39 WIESENGRUND-ADORNO AND GRETEL KARPLUS TO BENJAMIN HORNBERG, 2–4 AND 5.8.1935

Hornberg i. Schwarzwald.
Hotel Bären
2 August 1935–4 August 1935

Dear Herr Benjamin,

At long last I would like to say something to you today about your *exposé*,[1] which I have now studied very carefully and discussed with Felizitas again; she is in full agreement with the views expressed here. It would seem to be in keeping with the importance of the subject, which, as you know, I regard extremely highly, if I speak with total candour and proceed without further preliminaries to those questions which I believe are equally crucial for both of us. But I would like to preface the critical discussion by saying that although your method of working means that a sketch or 'line of argument' cannot properly convey an adequate impression, your draft nevertheless seems to me to be full of the most important ideas. Amongst these I would particularly like to emphasize the magnificent passage about living as a leaving of traces, the definitive remarks about the collector, the liberation of things from the curse of utility, and the dialectical interpretation of Haussmann. Your outline of the chapter on Baudelaire as an interpretation of the poet and your introduction of the category of *nouveauté* on page 20 also seem to me to be entirely convincing.

You will therefore already surmise what you can hardly have expected to be otherwise: that I am still concerned about the complex of issues designated by the rubrics of 'pre-history of the nineteenth century', 'the dialectical image', 'the configuration of myth and

104

modernism'. If I refrain here from making any distinction between the 'material' and the 'epistemological' questions, this will still be in keeping, if not with the external organization of the *exposé*, at all events with its philosophical core, whose movement is intended to eliminate the antithesis between the two (as in both of the more recent traditional sketches of the dialectic). Let me take as my point of departure the motto on p. 3, 'chaque époque rêve la suivante' [Every epoch dreams the one to come]. This seems to me to be an important key to the problem in so far as all those motifs in the theory of the dialectical image which provoke my criticism crystallize around precisely this *undialectical* proposition, the elimination of which might lead to a clarification of the theory itself. For the proposition seems to imply three things: a conception of the dialectical image as if it were a content of some consciousness, albeit a collective consciousness; its direct – and I would almost say developmental – relation to the future as utopia; and the idea of the 'epoch' as the proper self-contained subject of this objective consciousness. It seems extremely significant to me that this account of the dialectical image, which could be described as an immanent one, not merely threatens to diminish the original power of the concept, theological in character as it was, by introducing a simplification which undermines not so much its subjective nuance as its fundamental truth; and furthermore, it also fails to preserve that social movement within the contradiction for the sake of which you yourself have sacrificed theology here.

If you transpose the dialectical image into consciousness as a 'dream', you not only rob the concept of its magic and thereby rather domesticate it, but it is also deprived of precisely that crucial and objective liberating potential that would legitimate it in materialist terms. The fetish character of the commodity is not a fact of consciousness; it is rather dialectical in character, in the eminent sense that it produces consciousness. But if so, then neither consciousness nor unconsciousness can simply replicate it as a dream, but must respond to it rather with desire and fear in equal measure. But it is precisely this dialectical power of the fetish character that is forfeited in the replica realism (*sit venia verbo*) of your current immanent version of the dialectical image. To return to the magnificent language of the first draft of the Arcades[2] project: if the dialectical image is nothing but the way in which the fetish character is perceived in the collective consciousness, then the Saint-Simonian conception of the commodity world might well reveal itself as Utopia, but hardly as the reverse – namely as a dialectical image of the nineteenth century as *Hell*. But it is only the latter which could place the idea of the 'Golden Age' in proper perspective, and it is precisely this double sense which could also turn out to be extremely appropriate for an interpretation of Offenbach – that is, the double sense of the Underworld and Arcadia; both of these are explicit categories in Offenbach the ramifications of which could be pursued right down to the instrumental details of orchestration. Thus the abandonment of the category of Hell in your draft, and in particular the elimination of the brilliant passage on the gambler[3] (for which the passage on financial speculation and games of chance[4] is no substitute), seems to me to result not merely in a certain loss of lustre but one of dialectical consistency as well. Now I am myself the last person to be unaware of the relevance of the immanence of consciousness for the nineteenth century, but the concept of the dialectical image cannot simply be derived from it; rather, the immanence of consciousness itself, as *intérieure*, is the dialectical image for the nineteenth century as alienation. And there I shall have to leave the stake which the second chapter of my Kierkegaard book[5] enjoys in this new game. The dialectical image must therefore not be transferred into consciousness as a dream, but rather the dream should be externalized through dialectical interpretation and the immanence of consciousness itself understood as a constellation of reality – the astronomical phase, as it were, Hell wanders through mankind. It seems to me that it is only a map of such a journey through the stars which could provide a perspicuous vision of history as pre-history.

Let me now try and formulate the same objection from the diametrically opposed standpoint. In accordance with your immanent vision of the dialectical image (with which, to employ a positive term, I would contrast your earlier conception of a *model*), you interpret the relationship between the oldest and the newest, one which was already central to your first draft, in terms of a utopian reference to the 'classless society'.[6] The archaic thereby becomes a complementary addition to the new, instead of actually being 'the newest' itself, and is therefore rendered undialectical. However, at the same time, and equally undialectically, the image of classlessness is projected back into mythology, in so far as it is merely conjured up out of the *arche*, instead of becoming properly transparent as the phantasmagoria of Hell. Thus the category in which the archaic fuses with the modern seems to me more like a catastrophe than a Golden Age. I once remarked how the recent past[7] always presents itself as though it had been destroyed by catastrophes. *Hic et nunc*, I would say that this is how it presents itself as pre-history. And at this point I realize I am in agreement with the boldest passage in your book on Tragic Drama.

Now if the disenchantment of the dialectical image as a 'dream' only psychologizes it, then it inevitably falls under the spell of bourgeois psychology. For who precisely is the subject of this dream? In the nineteenth century it was surely nothing but the individual; but in the individual's dream no direct depiction of the fetish character or of its monuments is to be found. That is why the collective consciousness is then invoked, but I fear that in its present form this concept cannot be distinguished from Jung's conception of the same. It is open to criticism from both sides; from the perspective of the social process because it hypostatizes archaic images, whereas in fact dialectical images are generated by the commodity character, not in some archaic collective ego but amongst alienated bourgeois individuals; and from the perspective of psychology because, as Horkheimer puts it, a mass ego[8] only properly exists in earthquakes and catastrophes, while objective surplus value otherwise prevails only through and against individual subjects. The idea of the collective consciousness was invented to distract attention from true objectivity, and from alienated subjectivity as its correlate. Our task is to polarize and dissolve this 'consciousness' dialectically in terms of society and singular subjects, not to galvanize it as the imagistic correlate of the commodity character. The fact that such a dreaming collective serves to erase the differences between classes should already act as a clear and sufficient warning in this respect.

Finally, moreover, the mythic-archaic category of the 'Golden Age' – and this is what is socially decisive to my mind – has had fateful consequences for the commodity category itself. If the crucial 'ambiguity' of the Golden Age is under-emphasized (itself a concept which urgently requires theoretical elucidation and should certainly not be left unexamined), that is, its relationship to Hell, then the commodity as the substance of the age becomes Hell pure and simple, yet negated in a way that actually causes the primal state to appear as truth. Thus disenchantment of the dialectical image leads directly to purely mythical thinking, and then Klages appears as a danger, just as Jung did before. Nowhere does your draft contain more remedies than it does at this point. This would be a central place for the doctrine of the collector as the one who liberates things from the curse of utility. If I understand you properly, this is also where Haussmann would belong. His class consciousness, precisely by the very perfection of the commodity character in a Hegelian self-consciousness, inaugurates the explosion of its phantasmagoria. To understand the commodity as a dialectical image is also to recognize the latter as a motif of the decline and 'sublation' [Aufhebung] of the commodity, rather than its mere regression to an older stage. On the one hand, the commodity is an alien object in which use-value perishes, and on the other, it is an alien survivor that outlives its own immediacy. It is through commodities, and not directly in relation to

107

human beings, that we receive the promise of immortality; and to develop the relationship which you have rightly established between the Arcades project and the book on the Baroque, we could regard the fetish as a final faithless image for the nineteenth century, one comparable only to a death's-head. It seems to me that this is where the basic epistemological character of Kafka is to be identified, particularly in Odradek,[9] as a commodity that has survived to no purpose. Perhaps surrealism finds its fulfilment in this fairy-tale of Kafka's as much as baroque drama found its fulfilment in *Hamlet*. Within society, however, this means that the mere concept of use-value by no means suffices of itself as far as a critique of the commodity character is concerned, but only takes us back to a stage prior to the division of labour. This has always been the source of my real reservations about Berta,[10] and I have always been suspicious of his 'collective' and unmediated concept of function as examples of 'regression' in themselves. Perhaps you will gather from these observations, which essentially concern precisely those categories in your work which may correspond to those of Berta, that my opposition is more than some insular attempt to rescue autonomous art or anything of that sort, but rather addresses itself with the utmost seriousness to those motifs of our philosophical friendship which I regard as fundamental. If I were to close the circle of my critique boldly here at a single stroke, as it were, then I should have to try and grasp the two extremes. A restoration of theology, or better still, a radicalization of dialectic introduced into the glowing heart of theology, would simultaneously require the utmost intensification of the social-dialectical, and indeed economic, motifs. Above all, these must be grasped historically. The *specific* commodity character of the nineteenth century, in other words, the industrial production of commodities, would have to be developed much more clearly and substantively. After all, alienation and the commodity have existed since the beginning of capitalism itself, i.e. the age of manufactured objects which is also that of Baroque art, whereas the 'unity' of the modern age has consisted since then precisely in the commodity character. But it would only be possible to establish the complete 'primal history' and ontology of the nineteenth century through a precise definition of the industrial form of the commodity as something historically distinct from the older form. All references to the commodity form 'as such' lend that history a certain metaphorical character which in this crucial case cannot be permitted. I would surmise that the greatest interpretative results would be gained here if you follow your own procedure, namely the blind processing of material, without hesitation. If my critique, on the other hand, seems to move in a certain sphere of theoretical abstraction, that is indeed a problem, but I

108

know that you will not regard it merely as a problem of 'outlook' and thereby dismiss my reservations outright.

However, I would also like to add a few specific remarks of a more concrete nature, which will naturally be intelligible only against this theoretical background. As a title I would like to suggest *Paris, Capital of the Nineteenth Century*, and not *The Capital* – unless, that is, you revive the *Arcades* title along with Hell. The division into chapters according to particular individuals does not strike me as altogether appropriate: it suggests a rather forced attempt at systematization that makes me a little uneasy. Did you not previously have sections according to various materials, like 'plush', 'dust' and so forth? The relationship between Fourier and the arcades is not very satisfactory either. As an appropriate arrangement here I could imagine a constellation of various urban and commodity materials, something which could then be deciphered later in terms of the dialectical image and its theory.

With regard to the motto on page 1, the word 'portique' very aptly supplies the motif of 'antiquity'; and in connection with the idea of the newest as the oldest, perhaps an elementary treatment of the morphology of the Empire could be provided (like that provided for melancholy in the Baroque book). On page 2, at any rate, the conception of the State in the Empire as an end in itself should explicitly stand revealed as mere ideology, as your subsequent remarks imply you had in mind. You have left the concept of construction completely unclarified; as both alienation *and* mastery of material, it is already eminently dialectical in character and should therefore, in my view, be expounded explicitly as such (with a clear differentiation from the current concept of construction; perhaps the term engineer, which is very characteristic of the nineteenth century, would provide a suitable starting point!). Incidentally, I think that the introduction and exposition of the concept of a collective unconscious, on which I have already made some basic remarks, are not entirely clear. With regard to page 3, I would ask whether it really is the case that cast iron was the first artificial building material (what about bricks!); in general, I am not always comfortable with the notion of 'first' as used in the text. Perhaps this formulation could be added: every epoch dreams that it has been destroyed by catastrophes. Page 4: the phrase 'the new and the old are intermingled' is highly suspect to me, given my earlier critique of the dialectical image as regression. There is no real reversion to the old, but rather the newest, as semblance and phantasmagoria, is itself the old. And here I might perhaps remind you, without being too forward, of some formulations of mine, including certain remarks on the subject of ambiguity, in the *intérieure* section of the book on Kierkegaard. By way of supplementing these

109

here: considered as models, dialectical images are not social products, but objective constellations in which the condition of society finds itself represented. Consequently, no ideological or social 'accomplishment' can ever be expected of a dialectical image. My objection to your merely negative account of reification – the critique of the presence of 'Klages' in the draft – is based primarily upon the passage concerning machines on page 4. An over-valuation of machine technology and of machines in general has always been characteristic of bourgeois theories of the past; the relations of production thereby get concealed through abstract reference to the means of production.

Hegel's extremely important concept of second nature, which has since been taken up by Georg[11] and others, belongs on page 6. And presumably the 'diable à Paris' could lead on to Hell. On page 7, I would rather doubt that the worker really appeared as a 'stage extra' etc., 'for the last time' outside of his class. Incidentally, the idea of an early history of the *feuilleton*, about which there is so much in your essay on Kraus, is a rather fascinating one; this would also be the place for Heine. In this connection an old journalistic expression occurs to me: *Schablonstil* [clichéd style], the origin of which would be well worth pursuing. The term 'Lebensgefühl' [general feeling for or attitude to life], as used in cultural and intellectual history, is extremely suspect to me. It appears to me that your uncritical acceptance of technology at its first appearance is connected with your over-valuation of the archaic as such. I noted down the following formulation: myth is not the classless longing for a true society, but rather the alienated character of the commodity itself. On page 9, your conception of the history of painting in the nineteenth century as a flight from photography (to which the flight of music from 'banality' is an exact correspondence) is powerful but undialectical, for the share of the forces of production not incorporated into the commodity form in the stock of paintings cannot be grasped concretely in this fashion, but only through the negative presence of its trace (Manet would probably seem to be the exact site of this dialectic). This all seems to be connected with the mythologizing and archaizing tendency of your draft. Belonging to the past, the stock of paintings thereby becomes a series of fixed starry images in the philosophy of history, drained of their share of productive force. The subjective side of the dialectic vanishes before an undialectically mythical gaze, the gaze of the Medusa. The Golden Age, page 10, perhaps forms the proper transition to Hell. – I cannot grasp the relationship of the World Fairs to the workers; this sounds like conjecture and can only be presented with extreme circumspection. Of course, a great definition and theory of the phantasmagorical belong on page 11. Page 12 was a *mene tekel* [a warning] as far as I am concerned. Both

110

Felizitas and I well remember the enormous impression which the Saturn quotation once made upon us,[12] but the quotation has not survived the test of more sober reflection. The ring of Saturn should not become a cast-iron balcony, but the balcony should become the real ring of Saturn. And here I am happy not to offer you abstract objections of my own, but merely to confront you with your own achievement: the incomparable moon chapter in your Berlin Childhood,[13] the philosophical content of which properly belongs here. It was at this point that I recalled something you once said about the Arcades project: that it could only be wrested from the realm of madness.[14] That it has avoided this realm, rather than subjugating it to itself, is revealed by the interpretation of the Saturn quotation, which has rather recoiled from it. And this is the source of my real objections: for Siegfried[15] might well be delighted here, and that is why I must speak so brutally, given the enormous seriousness of the issue. As was probably your own intention, the conception of the commodity fetish must be documented with appropriate passages from the man who discovered it. The concept of the organic, which also appears on page 12 and suggests a static anthropology, is probably not a tenable one either, except perhaps in the sense that it merely existed as such prior to the fetish and thus is itself historical, like the idea of 'landscape'. The dialectical commodity motif of Odradek probably belongs on page 13. Once again the workers' movement appears here as something of a *deus ex machina*. Of course, as with a number of other similar formulations, the extremely concentrated style of the draft may be to blame here: this reservation is something that should also be applied to many of my other reservations. With regard to the construction of the passage on 'fashion', which seems to me to be extremely important, and which I think should probably be detached from the concept of the organic and brought into relationship with the living, i.e. not with some superior nature, the idea of the 'changeant' occurred to me – the shot fabric which seems to have had great expressive significance for the nineteenth century and was presumably bound up with certain industrial processes. Perhaps you will pursue this idea one day. Frau Hessel,[16] whose fashion reports in the *Frankfurter Zeitung* we always used to read with such interest, will certainly have some information about this. The passage where I am particularly unhappy about the overly abstract use of the commodity category is on page 14. I am doubtful whether this category appeared 'for the first time' as such in the nineteenth century. (Incidentally, I would say the same objection also applies to the *intérieure* and the sociology of interiority in my Kierkegaard book, and every criticism I have made of your draft also holds for my own earlier study.) I believe that the commodity category could be rendered much more concrete by reference to the specifically modern categories of world trade and imperialism. Connected with this is the Arcade as bazaar, and also antique shops as world trade markets for the ephemeral. The significance of ever diminishing distance – perhaps this touches on the problem of winning over aimless social strata and that of imperial conquest. These are simply suggestions. You would certainly be able to unearth incomparably more conclusive evidence from the material you have at your disposal and thereby determine the specific form of the nineteenth century world of things, perhaps by looking at it from the seamier side, from its refuse, remnants and debris. The passage about the 'office', too, probably lacks historical accuracy. To me the office would appear to be less a direct opposite to the home, than a relic of older forms of rooms, and probably baroque ones (consider the globes, the maps on walls, the railings, and other kinds of material). Regarding the theory of *Art Nouveau* on page 15: if I agree with you that this signified a decisive shattering of the interior, I can only reject the idea that it 'mobilizes all the reserve forces of interiority'. It seems rather to salvage them and actualize them through a process of 'externalization'. (The theory of symbolism in particular belongs here, but above all Mallarmé's interiors, which have precisely the opposite significance to those of Kierkegaard.) *Art Nouveau* replaced interiority with sexuality. It addressed itself to sexuality precisely because it was only in sex that private individuals could encounter themselves as corporeal rather than as inward. This is true of all *Art Nouveau* from Ibsen to Maeterlinck and d'Annunzio. The origins of Strauss and *Art Nouveau* lie in Wagner rather than the chamber music of Brahms. The use of concrete as material seems uncharacteristic of *Art Nouveau*, and presumably belongs in the strange vacuum period around 1910. Incidentally, I think that the real *Art Nouveau* probably coincided with the great economic crisis around 1900. Concrete belongs to the pre-war boom. Page 16: let me also draw your attention to the very remarkable interpretation of 'The Master Builder' in Wedekind's posthumously published works.[17] I am not aware of any particular psychoanalytic literature on the subject of emerging from sleep, but I shall look into it. However, is not all this dream-interpreting and newly emergent psychoanalysis, which expressly and polemically dissociates itself from hypnotism (as documented in Freud's lectures),[18] itself part of *Art Nouveau*, with which indeed it corresponds in time? This is probably a question of the first order and one that may prove very far-reaching. As a corrective to my fundamental critique, I should like to add the following here: if I reject the idea of the collective consciousness, this is naturally not in order to leave the 'bourgeois individual' untouched as the real substratum here. The interior should

112

be rendered transparent as a social function and its apparently autarchic character revealed as an illusion – not vis-à-vis some hypostatized collective consciousness, but vis-à-vis the actual social process itself. The 'individual' is a dialectical instrument of transition which must not be mythicized away, but can only be superseded. Once again I would like to emphasize most strongly the passage on 'the liberation of things from the bondage of utility' as a brilliant turning point for the dialectical salvation of the commodity. On page 17 I should be very pleased if the theory of the collector and of the interior as a kind of encasement could be elaborated as fully as possible. On page 18 I would also like to draw your attention to Maupassant's 'La Nuit',[19] which seems to me to be the dialectical capstone to Poe's 'Man of the Crowd' as cornerstone. I think the passage about the crowd as veil is magnificent. Page 19 is the place for the critique of the dialectical image. Undoubtedly you know better than I do that the theory as given here still fails to do full justice to the enormous demands of the issue. I should merely like to say that ambiguity is not the translation of the dialectic into an image, but the 'trace' of that image which itself must first be rendered dialectical by theory. I seem to recall that there is a convenient statement about this in the 'Interior' chapter of my Kierkegaard book. Concerning page 20, perhaps the last stanza of the great 'Femmes damnées' from the 'Pièces condamnées'. In my view, the concept of false consciousness should be treated with the greatest caution, and should certainly not be used any longer without reference to its Hegelian (!) origin. The concept of the 'snob' was originally a social rather than an aesthetic one, and was given currency by Thackeray. A very clear distinction is to be made between the snob and the dandy; the history of the snob should be investigated, and Proust furnishes you with the most splendid material in this respect. Your thesis on page 21 concerning *l'art pour l'art* and the 'all-embracing work of art' [Gesamtkunstwerk] seems untenable to me in its present form. The all-embracing work of art and aestheticism in the precise sense of the word are not identical, but rather diametrically opposed attempts to escape from the commodity character: Baudelaire's relationship to Wagner, therefore, is as dialectical as his association with a prostitute. I am very unhappy about the theory of speculation on page 22. For one thing, the theory of games of chance[20] which originally formed a brilliant part of the Arcades draft is missing; and another element which is lacking is a genuine economic theory of the speculator. Speculation is the negative expression of the irrationality of capitalist rationality. Perhaps it would also be possible to deal with this passage by means of 'extrapolating to the extremes'. An explicit theory of perspective would be required on page 23, and I believe you had something on that in the original

113

draft.[21] The stereoscope, invented between 1810 and 1820, is relevant in this connection. The fine dialectical conception of the chapter on Haussmann could perhaps be elaborated more precisely in the study than it is in the draft, where it has to be interpreted beforehand.

I must ask you once again to excuse the carping character of these comments; but I believe that I owe you at least a few specific examples of my basic criticisms. I shall be discussing the book[22] with my friend Wind at the Warburg Institute in London, and hopefully I shall be able to bring things off for you in person. I shall enclose the draft. Finally, I must ask you to forgive me for making a copy of this letter for Felizitas and myself, something quite exceptional for me. I hope you will think this justified given its substantive content, and I would like to believe that it will also help to facilitate further discussion in future. – I had merely asked Siegfried[23] to tender my apologies for the delay in responding to your draft by letter, and had said nothing about the origins, let alone the content, of the draft. Incidentally, he has still not responded to a substantial letter of mine, something which has irritated me considerably in my current situation.[24] Finally, I would also ask you to forgive the appearance of the letter itself. It was composed on a badly damaged typewriter and a written draft was impractical on grounds of length.

Felizitas and I are recuperating as well as these mountain surroundings allow. I have done no work whatsoever, except to draw up a plan for a projected edition of my essays on music[25] in book form. It is still uncertain whether anything will come of it.

In true friendship, yours,

Teddie Wiesengrund

Dear Detlef,

Many, many thanks for Baba.[26] Merely lots of greetings for today and best wishes for the rest of your holidays! I will reply soon, but at present I am still too immersed in the Arcades. Heartfelt wishes as ever,

Yours,

Felicitas (is it correct with the c or the z?)

5 August 1935

Dear Herr Benjamin, the attempt to reconcile your 'dream' moment – as the subjective element in the dialectical image – with the model conception of the latter has led me to certain formulations which I also communicate to you as the furthest I have been able to get for the present:

In so far as the use-value of things perishes from them, the alienated things are hollowed out and thereby come to acquire encoded meanings. Subjectivity appropriates these meanings by introducing intentional experiences of desire and anxiety into them. In so far as these relinquished things now stand in as images of subjective intentional experiences, they present themselves as still present and eternal. Dialectical images are constellations between alienated things and injected meanings, resting in a moment of indifference between death and meaning. Whereas the things are roused to the appearance of the newest, death transforms the meanings into the oldest.

1 *exposé*: The draft version seen by Adorno is printed in GS V [2], pp. 1237–49; the pagination of the typescript, to which Adorno refers in his letter, is given there in square brackets.

2 *first draft of the Arcades*: According to a verbal communication to Rolf Tiedemann, Adorno was thinking here of certain individual sections which Benjamin had read out to him in 1929: these are texts known as the Paris Arcades II (cf. GS V [2], pp. 1044–59.)

3 *the passage on the gambler*: cf. GS V [2], pp. 1056f.

4 *the passage on speculation and games of chance*: cf. ibid., p. 1247.

5 *the second chapter of my Kierkegaard book*: cf. GS 2, pp. 38–69; on the 'Interior', cf. ibid., pp. 61–9.

6 *reference to the 'classless society'*: cf. GS V [2], p. 1239.

7 *the recent past*: see letter 33 and the relevant note.

8 *Horkheimer ... mass ego*: cf. Max Horkheimer, 'Geschichte und Psychologie' [History and Psychology] in the Zeitschrift für Sozialforschung 1, issue 1/2 (1932), pp. 125–144; the passage referred to by Adorno is found on p. 136; it can now be found in Horkheimer, *Gesammelte Schriften*, vol. 3 (Frankfurt a.M. 1988), pp. 48–69 (the passage is on p. 60).

9 *Odradek*: For Kafka's prose piece, see also letter 27.

10 *Berta*: a pseudonym for Brecht, whose name, like that of Georg Lukács, was best avoided in a letter written in Germany and sent to an addressee abroad.

11 *Georg*: the reference is to Georg Lukács and his book *Geschichte und Klassenbewusstsein* [History and Class Consciousness] (Berlin 1923).

12 *the enormous impression the Saturn quotation once made upon us*: probably in 1929 in Königstein when Benjamin read out the text 'The Ring of Saturn or Something Concerning Iron Construction' (cf. GS V [2], pp. 1060–3, and the quotation itself p. 1060).

13 *the moon chapter in your Berlin Childhood*: cf. GS IV [1], pp. 300–2 and VIII [1], pp. 426–8.

14 *the Arcades project ... wrested from the realm of madness*: cf. Benjamin's formulation in GS V [2], p. 1010 and GS V [1], pp. 570f.

15 *Siegfried*: i.e. Siegfried Kracauer.

16 *Frau Hessel*: Helen Hessel, the wife of Franz Hessel, was one of Benjamin's Paris acquaintances; she worked in Paris as a correspondent for the *Frankfurter Zeitung*.

17 *interpretation of 'The Master Builder' in Wedekind's posthumous works*: cf. Franz Wedekind, 'The Writer Ibsen and "The Master Builder"', in *Gesammelte Schriften*, vol. 9 (Munich 1921), pp. 340–58.

18 *Freud's lectures*: a reference to Freud's *Introductory Lectures on Psychoanalysis* of 1916/17.

19 *Maupassant's 'La Nuit'*: see letter 33 and the relevant note.

20 *the theory of games of chance*: see the opening of this letter and the relevant note.

21 *theory of perspective . . . in the original draft*: cf. GS V [2], pp. 1949f.

22 *discussing the book*: in the postscript of his letter of 29 July to Gretel Karplus, Benjamin had written: 'Could you ask Teddie if he will be able to look (or has already looked) at Noack's piece entitled 'The Triumphal Arch' (Studien der Bibliothek Warburg)?' Cf. GS V [2], p. 1127.

23 *I had asked Siegfried*: in his unpublished letter of 5 July to Siegfried Kracauer.

24 *my current situation*: i.e. after the death of his aunt.

25 *a projected edition of my essays on music*: see letter 25 and the relevant note.

26 *Baba*: on the envelope of Benjamin's last letter to Gretel there is a depiction of an elephant driving an open car with the roof pulled back by its trunk. Benjamin had written underneath: 'The elephant, by the way, derives from one of the best of the recent French children's books and is called Baba' (unpublished; Benjamin to Gretel Karplus on 29.7.1935).

40   BENJAMIN TO GRETEL KARPLUS AND WIESENGRUND-ADORNO
    [PARIS, 16.8.1935]

Dear Felizitas,
    I think I am doing right if I consign these few lines into your hands.
    If, contrary to expectation, you should no longer both be there together when they arrive, you will surely pass them on directly to Wiesengrund yourself.
    They contain no detailed response to the substantial and marvellous letter which I received from both of you on the 4th. That shall

be reserved for later correspondence, not so much in any single letter as in a whole series of them in due course, a correspondence whose many currents and tributaries one day, and not too distantly I hope, will finally rejoin one another when we all have the opportunity of meeting once again in person.

No, not a detailed response then, but simply, if you wish, an acknowledgement of its arrival. But I do not merely wish to say that it is your hands which have received this letter. Nor merely your minds either. Rather, what I wish to express to you both, before touching upon anything else whatsoever, is the joy it gives me to see our friendship so confirmed and so many friendly conversations renewed through this letter of yours.

The most remarkable aspect of your letter, and something which is extremely significant and fruitful for me given your precisely formulated and penetrating objections, is the way in which it constantly brings the central issue into the closest possible connection with the previous history of our thoughts on this matter; that all of your reflections, or almost all of them, go precisely to the productive heart of the issue, and hardly a single one fails to do so. In whatever form your reflections will also continue to affect my thinking, and little as I can anticipate as yet what this means, at least two things seem quite certain to me: firstly, that your response can only serve to benefit the work, and secondly, that it can only confirm and strengthen the friendship between us.

If it were simply left to me, that would be all I should like to say for today. For anything else would easily lead us into further as yet unclarified matters that are difficult to contain and define. But since I would certainly not wish these lines to appear as too meagre a response, let me be bold enough to offer just a few quite provisional remarks – although this runs certain risks as well.

You will have to accept that they have a somewhat confessional, rather than straightforwardly substantive, character.

One thing I would like to say immediately: if your letter makes such emphatic reference to the 'first' sketch of the Arcades, I can confirm that absolutely nothing has been abandoned, and not a single word relinquished, from this 'first' version. And the piece you had in front of you is not, if I could put it this way, the 'second' sketch but rather a *different* one. The two sketches have a polar relationship to one another. They represent the thesis and the antithesis of the work. Consequently, as far as I am concerned, this second one is far from being a conclusion. The necessity for it lies in the fact that the insights contained in the first sketch cannot be articulated immediately – except perhaps in an impermissibly 'poetical' fashion.

Hence the subtitle, long since abandoned, of the first sketch: 'A Poetic Fairy-Tale'.

Now I have the two ends of the bow in hand – but still lack the strength to bend and string it properly. Only a long period of 'training' can prepare me for this, and directly working in the material itself is one element, amongst others, of the process. My unfortunate circumstances also mean that those other elements have had to recede in favour of the first one during the second period of my work on the project. I am aware of this. And the somewhat dilatory character of my method reflects this awareness. I do not wish to let any mistake disturb the calculated plan of the whole.

What are these other elements of 'training'? The constructive ones. If Wiesengrund expresses reservations about the way in which the chapters have been divided up, he has certainly hit the nail on the head. For as yet the arrangement still lacks the constructive moment. Whether the latter should be sought in the direction you suggest, I leave open for the present. But one thing is quite certain: what the constructive moment means for this book must be compared with what the philosopher's stone means for alchemy. The only thing that can really be said about this at present is that it will have to re-articulate the opposition in which my book stands in relation to all previous and traditional historical research in a new, succinct and very simple fashion. How this will be done remains to be decided.

After these remarks I do not imagine that I have to dispel any suspicions on your part that anything resembling personal stubbornness has affected my resistance to certain of your other objections. In this matter I cannot think of any vice from which I am further removed than that. And I pass over many points in which I find myself in agreement with you, saving these up for discussion later on. (And seldom more so than with respect to Wiesengrund's reflections on the theme of 'The Golden Age'.)

No, what I am thinking about at the moment is the passage in your letter where you discuss Saturn. I would certainly not deny that 'the molten iron balcony must become one of Saturn's rings'. But do I have to explain the following: that this transformation is certainly not a task which falls to any single approach – and least of all to Grandville's drawing – since it is essentially one that falls exclusively to the book as a whole. Forms like those suggested to me by 'A Berlin Childhood' can have no claim whatsoever on any part of this particular work, not even in the slightest degree. One important function of the second sketch is precisely to consolidate this insight for myself. The primal history of the nineteenth century which is reflected in the expression of the child playing on the threshold, reveals a quite different face than in those signs inscribed upon the paper of history.

118

These quite preliminary remarks are confined to certain very general questions. Without exploring the latter to their full extent, my remarks must leave all the detailed points unaddressed. I shall come back to many of them on a later occasion. But allow me to conclude, again at the risk of sounding rather confessional, by emphasizing a problematic which seems to me to be quite decisive. In mentioning this I would draw attention to two things: firstly, just how important Wiesengrund's description of the dialectical image in terms of a 'constellation' seems to me to be, but secondly, how indispensable certain elements I pointed out in this constellation appear to be: namely the dream figures. The dialectical image does not simply copy the dream – I never remotely intended to suggest that. But it certainly does seem to me that the former contains within itself the exemplary instances, the irruptions of waking consciousness, and that indeed it is precisely from such places that the figure of the dialectical image first produces itself like that of a star composed of many glittering points. Here too, therefore, a bow needs to be stretched, and a dialectic forged: that between the image and the act of waking.

[Yours, Detlef]

41 BENJAMIN TO WIESENGRUND-ADORNO
    PARIS, 27.12.1935

Dear Herr Wiesengrund,
    Before I pass on a message from Max,[1] which originally prompted me to write these lines, let me express the profound sympathy I felt for you on learning yesterday of the death of Alban Berg.[2]
    You know that whenever we talked about music, a field otherwise fairly remote from my own, it was really only when his work was under discussion that we reached the same level of intensity as we usually do in our discussions on other subjects. You will certainly still remember the conversation we had following a performance of Wozzeck.[3]
    Max asks that on no account must you leave the Continent without first informing him by telegram about where you can be contacted before the crossing. It is extremely important for him to speak to you while you are on the Continent, either in Holland or in Paris. (You can imagine how delighted I would be and just how much it would mean to me if it could be Paris.)
    He specifically wants you to pass this information on to me since he will keep me informed about his own whereabouts and the length of his stay in Holland, which begins at the end of the week.

Of course, Max realizes how much I would like the three of us to meet up in Paris for discussion.

Sincere regards to you and to Felizitas.

Your

WB

27 December 1935
Paris XIV
23 rue Bénard

1 *Before I pass on a message from Max*: Since the middle of December, Max Horkheimer had been staying in Paris and had obviously asked Benjamin to write to Adorno who was then at home for the winter vacation.

2 *the death of Alban Berg*: Berg, the friend and teacher of Adorno, had died on 24 September 1935.

3 *the conversation ... following a performance of Wozzeck*: Adorno and Benjamin had attended a performance of Berg's 'Wozzeck' together on 22 December 1925 in Berlin, the first performance after the premiere of the work on 15 December. Adorno gives some impression of the conversation with Benjamin in his unpublished letter to Berg of 27.12.1925: 'This time the great scene in the inn was quite clear: I do not know whether this was due to Kleiber or just to me, for in fact I now find the entire work to be concentrated in this central section; it is a quite brilliant and unparalleled stroke, and that is why it is so successful, to seize and assimilate here that primeval and diffusely elemental dimension: the exploitation of out of tune singing as a constructive motif is a metaphysically profound discovery and even goes beyond Mahler's own innermost intentions. I cannot find any other equally grand words to express this, and Benjamin, who might well strike you as a less suspicious witness than I – although he has a much better idea of what the work is about than any musician – felt exactly the same way. Thus it is certainly no coincidence that this scene stands precisely where it does: it is a caesura in Hölderlin's sense, and one which thereby allows the "expressionless" to break into the music itself.'

42 WIESENGRUND-ADORNO TO BENJAMIN
    [FRANKFURT A.M.,] 29.12.1935

29 December

Dear Herr Benjamin,

Let me thank you deeply from the heart for your lines, the first which have reached me concerning the death of my friend Alban Berg, and tell you how much this alone, as a token, has touched me. This latest blow is more than I can handle, even after all the experiences of the past year, and all I really have to offer today are fragments, as Berg himself once wrote in a dedication copy[1] of one of his scores in a very similar connection.

Hence this very brief reply. On Tuesday (the 31st) I am travelling to visit Gretel in Berlin, where I shall be staying until the 6th. Then I shall be back in Frankfurt. I was intending to stay there until the 10th, or the 11th at the latest, and then I would be off for London without further delay (my address: Albemarle Court Hotel, W2, Leinster Gardens; tel. Paddington 7228; the hotel's address for telegrams: Apporter, London). I have to be in Oxford by the 17th.

I had hoped to be able to meet Max in London. But since I want to arrange a meeting just as much as he does, I shan't be difficult about it, and will gladly meet him wherever he suggests. It is all the same to me whether I am in London or somewhere else between the 11th and the 17th, and if absolutely necessary I could always meet Max *beforehand*, whether in Paris or in Holland, on the 9th at the earliest let us say, and then possibly travel back to England with him. Nonetheless, I would be very grateful to receive a decision as quickly as possible, and preferably while I am still in Berlin. A meeting in Brussels would also be a possibility.[2]

All that needs to be said in this regard is: as far as London is concerned I have an invitation, but I could only make it to Holland or Belgium if Max arranges that officially as an invitation too, since I can only get a little financial assistance here and no one else invites me anywhere. I assume that Max knows this and will put the required funds at my disposal. Perhaps you could mention this to him in a way that spares my feelings; I certainly find it very disagreeable to depend on such things, but given the regulations now in force, there is really no other choice and I am sure he will understand the situation.

Please accept my heartfelt thanks in advance for this. I do not have to tell you how happy it would make me to see you again so soon. Is there then no possibility of your making a trip to England?

Your true and long-standing friend,

Teddie Wiesengrund

1 *fragments . . . dedication copy*: See Adorno's account in GS 18, p. 491; the dedication copy of the 'Three Fragments from Wozzeck' has not survived.

2 *A meeting in Brussels would also be a possibility*: Adorno's meeting with Horkheimer actually took place in Amsterdam in the middle of January, when their agreement regarding Adorno's essay on jazz initiated the period of Adorno's closer participation in the *Zeitschrift für Sozialforschung*.

Dear Herr Wiesengrund,

Many thanks for your letter of 29 December.

Given Max's current plans, I shall not be able to fulfil all those wishes we were harbouring for your return trip. Unfortunately his arrangements mean that the three of us will not be meeting up in Paris after all, as he too had hoped.

It rather looks as though he will stick with the meeting originally arranged for London, unless he should call you over from there to Holland instead. Since he is still not yet entirely clear about his future arrangements, he would like you to send him a telegram immediately if you find no message already waiting for you when you arrive at Albemarle Court Hotel. In that case his address will be: Amsterdam Carlton-Hotel.

I think Max will have my essay[1] with him when he meets you, and I am delighted that it will be appearing, and in French no less, in the Institute's journal. Be sure to ask him for the manuscript and write to me about it. At any rate, be sure to keep me promptly informed about the news in London.

As far as the external arrangements for a meeting outside England are concerned, I have already informed Max about this in the manner you suggested.

Tell Felizitas that she can expect to hear from me very soon.

And heartfelt greetings to you,

Yours,

WB

3 January

1 *my essay*: a reference to the first version of 'The Work of Art in the Age of Mechanical Reproduction' (cf. GS I [2], pp. 431–508). The French translation by Pierre Klossowski appeared in the Institute journal under the title: 'L'œuvre d'art à l'époque de sa réproduction mécanisée' (*Zeitschrift für Sozialforschung 5*, issue 1 (1936), pp. 40–66). Now in GS I [2], pp. 709–39.

London, 29 January 1936

Dear Herr Benjamin, I am writing you this card from an extremely dark café, hidden away in an alley in the very heart of the city, surrounded by domino-playing characters – a little place that I would love to disclose to you alone. And it seems to be just the place for me to get in touch with you again. I am back in Oxford again, totally immersed in work. The conclusion of my book appears to be imminent. I hope to be finished with the analyses within four weeks at the most; and I think I can dedicate the summer to concluding the final literary version. I do hope the work will objectively redeem at least something of what it has meant for me. In addition, I am also working on my contribution to the Berg monograph,[1] which I have been unable to ignore. I have had to take on the greater part of the musical analyses – good work for the night-time. This fact, in conjunction with the café, may help to excuse writing this card. It also expresses a request: could you make a copy of your piece on technological reproduction[2] available to me as soon as possible? The request is all the more urgent since the passages which Max has shown me[3] provoked a number of reservations in my mind (at least with regard to the style of formulation) which I can only properly explore or dispel after examining the whole essay. I should be extremely grateful if you could manage this. – Max will already have mentioned to you that there is a chance that I may be able to come to Paris[4] in March. This would delight no one more than your own true friend,

Teddie W.

1 *contribution to the Berg monograph*: reference to the project for a book on Alban Berg initiated by Willi Reich; cf. Willi Reich, *Alban Berg. Mit Bergs eigenen Schriften und Beiträgen von Theodor Wiesengrund-Adorno und Ernst Krenek* (Wien, Leipzig, Zürich 1937). Adorno was responsible for the analysis of the Piano Sonata, op. 1; the Four Songs, op. 2; the Seven Early Songs; the String Quartet, op. 3; the Four Pieces for Clarinet and Piano, op. 6; the Lyric Suite for String Quartet and the Concert Aria 'Der Wein'. These analyses were later incorporated in Adorno's own 1968 monograph on Berg (cf. GS 13, pp. 321–494).

2 *your piece on technological reproduction*: see the relevant note to the previous letter.

3 *the passages which Max has shown me*: during their meeting in Amsterdam.

4 *a chance that I may be able to come to Paris*: in the event Adorno did not manage to visit Paris.

45 BENJAMIN TO WIESENGRUND-ADORNO
PARIS, 7.2.1936

Dear Herr Wiesengrund,

Naturally enough I was extremely keen from the first to send you my new piece. When it was finished – for the first time, as it were – you were still in Frankfurt. I therefore gave it to Max in the hope

123

that your meeting would give you enough time to read the whole thing. When I learned from Max that this was not possible after all, my two copies were already completed.

Now you will probably be receiving within a few days not only the original, but also the translation which was undertaken at Max's behest by Pierre Klossowski.[1] We expect the piece will be quite safe in his hands; he not only possesses all the necessary linguistic skills for this, but also brings important theoretical prerequisites to the task.

I am very pleased to be able to report that my discussions with Max about the piece have been extremely fruitful and were conducted in the most cordial manner. And indeed some of the very questions which you originally provoked also proved very important for us. The results of these conversations – in which I think you will recognize something of your own contributions – to the extent that they have not actually led to reformulations in the text (in a very few places), have found expression in a number of notes which intersect as it were with the political-philosophical basis of the argument constructed in the text.

But over and beyond this particular text, I can say this time that the conversations and arrangements with Max[2] have helped to realize the goal towards which my own most urgent aspirations and your active friendship have for so long been striving. After the very last words we exchanged here in the Hotel Lutétia during your brief visit,[3] I hardly need to tell you just *what* it means for me to be able to work at last without having to deal with the harshest concerns of life. And since you too are becoming ever more closely involved with the Institute's work, I can only expect, without I hope being irresponsibly optimistic, good things to come of it, both with respect to our theoretical perspectives and to our practical position.

First of all it looks to me as though the preparation of a French translation of Max's essays,[4] something which I am about to try and negotiate with Groethuysen,[5] will prove an appropriate external occasion for the next early meeting with Max. I would be so pleased if you could spare some time to visit Paris. I would not be able to let you leave without first showing you something of my book's vivid documentation to be found, for example, in the Cabinet des Estampes.[6]

I hope you will read between these lines the gratitude which our current situation prevents me from expressing to you in person. In heartfelt friendship,

Yours,
Walter Benjamin

7 février 1936
Paris XIV
23 rue Bénard

124

1 *Pierre Klossowski*: the writer, painter and translator Pierre Klossowski (born 1905).

2 *arrangements with Max*: Max Horkheimer had confirmed his intention to help to alleviate Benjamin's financial situation. In his letter of 26 January, Adorno had written to Horkheimer: 'We spoke about 1000 francs – is it indelicate if I remind you of the sum? Since in the meantime he is unable to earn anything in addition to this, he would not be able to manage in Paris with less, even with the most drastic economies.' (Unpublished; 26.1.1936, Adorno to Horkheimer.)

3 *your brief visit*: Adorno had arrived in Paris on the evening of 11 December 1935 before proceeding to Frankfurt after a short stay.

4 *Max's essays*: a planned French translation of a selection of Horkheimer's essays from the Institute's *Zeitschrift für Sozialforschung*, which were going to bear the title of 'Essais de philosophie matérialiste', eventually collapsed through dilatoriness on the part of the publishers Gallimard.

5 *Groethuysen*: Bernhard Groethuysen (1880–1946), philosopher, pupil of Wilhelm Dilthey, Professor in Berlin 1931–1933, subsequently lived in Paris and acted amongst other things as an adviser to Gallimard publishing house.

6 *Cabinet des Estampes*: For Benjamin's time working in the *Cabinet des Estampes* of the *Bibliothèque Nationale*, cf. GS V [2], pp. 1323f.

46   BENJAMIN TO WIESENGRUND-ADORNO
      PARIS, 27.2.1936

Dr Walter Benjamin   Paris, 27 February 1936
                                            23, Rue Bénard

Dear Herr Wiesengrund,
    I had hoped to be able to send you my essay[1] and a covering letter before now. But I was unable to get hold of an extra German copy until the French translation was completed. Please forgive me if the copy I am sending you now shows traces of the translator's labours.
    Furthermore, if the task of translation were indeed completely finished in all respects, you would be receiving the German and the French simultaneously. As things stand at present, however, in spite of the fact that the work has already gone to press, I still have to hold on to the latter for a while in order to go through it one last time with the translator.
    Due to these circumstances I have also had to postpone the expression of my thanks for sending me your commemorative essays[2] on the death of Alban Berg. You would have heard something from me concerning these extraordinary pieces before now if I had not had to

125

keep snapping at my translator's heels for the last two weeks, all day long and a good part of the night as well. You are aware that the second of the essays is the more immediately accessible to me on account of its more familiar subject matter. I have therefore devoted most of my time to this one, and indeed it strikes me as an extraordinarily beautiful piece of work. There are many passages here that spoke intimately to me.

For example, right at the beginning, your description of the 'stony gentleness' which corresponds so wonderfully to the death mask;[3] and then that truly astonishing remark, which speaks to me so directly: 'he has undercut the negativity of the world with the hopelessness of his fantasy' – a perspective which vividly brings back to me the first encounter with the music of Wozzeck. As for some of the other remarks, I cannot help but think that you generally had me in mind when you were writing them, above all, of course, the reference to the 'friendliness of the cannibal'.[4] I was also particularly delighted about the connection in which you cite Berg's remark about the brass chord.[5]

Hopefully I shall not have to wait too long before receiving your next letter. No matter how brief the interval, I will await its arrival with impatience. The two weeks I spent in the most intense work with my translator have provided me with some distance from the German text, something which usually takes much longer to do with me. I say this not in order to dissociate myself from it in the least, but rather because it was only at a certain distance that I discovered *one* element in the text to which I would particularly like to see you as a reader do proper justice: specifically, its cannibalistic urbanity,[6] a certain circumspection and caution in the destructive approach, which will I hope betray something of the love it harbours for those things which are also closest to you.

I am waiting to receive the collection of Max's essays, the translation of which has been entrusted to me. Once the work is underway I assume we will definitely be able to see each other here. I believe and hope this will take place soon.

With sincere regards,

Yours,

Walter Benjamin

1 *my essay*: Benjamin sent Adorno a typescript of the second version of the essay 'The Work of Art in the Age of Mechanical Reproduction' (cf. GS VII [1], pp. 350–84).

2 *your commemorative essays*: see the two essays by Adorno which appeared under the pseudonym Hektor Rottweiler: 'Zur Lulu-Symphonie' [On the Lulu Symphony], in the Vienna music journal '23', 1.2.1936,

126

nr. 24/25, pp. 5–11 (now in GS 13, pp. 472–7) and 'Erinnerung an den Lebenden' [Commemoration of a Living Presence], in '23', 1.2.1936, nr. 24/25, pp. 19–29. – Adorno composed a second version of his commemorative remarks – 'Im Gedächtnis Alban Bergs' – in October 1955 (cf. GS 18, pp. 487–512), which was in turn revised for his 1968 monograph on Berg (cf. GS 13, pp. 335–67).

3 *the death mask*: Berg's death mask was also reproduced in the journal '23'.

4 *the 'friendliness of the cannibal'*: see Adorno's essay in '23', p. 27.

5 *Berg's remark about the brass chord*: '"Yes", he said, with a ferocity which buried every trace of Johannine gentleness with an avalanche, "once you should really hear what a brass chord of eight different notes really sounds like"; as if he were quite certain that no audience would be able to survive the experience.' (Ibid., p. 26.)

6 *its cannibalistic urbanity*: see Benjamin's characterization of the satirist in his essay 'Karl Kraus' (GS II [1], p. 355).

47   WIESENGRUND-ADORNO TO BENJAMIN
     LONDON, 18.3.1936

London, 18 March 1936

Dear Herr Benjamin,
   If I now prepare to send you some notes concerning your extra-ordinary study, I certainly have no intention of offering a critical analysis of it or a remotely appropriate response to it. The enormous pressure of work on me at the moment – the large book on logic, the completion of my contribution to the monograph on Berg, which is now ready apart from a couple of musical analyses, and the study on jazz[1] – makes any such endeavour impossible. This is especially true of a piece in the face of which I am very seriously aware of the inadequacies of written communication, for there is not a single sentence here that I would not want to discuss with you in detail. I cling to the hope that this will in fact prove possible, but at the same time I do not wish to wait too long before providing you with some kind of response, however inadequate it may be.
   Let me confine myself therefore to one fundamental theme. I can express my passionate interest and total approval with regard to that aspect of your piece which appears to me to fulfil your original intention – the dialectical construction of the relationship between myth and history – within the intellectual domain of the materialist dialectic: namely, the dialectical self-dissolution of myth, which is

127

viewed here as the disenchantment of art. You are well aware that the question of the 'liquidation' of art has been a motivating force behind my own aesthetic studies for many years, and that my emphatic endorsement of the primacy of technology, especially in music, must be understood strictly in this sense and in the sense of your second piece on technology.[2] It is not surprising if we find common ground between us here; and it doesn't surprise me since in your book on the Baroque you effectively distinguished allegory from symbol (in the newer terminology, from the 'auratic' symbol), and likewise in *One-Way Street* distinguished the work of art from the domain of magical documentation. It is a splendid confirmation – and I hope it does not sound too immodest if I say it is a confirmation for both of us – that in an essay for the Schönberg *Festschrift*[3] which appeared a couple of years ago, and with which you are unfamiliar, I proposed certain formulations concerning technology and dialectics, and our changing relationships to technology,[4] which are in total agreement with your own.

It is precisely this agreement which for me constitutes the criterion for the differences which I must also mention, with the sole aim of serving the shared 'general approach' which has now clearly begun to delineate itself. In doing so, I can perhaps begin by pursuing our old method of immanent criticism. In your earlier writings, of which the present essay is a continuation, you distinguished the idea of the work of art as a structure from the symbol of theology on the one hand, and from the taboo of magic on the other. But I now find it somewhat disturbing – and here I can see a sublimated remnant of certain Brechtian themes – that you have now rather casually transferred the concept of the magical aura to the 'autonomous work of art' and flatly assigned a counter-revolutionary function to the latter. I do not need to assure you just how aware I am of the magical element that persists in the bourgeois work of art (especially since I constantly attempt to expose the bourgeois philosophy of idealism that is associated with the idea of aesthetic autonomy as something mythical in the full sense). However, it seems to me that the heart of the autonomous work of art does not itself belong to the dimension of myth – forgive my topical manner of speaking – but is inherently dialectical, that is, compounds within itself the magical element with the sign of freedom. If I remember correctly, I think you once said something very similar about Mallarmé, and I cannot express my feelings about the entire piece more clearly than by telling you how much I would like to see a study of Mallarmé precisely as a counterpoint to this essay, a study which in my opinion you still owe us as a most important contribution to knowledge. Dialectical though your essay is, it is less than this in the case of the autonomous work of art itself; for it neglects a fundamental experience which daily becomes increasingly evident to me in my musical work, that precisely the uttermost consistency in the pursuit of the technical laws of auto-nomous art actually transforms this art itself, and, instead of turning it into a fetish or taboo, brings it that much closer to a state of freedom, to something that can be consciously produced and made. I know of no better materialist programme than that remark of Mallarmé's,[5] where he defines a work of literature as something that is not inspired but rather is made out of words; and the greatest of the reactionary figures, like Valéry and Borchardt (especially the lat-ter's essay on 'Villas',[6] which could be recuperated in a materialist sense in its entirety, in spite of one appalling comment about the workers), also harbour this explosive power within the innermost cells of their work. There is no one who will agree with you more than I when you defend *kitsch* cinema against the quality film; but *l'art pour l'art* needs just as much defending, and the united front which now exists against it and extends, I know, from Brecht right through to the Youth Movement, is itself encouragement enough to undertake a rescue attempt. You speak of play and semblance [Schein][7] as the elements of art; but I cannot see why play should be dialect-ical, while semblance – the semblance you once salvaged in the figure of Ottilie,[8] who now fares just as badly as Mignon and Helena – is supposed not to be. At this point, of course, the debate becomes immediately political. For if you legitimately interpret technical progress and alienation in a dialectical fashion, without doing the same in equal measure for the world of objectified subjectivity, then the political effect of this is to credit the proletariat (as the cinema's subject) directly with an achievement which, according to Lenin, it can only accomplish through the theory introduced by intellectuals as dialectical subjects, although they belong themselves to the sphere of works of art which you have already consigned to Hell. I do not wish to be misunderstood. I would not wish to secure the autonomy of the work of art as a special prerogative, and I agree with you that the auratic element of the work of art is in decline, and that not merely on account of its technical reproducibility, incidentally, but also through the fulfilment of its own 'autonomous' formal laws (this is the subject of a theory of musical reproduction[9] which Kolisch and I have been considering for years now). But the autonomy of the work of art, and therefore its material form, is not identical with the magical element in it. The reification of a great work of art is not simply a matter of loss, any more than the reification of the cinema is all loss. It would be a reactionary bourgeois gesture to negate the reification of the cinema in the name of the ego, and it would border on anarchism to revoke the reification of a great work of art in the spirit of an immediate appeal to use-value. *Les extrèmes me touchent,* as they do you – but only if the dialectic of the lowest has the same value as the dialectic of the highest, and not if the latter is simply left to decay. Both bear the stigmata of capitalism, both contain elements of change (but never, of course, simply as a middle term between Schönberg and the American film). Both are torn halves of an integral freedom, to which, however, they do not add up. It would be romantic to sacrifice one to the other, either with that bourgeois romanticism which seeks to uphold the 'personality' and such-like mystification, or with that anarchistic romanticism which places blind trust in the spontaneous powers of the proletariat within the historical process – a proletariat which is itself a product of bourgeois society. To a certain extent, I must charge your essay with this second form of romanticism. You have startled art out of every one of its tabooed hiding places – but it is as though you feared a sudden irruption of barbarism as a result (and who could share that fear more than I do?) and protected yourself by elevating the feared object with a kind of inverse taboo. The laughter of a cinema audience – I have discussed this with Max and he has probably related this to you already – is anything but salutary and revolutionary; it is full of the worst bourgeois sadism instead. I am very doubtful of the expertise of the newspaper boys in discussing sport, and in spite of its startling seductiveness, I cannot find your theory of 'distraction'[10] at all convincing – if only for the simple reason that in a communist society, work would be organized in such a way that human beings would no longer be so exhausted or so stupefied as to require such distraction. On the other hand, certain concepts of capitalist practice, like the 'test',[11] seem to have become almost ontologically congealed and to have started to function like a taboo – whereas if anything can be said to possess an auratic character now, it is precisely the film which does so, and to an extreme and highly suspect degree. To make one small additional point: the idea that a reactionary individual can be transformed into a member of the avant-garde through an intimate acquaintance with the films of Chaplin, strikes me as simple romanticization; for I cannot count Kracauer's favourite film director, even after *Modern Times*, as an avant-garde artist (the reason will be perfectly clear from my essay on jazz), and I cannot believe that the valuable elements in this piece of work will attract the slightest attention anyway. You need only have heard the laughter of the audience at the screening of this film to realize what is going on. Your attack on Werfel[12] gave me great pleasure. But if you consider Mickey Mouse instead, the situation is much more complex, and the serious question arises as to whether the reproduction on the part of each individual really does constitute that a priori you claim it to be, or whether this act of reproduction belongs instead to precisely that 'naive realism', concerning the bourgeois nature of which we found ourselves in complete agreement in Paris. After all, it is hardly an accident if *that* modern art, which you counterpose as auratic in character to technological art, is of such inherently dubious quality as Vlaminck[13] and Rilke. It is certainly an easy matter for the lower sphere to score a victory over art like that; but if we were to mention the names of Kafka, say, or Schönberg in this connection instead, then the problem would look rather different. Schönberg's music is emphatically *not* auratic.

What I should like to postulate, therefore, is *more* dialectics. On the one hand, a dialectical penetration of the 'autonomous' work of art, which transcends itself by virtue of its own technical procedures into a planned work; and on the other, an even stronger attempt to interpret the negativity of utilitarian art dialectically, a feature which you certainly do not ignore, but which you describe with rather abstract categories like 'film capital',[14] without tracking it back to its ultimate lair as a form of immanent irrationality. When I spent a day in the studios of Neubabelsberg a couple of years ago, what impressed me most of all was how *little* montage and all the advanced techniques you emphasize were actually used; rather, it seems as though reality is always *constructed* with an infantile attachment to the mimetic and then 'photographed'. You underestimate the technical character of autonomous art and overestimate that of dependent art; put simply, this would be my principal objection. But this objection could only be made effective precisely as a dialectic between the extremes which you tear asunder. And in my judgement, this would mean the total elimination of those Brechtian motifs which have already undergone considerable transformation in your work – above all, the elimination of any appeal to the immediacy of combined aesthetic effects, however they are produced, and to the actual consciousness of actual workers, who in fact enjoy no advantage over their bourgeois counterparts apart from their interest in the revolution, and otherwise bear all the marks of mutilation of the typical bourgeois character. This prescribes our own function fairly precisely – by which I certainly do not mean to imply an activist conception of 'the intellectual'. But nor can it mean that we should merely escape from the old taboos by entering into new ones – like 'tests', so to speak. The goal of the revolution is the elimination of anxiety. That is why we need not fear the former, and need not ontologize the latter. It is not a case of bourgeois idealism if, in full knowledge and without intellectual inhibitions, we maintain our solidarity with the proletariat, instead of making our necessity into a virtue of the proletariat as we are constantly tempted to do – that proletariat which itself experiences the same necessity, and needs us for knowledge just as much as we need the proletariat for the revolution. I am convinced that the further development of the aesthetic debate which you have so magnificently inaugurated, depends essentially upon a true evaluation of the relationship between intellectuals and the working class.

Please forgive the haste of these remarks. All of this could only seriously be addressed on the basis of those details where, not so magically after all, the good Lord dwells. It is only lack of time which leads me to employ the broad categories which you have taught me strictly to avoid. In order at least to indicate the passages I refer to, I have left my spontaneous pencilled annotations[15] in the manuscript, though some of them are too spontaneous to be readily communicable. I hope you will excuse this, as well as the rather sketchy nature of my letter.

I am leaving for Germany on Sunday. I may be able to complete my study on jazz there, something which unfortunately I did not find the time to do in London. In that case I shall send it to you without a covering letter and ask you to send it on to Max immediately after reading it (it will probably only amount to approximately 25 printed pages). All of this is still uncertain, however, since I do not yet know whether I shall find the time or, more particularly, whether the nature of the study itself would allow me to dispatch it from Germany without risking considerable danger. Max has probably told you that the concept of the clown[16] constitutes the focal point of the piece. I would be extremely pleased if it could appear at the same time as your study. Its subject is a very modest one, but it probably converges with yours in essential respects, and will attempt to express positively some of the things which I have formulated negatively here today. It offers a complete verdict on jazz, in particular by exposing the 'progressive' elements of the latter (the appearance of montage, collective participation, the primacy of reproduction over production) as façades of something that is in truth utterly reactionary. I believe that I have succeeded in effectively decoding jazz and defining its social function. Max was very taken with the piece, and I can well imagine that you will be too. Indeed, I feel that our theoretical disagreement is not really a discord between us, and that my own task is to hold your arm steady until the Brechtian sun has finally sunk beneath its exotic waters. And I hope you will understand my criticisms in this spirit.

I cannot conclude, however, without saying that I find your few sentences concerning the disintegration of the proletariat into 'masses'[17] through the revolution, to be amongst the most profound and most powerful statements of political theory I have encountered since I read *State and Revolution*.[18]

Your old friend,
Teddie Wiesengrund

I should also like to express my particular agreement with your theory of Dadaism. It fits in with the essay as perfectly as the passages on 'bombast' and 'horrors'[19] fit into your book on the Baroque.

1 *the study on jazz*: Adorno's essay 'On Jazz' – developed from a draft, written at Horkheimer's instigation, to form the basis of 'An Investigation into Jazz' – appeared under the pseudonym of Hektor Rottweiler in the Institute's *Zeitschrift für Sozialforschung 5*, issue 2 (1936), pp. 235–57; now in GS 17, pp. 74–100.

2 *your second piece on technology*: cf. GS VII [1], pp. 359ff.

3 *an essay for the Schönberg Festschrift*: cf. Adorno, 'Der dialektische Komponist', in *Arnold Schönberg zum 60. Geburtstag*, 13 September 1934, Vienna 1943, pp. 18–23; now in GS 17, pp. 198–203.

4 *formulations concerning technology . . . and our changing relationships to technology*: cf. GS 17, pp. 202f.

5 *that remark of Mallarmé's*: Mallarmé's response to Edgar Degas' sighing comment: 'Quel métier! [. . .] j'ai perdu toute ma journée sur un sacré sonnet, sans avancer d'un pas . . . Et cependant, ce ne sont pas les idées qui me manquent . . . J'en suis plein . . . J'en ai trop. . . .' [What a task! . . . I've spent the whole day long on one of these blessed sonnets and I've made no progress whatsoever . . . And yet I'm hardly lacking in ideas . . . I'm quite full of them . . . I've got too many in fact], as reported by Paul Valéry in his 'Degas Danse Dessin': 'Mais, Degas ce n'est point avec des idées que l'on fait des vers . . . C'est avec des mots' [But my dear Degas, one does not make poetry out of ideas, *but out of words*]. (Paul Valéry, *Œuvres*, tome 2. Édition établie et annotée par Jean Hytier, Paris 1960, p. 1208 [Bibliothèque de la Pléiade 148].)

6 *Borchardt . . . essay on 'Villas'*: cf. Rudolf Borchardt's *Schriften*, Prosa 1 (Berlin 1920), pp. 1–54; the *appalling remark* about workers is to be found on pp. 32f.

7 *You speak of play and semblance*: GS VII [1], p. 359.

8 *the semblance you once salvaged in the figure of Ottilie*: Adorno is referring to Benjamin's essay 'Goethe's Elective Affinities'; cf. GS I [1], pp. 123–201, particularly pp. 194–201.

9 *theory of musical reproduction*: in March 1935 Adorno and Rudolf Kolisch had resolved to carry out a project they had already entertained for some years and collaborate in writing 'A Theory of Musical Reproduction'. (cf. *Briefwechsel Adorno/Krenek*, pp. 72f.). The plan was never realized; the

substantial fragments towards articulating such a theory to be found amongst Adorno's literary remains arose later and independently of Kolisch.

10 *your theory of 'distraction'*: cf. GS VII [1], pp. 380f.

11 *concepts . . . like the 'test'*: cf. ibid., pp. 364f.

12 *Your attack on Werfel*: cf. ibid., p. 363.

13 *Vlaminck*: Benjamin does not actually mention the name of the painter Maurice Vlaminck in any of the surviving versions of his essay on the work of art.

14 *'film capital'*: cf. ibid., pp. 356f. (n. 2), pp. 370 and 372.

15 *my spontaneous pencilled annotations*: the typescript with Adorno's annotations has not survived.

16 *the concept of the clown*: cf. GS VII [1], pp. 377f. and GS 17, pp. 97–9.

17 *the disintegration of the proletariat into 'masses'*: cf. GS VII [1], pp. 370f (n. 2).

18 *State and Revolution*: Lenin's eponymous essay of 1917.

19 *the passages on 'bombast' and 'horrors'*: cf. GS I [1], p. 230.

48   BENJAMIN TO WIESENGRUND-ADORNO
     [PARIS, SUBSEQUENT TO 18.3.1936]

Dear Herr Wiesengrund,
    My heartfelt thanks for your lengthy and instructive letter of the 18th. It has opened up a wealth of perspectives – a mutual exploration of these surely calls for discussion as clearly and strongly as it proves resistant to any purely written exchange of ideas.
    Therefore, I would only like to say one thing for the present:
    A request that you seriously consider whether you might be able to travel back via Paris.[1] I believe a meeting between us at this point would be more desirable and more fruitful than ever. At the moment this would also give me enormous pleasure for quite personal reasons.
    If we could only spend a couple of days together, that would prove beneficial to my work for months ahead.
    Do let me know what you think! And in conclusion, please accept once again my very first thanks for your lines.
                                      Cordially yours,
                                           WB

1 *you might be able to travel back via Paris*: Adorno did not pass through Paris on his trip to Germany.

Merton College
Oxford
28 May 1936

Dear Herr Benjamin,
It is some considerable time since we last heard from one another. My own share in this silence is due solely to the enormous burden of work which continues to weigh upon me. I would be extremely interested to hear your response to my letter concerning film. In the meantime I have another piece for us to discuss, my essay on jazz, which is obviously very closely related to your own piece – so closely in fact that I am moved nonetheless to insist that the entire conception of my essay, and especially the section on the clown[1] and the critique of the allegedly collective labour involved[2] in jazz music, goes back to a time before I became acquainted with your work. In the interval you will have read the *résumé*[3] and played a part in the French version of the same: I would like to thank you very much indeed for that. But I am also very keen that you should get to see the text itself as soon as possible, since the *résumé* naturally gives little idea of this material. It is currently in press in Paris, indeed has probably already appeared in print. Please refer to me and get the publisher to send you an offprint, or, if this proves impracticable, the typescript of the piece.
There is very little to report as far as my everyday life is concerned, but all the more with respect to my spiritual existence. I completed my contribution to the Berg monograph, eight musical analyses, while I was still in Germany; the manuscript runs to about 60 printed pages. Although for the most part the material is strictly technical, or precisely because of this, I expect a great deal from the piece; it contains a number of things which are very important to me, and I think they will also touch upon your own interests. It will go to press in 8–14 days; I will ensure that you receive either the proofs or a carbon copy, and that as soon as possible. In the meantime, however, I must hold on to the copy I have here. – There is also an essay on Mahler[4] for the journal '23', which you will receive as soon as it appears – probably in the next few days.
For all this my principal work[5] has not had to suffer adverse consequences. I have been sitting on it for the last month and the analyses are now complete. The material has already been organized and very roughly schematized. I am now going to compose a substantial and detailed intermediate version between the original schema and the final definitive text. But I hope to accomplish all this during the

summer. It will certainly involve no small amount of effort to produce a reasonable book from all my inappropriately expanding notes
and materials. The whole piece is intellectually governed by the interpretation of logic as an expression of the social, and, in counterpoint
to this, by the precise formulation of a dialectical logic on the basis
of a critique of an advanced bourgeois conception of the domain of
logic. But it also contains a great deal on Art Nouveau, the nature
of fiction, neo-romantic forms of philosophy – as well as on the
philosophy of language and the liquidation of idealism which this
involves. The focal point is the analysis of categorial intuition as a
hypostatized aporia of idealism. I was particularly gratified to come
across some remarks in the introduction to your book on Baroque
Drama, which are also aimed against the idea of categorial intuition,[6]
and with which I concur entirely. I shall also be able to incorporate
the doctrine of truth and intention[7] which you unfolded there in the
course of my own argument, and especially in connection with a
critique of Husserl's conception of language as intentionality. But I
do not want to bore you here with general indications, which can
mean nothing outside the overall concrete context of the argument.

In my last letter to Max[8] I proposed the idea of a fundamental
essay on Baudelaire and the social theory of neo-romanticism[9] – one
in which, as I already suggested in my last letter to you, Mallarmé
could well be brought in too. Naturally I proposed you for the piece
– and especially since I imagine this would fit in very comfortably
with your work on the Arcades project, and might even represent
something like a partial publication of your material (precisely of the
chapter on Baudelaire). I would also be quite prepared to collaborate
here, if that should coincide with Max's intentions as well as your
own – without, of course, wishing to prejudice your earlier and even
better aspirations for the Baudelaire material. I would be very keen
to hear how the idea strikes you in principle. I should also take this
opportunity to tell you that my Berg monograph contains a chapter
on Baudelaire[10] (specifically about 'Le vin'), which defends the claim
that all neo-romantic poetry,[11] from Baudelaire through to George
and Borchardt, can be understood exclusively in terms of the idea of
translation.

I would also love to know how things currently stand with regard
to the essays on materialism. When I shall make it to Paris may
depend largely on them and the Baudelaire project. If it is not going
to be the end of June, then we shall have to wait until the autumn. In
all probability I shall have to forgo any thought of a vacation in
order to push my 'Prolegomena' to their final conclusion.

I received the Institute journal yesterday: I would like to read
the French version of your piece very carefully before expressing an

opinion. But at first sight I must say the translation makes a quite outstanding impression.

Please write back soon and let me know, in particular, how your work on the Arcades is progressing. – Yesterday I went to see Reinhardt's film of the Midsummer Night's Dream[12] – and a sorry story it was, too, supplying abundant confirmation *e contrario* for your own theory and especially your passage on Werfel.[13] Certainly a highly dialectical confirmation: for the film's ambitions to attain the 'auratic' dimension itself leads inevitably to the destruction of aura. Rather like the cinematographic Manet served up to us in Anna Karenina.[14] One must possess nerves of steel to be able to endure this kind of liquidation.

With cordial greetings from your old friend,

Teddie Wiesengrund

1 *the section on the clown*: cf. GS 17, pp. 97–9.

2 *the critique of the allegedly collective labour involved*: cf. ibid., pp. 87f.

3 *the résumé*: résumés in English and French were included along with German articles printed in the *Zeitschrift für Sozialforschung*.

4 *an essay on Mahler*: cf. Adorno, *Marginalien zu Mahler* [Comments on Mahler], in the Viennese music journal '23', 18.5.1936, nr. 26/27, pp. 13–19; now in GS 18, pp. 235–40.

5 *my principal work*: i.e. Adorno's book on Husserl.

6 *some remarks in the introduction to your book on Baroque Drama . . . aimed against the idea of categorial intuition*: cf. GS I [1], pp. 215f.

7 *the doctrine of truth and intention*: cf. ibid., pp. 215–18.

8 *my last letter to Max*: Adorno's (unpublished) letter to Horkheimer of 26 May 1936.

9 *a fundamental essay on Baudelaire and the social theory of neo-romanticism*: the project never materialized.

10 *my Berg monograph contains a chapter on Baudelaire*: the chapter in question discusses Berg's concert aria 'Der Wein', which is a setting of three poems from Baudelaire's cycle 'Le vin'; for the 1937 version of Adorno's interpretations cf. GS 13, pp. 509–14.

11 *which defends the claim that all neo-romantic poetry*: cf. GS 13, pp. 511f.

12 *Reinhardt's film of the Midsummer Night's Dream*: Max Reinhardt's film of Shakespeare's 'A Midsummer Night's Dream', made in 1935.

13 *your own theory and especially your passage on Werfel*: Adorno is referring to a passage in Benjamin's essay on The Work of Art in the Age of Mechanical Reproduction; cf. GS VII [1], p. 363.

14 *the cinematographic Manet served up to us in Anna Karenina*: Adorno is referring to the eponymous film of 1935 after the novel by Tolstoy, with Greta Garbo in the title role; the director was Clarence Brown.

2 June 1936   MERTON COLLEGE,
                                                       OXFORD.

Dear Herr Benjamin,
I have received a letter from Else Herzberger, who is now back in Paris (Hotel San Regis, 12 rue Jean Goujon, Champs Elysées). The letter has disconcerted me very much indeed. She writes about how difficult things have become with her, and asks whether I could possibly do something to help her out.

I had hoped that these arrangements, however modest, were secure enough to protect you from hardship. That was what occupied my discussions with Max, and I thought you would be able to confirm the same. After hearing from Else, I am extremely fearful that something has gone wrong, and would ask you therefore to let me know the situation immediately, so that I can intervene *at once* on your behalf if necessary. Else was clearly under the impression that I had left you in the lurch – something which distressed me considerably. I would therefore ask you to rectify this situation if possible. It goes without saying that I continue to defend your interests with respect to the Institute, just as I have always done.

In heartfelt solidarity,
                                              Your Teddie Wiesengrund

Dear Herr Wiesengrund,
This response to your letter of 28 May, for which many thanks, has nothing definitive to report. You will see that the most important substantive issues are dealt with more briefly than anything else. There are a number of reasons for this.

In the first place, there is the prospect you offered of arranging a meeting at the end of the month. I do not think we can assume that a precise contract concerning Max's essays will be ready before then. Nonetheless, I think it would be sensible to get arrangements moving for the volume all the same, and have written to New York today to that effect.

I would strongly request you to come at this time if you can make it, especially since I shall be leaving the city for a while in July if I possibly can.

This brings me to your letter of 2 June. I am extremely sorry to hear that even the slightest misunderstanding concerning our friendship and your own relation to Else H could have arisen. This can be dealt with easily and quickly, and I hope you will soon absolve me of any responsibility in the matter.

Once the pressure which had weighed upon me for so long on account of my financial situation was lifted, I experienced something that is not unusual in these circumstances: in a state of relaxation, my nerves began to give way. I felt as though all of my reserves were exhausted. I also felt the consequences which over a year's uninterrupted stay in Paris under such conditions had brought with it. I realized that I had to do something to repair the state of my spiritual health.

When I spoke to Max about the problem, I told him that travelling costs were not regarded as included in the minimum financial request which I had made and he had approved. And in fact I cannot finance a trip solely out of my own resources. On the other hand, I felt extremely reluctant – and I still feel reluctant today – to make another request so soon after an approval that was so important for me.

In this situation I thought of Else H and discussed the issue with Arnold Levy. He told me it would be a simple matter for him to broach the subject with his aunt. He must have done something of the kind in the meantime – although I was quite unaware of Else's presence here – and perhaps in a somewhat inappropriate manner. For it was certainly no part of my intention or design to give Arnold the impression that my situation was just the same as it was last year. I told him, rather, that a quite perceptible change had occurred. I fear that he felt it necessary to paint a rather vivid picture of the situation to Else H.

I am sorry that I have not yet been able to see Else H. I do hope to do so in the very near future, although I am not really in a position to arrange this for myself. Especially because I wish to communicate the undiminished image of both your friendship and of my own towards her. I also hope thereby to restore my own peace of mind, which would naturally be sorely disturbed by any awkwardness touching our personal relations with one another. But surely you need no reassurance from me that I shall continue to preserve that solidarity which you have also shown towards me, especially during the recent past?

I had hoped today to be able to include a small contribution of my own in the form of several paralipomena on the cinema.[1] Unfortunately,

I still have no copies to hand. They would probably belong in the overall context of our most recent work, although I do not wish to discuss this before reading your essay on jazz, the *exposé* of which has certainly aroused great expectations in me. Unfortunately, the Paris office has neither the manuscript nor the proofs at its disposal at present. Nonetheless, I should be receiving a text at the beginning of next week.

Until then I shall have to postpone any closer examination of your substantial letter concerning the theory of art, and preferably even longer still – namely, until our actual meeting in the near future, as I hope. At any rate, I cannot possibly imagine my own notes without reference to this letter any more. The positions expressed in it are clear to me even where they enter in opposition to my own. The details of the matter will need to be explicated with the greatest of care. I found your reference to Mallarmé immediately illuminating, since his work certainly reveals in exemplary fashion, if anything does, a purely dialectical aspect of art which is devoid of ritual.

Many thanks for your essay on Schönberg,[2] which you have rightly placed in this same overall context. And it is not merely your examination of Schönberg's musical technique which is important to me here; I was personally struck even more by the astonishing way in which you interpret the sequence of Schönberg's compositions, and your observation[3] that none of them ever really develops from its embryonic form to full maturity gives much food for thought. – I am looking forward to seeing the analyses of Berg and the Mahler text.

I find your suggestions for a collaborative study of Baudelaire extremely interesting, as you can well imagine I would. I can certainly understand the significance of Mallarmé's name in this connection, but I am not so clear about 'the social theory of neo-romanticism' here. I realize that it is rather difficult for you to develop the relevant connections in a letter, but I would ask you to try and do so in case our meeting does not transpire as we hoped.

For the rest, I am expecting to have first look at your critique of phenomenology. The social critique of logic is a totally new and fascinating enterprise. I have recently written a piece on Nicolai Leskov,[4] and although it does not remotely claim the range of my writings on the theory of art, it does reveal certain parallels to the thesis concerning 'the decline of aura' in so far as I emphasize that the art of story-telling is approaching its end.

Finally, cordial greetings to you as ever,

from your

Walter Benjamin

4 June
Paris XIV
23 rue Bénard

140

1 *paralipomena on the cinema*: cf. GS I [3], pp. 1044–51.

2 *your essay on Schönberg*: see letter 47 and the relevant note.

3 *your observation*: cf. GS 17, p. 199.

4 *a piece on Nicolai Leskov*: cf. Benjamin, *Der Erzähler. Betrachtungen zum Werk Nicolai Lesskows* [The Story-teller – Reflections on the Work of Nicolai Leskov], in the journal *Orient und Occident. Staat – Gesellschaft – Kirche. Blätter für Theologie und Soziologie*, Neue Folge, issue 3 (October 1936), pp. 16–33; now in GS II [2], pp. 438–65.

52 WIESENGRUND-ADORNO TO BENJAMIN
    OXFORD, 16.6.1936

16 June 1936   MERTON COLLEGE,
                                                OXFORD.

Dear Herr Benjamin,
    I have just received a telegram from Max asking me to find out from you whether you think it appropriate for me to come to Paris around now in connection with the translation of the essays on materialism.
    I hardly need to tell you how much I would like to come. But I think I could only justify the costs of such a trip to the Institute if the whole matter of translation is indeed so far settled that my presence there would effectively and immediately further the publication of Max's book in a French edition.
    For this reason I would ask you directly to let me know as soon as possible exactly how things stand, and also to express your own opinion concerning the objective justification of such a trip.
    I was thinking of coming around the middle of next week; perhaps you could arrange a hotel or some other accommodation that is not too expensive. I do not know whether the Lutétia[1] would be a possibility this time as well.
    I have also received a second, rather short, letter from Else in which she requested me, in a somewhat peremptory fashion, to assist you – and Kracauer – financially. The letter closes by saying: 'He who quickly gives, gives twice as much'.
    The situation is really quite grotesque. Painful though it is for me, I must now ask you to set the whole matter straight on your side, and to tell her that neither I nor Felizitas hardly require exhortations of this kind from her. It would seem to me more appropriate for you to do this rather than for me to write. If you feel it would be helpful for you, please talk the matter over with Levy-Ginsberg[2] as he is called:

141

above all with a view to finding some way of dampening down Else's pedagogic eros without adversely affecting your financial arrangements for the vacation at the same time!

I hope to receive a speediest possible reply from you concerning Paris.

Cordially yours as always,

Teddie Wiesengrund

1 *the Lutétia*: the Hotel Lutétia, where Horkheimer used to stay when visiting Paris, was one of the more luxurious establishments.

2 *Levy-Ginsberg*: Adorno is referring to Arnold Levy.

53 BENJAMIN TO WIESENGRUND-ADORNO
    PARIS, 20.6.1936

Dr Walter Benjamin   Paris, 20 June 36
                                                23 Rue Bénard

Dear Herr Wiesengrund,

I was very sorry and upset to hear that Else H. has now written to you a second time. The fact that she mentions Kracauer's name, as well as my own, rather suggests to me that her letters were motivated by interests other than those of helping me. This is all the worse for me, since I must still hold out for these interests.

Much as I feel genuinely indebted to her, I cannot possibly allow her, or anyone else, to disturb your friendship towards me or mine towards you. I hope I shall find sufficient diplomatic skill to express this clearly, and indeed definitively, to her at the nearest opportunity which presents itself.

When I received your letter, my first thought was to send a special offprint of my work directly to her, in order to get her to contact me. That I have been unsuccessful in this so far (in spite of attempting twice to call her) rather confirms my fear that I have provided her with a pretext in the matter. In these circumstances, it hardly seems likely that we can expect any assistance from her with regard to my vacation.

I have now asked Levy-Ginsberg to arrange a meeting between Else and me at the very first opportunity.

I cannot deny that in these circumstances your arrival here would be doubly important to me at this precise time. But we must naturally keep these issues separate nonetheless.

Yesterday I had a long conversation with Groethuysen, which has considerably clarified the current situation. Before translation begins we shall have to discuss a number of questions connected with preparing the volume for a French audience. All of this – the actual sequence of the essays, the chapter divisions, the various titles, the question of a preface – will basically be dealt with by the beginning of July. But we can only proceed with the translation of the volume itself when all these arrangements have finally been made.

Precisely from Max's point of view, as I imagine, your participation in these arrangements will prove more important than in the detailed questions of translation, which will only properly arise months later anyway. For this reason I believe that it is perfectly justifiable, and indeed desirable, as far as Max is concerned, if you could make it to Paris in early July. (It would not be such a good idea to plan your visit earlier than that,[1] because the work might not otherwise be sufficiently advanced.)

Please do not take it amiss if I conclude these lines, which must reach you as quickly as possible, with this extremely important matter. I would merely like to add that I am finally supposed to be receiving your essay on jazz through the Paris office tomorrow.

I now believe that my hopes for an imminent meeting between us are fully justified.

With heartfelt greetings as ever,

Yours,
Walter Benjamin

PS If you do come, could you bring Noack's 'The Triumphal Arch'[2] with you for me to borrow?

And at least as important for me as the former is also Panofsky's work on the development of perspective[3] in the history of art. Unfortunately I cannot remember the precise title of the book.

1 *to plan your visit earlier than that*: in fact Adorno did not visit Paris until October.

2 *Noack's 'The Triumphal Arch'*: cf. Ferdinand Noack, *'Triumph und Triumphbogen'* [The Triumphal Procession and the Triumphal Arch], published in *Vorträge der Bibliothek Warburg* 1925/26 (Leipzig and Berlin 1928), pp. 149ff.

3 *Panofsky's work on the development of perspective*: cf. Erwin Panofsky, *'Die Perspektive als "symbolische Form"'*, published in *Vorträge der Bibliothek Warburg* 1924/25 (Leipzig and Berlin 1927), pp. 258–330.

Walter Benjamin   Paris, 30 June 1936
                                          23 Rue Bénard

Dear Herr Wiesengrund,

I have heard nothing from you in response to my last letter and am therefore hoping all the more to see you, either at the end of this week or at the beginning of next.

The progress we have made in working on Max's essays most certainly justifies your visit. Right now I am on the verge of discussing the production of the book with Groethuysen. There are certain questions arising which, in accordance with Max's wishes, would certainly benefit from your assistance, if at all possible.

The final layout of the book must be more or less decided before the translation is undertaken. And I believe that your contribution is more important as regards the former than the latter – quite apart from the fact that the detailed questions arising from translation will not become pressing before the autumn anyway.

I have read the proofs of your essay on jazz. Would it surprise you if I tell you how enormously delighted I am to discover such a profound and spontaneous inner communication between our thoughts? Nor did you have to assure me that this communication already existed before you had looked at my work on film. The way in which you approach the matter has the kind of power and originality which only arises from the exercise of perfect freedom in the creative process – a freedom whose practice in both our cases only serves to substantiate the profound concordance between our own ways of seeing things.

In view of our imminent meeting, I do not wish to discuss any particular details of your work here. Nonetheless, I would not like to let this opportunity pass without saying at once just how much your own interpretation of syncopation in jazz[1] has helped to clarify for me the entire question of 'shock effects' in film. In general, it seems to me that our respective investigations, like two different headlamps trained upon the same object from opposite directions, have served to reveal the outline and character of contemporary art in a more thoroughly original and much more significant manner than anything hitherto attempted.

Everything else – and that means a great deal – must await mutual discussion.

I have now spoken to Else H. This was a week ago, outside Paris, in a situation quite favourable to a serious conversation. I spoke to her in definitive, and I hope extremely emphatic, terms about our relationship, and in particular about your relationship to me. I have the impression that my words affected her deeply and have, in any case, prevented any further such intervention in our affairs. Tillich was here; I managed to speak to him for a while. I would be extremely interested to compare my own impressions of him with your own.

Please be in touch as soon as possible.

Till we meet again, cordially yours,

[Walter Benjamin]

1 *your interpretation of syncopation in jazz*: cf. GS 17, pp. 74f.

55   WIESENGRUND-ADORNO TO BENJAMIN
     BERLIN, 6.9.1936

> Berlin-Halensee.
> Westfälische Strasse 27
> chez Karplus.
> 6 September 1936

Dear Herr Benjamin,

I feel rather guilty towards you with regard to my long silence, and can only offer the apology that your letter on Rottweiler's essay on jazz, which I was naturally extremely keen to look at, never actually reached me. In the meantime, so much material for mutual discussion, and even more material for work, has accumulated, that it seems a hopeless undertaking to try and address any of it in a letter. Today, therefore, let me simply atone for my guilt in not writing earlier by mentioning a trip to Paris.[1] It is possible for me to be in Paris at the beginning of October, namely, between the 4th and the 8th or 9th; I cannot make it later since I absolutely have to accept an invitation to Oxford on the 11th. I would be very pleased to know if this period would be convenient for you; I was thinking of arriving on the evening of the 4th. This visit would, of course, be conditional upon my being formally invited. Max has assured me that in principle the Institute is willing to meet the travel costs involved; this would have to be clearly sorted out beforehand, because as far as France is concerned, I certainly cannot rely upon transferring available funds, and in some cases it is necessary to present an officially documented invitation at the French Consulate as well as at Passport Control. Would you do whatever is required here in whatever way you and Max think most appropriate? If everything works out, and you can arrange to be in Paris at the right time[2] there is nothing more to hinder or prevent us meeting.

Nonetheless, I do not want to wait for this meeting before communicating to you at least a few observations on your essay on the story-teller.[3] In the first place, I can only express the fullest agreement with your claim from the perspective of the philosophy of history: that story-telling is no longer possible. This is indeed a familiar thought to me, already above and beyond the suggestions to that effect in 'The Theory of the Novel',[4] something which was evident to me for some years, even before I was capable of analysing it theoretically. I can well remember an occasion about twelve or thirteen years ago now, when my friend Reinhold Zickel was reciting his short stories,[5] in which the personal names were preceded by the definite article ('so spoke *the* Sunna' etc.); I strongly objected to such a familiar use of the article precisely because it laid fictive claim to a gesture of immediacy that already appeared obsolete then; and I am also aware that for this very reason I have long harboured a resistance to the supposedly great story-tellers like Keller and Storm, let alone Fontane. And when only recently I read the first sentence of Schnitzler's 'Away to the Country':[6] 'Georg von Wergenthin was sitting all alone at his table today', I was gripped by a similar sense of shock: where is the justification for writing about someone as if one really could talk about that individual, or even know who he was? (Unless I am much mistaken, the first sentence of the *Elective Affinities*, with its hesitant introduction of the characters' names, which you yourself have interpreted,[7] already testifies to Goethe's infallible sense for the philosophy of history, to his associated awareness of the impossibility of story-telling.)

However, I cannot follow your tendency to reduce the gesture of immediacy (if I may retain this irresponsible term here for the moment, and without having your text to hand), not so much to immediacy in the Hegelian sense, in the context of a philosophy of history, as to an essentially somatic gesture. And this difference of perspective has led me right to the heart of our debate with unusual directness. For all those points in which, despite our most fundamental and concrete agreement in other matters, I differ from you could be summed up and characterized as an *anthropological materialism* that I cannot accept. It is as if for you the human body represents the measure of all concreteness. But the latter is an 'invariant' factor which, as I believe, distorts the decisively concrete (that is, precisely the *dialectical* rather than the archaic image). That is the reason why I am always uncomfortable with the way in which you use the word 'gesture' and the like (although I would not wish to avoid the word as such: but everything depends upon the specific manner in which it

146

is determined); and if I am not mistaken, a certain *overexertion* of dialectic, in the sense of an overly hasty acceptance of reification as a behaviouristic 'test' for the body, is merely the inverted image of the undialectical ontology of the body which emerges in this work (it is thus the same objection which I made against the essay on Art in the Age of Mechanical Reproduction). I think that our discussions could prove fruitful (with respect to your *ultima philosophia*, the Arcades project) if I can succeed in making clear to you the inner unity of both these critical objections. And there is nothing I could wish more from a meeting between us.

There is little empirical news to relate about myself. I have, along with Gretel, abandoned the idea of a vacation entirely and have spent two months in Berlin exclusively engaged in work. About half of the basic version of the text is now ready. The first part presents a fully worked out plan, while the second already touches on the text proper. I have also undertaken a renewed and extremely fruitful study of Hegel. C'est tout. We have been living a life of almost unimaginable seclusion and have seen no one. From the health point of view Gretel is coping very well, although she is still suffering from the most idiotic professional problems. But perhaps the suppressed motto of Max's last book[8] hopefully applies here too: 'Tout cela sera balayé'.

In heartfelt solidarity as always, yours,

Teddie Wiesengrund

I realize that my claim concerning the inner unity of my two objections is expressed in a highly generalized and inadequate fashion here in the letter. This identity can perhaps best be grasped in relation to the question of aesthetic autonomy. Just as you seem simply to have leapt over the latter in your essay on the Work of Art in the Age of Mechanical Reproduction (and proceeded undialectically in *that* respect), its actual exclusion from your essay on the story-teller seems too 'gestural' to me. Johann Peter Hebel and the work of art as distraction: the latter is conceived as such only because the former has been positively identified as invariant according to the measure of the body. But the autonomy involved in reification is as much deserving of dialectical treatment as the behaviouristic features which are involved!

Gretel sends her greetings; she would really love to hear more about Borchardt,[9] and that goes for me too.

1 *a trip to Paris*: Adorno stayed in Paris between the 4th and the 10th.

2 *and you can arrange to be in Paris at the right time*: Benjamin was in Denmark with Brecht until the beginning of September, and then travelled on to San Remo.

147

3 *your essay on the story-teller*: at the beginning of July, Benjamin had sent Gretel Karplus a copy of the essay – probably a carbon copy of the typescript – which she then passed on to Adorno in Frankfurt.

4 *'The Theory of the Novel'*: an allusion to Georg Lukács, *Die Theorie des Romans. Ein geschichtsphilosophischer Versuch über die Formen der grossen Epik* (Berlin 1920).

5 *my friend Reinhold Zickel . . . reciting his short stories*: on Reinhold Zickel, cf. GS 20 [2], pp. 756–67; for the stories, cf. Reinhold Zickel, *Das Lirileirapodagrü oder Die neun Geschichten vom Echo. Ein phantastisches Karussell* (Frankfurt a.M. 1925). – Adorno was thinking of the final story entitled 'Sunna oder Das Lirileirapodagrü'.

6 *Schnitzler's 'Away to the Country'*: Schnitzler's novel *Weg ins Freie* had appeared in 1908.

7 *Elective Affinities . . . which you yourself have interpreted*: cf. the paragraph on names in Benjamin's study of Goethe's *Elective Affinities*, GS I [1], pp. 134f.

8 *the suppressed motto of Max's last book*: Horkheimer had originally intended to preface his essay 'Egoismus und die Freiheitsbewegung' [Egoism and the Freedom Movement] with this motto from André Gide; for the essay, cf. the Institute's journal, *Zeitschrift für Sozialforschung 5*, issue 2 (1936), pp. 161–231; now in Horkheimer, *Gesammelte Schriften*, vol. 4, pp. 9–88.

9 *Borchardt*: in her letter to Benjamin of 14 July, Gretel Karplus had asked: 'in your last letter but one you write that the last person . . . to exercise an influence upon you had died with Karl Kraus. I don't believe we have ever discussed this before, but did you forget about Borchardt when you made this claim? I find . . . that there are some very strong connections between the two of you, and he is one of the few people whom I would very much like to meet.' (Unpublished letter from Gretel Karplus to Benjamin of 14.7.1936.)

56 BENJAMIN TO WIESENGRUND-ADORNO
SAN REMO, 27.9.1936

Dear Herr Wiesengrund,
Many thanks for your letter[1] of 24 September.
I am writing back by return of post so that there shall no longer be any uncertainty about our meeting. This is something far too important for me even to envisage yet another postponement. I have therefore arranged, with the agreement of my wife, that Stefan[2] will come

148

and visit at Christmas rather than now. That means it is possible for me to be in Paris on 4 October. I shall be arriving at the Gare de Lyon at 22.50.

Even if you should arrive in Paris some hours before I do, there is no need for you to pick me up from the railway station. Unless, that is, you have nothing more urgent to do. But I assume that you would prefer to take a rest in a pleasant hotel after your tiring journey.

Since, according to Max's express desire and the arrangements he has made, you will be my guest while you are here in Paris – and I am particularly grateful to Max for facilitating this for me – you should take lodgings at the Hotel Littré, in the rue Littré, and mention my name to them on arrival. They will not ask more than 25 francs for a very comfortable room (unless the devaluation of the currency has already begun to take effect). Do not worry about the cost: I know the people there fairly well and will speak to them myself if necessary.

Once I have arrived, at around 11.15 or 11.30, I shall make my way to the Hotel Littré – it's not actually very far from rue Bénard.

The last letter I received from Etiemble[3] gives us particularly good reason to keep to our rendezvous. It contains the completely unexpected news that he is moving to Beauvais, and as soon as possible. This town is not that far from Paris, but I think this circumstance would only make collaboration more difficult, and there are some matters in which I would very much appreciate your assistance. And this also rules out the possibility of a meeting in Oxford. You can imagine how gladly I would otherwise have contemplated the idea, despite certain hesitations of a rather technical kind.

Anyway, let us stick with these hasty arrangements for today. I am looking forward so much to seeing you and will simply conclude here with all my usual greetings to you and Felizitas.

Yours,
Walter Benjamin

San Remo
Villa Verde
27 September 1936

1 *thanks for your letter*: the letter has not survived.

2 *Stefan*: Benjamin's son Stefan (1918–72) attended school in Vienna from the beginning of 1936 until 1938.

3 *Etiemble*: René Etiemble (born 1909), writer and literary historian, had studied law and oriental languages at the École Normale Supérieure in Paris. Etiemble was one of the prospective translators for Max Horkheimer's essays.

15 October 1936   MERTON COLLEGE,
                                                   OXFORD.

Dear Walter,[1]
Now that a peaceful crossing and three cordial days lie between
my last week in Paris and my life here in Oxford, I would like to
thank you once again from the heart for everything the week has
brought. The wealth of perspectives it opened up is the perfect equivalent to the personal warmth in which it transpired. I realize that I owe
all this to you.

Your requests have not been forgotten. The Mahler[2] has been
ordered; my travelling companion[3] for Sunday (who is, incidentally,
a rather interesting character: attached to the New Zealand delega-
tion, a reader here for Oxford University Press, and a Marxist) will
research Worth[4] for you; I am still trying to find out about the Noack
piece[5] at the moment; I would merely ask for your patience with
regard to the Kierkegaard book.[6] You should already have received
the apocryphal Hölderlin poem[7] in the meantime.

I have been reading Valéry[8] with great pleasure and not a little
anxiety. The connection between war and absolute poetry is indeed
striking here. Naturally, most of all in his essay on progress.[9] Nevertheless – or perhaps because of this – what an impressive figure!

Incidentally, have you seen a book by one Herr Kaufmann,[10] which
concerns itself particularly with Mallarmé, Valéry and the later Rilke?
It's going the rounds here at the moment. But the real sensation is
Huxley's new book,[11] *Eyeless in Gaza*, in which he is obviously making a vigorous attempt to respond to surrealist trends.

I am once again engaged in work. I am also trying to get a number
of my musical contributions wrapped up[12] as soon as possible.

Finally, may I bother you with a request? You know that my mother
is of Corsican, and thus officially of French origin. She was indeed a
French citizen until her marriage, and Agathe, who never married,
died as a French citizen. My grandfather was a military officer who
left the service relatively early, but had led a regiment in 1870 and
been gravely wounded (at Lille). All this can be proved if necessary.
What I would very much like to know is this: whether my origins
could procure me, as a university teacher exiled by the Nazis, a
speedier and perhaps even an immediate naturalization as a French
citizen; and further, whether at the age of 33 I might be liable to
military service in that case.

150

This question has become all the more urgent for me since a certain constellation of circumstances in Germany[13] has emerged – though I would ask you to keep the *strictest* confidence here, even with regard to Gretel – which makes it very doubtful that I shall now be able to return to Germany at all. The German funding source has enquired after my means of subsistence in England, and since I have only now, and not earlier, revealed the amount of financial assistance I have received from the Council, I have technically committed an offence (I had good reasons for not disclosing the information until now). They have already assured me that they will not actually treat it as an offence, although I have now had to make a quite considerable, but not intolerable, contribution in return. My father has been conducting the necessary arrangements in my name; there is no serious danger involved, but the situation remains rather uncomfortable. Especially since I shall have to apply for a new passport in January.

Under these virtually transformed conditions the question of French naturalization has become directly relevant. I would, therefore, be particularly grateful if you could possibly pursue this matter, without mentioning my name in any way. Brill[14] would seem to be the right person in this connection. In the first place, he is a lawyer, and would find this a good opportunity to play a useful and important role; and finally, of course, it is also a question full of practical consequences for the Institute. If you consider it appropriate, you could mention my name to *him* – and no one else! Many thanks in advance for this.

I wrote at once to Max[15] in *considerable* detail on Monday. I also mentioned Kracauer,[16] and followed your own formulation. I hope what I have written about him will prove beneficial to him. It was no easy task to formulate the matter.

I hope to hear from you very soon; also with regard to the question of translation. I shall at least advise Goldbeck[17] in a friendly manner to let you see some more material.

Have the Arcades been broached once more, or have they been pushed aside by your old attentions to Fuchs?[18]

In friendship,

Yours,

Teddie

1 *Dear Walter*: with Adorno's visit to Paris, he and Benjamin began to address one another by their first names.

2 *The Mahler*: see letter 49 and the relevant note.

3 *my travelling companion*: nothing further known about his identity.

4 *Worth*: the English 'dressmaker' Charles Frederick Worth (1825–95) had founded, together with the Swede Dobergh, a fashion house in the French

151

metropolis in 1858, and which continued to dominate Paris fashion for the next thirty years.

5 *still trying to find out about the Noack piece*: Adorno's (unpublished) letter to Edgar Wind is dated 29 October 1936.

6 *the Kierkegaard book*: Benjamin had probably asked Adorno in Paris for a copy of his book *The Construction of the Aesthetic*.

7 *the apocryphal Hölderlin poem*: Adorno cited the poem in 1956 in his anonymous 'Afterword' to Benjamin's *A Berlin Childhood Around 1900* (cf. Adorno, *Über Walter Benjamin*, pp. 74–6): 'The explosion of despair consolingly reveals that enchanted landscape which is invoked in an apocryphal poem that has been ascribed to Hölderlin. It sounds just like Benjamin's writing and he became particularly fond of it: "Mit Rosen umweben / Der Sterblichen Leben / Die gütigen Feen; / Sie wandeln und walten / In tausend Gestalten / Bald hässlich, bald schön. // Da wo sie gebieten, / Lacht alles, mit Blüten / Und Grün emailliert; / Ihr Schloss von Topasen / Ist herrlich mit Vasen / Von Demant geziert. // Von Ceylons Gedüfte / Sind ewig die Lüfte / Der Gärten durchweht / Die Gänge, statt Sandes, / Nach Weise des Landes / Mit Perlen besät. // Seit Salamo nahte / Dem luftigen Staate / Kein Aeronaut. / Dies hat mir, nach Schriften / In Mumiengrüften, / Eine Sylphe vertraut." [With roses they entwine / Our mortal life / The gracious spirits; / They wander and they rule / In myriad shapes and forms, / Now fair, now foul. // Where they hold sway / All things laugh / With blossoms and green grass enamelled; / Their citadel of topaz / Resplendent shines with vases / Are adorned with diamonds. // Ceylon's scents ceaselessly caress the garden air. / The paths are strewn, instead of sand, with pearls, / According to the custom of the land. // No flying man has yet approached this airy world since Solomon's time. / Or so a Sybil taught me, secretly, from images inscribed in mummies' tombs]' (ibid., pp. 75f). – For this poem, which is actually a 'shortened version' of a poem by Friedrich Mathisson entitled 'Feenland' [The Land of Spirits], cf. Hölderlin, *Sämtliche Werke*, GSA, vol. 2.2 (Stuttgart 1951), p. 984.

8 *I have been reading Valéry*: Benjamin had presented Adorno with Paul Valéry's *Pièces sur l'art* as a gift in Paris, a work which had appeared in its third edition in 1936. Benjamin inscribed the front end paper of the book with the words: 'In lasting commemoration of our Paris days in October 1936.'

9 *his essay on progress*: cf. Paul Valéry, 'Propos sur le progrès', op. cit., pp. 215–27.

10 *a book by one Herr Kaufmann*: cf. Fritz Kaufmann, *Sprache als Schöpfung. Zur absoluten Kunst im Hinblick auf Rilke* [Language as Creation. On Absolute Art with Special Reference to Rilke] (Stuttgart 1934).

11 *Huxley's new book*: the book by Aldous Huxley (1894–1963) appeared in 1936.

12 *a number of my musical compositions wrapped up*: Adorno is presumably referring to the series of aphorisms entitled 'Ensemble' (see letter 83
and the relevant note) and the piece entitled 'Why Twelve-Tone Music?'
(first published in GS 18, pp. 114–17), something he wrote in connection
with the collaborative work on dodecaphonic music which he was planning
with Krenek.

13 *a certain constellation of circumstances in Germany*: Adorno met the
costs of his stay in England from part of the family income which his father
possessed in England. He also received pro forma a grant from the 'Academic Assistance Council' in order to show the German funding source, if
necessary, how he was able to meet subsistence costs while he was abroad.
Adorno's failure to declare he stipendium, which was first disclosed to the
German authorities by Adorno's solicitor in autumn 1936, led to a fine of
1500 German Marks. However, Adorno's father succeeded through negotiations in reducing the figure to 150 Marks and dealing with the ensuing
difficulties.

14 *Brill*: Hans Klaus Brill was the secretary at the Paris bureau of the Institute of Social Research.

15 *I wrote at once to Max*: the letter is dated 12 October 1936; cf. the
excerpt in GS VII [2], pp. 864f.

16 *I also mentioned Kracauer*: during his stay in Paris, Adorno had discussed with Kracauer, amongst other things, the idea of Kracauer writing an
essay for the Institute's *Zeitschrift für Sozialforschung*; in December, consequently, Kracauer drew up an *exposé* entitled 'Propaganda and the Masses'
(cf. *Siegfried Kracauer 1889 bis 1966*, bearbeitet von Ingrid Belke und Irina
Renz, Marbacher Magazin 47 (1988), ed. Ulrich Ott (Marbach a.N. 1989),
pp. 85–90). – The substantial work which actually emerged was entitled
'Totalitarian Propaganda in Germany and Italy'.

17 *Goldbeck*: Fred Goldbeck (born 1902 in the Hague), a conductor and
writer on music, an early friend from Adorno's youth, went to Paris in 1925,
where he taught conducting technique at the École Normale de Musique
between 1936 and 1939. Adorno had suggested him as one possible translator for the French edition of Horkheimer's essays.

18 *your old attentions to Fuchs*: Adorno is referring to the essay on Eduard
Fuchs which Benjamin was intending to write for the Institute journal.

58 WIESENGRUND-ADORNO TO BENJAMIN
    OXFORD, 18.10.1936

18 October 1936.

Dear Walter, is it all right if I send you a small unedited piece herewith? – a short essay on Ravel (not the one you already know)[1]

153

which I composed three years ago, that is, before the onset of his illness and in total ignorance of the circumstances involved. Any thought of publication is quite out of the question now. The only person to possess a copy of the piece, apart from yourself, is Goldbeck, and fittingly enough in a much more inadequate version. I myself no longer have a copy; so it is therefore your own property in that unique sense which has now decisively disappeared according to your own theory of reproduction. Nonetheless, I would ask you to preserve the manuscript: as a small token of my grateful remembrance for those days in Paris, but also as a parting greeting from that sphere in which neither of us will be permitted to wander for some time to come.

In friendship,

Yours,

Teddie

Krenek has written a substantial essay[2] on Kraus, which repeatedly makes emphatic reference to you; it is a kind of pastiche of my own commemorative essay on Berg.[3]

1 *an essay on Ravel (not the one you already know)*: the essay on Ravel with which Benjamin was already familiar was the one Adorno published in the journal *Anbruch* in 1930 (cf. GS 17, pp. 60–5). – The characterization of what Adorno describes here as an essay on Ravel, the manuscript of which in Benjamin's possession has not survived, reveals some common features with the text of *the piece on Ravel* mentioned in letter 17; as does the reference to Ravel's illness of 1933, which Adorno seems to have interpreted as syphilitic in origin, with the theme of Adorno's piece 'Erotic Music' (GS 18, p. 273); the conclusion here – 'His deepest youthfulness lies in a fidelity to the image' – also partly corresponds to Benjamin's quotation in letter 60 – 'And those words concerning fidelity to the image "even when it falls wearily from our hands"'. The differences between the two texts – the passage on Stravinsky is missing in the surviving typescript copy (cf. letter 60) – would then be explicable in terms of alternative versions.

2 *Krenek has written a substantial essay*: cf. Ernst Krenek, 'Ansprache bei der Trauerfeier für Karl Kraus im Wiener Konzerthaus am 30. November', reprinted in Krenek, *Zur Sprache gebracht* (Munich 1958), pp. 224–8; cf. also Krenek, 'Erinnerung an Karl Kraus' in the Viennese music journal '23', 10.11.1936, nr. 28/30, pp. 1–16.

3 *my own commemorative essay on Berg*: see letter 46 and the relevant note.

Paris, 19 October 1936

Dear Teddie,

Many thanks for your letter. What delighted me most of all about it was the echo of those days in Paris which it vouchsafed to me. That was a time which brought things long since prepared to mature fulfilment. This was all the more important to me, since the mutual confirmation we found in one another's thoughts had followed hard upon a separation which seemed to put in question, not indeed our friendship, but the reciprocal attunement of our ideas.

Till we meet again soon!

Given the unpleasant situation you mentioned in your letter, the only positive thing I can see in the matter is that it might prompt you to move to Paris in the future. Whatever the precise situation about the personal background of yourself or your parents, I believe that a minimum three-year period of residence in France is an essential condition of naturalization. But I have got Brill to find out more about this, and about the other issues you raised in your letter. As soon as I hear something from him, I will let you know.

In general, the process of naturalization now goes rather more smoothly than it used to. But with a change of government here the present procedure could change once again. The sooner one applies the better.

Klossowski has produced a substantial translation sample, which strikes me as perfectly satisfactory from the point of view of content, and which Aron[1] regards as beyond reproach from the linguistic point of view. In both respects his sample translation is certainly to be preferred over Goldbeck's. I have also heard nothing further from the latter.

After I had sent Horkheimer a very detailed report about the translation situation (as we had agreed I would) on 13 October, I recommended Klossowski as translator in a letter of 17 October. Klossowski has also simultaneously contacted him on his own account.

I must thank you from the heart for the way in which you have responded to all my wishes and requests. And now I have something else to add – a personal wish. When you next write to Krenek, could you also possibly draw his attention to my Berlin Childhood Around 1900?[2] At the moment the manuscript is with Dr Franz Glück,[3] Vienna III, Landstrasser Hauptstrasse 140.

I have now received the fairy poem from Felizitas[4] – you have really thoroughly appreciated its relationship to me. I have given her a detailed report of the week we spent together.

I have still not seen Kracauer since our shared meeting together.

That is enough for today, with all my best wishes for the progress of your work and heartfelt greetings,

Yours,

Walter

1 *Aron*: Raymond Aron (1905–83), French sociologist and political theorist, was Professor at the École Normale Supérieure and the French representative of the Institute of Social Research.

2 *draw his attention to my Berlin Childhood Around 1900*: Adorno's letter to Krenek has not survived; for Krenek's response, cf. *Briefwechsel Adorno/ Krenek*, pp. 121–3 (the paragraph on Benjamin is to be found on p. 123).

3 *Franz Glück*: Franz Glück, born in 1899, the brother of Gustav Glück, was Director of Historical Museums in the city of Vienna. In 1930 Franz Glück had sent Benjamin, probably on the advice of his brother, who was acquainted with Benjamin, his selection of Adolf Loos' writings; they actually met in person in January 1931. – Franz Glück had been attempting to find a publisher in Vienna for Benjamin's *Berlin Childhood* since November 1935, but without any success.

4 *I have now received the fairy poem from Felizitas*: Benjamin is referring to the apocryphal Hölderlin poem mentioned in letter 57; cf. the relevant note.

60   BENJAMIN TO WIESENGRUND-ADORNO
      PARIS, 26.10.1936

Dear Teddie,

Your imaginative essay on Ravel is a particularly fine piece of work, and I genuinely understand the spirit in which you have bestowed it. Many heartfelt thanks.

The place where you invoke the contrast with Stravinsky is especially striking. And those words concerning fidelity to the image 'even when it falls wearily from our hands' reminded me of a remarkable passage in one of Seume's letters – one which you will soon come across in my collection of letters.[1]

In the meantime, you will have received the information you asked for from Brill. (I thought it expedient to mention your name to him to underline the urgency of the business.) Have you had any further thoughts in this regard?

I must not forget something else I wanted to ask you: have you ever heard of an English painter by the name of Martin,[2] who is said to have painted cities 'the way they comb away the columns of hair across their shoulders'? I found this reference in a long-forgotten author of the Second Empire period (Nettement).[3]

Has Krenek's essay on Kraus actually appeared in print yet? Naturally, I would be just as keen to read it even if it hasn't.

Etiemble has written again, promising me parts of the manuscript. Nothing has arrived as yet however.

For today all my greetings,

Yours,

Walter

26 October 1936
Paris XIV
23 rue Bénard

1 *one of Seume's letters ... my collection of letters*: cf. Detlef Holz [Benjamin's pseudonym], *Deutsche Menschen. Eine Folge von Briefen* [Germans: A Series of Letters] (Luzern 1933); now in GS IV [1], pp. 149–231; for the letter of Johann Gottfried Seume, cf. ibid., pp. 169f.

2 *an English painter by the name of Martin*: Benjamin is probably referring to the British painter John Martin (1789–1854). Amongst other things, according to the eleventh edition of the *Encyclopaedia Britannica*: 'He was occupied with schemes for the improvement of London.' The precise source of Benjamin's quotation has not as yet been identified.

3 *Nettement*: Alfred Nettement (1805–69), French historian and historian of literature, founded the journal 'L'opinion publique' in 1848, and was a parliamentary deputy between 1849 and 1852; for the works of Nettement which Benjamin read in connection with the Arcades project, cf. GS V [2], p. 1312.

61   BENJAMIN TO WIESENGRUND-ADORNO
     PARIS, 5.11.1936

Paris, 5 November 1936

Dear Teddie,

I hasten to send you these lines immediately before you leave.

As far as my son's behaviour is concerned, those effects have unfortunately begun to emerge, which I had only disclosed to you in the form of a vague and general fear. And perhaps I should speak here of his condition rather than his behaviour.

In any case, he can no longer be expected to look after himself properly. Some closer contact with him is absolutely essential, since this has been seriously interrupted for over a month now.

157

My wife still owes tax arrears in Germany; as far as I know, Austria is the only country which collaborates with Germany in tax matters. My wife cannot therefore go to Vienna.

It is proving very difficult for me to extricate myself from work; my wife has been helping me to endure the other travel difficulties. I just do not know how long this stay is going to keep me away from Paris.

The unknown problems awaiting me in Vienna are only worsened by the fact that the place is utterly alien to me. I have no real contacts there. I would therefore be extremely grateful if you yourself could facilitate a few openings for me by dropping a line to Krenek, or anyone else who might seem appropriate to you. Under certain circumstances it might prove important for me to acquire some testimonials before dealing with any authorities.

My address in Vienna is: c/o Dr Franz Glück, Vienna III, Landstrasser-Hauptstrasse 140. Please write to me there and send on Krenek's address to me.

By return of post you should receive a book that I hope will delight you.

Heartfelt greetings,

Yours,
Walter

Oxford, 7 November 1936

Dear Walter,

I was very concerned on reading your letter, although I could hardly be surprised after what you had already told me in Paris. I hope you will not regard it as beyond the limit if I remind you of two things in this connection: firstly, even if Stefan's case involves more than a neurosis, that is no cause for despair. Psychotic illnesses of this kind frequently arise in people of his age – that is precisely what gave the illness its name – before disappearing completely later on. And I am assuming that you will have Stefan looked at by a therapist in the first place, and not a psychiatrist. But I would also urgently advise you to have him thoroughly examined physically, in particular by a specialist in hormone research, internal secretions, etc. For it is also frequently the case that certain problems of sexual development can lead to consequences resembling psychosis, and I am aware of one case where someone was even seriously helped by operational intervention.

The physical aspect of treatment should therefore certainly not be neglected simply in favour of the psychological aspect.

Your book on 'Germans' has indeed been a great delight to me. I read it immediately after it arrived, from the first sentence to the last throughout the night. The expression of grief which the book exudes seems remarkably close to that of the Berlin Childhood, the composition of which may indeed have coincided in time with making the selection of the letters and writing the introduction to them. If the former piece reproduced images of a life which a certain class forbade itself to see without revealing any other life, so the perspective you cast on these letters reproduces, as it were, the very same process of concealment in objective form, where the Childhood had testified to its subjective form. One could also say that the decline of bourgeois life is presented here through the decline of the art of correspondence: in the letters of Keller and Overbeck, the class in question is already concealed, and the gesture with which it turns away – away from letter writing as a form of communication – is the gesture of its self-renunciation. If I tell you that the letter by Collenbusch, with its enormous postscript, and Goethe's letter to Seebeck, with the superb commentary, were those which excited me the most on first reading, you will be no more surprised by that than I myself was surprised when you immediately identified in my little Ravel piece the very sentence which prompted me to send it to you. – As far as the commentary on Goethe is concerned, I would just say this: do you know my previously unpublished remarks on late Beethoven,[1] which I wrote three years ago (which will at last now be appearing in Prague)? It is astonishing to see how closely they coincide with certain formulations concerning the inner involvement of the abstract and the concrete as expressed here in your own commentary. I think that Krenek possesses a copy (this material, which is enormously important to me, has nonetheless undergone much revision following a discussion I had with Kolisch):[2] he will certainly show it to you.

But let me come to the question of Vienna. This city, which I am more justified in calling my second home than Kracauer is justified in calling Paris his, has become extremely alien and dismal to me since Berg's death, and it will prove even more so to you after the death of Kraus. My two closest Viennese friends, Kolisch and Steuermann,[3] are both in America. So contact with Ernst Krenek now seems the most fruitful idea and could also be most stimulating for you on its own terms. The address is: Vienna III (Hietzing), Mühlbachergasse 6. Ring him as soon as you arrive, for he will receive you with full honours and will certainly prove extremely helpful to you in many ways. You should also contact Dr Willi Reich,[4] an early secretary and personal friend of Berg's, the editor of the journal '23', with

159

whom we are bringing out the Berg monograph, which was prompted by him. He is a delightful man and is also familiar with your name: you only have to ring him up. He is rather like a travel junction and will be able to introduce you to all kinds and manner of people. With Helene Berg, for example, whom you must certainly get to meet; you will probably put less value on meeting Werfel and Alma Mahler. Reich's address is: Vienna I, Hohenstaufengasse 10. Through him or Krenek you will also be able to make contact with Soma Morgenstern,[5] whose current address I do not know, but the genius loci absolutely demands that you spend one night with him in a café. – And then, of course, there is Freud. Although one cannot count on any fruitful results from talking to him, it is nonetheless worth seeing this rather ancient man who has himself destroyed our image of the father. I have no direct relationship with him, but Max will be able to arrange it, or perhaps even better Landauer,[6] whom you only have to drop a line to and mention me or Max. Dr Karl Landauer, Amsterdam, Breughelstrasse 10. – Otherwise, of course, Gretel, related as she is – poor thing! – to so many doctors in Vienna, will certainly be able to give you far better advice than I can concerning a city from which I have become so terribly alienated since Berg's death. In this connection I am also thinking of the extremely captivating Marie-Louise Motesiczky.[7] Also, you might want to consider one of Gretel's nephews, said to be an uncommonly fine doctor, with regard to Stefan's examination. Be sure not to miss the opportunity of talking quite directly to Krenek about the idea of publishing the 'Childhood' with Reichner, and likewise with Willi Reich. I take it as a favourable omen that your collection of letters has come out just at this moment: I think it is your first publication in book form since *One-Way Street*. I would give a copy to Krenek (which is not spelt with ck!) who will genuinely know how to appreciate it. Krenek and Reich will also certainly make the manuscript or the first proofs of my book on Berg available to you.

I wish you all the best from my heart. Did you receive the Noack piece?[8] No one could possibly have been more importunate than I was at the Warburg Institute on your behalf. I also hope you have received the essay on Mahler by now. On hearing back from Max, I wrote an extremely positive letter to Kracauer, although I have still not been graced with a response.

Your faithful friend,

Teddie

I also wanted to say just how entirely I agree with what you have to say about the limits of humanism: and almost about humanism and poverty. This is the true deciphering of Goethe's house in Weimar,

160

and especially the room in which he died. And the great art involved in expressing all this through a letter from Kant's brother!

1 *unpublished remarks on late Beethoven*: i.e. Adorno's essay 'Beethoven's Late Style', written in 1934 (cf. letter 17 and the relevant note).

2 *Kolisch*: the musician Rudolf Kolisch (1896–1978) belonged to Schönberg's circle, whose compositions Kolisch frequently played as first violinist and leader of the Kolisch Quartet; Adorno had been on friendly terms with Kolisch since his composition studies with Berg in Vienna.

3 *Steuermann*: for the composer and pianist Eduard Steuermann (1892–1964), with whom Adorno had studied piano in 1925, see Adorno's essay 'The Death of Steuermann' (GS 17, pp. 311–17).

4 *Willi Reich*: the Viennese born Willi Reich (1898–1980) was also a pupil of Berg, and worked as a music critic and general writer on music between 1924 and 1937; in 1937 he emigrated to Switzerland and subsequently taught the history of music in Zürich from 1967.

5 *Soma Morgenstern*: Adorno had become acquainted with Soma Morgenstern (1890–1976) during a stay in Vienna in 1925; Morgenstern later worked as the Vienna cultural correspondent of the *Frankfurter Zeitung*; in 1938 he emigrated, first to France, and then in 1941 to New York.

6 *Landauer*: the psychoanalyst Karl Landauer (1887–1945) worked in Frankfurt between 1919 and 1933; he had also collaborated with Horkheimer from 1927; in 1933 he emigrated to Holland via Sweden, and in 1943 was transported to the concentration camp Westerbork, later known as Bergen-Belsen, where he died of hunger in January 1945.

7 *Marie-Louise Motesiczky*: a Viennese painter, born in 1906, who, after completing her studies in The Hague, Paris and Vienna, also studied with Max Beckmann in 1927/8.

8 *Did you receive the Noack piece?*: Noack's book on 'The Triumphal Procession and the Triumphal Arch' was sent to Benjamin from the Warburg Institute on 5 November.

63   WIESENGRUND-ADORNO TO BENJAMIN
     OXFORD, 28.11.1936

Oxford, 47 Banbury Road
28 November 1936.

Dear Walter,

It has been weeks since I heard a word from you[1] and I am extremely concerned. Immediately after receiving your last letter, I wrote to you in some detail at your Vienna address[2] and simultaneously contacted Krenek and Dr Reich to let them know the situation.[3] Not only have I heard nothing from you, but they too (and Gretel as well, as far as I am aware) have also had no news from you. I can think of no other explanation than that matters with Stefan have become so problematic that you have lost all desire to communicate at the moment. My own inclination to write letters is itself far too subject to difficult lapses for me to lack all understanding for such things. Nonetheless, I would dearly ask that you contact me in some way, even if only by postcard.

My request has a further intimate reason as well. I have asked Horkheimer whether the Institute would like me to go to Paris in the second week of December, and have just received affirmative confirmation to this effect by telegram – as long as you will be in Paris at that time, that is, between about the 8th and the 15th. My precise arrangements,[4] therefore, depend entirely upon hearing something from you. There will be a lot to do. Max has agreed to resume work on the essay on 'Egoism and the Freedom Movement', and would have liked to see it translated first; we shall have to deal with the question of renumeration for Klossowski, but above all we shall also have to reorganize the review section of the journal.[5] I would also like to have determined the precise modus procedendi with regard to my substantial essay on Mannheim,[6] which will probably be finished in Germany and which I would then like to send on to you directly. In addition to this, there are several philosophical issues which are now clamouring for mutual discussion more than ever. The importance of that last week in Paris was far too great for me to forgo any similar opportunity with an easy conscience.

My own work is advancing nicely. I am currently immersed in the plan of my seventh chapter and have just sketched out an attempt to reformulate the problem of ideology. The most significant événement of the last week was a visit from Alfred Sohn-Rethel,[7] who first wrote me an extremely stimulating letter about his own project and then came and discussed the project itself with me in some detail. From a quite different angle, he has arrived at certain conclusions which are remarkably similar to those of my own current efforts. I regard this mutual discussion between us as very important for the issues in question.

It seems that Kracauer is now coming slowly, very slowly, to see reason. Schoen, who has also paid me a visit here, behaves quite admirably in every respect. It is a pity that his intellectual powers are not greater.

I have attempted to identify the results of our mutual discussions of my essay on jazz.

In order to increase the probability of your actually receiving this letter, I have prepared two copies, which I am sending to your Paris

162

and to your Vienna address simultaneously. Please write back to me at my private address, 47 Banbury Road, rather than at the College, where things are sometimes delayed.

With heartfelt greetings as ever,

Yours,

Teddie

You must certainly have received the Noack by now.

1 *weeks since I heard a word from you*: see letter 64 following.

2 *I wrote to you ... at your Vienna address*: probably a reference to letter 62.

3 *contacted Krenek and Dr Reich ... the situation*: for Adorno's letter to Krenek, see the relevant note to letter 59.

4 *My precise arrangements*: Adorno actually spent a few days in Paris starting on 9 December.

5 *the review section of the journal*: on Horkheimer's initiative, Adorno and Benjamin were planning a reorganization of the review section of the Institute's *Zeitschrift für Sozialforschung*. As a result, Benjamin sent the 'Proposals for the Review Section of the *Zeitschrift für Sozialforschung*' (cf. GS III, pp. 601f.), which he had co-authored with Adorno, to Horkheimer on 17 December (cf. ibid., pp. 707f).

6 *my substantial essay on Mannheim*: Adorno's essay 'The New Value-Free Sociology', first mentioned in letter 23.

7 *a visit from Alfred Sohn-Rethel*: Sohn-Rethel visited Adorno in Oxford on 22 November. – The *extremely stimulating letter* about his own project has not survived (cf. *Briefwechsel Adorno / Sohn-Rethel*, pp. 11f, footnote.

64   BENJAMIN TO WIESENGRUND-ADORNO
     SAN REMO, 2.12.1936

Dear Teddie,

You must have been waiting some time to receive thanks and confirmation of your letter of 7 November. You should indeed have had my thanks for the concern it expressed, and the thoughtful considerations it contained, long before now. But I shall explain why my response has been so long in coming.

As far as the external circumstances of the matter are concerned, everything has turned out otherwise than expected. I hasten to add that this is not true of the inner concatenation of the elements involved. Unfortunately, the trip did prove to be just as necessary as

163

I suspected, even though Stefan's condition is not quite as bad as my worst fears had suggested. I have not lost all contact with him. But there are some undeniable disturbances in his volitional powers. I am well versed enough psychiatrically to see that a proper medical opinion is absolutely required, but not enough to prejudge the outcome. There are also certain other symptoms, in addition to disturbance of the will, which need to be clarified – not to mention graphological ones.

I am writing to you from San Remo; I never went to Vienna. My wife wanted to clear up certain personal difficulties between Stefan and herself and urged me to arrange a meeting in Italy. But then Stefan could not be persuaded to come. This resulted in two extremely upsetting and enormously difficult weeks of attempted mediation on my part, until I finally managed to meet Stefan, initially on my own, in Venice. As far as my own personal contact with him is concerned, the meeting went quite well. I then brought Stefan to meet my wife in San Remo and here he will stay until Christmas. Around that time I shall have to travel down here again for a few days. (I return to Paris at the end of this week.)

The question of a medical examination poses considerable difficulty. Bernfeld[1] is living in Menton, but is away at the moment anyway. If we cannot get in contact with him, my wife will have to decide to approach a Swiss doctor.

As you can well imagine, I have not been able to do very much work. On the other hand, I have read a very substantial book by Dickens,[2] the first thing of his I have seen since 'The Old Curiosity Shop', which I got to know in Germany after studying your fine essay on the subject. This is a book with some significant constellations and rather wonderful figures – however inadequate the overall composition, and especially at the end.

Krenek has sent me his commemorative piece on Kraus; I was much impressed by the enormous loyalty with which he discusses his personal relationship to Kraus. I will read your own letter in the same issue[3] in the next few days, followed by the essay on Schönberg[4] when I get back.

This brings me to the very fine things you said about my book of letters. The history of the letter form which you revealed in it bespeaks a profound insight. And equally so, although I hardly need to say it, with regard to the relation you establish between this book and the 'Berlin Childhood'. (I would have dearly loved to promote its cause in Vienna; and your letter generally only makes me rather regret not being able to make the trip to Vienna. I shall be sending my book to Krenek.) You were also right about the gestation of the book; the preface is the only really recent part.

164

Finally, my thanks for the Noack. Studying it was the one way in which I was able to salvage even some fragments of this time for my Arcades project.

Let me close now with all the usual heartfelt greetings.

Yours,

Walter

2 December 1936
San Remo
Villa Verde

1 *Bernfeld*: Siegfried Bernfeld (1892–1953), Austrian psychologist and pedagogue, a leading member of the Youth Movement and personally known to Benjamin from this period; he worked at the Institute of Psychoanalysis in Berlin from 1925, and finally emigrated to the United States in 1935.

2 *a very substantial book by Dickens*: probably the French translation of 'Great Expectations', which Benjamin entered under the title 'Les grandes espérances' as number '1589' in his 'List of Books Read' (cf. GS VII [1], p. 472).

3 *your own letter in the same issue*: cf. Hektor Rottweiler [Adorno's pseudonym], 'Musikpädagogische Musik (Brief an Ernst Krenek)', in the Vienna music journal '23', 10.11.1936, nr. 28/30, pp. 29–37; now in GS 18, pp. 805–12.

4 *the essay on Schönberg*: the essay entitled 'The Dialectical Composer', mentioned for the first time in letter 47.

65 BENJAMIN TO WIESENGRUND-ADORNO
    PARIS, 29.1.1937

Dear Teddie,

Yesterday you were the cause of great pleasure to me. One day I shall tell you myself the full story about the role which 'Les liaisons dangereuses'[1] has played for me. Suffice it to say that, as things fell out, I had never read the book until now. Your gift has opened up for me an unexpected path, though one I can certainly pursue, into the work of Laclos. Many thanks!

I read Les Mariés[2] in San Remo; it gave me great pleasure, although it naturally produced some dark clouds of reflection, too. I am still not entirely clear as to what I think about it.

As far as my son is concerned, the situation is rather gloomy, I am afraid. I do not think there is any chance of his completing his school studies. It is impossible for him to stay in Vienna any longer, and equally impossible in San Remo. But there are also very good reasons against his going to Paris. At the moment it is quite impossible for me to see a clear way ahead.

This is a real burden to me. And the terrible weather here is doing nothing to improve my general outlook. In periods like this it is advisable to keep working. I have started on the Fuchs text, but I think it will take me another three weeks to complete it.

You will get in first with the Mannheim piece, which I am very much looking forward to looking at.

The wish to see you in March, at the latest, is now increased by my desire to hear more about the Berlin story to which you alluded.[3]

I am very glad that everything went well for you there.

I must also thank you for sending me the material from the bank.[4]

Finally, the response to our proposals from Max's letter:[5] 'Thank you very much for the proposals concerning the review section. We shall be discussing the whole question in detail, and hopefully by the beginning of 1938 at the latest, the journal will have assumed the form which we all wish to see it have.'

That's all for today.

In friendship as ever,

Yours,

Walter

29 January 1937
Paris XIV
23 rue Bénard

1 *'Les Liaisons dangereuses'*: Adorno had obviously sent Benjamin a copy of the eponymous novel by Choderlos de Laclos.

2 *Les Mariés*: the novel 'I promessi sposi' by Alessandro Manzoni.

3 *the Berlin story to which you alluded*: the letter which accompanied Adorno's gift of the book has not survived.

4 *the material from the bank*: nothing further known.

5 *the response from Max's letter*: Horkheimer's (unpublished) letter to Benjamin of 30 December 1936, was responding to Benjamin's and Adorno's 'Proposals for the Review Section of the *Zeitschrift für Sozialforschung*' (cf. letter 63 and the relevant note).

66 WIESENGRUND-ADORNO TO BENJAMIN
    OXFORD, 17.2.1937

Oxford, 17 February 1937.

Dear Walter, many thanks for your words and my best wishes towards finally hunting down the fox [Fuchs] – and herewith my own little quarry,[1] namely Herr Mannheim, who unfortunately cannot even supply the sort of pornographic illustrations that would be the only possible justification for his books. I must ask for your patience given the uncorrected state of the copy: unfortunately, I was only able to enter the quite considerable substantive and stylistic corrections into the copy already destined for New York. It would have taken hours of work to do the same with this one. But nonetheless I think you will get something out of it, even in this rather crude state, and be able to forgive me the absence of elegance in this case.

I am still not even sure whether the work will actually appear: Max certainly confirmed on the telephone that they would be publishing it, but I have heard nothing else from him since, and am now somewhat concerned about the fate of this essay,[2] which I would dearly like to see in print (Mannheim's reaction[3] to the manuscript has only confirmed me all the more in this). Would you be able, without too much trouble, to find out from Brill whether the final manuscripts for the issue currently being prepared have now gone in, and if so, whether mine was included amongst them (and in a tactful manner, since Max has already promised me a letter and I certainly won't hear anything before the end of next week)? And while I am making requests: could you get Brill to send an issue of the journal containing 'Egoism and the Freedom Movement', or at least an offprint of the same, in my name, to Dr Marianne Marschak,[4] Oxford-Headington, 17 Stephen Road. Many thanks in advance for this.

If you wish, you could pass the Mannheim essay on to Kracauer, for there are many good reasons why I should really like him to read it; but only do so on condition that he reads it very soon (within reasonable limits, but without pleading the case of massively urgent work instead) and returns it to me forthwith. It is the only copy in my possession.

I am really very much looking forward to seeing the Fuchs piece; I am also hoping to receive Alfred Sohn's essay[5] very soon. My major project is coming on well; indeed, I am now beginning to feel really rather stressed. Especially as far as Stefan is concerned, I wish you all the best. I think I may get to see Bernfeld in the next few weeks; if you would like me to discuss anything with him, just let me know.

Cordially yours, as ever,

Teddie

1 *my own little quarry*: the typescript of the essay on Mannheim which Adorno sent to Benjamin has not survived.

2 *the fate of this essay*: the piece did not in fact appear in the *Zeitschrift für Sozialforschung*.

3 *Mannheim's reaction*: on 8 February, Karl Mannheim had written a detailed (hitherto unpublished) letter about the essay, in which he avoided discussing the substantive differences between them, and accused Adorno of unintentionally accentuating the purely negative aspects of his method.

167

4 *Marianne Marschak*: Marianne Berta Kamnitzer (born 1901) had married the economist Jacob Marschak and emigrated to England with him in 1933.

5 *Alfred Sohn's essay*: the piece which Alfred Sohn described as his 'Paris exposé' was only completed at the end of April (see letter 73 and the relevant note).

67 BENJAMIN TO WIESENGRUND-ADORNO
    PARIS, 1.3.1937

Dear Teddie,

I am sure you will have interpreted the simple reason for these several days of silence on my part in the most plausible manner. Once the progress of my work on the Fuchs piece reached a critical stage, it tolerated no other competitors, either day or night.

And if I had nothing else to be thankful for after completing the work, there would still remain even now the particularly elevated mood in which I was able to start reading your piece on Mannheim. Only now, for the first time, have I fully realized just how profound the analogy between our respective tasks, and the position in which these tasks have placed us, really is. In the first place, there were those chemical analyses which had to be performed on the whole 'disgusting concoction', as Kant would say, all those stale dishes of ideas from which every Tom, Dick and Harry have long been feeding. Everything from this squalid kitchen had to be subjected to laboratory analysis. And then, secondly, there was that show of urbanity which we had to cultivate towards the dubious kitchen chef himself, something you practised rather less, but which I unfortunately practised in great abundance. In this connection, I believe we can mutually confirm that we both revealed an honourable composure that was not always easy to maintain.

And I can see that we have also shared the same dexterity in advancing our ownmost thought, inconspicuously in each case, but without making any concessions. And at least in your work I discover certain far-reaching formulations, about which there would truly be so much to say if I even attempted to express my sympathy for them. Rather, in these things I find you have addressed *meam rem* with an extraordinary intimacy, which discloses to my mind quite original aspects of the matter. I will just select two particularly important remarks, which I joyfully received like a gift, if I may put it that way: your claim (p. 16)[1] that the priority of social being over consciousness possesses an essentially methodological significance; and the banning of 'examples' (p. 19)[2] from the domain of dialectical method. Insights like this are music to the mind, and one which gives me the deepest pleasure.

168

As I am sure you realize, I regard the treatment you have meted out to Mannheim as no more, and possibly much less, than he deserved. (I like to imagine the English edition of his book as MacDonald's own *livre de chevet*.) Your passage about the huntsman[3] is quite marvellous (Mannheim's must come from Struwwelpeter). For the rest, I think your review provokes far more contempt for this book than it openly expresses, and that surely proves that you have solved the stylistic problem.

You will notice that I speak here *en connaissance de cause*. And in fact, I cannot deny that in my own work on Fuchs, a certain feeling of contempt kept on growing the more familiar I became with his writings. I hope this feeling is no more perceptible in my work than with the corresponding case in yours. There are also points of contact between us in rather unexpected places – like the way in which we both mention Wedekind.[4] It is almost like getting out of some dive in order to breathe a little fresh air.

The image of the dive has often been a source of consolation to me in my work. For with the latter I am rather like someone who, in a den of ill repute, comes upon the stricken body of a sad old acquaintance from earlier and better times; and the unfortunate man expresses his dying wish to be buried in a mountain cemetery; getting the body up there is no easy task; and we can only hope that the funeral attendants enjoy the splendid view to be had from the top. I have often had such thoughts as these, *kata phrena kai kata thumon*,[5] as I write.

The piece will go off to you by the immediate post. What you said of your manuscript can also more or less be said of mine. As you suggested, I will pass on your piece for Kracauer to read the next time I see him. – The manuscripts of the next issue of the Institute journal have not yet arrived at the rue d'Ulm.[6] I do hope you have received favourable news from Max in the meantime. On the other hand, I cannot conceal my own feeling that any such delay in the publication of your work might turn out for the best, if it means that both your work and mine can appear together in the same issue.

In the meantime I have compiled a bibliography of Jung's writings. (This was no easy matter, since the most important pieces are scattered all over the place.) The more I think about your suggestion,[7] the more it strikes me as a good idea. I have written to Max to say as much.[8]

Sohn-Rethel has quite vanished into the mist. Let us hope that he will emerge all the more radiantly from the shadows in the end.

I have made the acquaintance of Jean Wahl,[9] Professor of Philosophy at the Sorbonne. The next time you are here[10] we should not miss the opportunity of arranging a pleasant, if not particularly crucial, meeting. And when will that be?

169

With this question, resonating as it does throughout my letter, I will close here.

Cordially yours,
Walter

1 March 1937
Paris XIV
23 rue Bénard

PS 'Egoism and the Freedom Movement' has been sent off to Frau Marschak. – I would love to know: *what* precisely was Mannheim's reaction to your essay?

1 *your claim (p. 16)*: cf. GS 20 [1], p. 34.

2 *the banning of 'examples' (p. 19)*: cf. ibid., pp. 38f.

3 *Your passage about the huntsman*: cf. ibid., p. 39.

4 *the way we both mention Wedekind*: cf. GS 20 [1], p. 23; for the passage on Wedekind in Benjamin's essay on Fuchs, cf. GS II [2], p. 496.

5 *kata phrena kai kata thumon*: an expression in Ancient Greek meaning 'in one's heart and in one's understanding'.

6 *the rue d'Ulm*: the address of the 'École normale supérieure', where the Paris office of the Institute was also situated.

7 *your suggestion*: Adorno had suggested to Benjamin the idea of writing an essay on Jung.

8 *I have written to Max to say as much*: cf. GS VII [2], p. 866.

9 *Jean Wahl*: the French philosopher Jean Wahl (1888–1974) had been teaching at the Sorbonne since 1936; during the German occupation he was dismissed from his post as a Jew and imprisoned on account of criticisms of Franco-German collaboration; after his release he left France for the United States.

10 *The next time you are here*: Adorno visited Paris on 18 March for a few days.

68 BENJAMIN TO WIESENGRUND-ADORNO
[PARIS,] 16.3.1937

16 March 1937

Dear Teddie,

You must have waited very impatiently to receive S.-R.'s manuscript. And I have to confess that I myself bear some responsibility for the delay.

170

I *hope* the conversations I have had with S.-R. about the subject have actually been helpful for his essay, but I *know* in any event that they have certainly slowed things down as well. Although I feel far from competent as far as the full range of his developing investigation is concerned, I think I have now gained a much clearer idea of its specific importance. And this has only confirmed your own promising expectations of the work.

There is, of course, no question of these lines giving you even the remotest idea of the questions on which our discussion – perhaps our debate – properly turned; I could only do that in direct conversation face-to-face. For the moment I will simply confine myself to asking your advice about the precise *modus procedendi* for bringing the essay to the attention of M. H.[1] This *modus procedendi* is, as we know, of decisive importance; in the first place, on account of the delicate nature of the significant content itself, and in the second place, on account of the delicate nature of S.-R.'s personal situation (as for the latter, I have learned from him that the residence permit for his wife and daughter in Switzerland runs out at the end of May, and this is causing him very serious concern).

But to come straight to the point, I must confide to you that I can only harbour any real hope for the work being accepted if it is accompanied by some enthusiastic advocacy – in the first instance from the author, in the second instance from you, and in the third instance, in the area of my own competence, from me.

You will be able to decide after reading the manuscript whether I am perhaps being overly cautious here. You already possess the necessary materials; and in particular you also have far more understanding than I do of the relevant logical, and epistemological, positions of M. in this respect. I cannot conceal from you that, for my part, the theoretical derivation of ratio 'as such' and of logic 'as such' undertaken in this essay seems problematic to me, however justified the original intention behind it may be.

My debate with S.-R. has revealed other problem areas as well. Problem areas of this kind will always arise with any investigation of this range and importance. And this is precisely what makes me doubt whether any decision about the continuation of his work (especially since questions of bare survival seem to be connected with it) could properly be made without the said enthusiastic advocacy on your part. The work will require this advocacy all the more since it touches upon so many different areas of competence: and in particular the economic competence of P.[2]

I would propose the following: that you try and effect provisional financial support for S.-R.[3] during the months that may well transpire before M.'s trip to Europe, support that should in no way prejudice possible ratification of his research later on. Audacious though such an attempt may seem, I think it would be much more promising than subjecting S.-R.'s manuscript to an examination at which the author could not be present to support his case. In this connection, I would emphasize again that the actual problem seems to me to lie less in the way that S.-R. approaches the central question than in the magnitude of the question itself.

I am sending this letter, which S.-R. himself was kind enough to type for me, to O. in the hope that it will still reach you there. Has it actually been decided that you will be travelling to F.[4] without passing through Paris? You know just *how* much I would regret it, if that were the case. This letter gives you more than abundant proof of that.

I am looking forward very much to hearing what you have to say about 'Eduard Fuchs'.

And in closing a request: could you possibly let me borrow Valéry's 'Pièces sur l'art' for my next review of books?[5] I have already worked through it once, as you will certainly have noticed.

All the usual cordial greetings from me, and those of S.-R. as well,

Yours,

Walter

1 *M. H.*: i.e. Max Horkheimer.

2 *P.*: i.e. Friedrich Pollock.

3 *provisional financial support for S.-R.*: in April Sohn-Rethel received a payment of 1,000 francs for his *exposé* from the Institute of Social Research, and the same again in May thanks to Adorno's initiative.

4 *O./F.*: abbreviations for Oxford and Frankfurt.

5 *for my next review of books*: cf. *Zeitschrift für Sozialforschung* 6, issue 3 (1937), pp. 711–15; now in GS III, pp. 511–17. – The review in question does not actually discuss the book by Valéry mentioned in the letter.

69 GRETEL KARPLUS AND WIESENGRUND-ADORNO TO BENJAMIN
  WÜRZBURG, 31.3.1937

Würzburg, 31 March 1937.

Dear Walter,

A card just to let you know we have arrived safely and communicate our greetings on this trip through the Franconian towns, which should take us at least as far as Bamberg and Nürnberg. I am delighted by the success of your work:[1] let us hope that its subject[2] also feels the same way about it.

How much I would love to accompany you for a second time up the stairs of that suburban dwelling. Here, by way of compensation, is a view of a rather more urban one.[3] With heartfelt greetings,
Teddie

Dear Detlef,
Thanks for your letter over Easter, which will receive a proper answer when I am back in Berlin. Lots of love for now, your Felicitas

1 *the success of your work*: Horkheimer had expressed an extremely positive response to Adorno and Benjamin with regard to the latter's essay on Fuchs.

2 *let us hope that its subject*: during Adorno's visit to Paris between 18 and around 22 March, he and Benjamin had gone to see Eduard Fuchs in his Paris apartment.

3 *a view of a rather more urban one*: the postcard carried the picture of the *Haus zum Falken* in Würzburg.

70 BENJAMIN TO WIESENGRUND-ADORNO
[PARIS,] 13.4.1937

Dear Teddie,
Just a few lines in order to comply with a request which Friedrich[1] has just made to me. (I have not actually seen him during his present stay yet, but he contacted me by telephone.)
He wants me to inform you that he will not be able to come via London, and he would not wish this news to be misinterpreted. He is extremely pressured for time, and illness had already delayed his trip here as it was. It is still not entirely clear when he will leave Paris, but possibly at the end of this week.
He wants me to tell you that on his part there is nothing really urgent that needs discussing at present. And much as he would have liked to get to see you – and I am supposed to emphasize this very strongly to you – he wouldn't want you to cut short your own holiday on his account. What has motivated him in this, is his certainty of seeing a lot of you very soon in any case.
I must thank Felizitas and yourself for the Franconian greetings. Although we met such a short while ago, I feel there is already so much more for us to talk about. The more often we get to see one another, the more crucial our meetings will come to seem to us.
Unfortunately, Kolisch's stay already comes to an end this Friday. He was unable to arrange a meeting before Friday. And indeed I have only just had a phone call from him. Nobody will be sorrier than I

am to attend his last concert[2] appearance here. I shall get to see him after the concert – although I fear he will then be surrounded by a mighty halo, something which hardly accords with your wishes, perhaps not with his, and certainly not with mine. However, he believes that he will be back here to perform again in the very near future.

Best wishes to Felizitas and yourself,

Walter

13 April 1937

1 *Friedrich*: i.e. Friedrich Pollock.

2 *Kolisch's stay . . . his last concert*: nothing further known.

71 WIESENGRUND-ADORNO TO BENJAMIN
    FRANKFURT A.M., 15.4.1937

Frankfurt.
15 April 1937.

Dear Walter,

Many thanks for your news. It was originally my intention to come to Paris on Saturday, and a postcard from Brill gave me no good reason for second thoughts, either. But after receiving your letter, it certainly does seem as though my visit would interfere with the arrangements Fritz has already made. And that alone – rather than my holiday, for example, which I now regard as over anyway – has led me to abandon this intention. Thus I would ask you to greet Fritz for me in the warmest terms, to tell him how much I regret that a meeting between us proved difficult for him at present, and to express my hope that we shall indeed get to speak to each other very soon. Above all, I am simply concerned that he should know that my own arrangements are still very much at his disposal, in spite of the changing plans, and that the only reason I didn't come was out of consideration for him. I also hope he is well-recovered by now.

So I shall be remaining here, certainly until the beginning, and perhaps until the middle of next week. It is a shame your meeting with Kolisch will prove such a fleeting one; but perhaps you will get more out of the meeting – and the concert – than was expected after all. Please do pass on my warmest greetings to him.

I feel much restored and hope to get back to my work properly now. Until then I am busy studying *Lulu*,[1] and reading Huxley[2] and *Les liaisons dangereuses*. Gretel, who also benefited a great deal from this fortnight's rest, is now back at home.

I must go to the dentist today, which reminds me of your own problems in this area. I would make sure you talk to Fritz about it.

Have you heard anything from Friedel?[3]

I am sure I do not have to tell you how sorry I am not to be able to get to Paris. But without an official invitation it is quite impossible and, *rebus sic stantibus*, this is not really something that can be pressed.

Heartfelt greetings as always,

Yours,
Teddie.

1 *I am busy studying Lulu*: Adorno is referring to the piano score of Berg's opera.

2 *reading Huxley*: it is no longer possible to determine which of Huxley's books Adorno was reading.

3 *Friedel*: i.e. Siegfried Kracauer.

72   WIESENGRUND-ADORNO TO BENJAMIN
OXFORD, 20.4.1937

Oxford, 20 April 1937.

Dear Walter,

Since my friend Opie[1] arrived in Frankfurt on Friday, and didn't want to continue his travels until Sunday, I only got back here yesterday evening, after a two-day car trip which proved remarkably enjoyable in every respect. But I am about to go to London for a couple of days, where I have a few extremely important matters[2] to sort out. Would it be a major inconvenience if I asked you to send on all the stuff I left in Paris to my London address as quickly as possible, by recorded and express delivery? I really need my list of addresses *very* urgently. Here is the London address again:

Albemarle Court Hotel.
18 Leinster Gardens.
W. 2

I would simply ask you to send on the dark green English registration book, which I specially gave you to look after for me, to my Oxford address, 47 Banbury Road, by recorded but not express delivery, as we had arranged before. Many thanks in advance for your great assistance here.

In Germany, once again everything went as smoothly as you can imagine. I didn't have to open my luggage for inspection either on the way in or coming back.

I returned here to find two letters from Max, and was particularly delighted to see how taken he is with your Fuchs piece. I shall not be letting this opportunity pass. As far as the piece on Jung is concerned, however, he expresses some reservations: he would far rather have the chapter on Baudelaire right away. But there are so many good reasons – touching upon the Institute and also, above all, upon the interests of the Arcades project itself – for you not to abandon the idea too hastily. I will be writing to him again from London in this regard, and I will naturally keep you informed about things throughout.

Kracauer will be getting a few lines from Max, which will make it very difficult, as far as I am concerned, for him to appeal to the plein pouvoir he has supposedly received from Max. – I would like to know what's happening with Alfred Sohn. Of course, his *exposé* still has not arrived.

The date for my American trip has now been fixed for the middle of June; but I think I will be able to make it over to Paris before then in any case, and perhaps with Gretel.[3] She will be visiting me here beforehand. Our all too brief fortnight of leisure was very good for her. There is so much we could tell you about this period – and about our visit to the Nazi Party Congress grounds in Nürnberg, for example.

Could I also ask you on my behalf to thank Brillo[4] for his news, and to tell him that shared arrangements have kept me from making it to Paris; further, that I would like him to send the proofs of the impending issue of the journal, and especially Marcuse's essay,[5] to me here in Oxford?

All my best wishes to you personally and with regard to the work. My own schedule for work has had to be revised somewhat: now I shall be writing the English dissertation version[6] of my book first. I shall probably only be writing the definitive version of the final chapter[7] – or its equivalent – in German, which we also hope to publish in the journal (and if possible in this year's third issue), under the title 'A Critique of Transcendental Subjectivity'.

Max's sense of disappointment concerning the larger part of all the so-called sympathizing intellectuals is so great, and his attitude to your own things so positive, that I really no longer have any doubt that the external consequences thereof will also be revealing themselves in the not-too-distant future. It hardly needs saying that I, for my own part, will be doing everything I can to encourage this.

Heartfelt greetings from your old friend,

Teddie

176

1 *my friend Opie*: the economist Redvers Opie (born 1900) was the Bursar of Magdalen College, Oxford.

2 *London . . . a few extremely important matters*: Adorno wished to arrange a temporary visitor's visa for the American trip planned for June, as well as a long-stay visa for France.

3 *Paris . . . perhaps with Gretel*: in fact Adorno visited Paris at the beginning of July without Gretel.

4 *Brillo*: i.e. Klaus Brill.

5 *Marcuse's essay*: cf. Herbert Marcuse, 'Über den affirmativen Charakter der Kultur', in *Zeitschrift für Sozialforschung* 6, issue 1 (1937), pp. 54–92. See 'The Affirmative Character of Culture', in H. Marcuse, *Negations* (Harmondsworth 1968), pp. 88–133.

6 *the English dissertation version*: Adorno never actually composed this version, which was to have been entitled 'The Principle of Intentionality and Categorial Intuition'.

7 *the final chapter*: the essay version of the final chapter, which was revised many times and only completed in 1938, did not appear in the *Zeitschrift für Sozialforschung*; for Adorno's 1938 version, cf. 'Zur Philosophie Husserls' (GS 20 [1], pp. 46–118).

73 BENJAMIN TO WIESENGRUND-ADORNO
PARIS, 23.4.1937

Dear Teddie,

I was delighted with everything your letter contained and the prospects it seemed to offer for the future – above all a meeting between the three of us, with Felizitas; but at the very least your own arrival here (I gathered that much from Pollock too). It was also very good to learn that your days in Germany passed off without too much cause for anxiety. If you manage to return to the same area, there are some irresistible reasons for you to visit Lemgo[1] in Westphalia.

What I so much desired seems to have come about: namely, that your critique of Mannheim and my piece on Fuchs will appear as neighbours after all. I was naturally quite delighted about the unconditional approval which Max has had communicated to me. And Fuchs has written me a friendly letter.

Pollock himself arranged an opportunity for me to discuss my current situation. At his request, I have drawn up a modest and precise budget[2] for him, which gives him to understand that I am short 400 francs a month – essentially, though not exclusively, as a result of inflation here. In the first instance he has approved a one-off payment of 1,000 francs to help me out. I am still waiting to hear about any further decision.

My discussion with Pollock basically centred upon the subject of my next piece of work. Resistance to the theme we had in mind is obviously quite considerable. I have the impression that at the moment some difficult arguments between Max and Fromm are going on concerning an entire set of problems that also involves Pollock. My last letter to Max contained three proposals,[3] and in his reply to me, which only arrived a few days ago, Max has responded positively to the third one: namely, to write the chapter on Baudelaire first. Certainly your own suggestion struck me firmly as the most appropriate one, and certainly also as the most urgent one as far as the work is concerned. On the other hand, it is also true that the essential motifs of the book are so interconnected that the various individual themes do not really present themselves as strict alternatives anyway.

Max was just as enthusiastic about the Jochmann[4] as we both hoped he would be. He has commissioned me to write an introduction to the essay. In the meantime, I have also unearthed some more interesting information about the author.

Short though my meeting with Kolisch turned out to be – it took place in the green room during the interval – it certainly did seem to stand under a friendly star. I am very much looking forward to seeing him again, something which can hardly be that far off.

Sohn-Rethel has completed his manuscript.[5] I have not been able to get a look at it. Let us hope for the best!

I have read Brentano's 'Trial Without a Judge'[6] – an extremely well-written, but unfortunately also utterly confused piece of work. At the moment, and very much to the advantage and benefit of the Arcades project, I am studying Chesterton's book 'Dickens':[7] an extraordinary work with the irresistible music of healthy common sense.

Let us wish one another good luck in the progress of our work!

With heartfelt greetings,

Yours,

Walter

23 April 1937
Paris XIV
23 rue Bénard

1 *irresistible reasons . . . to visit Lemgo*: the significance of this remark remains unclear.

2 *a modest and precise budget*: Benjamin estimated that he required the sum of 1,390 francs as a monthly minimum.

3 *my next piece of work / three proposals*: on 28 March Benjamin had
written to Horkheimer: 'To put it in a formula: I think that the definitive
and binding plan of the book [sc. the Arcades], since the preliminary material studies for it are complete apart from one or two very limited areas,
should really emerge from two fundamental methodological investigations.
The one would be concerned firstly with the critique of pragmatic history,
and secondly with the critique of cultural history, as this critique presents
itself to the materialist; the other would be concerned with the significance
of psychoanalysis for the 'subject' in the light of materialist historiography.
If you feel any hesitation about my handling this second theme without first
having the opportunity to discuss it with me in person, then we could also
consider the possibility of working up the first theme I mentioned – the
opposition between the bourgeois and the materialist presentation of history
– as a preface to my book. But I would definitely have certain reservations
about taking up an individual chapter of the book before the overall plan
of the latter was entirely determined in my mind. – If you feel in the last
analysis that you would not really welcome this alternative way of proceeding, then I would suggest to you, plunging *in medias res*, that I should write
the chapter on Baudelaire in advance of the rest' (GS V [2], p. 1158).

4 *the Jochmann*: i.e. Carl Gustav Jochmann's essay 'Rückschritte der Poesie'
[Regressions in Poetry], of which Benjamin had sent Horkheimer an abbreviated copy on 28 March.

5 *Sohn-Rethel / his manuscript*: Benjamin is referring to the 'Paris Exposé',
which was published in 1971 under the title 'Zur kritischen Liquidation des
Apriorismus. Eine materialistische Untersuchung (mit Randbemerkungen von
Walter Benjamin)' [The Critical Dissolution of A Priorism. A Materialist
Investigation (with Marginalia by Walter Benjamin)]; cf. Alfred Sohn-Rethel,
*Geistige und körperliche Arbeit. Zur Epistemologie der abendländischen
Geschichte* [Mental and Physical Labour. The Epistemology of Western His-
tory] (Weinheim 1989), pp. 153–220.

6 *Brentano's 'Trial Without a Judge'*: the novel *Prozess ohne Richter* by
Bernard von Brentano (1901–64) had just appeared.

7 *Chesterton's book 'Dickens'*: cf. G. K. Chesterton, *Charles Dickens*. Traduit
par Achille Laurent et L. Martin-Dupont (Paris undated).

74   WIESENGRUND-ADORNO TO BENJAMIN
     OXFORD, 25.4.1937

Oxford, 25 April 1937

Dear Walter,
    Many thanks for your letter and the material you sent to me in
London and here in Oxford. But firstly, as far as the latter, essentially
practical matters, are concerned: did I not also give you my personal

179

copy of the essay on jazz (as an offprint)? This particular copy is especially valuable to me since it also contains some of the additional remarks[1] which at last I now need to finalize. Many thanks in advance for this, too.

In the meantime I have written in some detail to Max,[2] and thereby done something, I think, to encourage a reliable improvement in your financial situation. Fritz also seems to have taken certain steps in this regard already. Let us wait and see whether my intervention leads any further. – Once again, I have explicitly argued the case why I would really prefer to see the piece on Jung taken in hand before the whole question of the Arcades itself is properly addressed. Max will certainly communicate his opinion on this to me in any case. And incidentally, as far as Fromm is concerned, Max writes that he shares my objections to Fromm's latest piece[3] (which I had communicated from Paris). – In the meantime I have read Marcuse's essay on culture. I find it rather tame: basically derivative things borrowed from Max and filled out with a lot of Weimar cultural stuff, the work of a converted, if indeed rather zealous, senior school teacher. And naturally, given the magnitude of its object, hopelessly off the mark. If only he had confined himself to elaborating the critique of the ideological *concept* of culture. Instead of that, he also incorporates cultural *contents*, which here amounts to everything and nothing. The stuff on art in particular, and its transfiguring effect etc., is quite hopeless. With young men like this, one has the feeling that they have had no further aesthetic experience since the time they first began to resent their senior German teacher at primary school. And in that respect they naturally find it rather easier to liquidate art than we do. What do you think of the work? It will not exactly be easy for me to tell Max what I think without encouraging him to number me amongst the grumblers and cavillers – especially since he already knows my views about Löwenthal's work[4] and my objections to Fromm, and hardly needs to be told about my attitude to Neurath and Lazarsfeld.[5] Nevertheless, I will find it difficult not to reveal what I think. Camp followers like Löwenthal, and now, unfortunately, Marcuse as well, represent a real danger. But just how difficult it is to defend ourselves precisely against those who imitate us, I know all too painfully from the cases of Sternberger and Haselberg.[6] And you are quite right, when you yourself have constantly and silently endorsed the demand to do so, more so indeed than I would have admitted only a year ago.

I am extremely keen to see Sohn-Rethel's work; I assume that you will get to see it before I do. If Max's response should turn out to be negative[7] – which is certainly quite conceivable, although the extremity of Alfred's gifts alone should guarantee him a hearing when one considers his distinctly average younger competitors – then I would be willing to try something else on Alfred's behalf, but please don't mention anything like that to him as yet.

I shall be resuming my own work tomorrow. First I shall select the appropriate sections for the English version and start to organize the material. At the same time I shall also start writing up the final chapter in essay form as the 'critique of transcendental subjectivity'. In addition, I will also have to take a bite into a rosy-looking, but extremely sour, apple with my critique of Ernst's book.[8]

If you should actually get involved in discussion with Fuchs, I would offer you the slogan 'Leninist Auto-critique'. I think that would be enough to establish the appropriate distance from him. I would so much love to see his letter.

From Gretel I have been hearing nothing but good things. – In London they have granted me not only a temporary visiting visa for America, but also a long-stay French visa for two years, something which I am especially pleased about with regard to maintaining the rhythm of our own meetings. I will certainly be making good use of it in June.

Krenek has just published a book[9] which makes the friendliest reference to myself, and which contains some excellent material in the section on the technical aspects of music. On the other hand, I am not very comfortable with the aesthetic ideas he expresses, and least of all where he appropriates some of our own themes in his own manner.

Let me close with a discreet prayer to the Almighty that he may protect us from our friends. As far as our enemies are concerned, I am currently relying on the 'Hood'.[10]

With heartfelt greetings,

Yours,

Teddie

1 *the essay on jazz / the additional remarks*: Adorno is referring to the 'Oxford additions' made to the essay 'On Jazz', which he included in the volume *Moments musicaux* in 1964; cf. GS 17, pp. 100–8.

2 *In the meantime I have written . . . to Max*: Adorno's letter to Horkheimer is dated 23 April; for the passage referring to Benjamin, cf. GS VII [2], pp. 867f.

3 *Fromm's latest piece*: cf. Erich Fromm 'Zum Gefühl der Ohnmacht' [On the Feeling of Powerlessness], in the *Zeitschrift für Sozialforschung* 6, issue 1 (1937), pp. 95–117.

4 *Löwenthal's work*: cf. Leo Löwenthal, 'Knut Hamsun. Zur Vorgeschichte der autoritären Ideologie' [Knut Hamsun. The Prehistory of Authoritarian Ideology], in the *Zeitschrift für Sozialforschung* 6, issue 2 (1937), pp. 295–343; now in Leo Löwenthal, *Schriften*, edited by Helmut Dubiel, vol. 2: *Das bürgerliche Bewusstsein in der Literatur* (Frankfurt a.M. 1981), pp. 245–97.

5 *my attitude to Neurath and Lazarsfeld*: Adorno is thinking of articles they published in the Institute's journal; cf. Otto Neurath, 'Inventory of the Standard of Living', in *Zeitschrift für Sozialforschung* 6, issue 1 (1937), pp. 140–50; and Paul Lazarsfeld, 'Some Remarks on the Typological Procedures in Social Research', ibid., pp. 119–38.

6 *Haselberg*: Peter von Haselberg (born 1908) studied with Adorno during the years 1931–3.

7 *Sohn-Rethel's work / If Max's response should turn out to be negative*: for Horkheimer's critical letter of 24.5.1937, cf. *Briefwechsel Adorno / Sohn-Rethel*, pp. 61f. – Adorno subsequently encouraged Walter Adams, General Secretary of the 'Academic Assistance Council', to consider granting financial assistance to Sohn-Rethel (see letter 83 and the relevant note).

8 *my critique of Ernst's book*: Adorno never wrote his intended review of Ernst Bloch's *Erbschaft dieser Zeit*.

9 *Krenek has just published a book*: cf. Ernst Krenek, *Über neue Musik* (Vienna 1937); and Adorno's review of the same in the *Zeitschrift für Sozialforschung* 7, issue 3 (1938), pp. 294–6: now in GS 19, pp. 366–8.

10 *the 'Hood'*: the reference to the monk's cowl here is an allusion to 'Comité Secret de l'Action Révolutionnaire', a clandestine French organization of the far-right established in 1932, which called itself the 'Cagoule' (the French equivalent of 'hood'). Members of the society – the 'Cagoulards' (cf. letter 94) – carried out attacks on representatives of the left. The organization was finally destroyed by the government of Léon Blum in 1937.

75 BENJAMIN TO WIESENGRUND-ADORNO
    PARIS, 1.5.1937

Dear Teddie,

Before anything else, congratulations on obtaining your two-year visa. So we shall get to see each other before your trip to America after all! And Felizitas will also make an appearance at last!

For the rest, I would like to begin these few lines with an apology and an expression of thanks. An apology for failing to send back your personal copy of the essay on jazz, which I hereby dispatch to you by registered delivery with the same post. And thanks for the lines you wrote to Max on my behalf. Since Pollock's return I have heard nothing from New York. I am also still waiting to hear about the other questions for the future, which he suggested would receive the most careful and sympathetic consideration.

Pollock had already given me to understand that Max had certain reservations about the idea of writing my next pieces on Jung and Klages, and that the reasons for this are connected with internal debates within the New York circle itself; and in the meantime this has subsequently been confirmed by a letter from Max.[1] I have explained to Max himself the reasons[2] why I so unreservedly supported your proposal, and also expressed my readiness in the meantime to take up the Baudelaire work immediately, if he thinks that is appropriate.

I have found some new material for my introduction to Jochmann's essay.

I imagine that Sohn-Rethel's manuscript will probably have reached you shortly before these lines of mine. He was unable to spare a copy for me, so I still haven't seen it myself. But I have got plenty of other reading to do, and in the first place Kracauer's book.[3] I am not yet half way through, but I see no reason to take back anything I said about my first impression, as already expressed to you.

I have taken only a cursory look at Marcuse's essay. Do I have to tell you that my own prejudgement has long since concurred with you, just as my explicit judgement most assuredly will too?

In conclusion, my best wishes for your English text and all my greetings as usual,

Yours,
Walter

1 May 1937
Paris XIV
23 rue Bénard

1 *a letter from Max*: Horkheimer's letter to Benjamin is dated 13 April 1937. (For an excerpt of this letter, cf. GS I [3], p. 1067.)

2 *I have explained to Max himself the reasons*: in Benjamin's letter to Horkheimer of 28 February 1937; cf. the excerpt in GS VII [2], p. 866.

3 *Kracauer's book*: cf. Siegfried Kracauer, *Jacques Offenbach und das Paris seiner Zeit* (Amsterdam 1937). – For Adorno's review, cf. *Zeitschrift für Sozialforschung* 6, issue 3 (1937), pp. 697f; now in GS 19, pp. 363–5.

76   WIESENGRUND-ADORNO TO BENJAMIN
     OXFORD, 4.5.1937

4 May 1937   MERTON COLLEGE,
                                              OXFORD.

Dear Walter,

Just a few lines to thank you for the letter and my personal manuscript, and at the same time to communicate something of the extremely embarrassing situation in which I have been placed by the Offenbach piece. It has far exceeded my worst expectations. It is only the fortunate circumstance that I do not have the copy to hand which prevents me from quoting to you some of the many remarks which are worthy of Mannheim, and which make the reader blush all the more vigorously, if only because they seem to cause no embarrassment to their author. The few passages which touch on music are crassly erroneous. And the arrangement of the whole, announced in the shameless and idiotic preface as a 'biography of society', is also worthy of the details. The social observations are no more than old wives' tales, the foolishness and superficiality of which find their only equivalent in that blinking petty bourgeois look with which, half admiringly and half resentfully, he squints at 'society' and indeed the demimonde – which, incidentally, Kracauer supplies with the feminine article. No, if Kracauer really does identify with this book, then he has definitely erased himself from the list of writers to be taken at all seriously. And I am myself seriously considering whether or not I should break off relations with him. For to carry on as before would almost be more hurtful still: it would mean that one could no longer respond properly to anything he might perpetrate in the future. In any case, something has to be done. I have already sketched one letter only to discard it. I am wondering now whether or not a joint intervention by Ernst, you and me might be able to influence him. Or should we wait until I come to Paris? But then Kracauer's dependence on the Institute makes that particularly difficult for me. I can only shudder to think of the impression the product will make on Max. Indeed, the piece is so irredeemably terrible that it could easily become a best-seller, and that would surely relieve all our worries. In the meanwhile I look forward to receiving some urgent advice from you.

With heartfelt greetings as ever,

Yours,

Teddie

77   BENJAMIN TO WIESENGRUND-ADORNO
     PARIS, 9.5.1937

Dear Teddie,

For some days I have been harbouring the vain hope that I might find an opportunity to dictate the following letter, which naturally cannot be all that brief. However, I have had to write it out by hand after all. But I would have liked to receive something rather easier to work with than a hand-written letter from you too. –

Your lines on the 'Offenbach' piece arrived barely an hour after I had confided my own impression on reading it to Sohn-Rethel, the first person I have spoken to about the work. Before telling you about my impression in detail, I can communicate the general drift by acknowledging what I take to be the essential tenor of your letter: how are we to proceed in response to this impression?

If I could really give you an answer to this question, my letter would be much shorter than it is. I have written in such detail because I want you to understand that my own perplexity here arises from a situation which must very much resemble that which prompted your letter to me in the first place. To put it briefly, as far as the principal problem is concerned, I can only respond to your question with another one. You ask: what is to be done? And I would ask: is anything to be done?

If my relationship to Kracauer were an isolated and self-contained one, I would have no hesitation in answering this question – my own – in the negative. And it is easy to explain the reason why, for my substantive considerations of the book give way to my psychological considerations about the author: with this book Kracauer has essentially resigned himself. He has composed a text that only a few years ago would have found its most ruthless critic in the author himself. And after a ten-year delay, he has finally joined the hosts of those biographers who once rode out under the banner of the blessed Ludwig[1] and found their valiant champions in Marcuse,[2] E. A. Rheinhardt[3] and Frischauer.[4] – The situation is perfectly obvious. If I was to respond to him solely for my own part, I would certainly not be able to ignore the complementary circumstances: in a time of dire need, Kracauer believed that he had to establish some positive access to the book market. No one could possibly have wished more sincerely than I that a certain cynicism – not to mention humour – on his part might have rendered this predicament more bearable, not only to him, but also to his friends. Unfortunately, such an attitude could never be expected of him in the first place.

All of these considerations would lead me – still assuming that I was dealing with him solely on my own account – to accept in silence his quite explicable state of discouragement for the moment and, without dropping him, to await further developments in the situation.

Unfortunately, the assumption I have been making here does not really hold. I cannot regard my dealings with Kracauer solely in my own terms – not merely from the personal angle, but with respect to substantive issues as well: the position which Kracauer has abandoned was not his alone, but was one which we all shared. That is the important thing here. And now I consider it carefully, I properly realize for the first time why Kracauer was able, and indeed why he was forced, to isolate his work so totally from all our discussions during the years in which he was preparing this book.

185

But I now come to considerations of a more material nature, which I can naturally only sketch briefly here. He has simply made an example of the thing: and as a result it is quite impossible to say anything essential about Offenbach's work, objectively or theoretically, if the music is ignored. One can, on the other hand, certainly say something about it subjectively and practically, as Karl Kraus has shown. Karl Kraus responded to Offenbach's operetta[5] in his own way: he was quite prepared, indeed he was wildly determined, to compromise himself with the work. But Kracauer wants to save the fallen maiden. His whole enterprise proves, against his intention, that no 'salvation' of Offenbach's operetta is possible without providing a musical analysis of the piece.

Once this attempt at salvation breaks down, it merely reappears in distorted form, namely as apologia. And I perceive the essentially fatal nature of the book to lie in precisely this, its apologetic character. It is especially flagrant in those passages which touch upon Offenbach's Jewish origins. For Kracauer, the Jewish element remains rooted in origins. He doesn't even dream of recognizing it in the work itself. – But I cannot see his theory of operetta as anything but an apologia either, one repeated endlessly with wearying persistence and without the slightest hint of musical variation. The concept of rapture [Rausch], which is supposed to support this theory, at least as it appears here, is nothing but a messy box of chocolates.

In addition, one has to say that it is hardly possible to find a period in which any attempt at apologetics would be more fruitless than our own. Everything which comes to *appearance* [Schein] in the Second Empire is obvious and offensive. Of course, Kracauer has noticed this himself. But since he only really attends to the appearance, he cannot help being stupefied by the latter either. That is the price he is forced to pay for the apologia. Lovely though many of the things in his sources are, they only appear shabby and mean in the text itself. And hardly any of the numerous anecdotes make a proper effect when they are reproduced.

Thus I cannot believe that our judgements about the book diverge in any way. In particular, I dislike the frequent offences against German itself. Perhaps they are sometimes quite deliberate, and I can hardly imagine that a writer like Kracauer could commit to paper a phrase such as 'make a cracking impression' without any forethought. I have the rather evil suspicion that the ressentiment of the emigré is simply finding an opportunity to express itself at the expense of the German language, and that is no longer an amusing matter.

Bloch mentions the book very briefly in his last letter[6] to me; he says that he would really like to know what you make of Kracauer's remarks concerning 'The Tales of Hoffmann'; he rather reserves judgement himself. (Incidentally, I regard the narration of Offenbach's last week of life as one of the few good passages in the book.)

And now in conclusion, and in spite of everything, I return to the question: is there anything to be done? I do not know if we can even contemplate making a decision before we get the chance to speak to one another. For my part I would simply say, *en attendant*, that nothing definite should be decided as yet.

Have you got any firmer idea about the date of your arrival here?[7] Be sure to give yourself as much time as possible. We shall have to discuss, amongst many other things, the question of finding a publisher for Max's essays since the translation will be ready in a few days.

Please write and tell me something about Berlioz. He crops up in the Offenbach piece; I have long wanted to know who and what he really was.

Heartfelt greetings,

Yours,

Walter

9 May 1937
Paris XIV
23 rue Bénard

1 *the blessed Ludwig*: an allusion to Emil Ludwig (1881–1948), who wrote one biography entitled *Der Menschensohn* [The Son of Man] (1928), as well as biographies of Goethe, Napoleon and Bismarck.

2 *Marcuse*: Benjamin is referring here to Ludwig Marcuse (1894–1971).

3 *E. A. Rheinhardt*: Emil Alphons Rheinhardt (1889–1945), who was murdered in Dachau concentration camp, was the author of *Das Leben der Eleonora Duse* (Berlin 1928), *Napoleon III und Eugenie* (Berlin 1930) and *Der grosse Herbst Heinrichs IV.* (Vienna 1935).

4 *Frischauer*: the Austrian writer and journalist Paul Frischauer (born 1898), who worked for the *Berliner Tageblatt* and the *Vossische Zeitung*, emigrated to England in 1934. He had written books on Prince Eugen (Vienna 1933), Garibaldi (Zürich 1934) and Beaumarchais (London 1935).

5 *Karl Kraus / Offenbach's operetta*: cf. the passage in Benjamin's essay 'Karl Kraus' (GS II [1], pp. 356f).

6 *Bloch mentions the book ... in his last letter*: Bloch's letter is dated 26 April 1937 (cf. Ernst Bloch, *Briefe 1903–1975*, vol. 2, pp. 667f).

7 *the date of your arrival here*: Adorno stayed in Paris from 2 July for a while before travelling on to New York.

187

Oxford, 47 Banbury Road.
12 May 1937

Dear Walter,

In the last few days I received a letter from Max[1] which contains some things of interest to you.

First of all, concerning the *Essais de philosophie matérialiste*, Max is still assuming that Klossowski's translation has to be checked through (and which, in fact, is already finished). He asks whether you or Klossowski, or both of you together, have produced a list of passages which involve unnecessary repetitions or things which might prove particularly obscure to French readers; he thinks it might also be necessary to supply some elucidating references to various authors and books less well known in France. And finally, there is the question of the introduction. Max would very much prefer one to be written by a French author; I have strong reservations about the idea myself, especially since I cannot think of anyone really suitable (Wahl?); I think that Max will have to write it himself in the end. He would like you to discuss all these matters with me in Paris in June, and I will then help to sort out any further problems with him when I get to New York. Perhaps you would be kind enough to note down what strike you as the most important questions, and perhaps consider drawing up that list of passages.

I also quote to you a further section from his letter verbatim: 'I have just received a letter from Benjamin saying that he is in full agreement about the Baudelaire theme. If you (i.e. Teddie) should prefer to ignore my proposal and return instead to the theme of images, then I have no real objection. I would simply be grateful, in that case, if I could receive a short outline containing the basic ideas involved as soon as possible. I leave it to you two to make the final decision as to what must be done now, but would still like to register my preference for the Baudelaire idea as things currently stand.'

In reply I have once again communicated my reasons for preferring 'The Archaic Image' as a subject, and told him that I shall be discussing the entire matter with you in detail; I cannot tell whether the decision can still be postponed until I am in New York, since I am not familiar with the precise state of your own work at the moment. I would not wish to pressure you about this, but you know why I prefer the subject of the archaic image, and I do not think it would

188

cause any serious problems for Max after everything he has written. There would then naturally be an even greater obligation to ensure a really decisive methodological 'achievement' with the work. But if you still want to stand by our original idea, and hold the view that this piece of work is substantively no less important than the chapter on Baudelaire, then I would ask you to send Max the small outline in question as quickly as possible, and also to inform me in some detail of his precise objections, which I am still in the dark about.

My travel arrangements are now more or less definite. Gretel will be arriving here[2] in less than a fortnight, at Opie's invitation. We shall then spend a couple of days in London before coming finally – probably around 2 June – to Paris. I shall not be going to Germany, but travelling on directly to New York on 9 June on the Normandie. I shall be staying there for a fortnight and coming back with the Normandie on 30 June; and perhaps then another couple of days in Paris before I visit Germany.

I have now decided to write Kracauer[3] a most principled and extremely frank letter about his abomination. I would dearly like to have known your own position in this matter first – especially concerning the idea of a shared intervention with Ernst Bloch. In any case, with all the discretion which necessarily arises from indiscretion, I shall be sending you a copy of my letter. – I have also expressed myself to Max in very clear terms about Marcuse's piece of work.

I shall be writing to Sohn-Rethel[4] this very afternoon.

Until we see each other very soon. Heartfelt greetings as ever,

Yours,

Teddie

1 *a letter from Max*: Horkheimer's (unpublished) letter to Adorno of 4 May 1937.

2 *Gretel will be arriving here*: Gretel's planned visit in May did not materialize. She left Germany three months later and arrived in London on 20 August.

3 *I have now decided to write Kracauer*: Adorno wrote to Kracauer the next day, on 13 May 1937. This letter (also referred to in letter 79 below) has not yet been published, but is mentioned repeatedly in the secondary literature, e.g. the Marburger Catalogue, *Siegfried Kracauer 1889–1966*, p. 91.

4 *I shall be writing to Sohn-Rethel*: Adorno's letter to Sohn-Rethel has not survived (cf. *Briefwechsel Adorno/Sohn-Rethel*, p. 59).

Oxford, 13 May 1937

Dear Walter,

Here is the copy of my letter to Kracauer. It was already written in outline by the time your letter arrived. We appear, therefore, to be entirely d'accord with one another. I was unable to keep my silence any longer, but this doesn't necessarily rule out the further possibility of a shared intervention on our part. But I feel that for Kracauer's own sake something has to be done. To accept his book in polite terms, or simply in silence, would be tantamount to abandoning him anyway. – Naturally enough, I would ask you to be very discreet about my letter to K., and in particular not to let Ernst know that you have read it; otherwise he would be sure to mention it tactlessly on some occasion or other. And please send it back to me when convenient. – It is interesting that you too suspected a certain revenge against the language here. I have often had the same feeling myself.

I find it quite difficult to respond to your enquiry about Berlioz. I am not really sure what to think about him myself. He is certainly a remarkable figure. A musician who accomplished something of decisive importance from the technical point of view: namely, the discovery of musical colour as a value in its own right. Before him, features of musical colour were more or less an effect of compositional structure, but with him they really become quite central. He discovered the various instruments as *valeurs*, equivalent to those involved in painting; he effectively created the kind of orchestra which Wagner, Liszt and Strauss immediately take for granted; he inaugurated the practice of orchestration as a specific discipline.[1] But with him, all this is always connected with a peculiar incapacity in the art of composition itself, which constantly borders on dilettantism and indeed often exceeds it. He has the worst musical manners in the world: all of the noise and spurious glitter of Wagnerism can be traced back to him, and there are also depths of triviality here which are quite remarkable and have remained characteristic of Strauss and this entire school of composing. As far as musical form is concerned, he introduced the principle of the *imprévu*: of sudden surprise, of new effects or *nouveauté*, precisely in the sense of your Arcades, and is always willing to sacrifice the logic of construction (his term) to this principle. All of his music hovers between the poles of the banal and the surprising: he was the first person to introduce the notion of the artistic 'sensation', probably earlier than in the case of literature (if I am not mistaken, his *Symphonie phantastique*[2] appeared before, or

190

very shortly after, the death of Beethoven). He is the only real representative of the eccentric 'clown' in the field of music; there are certain connections with Poe (though not with Baudelaire: there is absolutely nothing Parnassian about him). The strange thing is that, despite the banality, despite the closeness to the kind of orchestra you find in spas, despite the sudden leaps which make his music sound as though it had already begun to disintegrate in the very process of performance, despite all of this, every single bar can instantly be recognized as quite characteristic of him. There are many things, like the slow movement of the *Phantastique*, which are very remarkable and quite beautiful. I do not know his later works, but they would probably repay close study. He also wrote an autobiography that is well worth reading.[3] Historically speaking, he made an impact on his time like no one else, in a certain sense even greater than Wagner did on his; and yet hardly one properly completed work has survived. Perhaps these really rather spontaneous remarks will do a little to encourage you to explore his work.

Heartfelt greetings as ever,

Yours,

Teddie

Ernst Bloch can certainly be told that I repudiate the Offenbach piece entirely. Reading the book 'The Nightside of Paris' by Edmund B. d'Auvergne (London, undated, but probably around 1910), I came across the information on p. 56 that the inscription over the gate of the old Chat noir (Rue Victor-Massé) once read: Passant, sois moderne! Perhaps you could use this yourself.

1 *orchestration as a specific discipline*: cf. Hector Berlioz, *Grand traité d'instrumentation et d'orchestration modernes* (Paris 1843).

2 *his Symphonie phantastique*: Berlioz's op. 14 of 1830.

3 *an autobiography well worth reading*: i.e. the *Mémoires*, which Berlioz (1803–69) completed in 1864 and which were published posthumously in 1870.

80   BENJAMIN TO WIESENGRUND-ADORNO
     [PARIS,] 17.5.1937

Dear Teddie,

I have your letters of the 12th and 13th in front of me. The first and most important thing I gather from them is the expectation of seeing you in the early days of July. The dates you mention suggest that you have given yourself about eight days in Paris. Today I would merely ask you, and in good time I hope, not to allow this time to be cut short in any way by further arrangements, whatever they may be. For we will experience these days, I am quite sure of that, as very short anyway.

Klossowski's translation will be ready when you arrive; I shall deal with the list you mentioned.

We shall talk properly about the subject for my next piece of work when you are here. The question is too complex to elucidate by letter. Today I would merely like to assure you – which should be self-evident anyway – that the engagement between the dialectical and the archaic image still circumscribes, now as before, one of the decisive philosophical tasks of the 'Arcades'. But this also means that it is quite impossible for me to express my theses on this subject within the context of a short improvised *exposé*. On the contrary, I cannot possibly formulate these theses prior to a thorough critical examination of the theoreticians of the archaic image. But their writings – and this is something that I have only recently realized – are not represented in the *Bibliothèque Nationale*. Max's instructions had led me to postpone these bibliographical matters. I certainly do not regard these difficulties as remotely all-important, but they do require that a *clear* and positive decision be made within a matter of weeks.

In this regard, we shall have to discuss together to what extent the work on Baudelaire could, for its part, serve to promote the crucial methodological interests of the Arcades project. If I could put the whole question in a formula, in anticipation of our discussions, it would be this: as far as the organization of my work *in the long term* is concerned, I regard the work concerning the archaic image as the most pressing thing. But in the interests of producing a publishable manuscript in the more or less foreseeable future, I feel the work on Baudelaire, which would of course possess an importance of its own, seems like a good idea.

And now a couple of words about the things you sent me. I have just received your 'additional remarks'[1] this very moment. I only read a few of them before breaking off, since I would be denying myself considerable pleasure if I had to examine them too hastily. But I have already seen enough to feel certain that with these 'remarks' you have attained the greatest vividness of presentation imaginable. The gesture of your thinking is not that clumsy one of suddenly 'unmasking' your interlocutor, but rather that of a fleeting glance exposing truth. You have brilliantly described the archaic image of 'The Jew in Thorns',[2] and similarly the way in which the lights are extinguished at the end of a Debussy piece.[3] Your observation that 'the jazz subject leaves the Salon only to join the March'[4] seems to me to capture the political symptomatics of jazz perfectly. If you substitute the bar keeper for the jazz subject, he behaves in a similar way, in so far as

192

he throws himself straight into his SA uniform. The profound understanding with which you open your arms to the 'Puppchen'[5] already inspired me with admiration in Paris, as you will surely remember. And so forth: we shall have a lot to talk about here.

Many thanks for your remarks about Berlioz. I shall try and get hold of his autobiography some time. Your reference to the old inscription of the *Chat noir* has already found its way into my own papers.[6] Merci!

And in conclusion, I would like to share more than the fact that I agree with your judgement concerning the Offenbach piece and the way in which you have formulated it, but also the fact that I sympathize with the manner in which you propose to communicate your judgement to Kracauer. It is obvious that I would never have been able to attempt anything of the kind. But I can see how it was possible for you to do so, and this has also made my own position with regard to Kracauer a more defensible, and more clearly defined, one than I could hope (although I shall not say anything whatsoever to him to suggest that I have read your letter). At the same time, he has to know, and should know, that I am aware of the nature of your judgement. I have not seen him since reading the book, but I expect to be meeting him next week. – A few days later than that, and we will be seeing one another as well.

Heartfelt greetings until then,

Yours,
Walter

17 May 1937

1 *your 'additional remarks'*: see letter 74 and the relevant note.

2 *the archaic image of 'The Jew in Thorns'*: a sentence in the third of the 'Oxford Additions', which Adorno later deleted from the manuscript, read: 'The mythological model for jazz would be "The Jew in Thorns" who, riveted to a single spot, is forced to dance until he falls down dead.' – For the story 'Der Jude im Dorn', cf. *Kinder und Hausmärchen. Gesammelt durch die Brüder Grimm*, edited by Carl Helbling, vol. 2, 14th ed. (Zürich 1991), pp. 138–44.

3 *the way in which the lights are extinguished at the end of a Debussy piece*: cf. GS 17, p. 101.

4 *your observation that 'the jazz subject leaves the Salon only to join the March'*: cf. ibid., p. 102.

5 *the 'Puppchen'*: cf. ibid., pp. 103f, where Adorno dissects the popular song of the same title.

6 *your reference to the inscription . . . already found its way into my own papers*: cf. GS V [2], p. 687.

Dear Teddie,

I am writing this letter a day after your arrival in New York. I like to imagine that you will retain very fond memories of the crossing. And I hope that the days you have spent in New York since then have proved equally pleasurable.

By the time you receive these lines you will already have spoken about me to Max. And the contents of the accompanying letter[1] will therefore also be quite familiar to you.

In the first instance it seems to amount to this: Max and Pollock are both quite clear that 1,500 francs are insufficient as a financial minimum for anyone who is prepared to undertake the tasks the Institute is ready, fortunately enough, to set before me. The explicit recognition of this obvious economic fact in the accompanying letter suggests just how grateful I should be for further assistance.

In addition, I do not want to lose sight of the fact that any attempt to regularize my financial situation on the basis of the French franc does not, perhaps, strike me as particularly desirable at the present time. Since you left Paris, there has been growing uncertainty about the continuing outlook for the French franc. Even if it does remain stable, it does not look as if prices will be able to remain so.

Perhaps you will recall, my dear Teddie, what I said to you that time in the hall des Littré: there is no need for you to demonstrate your solidarity with me. That we both know this, and that the one shares the knowledge of the other here, proves to be of enormous value now that the particular importance which attaches to your own voice in my affairs and interests is clearly visible.

Pollock's letter, which was written before you were able to speak in this way on my behalf, leaves me a certain space for manœuvre, and perhaps thereby lends a deeper chance of resonance to your own words as well.

Let me conclude with this hope, which also harbours my heartfelt best wishes to you.

Yours,
Walter

15 June
Paris XIV
23 rue Bénard

---

1 *the accompanying letter*: the letter from Friedrich Pollock to Benjamin, which is mentioned below in this letter to Adorno and which has not survived.

Barbizon – Plaza – Hotel

101 west 58th street . . . central park south . . . new york

17 June 1937

Dear Walter,

Just a quick line to let you know that things are going well for you.
I cannot give you any definite information yet, but the situation seems
to be developing in precisely the way I expected. Especially with
regard to the hierarchy of the three contributors[1] in question. Since
there is not much hope for the other two, so much the more positive
the atmosphere looks for you.

My own affairs are satisfactory as well. I can say – in confidence! –
that I shall stay in Europe for another year or two in order to oversee
the management of the Institute's affairs there. This arrangement
should end up suiting all of us.

The journey was pleasant, but my stay here even more so. It is all
certainly very tiring. There is a monstrous amount of work to do –
hence my brevity here.

I shall be sailing back on the Normandie on the 30th. It does not
look as though I shall be able to visit Germany[2] any more.

With heartfelt greetings,

Yours,

Teddie

1 *the hierarchy of the three contributors*: Adorno is referring to Benjamin,
Kracauer and Sohn-Rethel; cf. the following letter.

2 *It does not look as though I shall be able to visit Germany*: Adorno did
not in fact return to Germany before the war.

FRENCH LINE   à bord, le 2. juillet, 1937
                                               'Normandie'

Dear Walter,

Let me keep you informed about things today during this my return
crossing.

And first of all to financial matters. There is now a firm intention to do everything possible to assist your situation. At the same time, however, there is also a prevailing *general* tendency at present to cut down on the enormously overburdened budget. After the last special payment of 2,000 French francs, it was therefore impossible for me to get Pollock to increase the amount to the sum I desired[1] immediately, although Horkheimer was quite positive about the proposal and everyone else supported me as well (including Löwenthal, who, I would like to stress, has been extremely loyal in all matters relating to you and me). Nor is there any question of ill will on Pollock's part, but simply an expression of his concern as head of Institute finances – a concern which I, too, have begun to experience. But I believe that I can assure you – *in confidence* and in an unauthorized capacity, albeit with the very *strongest* of reasons – that from 1 January they will agree to an arrangement[2] which corresponds largely – if not entirely! – with my hopes. In particular, I have succeeded in convincing the Institute that the whole system of 'one-off' payments, for which Pollock has a financially induced weakness, cannot really be permanently sustained: it just does not give you that feeling of security which the prosecution of your work properly requires, and what the Institute manages to save in that way cannot determine the whole course of its future policy. So things are really looking quite good; it is simply a question of balancing the books for another couple of months. Perhaps we can even succeed in getting Else involved. I have forged a secret agreement with Max.

In connection with the idea of some such definite arrangement, there are certain demands with regard to the Institute which will have to be met. In the first place, there was so much more interest in the Baudelaire than there was in Jung or Klages, that in your *own* interests I really did not feel that I ought to insist on the matter. If the Baudelaire piece could be produced in effective form soon, that would certainly prove a major advantage in every respect. And then there is also the question of the journal's review section to be considered. I shall only be able to undertake the fundamental reorganization of the way we do French reviews when I get to Paris (*a matter of some discretion*!!!); our guidelines[3] have already been accepted in principle. More important at the moment is your own more *intensive* collaboration in the review section. It would certainly be highly desirable if you could see your way to writing *more* reviews – even quite independently of deadlines; you would be granted the greatest freedom in the selection of material, German and French alike. But it would also be advantageous – and the same demand holds for me too – if you could prepare one or two quite substantial 'exemplary reviews' for each issue of the journal (like Max's current review of Jaspers,[4] for example); the ultimate intention here is to bring the reviews appearing in *German* qualitatively into line with the standard of the other substantive *German* contributions. This is a matter of considerable importance. I would also ask you to keep an eye out for highly qualified potential French contributors. With respect to the initial selection here, we shall certainly not be able to ignore Aron, who is, incidentally, already beginning to be something of a problem; but we cannot leave this entirely to him anyway. I have mentioned Caillois[5] and Bataille[6] (?); Klossowski has to be reminded about an essay 'De Sade à Fourier'[7] which he promised us some time back (unless, of course, Max himself decides to write the major essay on Sade).[8] I have also met Etiemble, who made an *excellent* impression upon me (particularly from the political point of view), as he also did upon Max: can't we mobilize him as well, Groethuysen *à part*, in some way or other? Please give these matters a little thought, without actually starting on anything until I get to Paris at the end of July.

And here I come to the egotistical part of my epistle. For in a highly official capacity, I shall be representing the Institute at the Congress of Logical Positivists[9] and at the major Philosophy Congress[10] that will follow – and will also have to write a detailed report of the proceedings. It would be a great relief to me if you could attend as well, and would please Max, too, if you could offer me some assistance in the business. Is this a lot to ask? I don't know the exact dates involved as yet, but you will be able to find this out from Brillo. Many, many thanks. I think Felizitas will also be coming along.

The publication of the Fuchs article will be delayed once again, albeit for a reason which it would be very difficult to challenge. For F. is currently engaged in negotiations concerning the acquisition of his collection, and we do not want to prejudice the proceedings in any way (Pollock's idea). All the same, it might be a good idea if you could also write him a couple of friendly lines in this connection. In San Remo, which is where I hope you are, you are certainly well out of firing range.

'Mass Art under Monopoly Capitalism':[11] I can organize the thing in such a way that it will not involve any *substantial* increase in costs – or much further work on the part of the small numbers of Institute staff. And you will only be able to take over the detective story, for example, as long as it does *not* interfere with your work on the Arcades or the Baudelaire material; Max will *hardly* be in a position to write about film etc. Today I would like to ask you for some suggestions regarding the following subjects:

197

The detective story
Neue Sachlichkeit [The New Realism]
The art trade
Radio
Illustrated journals (international)
Film in the narrower sense

The only potential collaborators at present are Bloch and Giedion:[12] I do *not* wish to approach Kracauer before his piece on propaganda[13] is finished. It would be a precise question of commissioning *essays* rather than offering grants; the relevant plans would have to be submitted to me first; payment would only follow on receipt of the completed manuscripts ready for printing. There would also have to be the possibility of publishing the essays in the journal *and* in book form. There is *no* more question of Schoen participating here than in *anything else* pertaining to the Institute (discretion is especially required in his regard). I regard the success of this plan as an extremely *urgent* matter.

My own affairs have been coming along satisfactorily. I shall effectively be in charge of the Institute's affairs in Europe over the next couple of years. But in order to spare any difficult situations, it would be best if that is *not* explicitly seen to be the case, and if no questions of rank or status are raised. I shall be living in London, but I shall now be coming to Paris and Geneva much more frequently than before. As I said, I have also felt the effect of cut-backs at the Institute, but I hope that I shall be able to manage with Gretel. After another two years I shall probably go to New York. There is not much I can report about the city: your interpretation of the old saying that 'Once is Never'[14] has proved entirely correct here. The atmosphere at the Institute is *extremely* agreeable. The real difficulty for us here (for Max and especially for me) is the revisionism inspired by Fromm and its tendency to produce factional strife. Max has written a very important essay on the place of theory,[15] and with an oppositional standpoint with regard to the East for the very first time; Löwenthal's piece on Hamsun[16] represents good progress; the appearance of my essay on Mannheim is now in question again because of certain objections I have raised myself.

I was able to procure a little help for Sohn-Rethel.[17] Collaboration in the journal is still open as far as Kracauer is concerned, but any really *firm* or long-term connection is out of the question.

You can reach me most easily by mail at the Albemarle Court Hotel, 18 Leinster Gardens, London W2, where I shall be staying for a few days at least. – I would be delighted to hear something from you soon. Hopefully you will be feeling much restored by now.[18] I

198

find the truly restful sea voyage is the only way of replenishing my energies for work. Please pass on my greetings to Dora Sophie for me.
Heartfelt greetings until very soon,

Yours as ever,
Teddie

Kolisch has arrived in New York on time. – Would you be good enough to send Max my 'Ensemble' piece,[19] together with a request for its safe return?

1 *increase the amount to the sum I desired*: Adorno seems to have regarded 120 US dollars as the necessary minimum, as appears from letter 92, where Benjamin describes the contribution of 80 US dollars, which he received as a monthly payment from November 1937 onwards, as *approximately three-quarters of what you originally envisaged*.

2 *from 1 January they will agree to an arrangement*: in fact, the new arrangement already came into effect in November 1937; cf. letter 92 and the relevant note.

3 *the journal's review section / our guidelines*: cf. GS III, pp. 601f.

4 *Max's review of Jaspers*: cf. Max Horkheimer, 'Bemerkungen zu Jaspers' "Nietzsche"', in the *Zeitschrift für Sozialforschung* 6 (1937), pp. 407–14; now in Horkheimer, *Gesammelte Schriften*, vol. 4, pp. 226–35.

5 *Caillois*: Roger Caillois (1913–78), who graduated from the *École Normale Supérieure*, founded the *Collège de Sociologie* together with Georges Bataille and Michel Leiris in 1937; Benjamin occasionally attended the events organized there.

6 *Bataille*: Georges Bataille (1897–1962) managed to conceal a quantity of Benjamin's papers after the latter's flight from Paris in May 1940, especially the 'Notes and Materials' for the Arcades project, in the *Bibliothèque Nationale*, where he worked.

7 *Klossowski / 'De Sade à Fourier'*: nothing by Klossowski actually appeared in the Institute journal; Klossowski did eventually publish an essay with the title 'Sade et Fourier' in 1974.

8 *unless . . . Max decides to write the major essay on Sade*: Horkheimer never wrote this projected essay; cf., however, the chapter 'Juliette or the Enlightenment and Morality', in *Dialectic of Enlightenment*.

9 *the Congress of Logical Positivists*: the 'Conference of the International Congress for Unified Science' took place in Paris between 29 and 31 July. Adorno informed Horkheimer about the discussions which he and Benjamin had with participants at the Congress in a report he composed together with Benjamin.

10 *the major Philosophy Congress*: the IXth International Congress of Philosophy took place in honour of Descartes, whose *Discours de la méthode* had

appeared 300 years before. – The opening section of the report which Adorno and Benjamin composed for Horkheimer reveals something of the general atmosphere: 'The *Congrès Descartes* is something of a mass event. The number of people attending is said to be around 800 (active and passive participants). More than 280 papers will be given: one from each speaker. The papers are organized in such a way that in the mornings, on average 3 papers of a general representative character are presented in plenum; in the afternoons, about 8 or 9 papers are presented simultaneously within the various section areas. Under these conditions it is quite impossible to produce a report about the contents of all the papers, but it is also unnecessary, since a great number of the contributions were already available in written form to the participants before simply being read out (something which contributed considerably to the prevailing sense of demoralization). [...] The discussions proceeded in a similarly unreal fashion, and were marked by a complementary combination of a Babylonian confusion of languages, on the one hand, and a generalized feeling of solidarity on the other.' (Unpublished; Adorno's literary remains contains a copy of the typescript.)

11 *'Mass Art under Monopoly Capitalism'*: Adorno was planning to publish a volume of collected pieces by different authors under this title, including Benjamin's essay on 'The Work of Art in the Age of Mechanical Reproduction', Adorno's own essay 'On Jazz', and a number of other essays on the critique of the culture industry still to be commissioned. Adorno had already encouraged Kracauer to write a major piece on architecture in January 1937. Horkheimer had agreed to write the general introduction to the volume, but the project was never realized because of the deterioration of the Institute's financial circumstances.

12 *Giedion*: Siegfried Giedion (1888–1968), Swiss art historian, First Secretary of the CIAM (*Congrès Internationaux d'Architecture Moderne*) in 1928, Professor at Harvard University from 1938; his book *Bauen in Frankreich. Eisen, Eisenbeton.* [French Architecture in the Medium of Iron and Concrete] had appeared in 1928.

13 *Kracauer / his piece on propaganda*: see letter 57 and the relevant note.

14 *your interpretation of the old saying 'Once is Never'*: cf. Benjamin's *Denkbild* [Intellectual Cameo] with this title, which was first published in 1934 (cf. GS IV [1], pp. 433f).

15 *Max has written a very important essay on the place of theory*: cf. Max Horkheimer, 'Traditionelle und kritische Theorie', in the *Zeitschrift für Sozialforschung* 6, issue 2 (1937), pp. 245–92 now in Horkheimer, *Gesammelte Schriften*, vol. 4 (Frankfurt a.M. 1988), pp. 162–216.

16 *Löwenthal's piece on Hamsun*: see letter 74 and the relevant note.

17 *a little help for Sohn-Rethel*: for a year the *Institute of Social Research* contributed the sum of £60 to the grant which the 'Academic Assistance Council' had offered Sohn-Rethel (cf. *Briefwechsel Adorno/Sohn-Rethel*, p. 65).

200

18 *Hopefully you will be feeling much restored by now*: Benjamin was on vacation in San Remo.

19 *my 'Ensemble' piece*: cf. Hektor Rottweiler [Adorno's pseudonym], 'Ensemble', in the Viennese music journal '23', 15.9.1937, nr. 31/33, pp. 15–21; now in GS 16, pp. 275–80 and GS 18, pp. 39f. – The original edition of the piece bears the dedication: 'For Detlef Holz'.

84 BENJAMIN TO WIESENGRUND-ADORNO
    SAN REMO, 10.7.1937

Dear Teddie,

I must begin by saying how pleased I am that you will be staying in Europe for the moment. Let us hope that Felizitas does not find the whole business too difficult. As you will know, I am absolutely convinced that this arrangement is extremely welcome from the substantive point of view. Thus the bridge to Europe will not be broken after all, but rather fortified!

I think I can also congratulate myself on the final outcome. I am certain that the epistemological foundations of the Arcades can be laid during the next two years. And you know how much I count upon our continued discussions in this connection.

There were some clouds hovering over your report. I hope these do not affect the payments due to you, and that Felizitas, as I believe, will now be able to look forward to the future with you without concern. The postponing of the essay on Jung in favour of the work on Baudelaire is a kind of cloud, on the other hand. Realization of the intention so important to both of us, namely, to develop the epistemological foundations of the Arcades as soon as possible, will now inevitably be delayed. Your news arrived to find me in the midst of intensive and by no means unfruitful study of Jung. When you visit me in Paris, you will be able to look at the extremely instructive volumes of the 'Eranos-Jahrbücher', the official organ of Jung's circle. And we will talk about the Baudelaire business.

If the financial part of your report clearly revealed these clouds, I was not really very surprised. You will gather that from the few lines with which I passed on Pollock's letter. But I shall concentrate on the rather brighter parts of your letter. The first concerns the future arrangement of the money question. I can only hope with the very greatest hope I can muster that it will all be settled by the New Year. I don't think I can rely on the present arrangement for much longer; as a result of the massive price increases here and the devaluation of the franc, my financial position, solely with regard to the current fixed arrangement,[1] has become a lot weaker in the last few months

201

than it was nine months ago. And here the one-off payments have certainly helped me to regain my balance, but not much more than this. I also regard it as a rather unfortunate circumstance that postponing the arrangement for a regular fixed payment could mean uncoupling it from the state of the French franc if its stability has not been restored before that time. Thirdly and finally, I shall place my hopes for the coming winter months in your 'conspiracy'. For indeed things will be more or less impossible here without a little Camorra-like fraternal assistance!

Coming now to the question touching my collaboration in the review section of the Institute journal, nothing could be more pleasing to me than the prospect of dealing with individual books in a much more detailed manner. Löwenthal had earlier rather given me to understand that this was not exactly required; on the other hand, as you know, it is the most appropriate way for me to work. As a first trial in this respect, I would suggest a review of Brunot's book,[2] 'The French Language in the Age of Revolution'. If I am not mistaken, the new issue of the journal will contain my review of Maublanc's anthology of Fourier's writings,[3] which already approaches the maximum length for these things. We will easily be able to sort out the questions arising here in discussion when we meet. The question about potential French participants is rather more difficult. We tend to be faced here with the inflexibility of an orthodox left intelligentsia crippled by the Russian developments on the one hand, and with the often unconscious fascist sympathies of the more independent writers on the other.

Similar problems also arise outside France. You only have to consider Giedion, whom you mentioned as a possible contributor for the collection 'Mass Art in the Age of Monopoly Capitalism'. Giedion is certainly a major talent, as his book *Architecture in France* shows. But he could only be approached as a contributor if we can find out more about his current views. – It will certainly be no easy matter to organize the collection. As far as the theme of 'Illustrated journals' is concerned, Grete de Francesco has the technical and professional expertise required. Let us wait for her new book[4] The *Charlatan* to appear in order to see if she has the necessary ability.

You write that you got on rather well in conversation with Etiemble. I felt very much the same way when I spoke to him. His sense of political independence is, fortunately, known to me as well. I can see no reason why he could not contribute to the review section either. My experience with young Frenchmen like him, however, has also convinced me of the importance of maintaining a certain reserve in their regard. You will certainly be able to tell me more about the difficulties with Aron when we see one other.

202

Which brings me to our imminent reunion. I hope it will not interfere with your arrangements if our meeting this time does not coincide exactly with your arrival in Paris. Stefan has to sit his final summer examination on 26 July and thus will not be arriving here until the 28th. It is extremely important that I get to spend at least a few days with him. As far as our own meeting is concerned, I certainly hope that we shall be able to spend a good week together in Paris. Klossowski will find out about the date of the Congress from Brill.

As far as the Fuchs piece is concerned, I am, unfortunately, rather pessimistic. The 'crucial negotiations' you mention have been going on for four years now; and there is nothing to suggest that they will come to an end before the Third Reich itself. Of course, it is part of people's tactics never to come to a final decision in such things. I am not sure whether Pollock's decision to postpone my essay arises from a desire on his part or that of Fuchs. Until I know that, I cannot really write to Fuchs myself; and if the former is indeed the case, then I would not like to write anyway. For then I would only be the messenger of bad news. – It is hardly consolation to see that our two essays, instead of appearing together, will at least be failing to appear together.

Have you visited Leyda[5] in New York yet? I assume you will hardly have had the time.

Has Max read the introduction to the Jochmann piece?[6] – I will only be able to send your 'Ensemble' piece to him when I get to Paris.

My former wife returns your friendly greetings with her own.

A heartfelt handshake from me and welcome back to Europe,

Yours,
Walter

10 July 1937
San Remo
Villa Verde

1 *the current fixed arrangement*: Benjamin's monthly grant of 1,500 francs.

2 *a review of Brunot's book*: for Benjamin's review of Ferdinand Brunot, *Histoire de la langue française des origines à 1900*, vol. 9, part 2 (Paris 1937), cf. the *Zeitschrift für Sozialforschung* 8, issue 1/2 (1939), pp. 290–2; now in GS III, pp. 561–4.

3 *anthology of Fourier's writings*: cf. Felix Armand and René Maublanc, *Fourier*, 2 vols. (Paris 1937); for Benjamin's review, cf. the *Zeitschrift für Sozialforschung* 6, issue 3 (1937), pp. 699f; now in GS III, pp. 509–11.

4 *Grete de Francesco / her new book*: the Austrian writer and journalist Grete de Francesco worked for the *Frankfurter Zeitung*; her book *Die Macht des Charlatans* appeared in Basel in 1937.

5 *Leyda*: Jay Leyda (born 1910) had graduated from Eisenstein's class at the Moscow School of Film; in 1936 he became Assistant Curator of the newly founded film department of 'The Museum of Art'. – In December 1936 Leyda had made enquiries at the *Institute of Social Research* concerning Benjamin's 'The Work of Art in the Age of Mechanical Reproduction' and announced his plan to translate the piece into English (cf. GS I [3], pp. 1029f). Benjamin wrote to Leyda on 17 May 1937 and offered him the German and the French versions of the essay as the basis for his translation. The plan never came to fruition.

6 *Max / the introduction to the Jochmann piece*: for Horkheimer's attitude to Benjamin's 'Introduction to the Jochmann Essay', cf. GS II [3], p. 1395.

85 BENJAMIN TO WIESENGRUND-ADORNO
    [SAN REMO, AROUND THE MIDDLE OF JULY 1937]

Dear Teddie,

You may well have received an incomprehensible telegram[1] from me recently. It was sent to your name at the Institute's Paris address and requests you to call me in San Remo.

The reason for the telegram was a communication from Brill, who notified me on 13 July that the Congress[2] was taking place that very week. That is why I assumed you would be in Paris and therefore sent the telegram there.

I received Brill's information with considerable consternation, since I had spoken to Herman Reichenbach[3] in Paris before my departure and he had told me that the Congress was planned for the end of the month.

In the last few days we have had a letter from Stefan, which gives us to understand that he will not be arriving here until 4 August. This has dashed my hope of seeing him before I return to Paris. On the other hand, I really cannot miss the opportunity of speaking with him. I have no option but to return here after the end of the Congress. This double trip naturally upsets my plans quite a lot. But it also means that we will still have all the time we want to discuss the Paris matters. I shall be arriving in Paris on the 28th at the latest, and hope to have received some word from you by then. If I am not expected to pick you up at the railway station, then I shall certainly get to see you at the Littré. Please write to me, as soon as possible, at the rue Bénard to let me know the exact time of your arrival, and your address if you are not going to stay at the Littré. I also think it would be a good idea for you to book a room in advance, since there are lots of similar congresses taking place in Paris at the moment.

Till we meet again very soon,

Yours,
Walter

1 *an incomprehensible telegram*: this has not survived.

2 *the Congress*: the Congress of Logical Positivists mentioned in letter 83.

3 *Herman Reichenbach*: the musicologist Herman Reichenbach (1898–1958) was the brother of the philosopher Hans Reichenbach (1891–1953), who was participating in the Congress along with Rudolf Carnap and Otto Neurath.

86 BENJAMIN TO WIESENGRUND-ADORNO
SAN REMO, 21.8.1937

Dear Teddie,

I have just received news from Brill that Max will be in Paris between 31 August and 6 September. I am travelling back there myself in a week's time. The possibility of visiting him in Geneva is something that I would only consider if the reunion I am looking forward to in Paris does not work out.

In the meantime, the project I was counting on[1] for the anxious winter months ahead has come to nothing. Scholem's wife[2] has fallen gravely ill in her home country – Poland – and he himself is about to go and see her. I don't really know where to turn.

The first thing I broached after my return was your 'Berg' piece.[3] It is quite easy for me to express the crucial significance which reading it has had for me: you have clarified my suspicion that the overwhelming impression which Wozzeck made on me that evening in Berlin[4] revealed an inner involvement that I was hardly conscious of, even though it can be specified down to the last detail.

Amongst the recurrent themes of these studies, that concerning Berg's relationship to the tradition struck me in a particularly forceful way, not least where you build on your interpretation of Mahler. The basic conception here: how the almost indescribable technical labour of Schönberg's pupil brings the tradition of the nineteenth century to rest in the name of the master and thereby sounds its final lament, is as convincing to me as Berg's music itself proved to be, despite the fact that I lacked all ready access to it.

I am trying to formulate the matter as best I can; but I feel that for all its clumsiness, the little I have said may express more than some fuller statement of agreement that would betray nothing of that peculiar haste with which I tend to address those areas on which I do not really feel competent to dwell. You are capable, on the other hand, of penetrating to the very heart of the labyrinthine structure of the work, of gradually unfolding the crimson thread of an another's life, and this is precisely your gift. Reich's contributions,[5] on the other hand, are simply the blind corners which no labyrinth can do without.

But I would not wish to curtail even my provisional response to your work here without telling you just how clearly I perceived central and animating concerns of my own thought in your gloss on *Wozzeck*[6] on page 48. I would particularly like to speak to you at the earliest opportunity about this passage and that concerning the opening up of time. Then you will be able to explain to me the concept of the 'tiniest transition', a concept which I myself would rather like to borrow from the language of musical composition (if that makes sense?). For the rest, your interpretation of Berg's Wine Aria[7] alone amply confirms that we share a lot of common ground in this book, which strikes me – albeit through a glass darkly – as one of the finest things you have written.

Along with the copy of the Berg, you will also be receiving, as requested, the proofs of Grete de Francesco's book on the charlatan. I am quite taken with the unusual theme of the book itself, and with the combination of carefulness and perceptiveness with which the author has approached the material. Unfortunately, it is rather disappointing in other respects. It basically suffers throughout from the unfortunate idea of presenting the charlatan as spiritually akin to the dictators of today, and imagines that criticizing the one is tantamount to scourging the other. The reasoning behind this is politically null and void, and only prevents her account from even approaching the most fundamental and interesting aspects of the figure of the charlatan. I think I am hardly wrong in assuming that even the publishers who commissioned the book would not have been unduly concerned if it had also revealed certain positive features in the phenomenon of the charlatan. Instead, the book is grounded in a kind of gloomy moralizing which no longer permits the appearance of any specific historical or local colour – even if such a thing were remotely intended in the first place. The inadequacy of the entire treatment is most tangibly revealed in the chapter on automation. If Ernst Bloch had ever written his 'Noble Couple',[8] we would certainly have received something rather more illuminating about the charlatan. – I don't need to say that the book has done nothing to reduce my sympathy for Grete de Francesco. But it looks questionable to me whether we shall actually be able to rely on her with regard to the more difficult projects. –

As far as Stefan is concerned, there is an imminent decision to be made, one which is causing me some anxiety – namely, whether he should attempt to sit his final school examinations. It is not clear to me whether the great difficulties which are involved here spring from his obsession with doing something 'practical', or from lack of concentration and application. But the question remains to be addressed all the same. Insubstantial though the immediate advantage of taking his exams may be, considerable disadvantage may arise if he cannot provide evidence of the qualifications later on. Stefan's health, and even the state of his nerves, seems to have improved a great deal.

I am sure that Felizitas is already with you. I hope that we shall all be able to meet in Paris before the wedding.[9] Please extend my heartfelt greetings to her.

Yours,

Walter

21 August 1937
San Remo
Villa Verde

1 *the project I was counting on*: a planned visit to Scholem in Palestine.

2 *Scholem's wife*: Scholem's second wife Fania, who was related to Sigmund Freud.

3 *your 'Berg' piece*: the monograph on Berg first mentioned in letter 44.

4 *that evening in Berlin*: see letter 41 and the relevant note.

5 *Reich's contributions*: Willi Reich wrote the pieces on 'Wozzeck', 'Lulu' and the Violin Concerto.

6 *your gloss on Wozzeck*: cf. GS 13, p. 409.

7 *your interpretation of Berg's Wine Aria*: see letter 49 and the relevant note.

8 *Bloch / his 'Noble Couple'*: cf. Bloch's *Das Prinzip Hoffnung* [The Principle of Hope], where several pages are dedicated to the 'Noble Couple'.

9 *Felizitas / the wedding*: the marriage between Adorno and Gretel Karplus took place in Oxford on 8 September. Max Horkheimer and Redvers Opie were witnesses; see the following letter.

87   THEODOR AND GRETEL WIESENGRUND-ADORNO TO BENJAMIN
    LONDON, 13.9.1937

21, PALACE COURT   13 September 1937.
HYDE PARK. W2.
BAYSWATER 3738.

Dear Walter,
    Your silence hangs over us like a black storm cloud, and this little slip of paper has no other desire in life than to act as a lightning conductor. I hope that the metaphorical impossibility of disarming lightning with paper does not correspond to the real one of dispelling your anger.

207

And I can see two reasons for such anger. Firstly, the fact that I have taken so long to respond to your letter about the Berg book. My silence is due neither to any lack of sympathy with what you said, nor of gratitude for the fact that you said it. The complex reasons for this sin result entirely from the complex circumstances of another one: namely, my marriage and everything that was connected with it, and indeed still is – like moving in to our new place around the middle of October. For today let me simply say that the concept of the tiniest transition in music does not properly belong to me – nor indeed to the standard language of musicology. It was Wagner who defined music as 'the art of transition', and there is no question that precisely those aspects of Berg's general procedure do point back to him. But of course, it is merely the infinitesimal reduction and compression of such transitions which is quite specific to him.

I must ask you for a little patience yet with regard to receiving a personal copy. I am expecting them to issue the book in Germany any day now, and it will be a great relief if I can manage to get all my copies for friends from Germany itself. Incidentally, neither the copy I lent you, nor indeed the proofs of Francesco's book, have actually arrived. Perhaps this is due to the change of address. I will make some enquiries and would ask you to do the same if you can.

The marriage took place in truly total privacy on the 8th – and in Oxford, where my friend Opie invited us to lunch in Magdalen College. Apart from him, Gretel's mother and my parents, no one else was present except Max and Maidon. No one else knew anything about it, and we could not let you know the details without producing more personal difficulties than the occasion warranted, to which of course we ascribe no significance beyond that of merely formal legitimation. I implore you to regard the matter as it really is and without taking offence: for that would be doing us an injustice. We both belong to you, and we have left Max in no doubt about the fact either; and indeed, I feel that I can now include him in the sentiment as well.

Now you will certainly have plenty of opportunity to speak to him as much as you like. As far as the question of Baudelaire or Jung is concerned, he has explained that he would prefer to have the Baudelaire first. But I am convinced that the Jung piece could prove to be your next essay after all, as long as you explicate the various aspects of the idea to him and point out its methodological significance for the Arcades. The Mannheim piece will almost certainly be turned into a gloss like that on Jaspers. Gretel was greatly opposed, by the way, to publishing it in its present form anyway. Unfortunately, Max has not had the chance to read the essay on Husserl[1]

208

yet. In the meantime, I myself have only written a few critical pieces,[2] including a fairly substantial one for the Cassirer Festschrift, together with a lot of notes on Wagner.[3]

It is quite possible, though by no means certain, that I shall be coming to Paris sometime during the next ten days, and indeed with the express intention of having a discussion with you and Max together.[4] Whether we can manage it depends entirely on him and how much time he has at his disposal. I do not have to tell you how pleased I would be if this works out.

I have already spoken to him about Mlle Monnier;[5] please don't forget to discuss this with him. As far as the acquisition of books is concerned, there is a certain difficulty, since we may already have the number required. In the first instance, Max will put 1,000 French francs at your disposal for procuring the appropriate books. They should all go to the Institute library, and Max thinks it best if the acquisition chiefly concerns books relevant to the Arcades. If the sum in question is all used up, we will have to take stock.

With regard to the proofs of the Institute journal, Max suggests the following procedure as a way of simplifying matters: all the proofs should come to me as the person responsible for the journal here in Europe. I will then send you everything which I think will be important to you, you pass on any comments and observations to me, which I will then send on to New York with my own as well. That will save time collating material – and spare you from having to read certain things like the English essays by Neurath and Lazarsfeld[6] . . . I imagine that you are quite happy with this solution of ours. It will ensure that there are no more delays like those involved in the Hamsun piece.[7] – Max has now abandoned the idea of sending Leo[8] to see you in Paris on a kind of apprenticeship. Perhaps you will be able to speak to him about this. I do not believe I am committing an indiscretion if I tell you now that Max's reasons have nothing to do with me or you.

I have also spoken to him at length about our legal representative. Max has got the picture of the situation, but also has good reason, so it seems to me, to retain his services. Perhaps Max will be able to do something to smooth the way for further communication a little. He tells me that Brill has on occasion adopted the tone of 'I insist . . .' towards him and Pollock in just the same way he does with you and me. But he also says that Brill expresses the most enthusiastic opinion of your work in every letter he writes. Max believes that he is basically driven by an excessive tendency to devote himself to other people, something which he then attempts to compensate for by being difficult. I think the best thing is for you yourself to discuss the whole

209

business with Max as openly as I have myself. And anyway, it really looks as though the affair will soon lose its sting, if your external circumstances really are as we imagine them to be.

We had hoped to go on holiday for a few weeks. But there is no prospect of that now, given the idiotic problems we have had with accommodation and everything connected with it – and we might just as well freeze here as in Devonshire, and we now have ample opportunity to do so. At the moment I feel like the proverbial ass stranded between two bundles of hay: I have so much work to do I don't know where to begin. One of the first things I have planned to do is to undertake the systematic study of *Capital*. – Apart from producing my English dissertation,[9] the longer version of the Husserl piece and the Wagner book, I am also planning to write an essay on determinism.[10] – Max himself has decided, fortunately enough, to write the book on the bourgeois character[11] instead of Fromm.

Finally a minor request: could you possibly exchange a friendly word with him about the Husserl piece? The fate of none of my writings has ever concerned me as much as this one does.

That's all for today – hopefully à bientôt, with the Arcades for company, in a quiet little pub in Armagnac.

In friendship as always,

Yours,
Teddie

Dear Detlef,

The rebus is your category rather than mine. I am unable to solve the riddle which your silence poses for me, and in the meantime it is all proving just as ambiguous as allegorical interpretation is according to your theory. Won't you offer me a little help as I tumble through your images? I would be very grateful for that, and equally to hear something from you generally. Lots of love, your

Felicitas

1 *the essay on Husserl*: the piece in question was finished at the end of July; see letter 72 and the relevant note.

2 *a few critical pieces*: that on Krenek's book (see letter 74 and the relevant note), that on Kracauer's book on Offenbach (see letter 75 and the relevant note), and that included in the *Festschrift* for Cassirer, entitled *Philosophy and History. Essays Presented to Ernst Cassirer*, ed. Raymond Klibansky and H. J. Paton (London 1936). cf. *Zeitschrift für Sozialforschung* 6, issue 3 (1937), pp. 657–61; now in GS 20 [1], pp. 221–8.

3 *notes on Wagner*: during his stay in London, Horkheimer had negotiated with Adorno concerning the idea of the latter writing a study of Wagner;

cf. Adorno's *Versuch über Wagner* [An Essay on Wagner], some chapters of which appeared in the *Zeitschrift für Sozialforschung* under the title 'Fragments on Wagner'; now in GS 13, pp. 7–148.

4 *a discussion with you and Max together*: Adorno's projected trip to Europe did not take place.

5 *Mlle Monnier*: on Benjamin's recommendation, Horkheimer wished to establish closer relations between writer and bookseller Adrienne Monnier and the *Institute of Social Research*, not least in order to counteract the missing presence of the *Zeitschrift* in Paris, and to meet the lack of qualified French contributors to the journal.

6 *English essays of Neurath and Lazarsfeld*: see letter 74 and the relevant note.

7 *the Hamsun piece*: see letter 74 and the relevant note.

8 *Leo*: i.e. Leo Löwenthal.

9 *my English dissertation*: see letter 72 and the relevant note.

10 *essay on determinism*: Adorno never composed this essay.

11 *a book on the bourgeois character*: the book remained unwritten.

88   WIESENGRUND-ADORNO TO BENJAMIN
      LONDON, 22.9.1937

                                              21 Palace Court
                                              London W 2.
                                              22 September 1937.

Dear Walter,
    Your lines[1] were a source of great pleasure to us. We were becoming rather anxious about your silence and are all the happier to learn that it harboured no special negative significance. In the meantime, and after a most remarkable postal delay, the Berg piece and the Francesco proofs have actually arrived – the stamps were all torn off. Thank you very much for both. The Berg piece cannot be advertised or reviewed in Germany, but it can be sold there; so I hope very soon to have some copies here at my disposal, and naturally I shall set aside the first one specially for you. I have read about one-third of the Francesco book. Without wishing to ignore the culture and industry that have gone into the work, I cannot but share your own view that there is really little question of considering the author for our planned book. Above all on account of a naivety in its philosophical approach to history, which constantly reduces the figure of

211

the charlatan to the dimension of 'the universally human'. And that is precisely why this crudely fashioned network of analogies proves so impotent where Hitler is concerned.

I have written to Dudow[2] in some detail; perhaps he gave you the letter himself. I also sent the letter, along with Dudow's essay, to Max, and have just heard from him today to say that he has sent them both on to New York. As far as Dudow is concerned, I am also extremely pessimistic about our planned book, although I did not express any firm decision in the letter.

In the meantime we have both read Caillois' *La Mante*[3] with the greatest care. It struck me quite positively in a sense – positively because, despite the fact that he denigrates psychoanalysis with a frivolousness worthy of Prinzhorn,[4] Caillois is not interested in dissolving the myths within the immanent sphere of consciousness, or in reducing their significance through an appeal to 'symbolism', but is really seeking to grasp their actuality. Of course, this is a kind of materialism he shares with Jung, and certainly with Klages. And unfortunately he shares more than that. Namely, that anti-historical, and indeed crypto-fascistic, faith in nature which is hostile to all social analysis, which eventually leads him towards a kind of 'national community' [Volksgemeinschaft] based on biology and imagination. Of course, it would also correspond to our own approach, to shatter the reified separation of spheres like the biological on one side and the socio-historical on the other. But I fear that Caillois himself unwittingly and rather naively leaves this reification in place, in so far as he certainly introduces a historical dynamic into biology, but then fails to introduce the latter into the historical dynamic as well. And I would even go so far as to ask myself whether, in a world where man as *zoon politikon* is really alienated from the biological dimension, the separation of realms here does not also merit a good dialectical justification, and whether indeed the premature liquidation of this separation would not simply result in another harmonizing perspective on the world. In a word, the whole thing is too cosmic for me. And if, in fact, there is only the slightest difference between a head-eating mantis and man himself, while the imagination with all its depths belongs to the cosmos, then I simply have to respond to Caillois with the familiar words of another equally enlightened Frenchman: Vive la petite différence. And the most original-looking part of the general idea, the attempt to identify the relationship between human imagination and zoological behaviour, reveals itself on closer inspection as nothing but a fashionably revamped version of one of Freud's worst theories, that of sublimation – and perhaps that is connected with the remarks about the self-generating absurdities of psychoanalysis. As is so often the case, once the automatic ambience

212

of scientific knowledge is removed, we find an intellectual banality which turns all debate inter pares into a question of polite exchanges between people speaking different languages. If I had to counter him from the political perspective, on the other hand, I would not reproach him, as he himself might expect, with nature mysticism, but rather with an old-fashioned form of vulgar materialism meretriciously clothed in erudition. As you see, I can only reinforce your own considered judgement that the man really belongs to the other side with the *rudesse* so characteristic of me.

My attitude to some of the issues addressed by Caillois, as well as to the dialectic of the taboo, can also be gleaned from the six and a half typed pages of a manuscript on the philosophy of music – entitled 'Second Night Music'[5] – which I have sent to Max today with the request that he also make it available to you. I do not want to say anything further about the text itself, apart from confessing to you that I have rather overburdened it. I hope you have already received the published version of 'Ensemble'. The Wagner piece is beginning to take shape, after much collecting of materials and many discussions with Max, and will be focused around the concepts of progress and reaction (and incidentally, if I am not mistaken, the concluding part of my Second Night Music also contains certain things which will be of interest for your own theory of progress).

I also have a request today: I have developed the vague, and surely for that reason all the more reliable, impression that Löwenthal is proving the centre of some resistance in New York to my Husserl piece;[6] Max has still not read it. Could I sincerely ask you, without mentioning these things, to be an enthusiastic spokesman for the essay, and to contribute as much as you can to its further dissemination? You would thereby really be doing me an enormous favour: I have never been quite so concerned about the fate of one of my writings as I am in this case, and this is partly because I would not wish to see it subjected to procedures which would not bother me at all in relation to the Mannheim piece. I shall now be shortening the latter and revising it with great care.

My request is also coupled with one from Gretel. She has only read your essay on the theory of reproduction in French, and quite rightly believes that one should really know any text of yours in the original. Would you be able to provide one for her? That would be very kind and friendly of you.

Today we received, for the first time in a long while, a substantial letter from Ernst Bloch.[7] It contained some important news: a child by the name of Johann Robert[8] and two book manuscripts,[9] one 900 pages and the other 700 pages long; the former is entitled the 'Theory and Praxis of Matter', the second 'Enlightenment and the Red Mystery'. A publisher also seems to have been found for them, and apparently Malik is planning to produce a 'Collected Edition'. Otherwise the letter is uncommonly friendly.

When, or indeed whether, I shall get to Paris[10] still remains uncertain. There are two possibilities at the moment: either that sometime during the next eight days Max will invite me to come for a couple of days, or that I might turn up during the second week of October, which is when Krenek will also be there. However things work out, let us hope a meeting will transpire soon, and that in peace and quiet for both of us. My own peace and quiet has certainly been disturbed by thinking about Kracauer's work.[11] I suppose that I now really will have to take some decisive action in the matter.

That is it for today. I would be grateful to hear from you soon and at some more length. There are two things in particular which strike me as important: how things stand with your arrangements for the rest of the year, and how your work on Baudelaire and the Arcades is coming along. Have you spoken to Max about the more external matters?

Lots of love from both of us,

Yours as ever,
Teddie

1 *Your lines*: these have not survived.

2 *Dudow*: the Bulgarian-German film director Slatan Dudow (1903–63) had begun working in theatre and film in Berlin in 1922, with Brecht amongst others. He emigrated to Paris in 1933.

3 *Caillois' La Mante*: cf. Roger Caillois, *La Mante religieuse. Recherche sur la nature et la signification du mythe* [The Praying Mantis. An Investigation into the Significance of Myth] (Paris: La Maison des Amis des Livres 1937); for Adorno's review, cf. *Zeitschrift für Sozialforschung* 7, issue 3 (1938), pp. 410f; now in GS 20 [1], pp. 229f.

4 *with a frivolousness worthy of Prinzhorn*: Adorno is thinking of those passages in Hans Prinzhorn's book, *Charakterkunde der Gegenwart* [Contemporary Theories of Characterology] (Berlin 1931), which he had described in 1933, in a review of this and various other books for the *Zeitschrift für Sozialforschung*, as 'Superficial, and sometimes crudely distorting [Freud, whose characterological theory is not even seriously mentioned, but merely abused and insulted]'. (Now in GS 20 [1], p. 217.)

5 *'Second Night Music'*: this piece remained unpublished during Adorno's lifetime; it was first published in GS 18, pp. 45–53; for the passage on the dialectic of the taboo, cf. ibid., pp. 48f.

6 *some resistance . . . to my Husserl piece*: see letter 90.

7 *a substantial letter from Ernst Bloch*: Bloch's letter from Prague of 18 September; cf. Bloch, *Briefe*, vol. 2, pp. 438ff.

8 *Johann Robert*: Jan Robert Bloch was born on 10 September 1937.

9 *two book manuscripts*: Theory and Praxis of Matter (later entitled *The Problem of Materialism, Its History and Substance*) and *Enlightenment and the Red Mystery*, a work which, according to the editor of Bloch's correspondence, can no longer be identified (cf. ibid., p. 439, n. 10).

10 *When, or indeed whether, I shall get to Paris*: Adorno did not actually travel to Paris in the autumn of 1937.

11 *Kracauer's work*: the essay on 'Propaganda and the Masses' first mentioned in letter 57.

89   BENJAMIN TO THEODOR AND GRETEL WIESENGRUND-ADORNO
     PARIS, 23.9.1937

Dear Teddie,

When your letter of 13 September arrived, for which many thanks, I had already been carrying around a letter addressed to you[1] some days since, although I had not been able to decide whether to send it or not.

On arriving back in Paris, I was subjected to something which, under current circumstances, proved a rather painful blow to me. Because of an utterly disloyal, but also quite irreversible, arrangement, I had effectively lost my Paris apartment in the rue Bénard to a more acceptable tenant, who was only able to make an unmatchable offer because, being in receipt of an expulsion order himself, he was particularly anxious to find unofficial accommodation.

This could hardly have come at a worse time than now, when the cost of hotels here in Paris, and even the cost of far less salubrious quarters as well, has risen by fifty per cent or more on account of the Great Exhibition.[2] The prospect of finding an even remotely decent lodging was so far beyond my financial means that I felt forced to accept compensation of around two hundred francs from the new tenant even to encourage me to find a reasonable room to rent. And precisely what might have been expected duly transpired: I was unable to recover my 600 francs. My time has thus been taken up with fruitless attempts to do so, and with a kind of constant haggling in hotel lobbies which sometimes came close to begging.

You will understand why I found it rather difficult to send you a letter written in circumstances such as these. And then finally, a few days ago, I received an offer from Else Herzberger suggesting that I

215

could stay in her maid's room for the duration of her American trip. (The room is not actually in Else H.'s apartment, but located outside on its own in the forecourt.) Once the resident maid has moved out, my address will be Boulogne (Seine), 1 rue de Château.

I actually had the opportunity to discuss all this with Max only yesterday. No one knows better than you do just how deeply I desired, and just how firmly I intended, on my part not to make any further requests in the financial domain. But this final and unexpected eventuality has left me with no choice after all.

My intention now, as I told Max, is to protect myself as soon as possible, albeit in the most modest way, from any similar eventualities and to rent a self-contained studio or one-room apartment. I shall also have to find some furniture. Max has shown the greatest understanding for my position as I explained it to him, and told me he would take the appropriate steps as soon as he gets back. He also confided to me that – quite independently of the devaluation of the franc – they were already intending to reconsider the existing arrangements by the end of the year anyway. And if they actually break down before then, I have shown sufficient foresight to ensure that I will myself be able to get through the extremely difficult coming September without having to ask Max for any immediate assistance.

One of the immediate consequences of the current situation is that I shall only be able to devote a part of the next few weeks to my work. I have to find an apartment, and that will not be a particularly easy matter. I hereby send my own best wishes for both of you on moving into your new place. Which brings me to your last letter. You now know that it was not hurt feelings on my part so much as other, more unavoidable, problems which accounted for my silence. So we shall say no more about that!

I am really very grateful to you for having discussed my affairs with Max at some length in London. In Paris we have only been able to spend a single evening together, and precisely because it passed so enjoyably in a new and congenial atmosphere between us, we didn't really get to discuss all the technicalities which we should have done. But your letter told me what I needed to decide about procuring the relevant books for the Arcades, and I can congratulate myself on that. As far as Adrienne Monnier is concerned, I shall do everything I possibly can to facilitate a meeting between her and Max over the next few days. In any case, the whole question has turned out favourably from our point of view. And furthermore, the suggestion that I should receive the proofs of the journal directly from you strikes me as the best arrangement imaginable.

As I said, questions of this kind were barely touched upon in my conversation with Max, which actually lasted well into the night. This was very important for me because Max was able to inform me, for the first time, about the remarkable legal and financial arrangements which have been responsible for securing the Institute's continued existence. The whole subject is fascinating in itself; in addition to this, I have rarely seen Max in a happier state of mind. First we spent some time in a small restaurant in the place des Abbesses, which I have already earmarked for when you and Felizitas come to visit next. Unfortunately, it looks as though we shall have to be patient about this for a while. On the other hand, when the moment does arrive, I hope to be able to receive both of you in an apartment of my own.

As far as the Berg is concerned, I wrote to my former wife immediately asking her to make some enquiries at the post office in San Remo. I have not heard back from her yet, but I do hope you have received the book in the meantime.

It would give me great pleasure to hear from you very soon, especially at the moment. Please write to me at the rue Nicolo – any letters will be sent on to me in Boulogne if necessary.

Heartfelt greetings,

Yours,
Walter

Dear Felizitas,

The request with which I have just concluded my letter to Teddie is also explicitly addressed to you. Please write soon, but at some length if possible.

You have seen how simply the business with the rebus has turned out. In order to prevent similar awkward passages – which I soon hope to avoid completely – bringing me to a standstill in this way, please do everything you can to keep our correspondence more vigorous than it has been while you were in Berlin. I shall not be tardy in my replies.

Lots of love for today,

from Detlef

23 September 1937
Paris XVI
Villa Nicolo
3 rue Nicolo

1 *a letter addressed to you*: the letter has not survived.

2 *the Great Exhibition*: the World Exhibition in Paris, which had been open since the end of July.

Boulogne s. Seine
1, rue du Château, le 2/10/37

My dear Felizitas,

Whenever in future I address my letters now to one or now to the other of you, they will still generally be directed to you both. Since I do not wish to abandon the usual way of beginning a letter, I hope you will forgive me alternating in this way.

The irregular character of my correspondence, deviating as it has even from its usual rhythm, and my change of address, all this doubtless tells you that things could be better with me. Max is aware of the situation, and I am expecting him to intervene on my behalf in the course of this month.

I am temporarily living, as I mentioned, in the *chambre de bonne* belonging to E. H.[1] As soon as I am financially fixed up through Max, I shall be looking around for a one-room apartment.

As things have fallen out over the last few weeks, you will hardly expect to hear any further news about the Baudelaire or the Arcades. And fortunately it has turned out that some more immediately pressing work[2] has come into prospect. Max arranged a meeting between Oprecht[3] and myself, and we have decided to try and write a substantial informative essay on the power and influence of the Institute of Social Research for the journal *Mass und Wert* [Measure and Value]. We have not overlooked the editorial and production difficulties involved. But I think the influence of Oprecht will be quite sufficient to resolve them.

I am doubly sorry that, given my present situation here, I cannot even compensate you by sending on any older material either. The final version of the essay on Mechanical Reproduction only exists as a single copy; I am afraid you will have to wait until you come to Paris to see it. – Teddie encouraged me to hope this might happen in the second week of October. If only it could really transpire this time!

I spent a very long evening with Max, as I reported earlier. I saw him again briefly on the afternoon of the next day and we went to visit Mlle Monnier. The arrangement which Teddie did so much to encourage in the first place has thus come to a most satisfactory conclusion. If October does bring you both here, it will certainly also bring you to the rue de l'Odéon.[4]

Now to your work on Husserl. (And here I would ask you, dear Teddie, to permit me to change the style of address[5] in mid-correspondence). Max informed me – and without my having in any

218

way to prompt him with a direct question – that there are indeed objections being made to your piece in New York. Whether they effectively originate from Löwenthal, I don't know, but Max gave me a rough idea of their character. The general assault on idealist epistemology, which itself appears to be definitively liquidated in the form of phenomenology, has clearly provoked a response there by virtue of its very range and breadth. Max immediately gave me the rather self-evident assurance that he would be studying the work with the greatest care and attention in due course. Your basic argument is surely quite familiar to him after your conversations in New York. Nonetheless, I would not put too much weight upon these provisional impressions, especially since you will soon be hearing some accurate news from New York.

I was no longer able to borrow your piece 'Second Night Music' from Max. But I think I can expect an offprint of the same in the very near future. Also, many thanks once again for the 'Ensemble' piece.

Dudow was extremely pleased with your letter. I would very much have liked to introduce him to Max. But there was simply not enough time. The idea of your essay collection on mass art appealed to him as strongly as it did to me. If only I knew how we should proceed now, either with or without him!

Nothing has been seen of Sohn-Rethel. And Kracauer is also extremely difficult to get hold of. And since I have no telephone, I am very much dependent upon the initiative of others.

As Teddie will realize, I concur with his criticisms of Caillois, and particularly of the political limitations and effect of his work. However, I am not entirely convinced that one should really describe it as 'vulgar materialism'. Whatever the diplomatic difficulties which may be involved in pursuing a dialogue with him 'inter pares', I would nonetheless urge that the idea is not simply abandoned.

Do write to me soon, once you are settled into your new apartment, and share your impressions now you have got to know London rather better. And let me know whether you still occasionally travel to Germany.

Could I also take this opportunity to ask about the French books[6] you have been keeping for me? I would be very pleased if you have them there with you in London. Perhaps you could possibly have them sent on to me as registered parcels?

The political prospects are looking extremely dark for anyone who really feels at home in Paris. You venture out into the street and see these characters from the American Legion,[7] and have the feeling you are entirely surrounded by fascism. I hope I shall soon be able to insulate myself against such impressions once I get down to work.

Please write without delay, and accept my heartfelt greetings

[Walter]

1 *E. H.*: i.e. Else Herzberger.

2 *some more immediately pressing work*: cf. Walter Benjamin, 'Ein deutsches Institut freier Forschung' [A German Institute for Free Research], in *Mass und Wert* 1, issue 5 (1937/38), pp. 818–22; now in GS III, pp. 518–26.

3 *Oprecht*: the Zürich publisher Emil Oprecht, whose company published the Institute journal.

4 *rue de l'Odéon*: the site of Adrienne Monnier's book store.

5 *permit me to change the style of address*: in the German, Benjamin here reverts from the familiar second-person subject pronoun (Du), with which he addresses Felizitas (Gretel), to the more formal third-person subject pronoun (Sie), with which he habitually addresses her husband.

6 *the French books*: Benjamin is referring to Gretel Adorno's letter of July in which she had reported: 'There are still the following books here: Balzac, *Contes Drolatiques*; *Peau de Chagrin*. Flaubert, *Madame Bovary*; Asselineau, *Mélanges Bibliotheque Romantique.*' (Unpublished letter from Gretel Karplus to Benjamin of 15.6.1937.)

7 *the American Legion*: an association of American war veterans founded in Paris in 1919.

91 WIESENGRUND-ADORNO TO BENJAMIN
    [LONDON,] 22.10.1937

22 October 1937.

Dear Walter,

Please find enclosed the new and final version of my Mannheim piece,[1] which will now be appearing with a few minor alterations. I am very keen to learn whether you will also prefer this version, as Gretel and the others in New York did, to the original one – for which I still continue to feel a certain devotion. If you have any relevant alterations of your own to suggest, as long as they would not require too much further revision to the text, I would be very grateful if you could send them to me, along with the copy I gave you. But only if this really seems worthwhile; I would certainly not want to impose any additional work on you on my account.

I hope that you will also soon be receiving my remarks on Beethoven[2] as well as the Second Night Music.

Sohn-Rethel informs me that you are still having to cope with the problems of finding accommodation and that you are really quite depressed as a result. In this connection, it might be worth something to you if I pass on to you some remarks in Max's last letter to me:[3] 'Amongst the best things I have to relate are the hours I spent with

Benjamin. He is really much closer to us than anyone else. I shall do everything in my power to help him out of his current financial distress.' These remarks are all the more significant in that the Institute has naturally felt the full impact of the slump too, and the rest of us shall all have to be prepared for reductions rather than increases in future.

My preparatory studies for the Wagner piece are coming on vigorously. The Husserl essay will not now be appearing, at least not in its present form. The principal objection is the one which you also raised, and Gretel quite independently as well, namely, that substantial parts of it are unintelligible without a detailed knowledge of Husserl's own texts, something which cannot really be expected on the part of the journal's readers. I shall attempt to remedy this problem, but I am certainly not yet sure at the moment whether I shall be successful in doing so.

We have received a friendly letter from Ernst Bloch[4] in which he promises to send on substantial portions of his book on materialism, all expressed in surprisingly moderate language. The letter also contains a bitter attack on Lukács, which certainly gives some food for thought.

Heartfelt greetings from the both of us,

Your old friend,
Teddie

1 *the new and final version of my Mannheim piece*: Adorno had undertaken the revision and shortening of the essay, which now received the title 'The New Value-Free Sociology' (cf. GS 20 [1], pp. 13–45), in the second half of September; this *final version* was actually set after a few editorial changes, but was not actually published.

2 *my remarks on Beethoven*: i.e. Adorno's essay 'Beethoven's Late Style'; see letter 17 and the relevant note.

3 *Max's last letter to me*: the passage cited derives from Horkheimer's (unpublished) letter to Adorno of 13 October 1937.

4 *a friendly letter from Ernst Bloch*: the letter in question has not survived.

92   BENJAMIN TO WIESENGRUND-ADORNO
     BOULOGNE SUR SEINE, 2.11.1937

Dear Teddie,

It would require a far longer letter than I am in a position to write at present, if I were to relate all the circumstances which have stood in the way of communication. You will have learnt something about this from Sohn-Rethel.[1]

For indeed, if I really look my gift horse in the mouth (Else Herzberger's room), I can see myself sitting here, wide awake since six o'clock in the morning, listening away to the oceanic rather than intelligible rhythms of the Paris traffic, which rumbles in through the narrow asphalt aperture right in front of my bed. In front of my bed – for the bed stands right there where the window is. If I lift the shutters, the street itself is a witness to my literary labours, and if I close them, I am immediately exposed to the monstrous climatic extremes which the (uncontrollable) central heating creates in this spring-like October.

I could congratulate myself if, indeed, it were only our correspondence which had suffered during these last few weeks. Of course, I flee straight to the *Bibliothèque Nationale* every morning, but one can hardly bear to spend the entire day there. I have been very unsettled, although this has certainly developed my familiarity with the housing market here. Nonetheless, I have still not found anything. And recently the kind of place which I am looking for has become rather more difficult to find. The dubious semi-demi-socialism of the Blum government[2] has produced, along with many other problems, a persistent stagnation in the building industry. And it is really only very recently that they have started to provide extremely small apartments.

When I heard the decision from New York[3] – which gives me approximately three-quarters of what you originally had in mind for me – my aforementioned miseries certainly retreated into the shade produced by this new source of light. And I was all the more keen to get down to work. And indeed, I have just completed the first of the Parisian letters on literature[4] which I promised Max when he was here. It is not intended for publication. As far as the content is concerned, you will be particularly interested in my critique of Jean Cocteau's new play,[5] 'Les Chevaliers de la table ronde'. It is a truly dreadful piece, which only seems to confirm Cocteau's *déchéance* as far as I am concerned. I shall tell you more about it in person when we meet.

Perhaps this will not be too far off. The invitation from Felicitas[6] to come and look around London strikes me as a very attractive one. And it would certainly make sense for me to come across before I have found an apartment here. I am planning to leave Paris as soon as Else Herzberger returns. Then I would first of all go and visit Brecht,[7] and stay with him over Christmas, while arranging to have my books transported[8] to Paris. I could then probably make it to London[9] sometime in January. Let me know what you both think about the idea. But bear in mind that my possibilities for travelling abroad can now only be counted upon until the middle of next year – for then my passport runs out. On the other hand, I will not be

222

leaving my apartment here – if I am fortunate to get possession of one – before I have seen to everything that is involved.

All these plans are subject to certain reservations. For I do not wish to leave the city before handing in my application for naturalization.[10] Yesterday I received Valéry's signature in support, certainly the most important I have been able to procure so far. But I should also like to smooth the paths a little in the Ministry of Justice before I take the official step.

Valéry's signature has necessitated certain negotiations on my part. The transportation of my effects from rue Bénard caused some difficulties. And in addition there were visits – by Brecht, Lieb and Marcel Brion.[11] In short, the last few weeks have been fairly fraught. Of course, Groethuysen had to make an appearance in this atmosphere as well. Max has put him – for largely incomprehensible reasons – in charge of things[12] once again. A new and more subtle form of sabotage was the result, as I had fully expected. 'One can never' – this is how it formally ran – 'predict the exact date of publication for any book accepted by the NRF.' I am sure that Alix Guillain,[13] stickler for regulations as he is, has had his share in these machinations. Fortunately enough, the negotiations with Groethuysen are officially in Aron's hands and not in mine.

And now I also remember your request to find out as much as possible about Kracauer's work[14] when I get together with him. I am afraid, to be blunt, that I have not seen him for a month and a half now. The last time we met was in Max's presence, and I proposed a rendezvous to him then. He could find no time for it in the next fortnight – that was his response. What I may have done to offend him is quite impossible to discover. It was all a bit much to take. So now I am waiting very patiently to hear from him some time. Please pass on my all the more agreeable greetings to Sohn-Rethel. I hope you have been able to spend some pleasant evenings in his company. I have heard from his daughter that – more fortunate than I in this – he has already found an apartment. Give him my best wishes in this respect, and remind him about the 'Thurn Forest'[15] (he will certainly understand what I mean!).

In the rather extensive meantime I have received three works from you. I recognize many extraordinarily important themes in your Night Music:[16] both in the remarks concerning Schönberg's expressive style and in those about taboo and kitsch. We shall certainly have to return to the latter next time we talk to one another. I hope the same with regard to your final reflection: I think I recognize the crucial intention here, although it partly escapes me with precise respect to the musical material itself. The Beethoven piece is thoroughly transparent and strikes me as particularly fine in its execution.

The essential point still exercises its undiminished effect in the new version of your Mannheim essay. And if I am not mistaken, some of the newer formulations are actually amongst the most powerful of all. I particularly liked the passage about the head of the grand bourgeois household,[17] and especially the final section. – I feel I can say in favour of the new version that it possesses a rather more official and representative character than the original one, which the academic style had lent a rather private tone in places. However, the transition you have made from the original version to the present one does not strike me as particularly felicitous at the beginning. I have permitted myself to make a suggestion for omission here at the beginning, and have clearly marked your returned copy accordingly for the sake of brevity. I don't think my suggestion adversely affects anything, but reduces not so much the sharpness as the violence of your approach. A couple of suggestions about vocabulary:[18] on page 3, line 15, second word, I would substitute 'dark' for 'light', and likewise on page 10, line 8 from the bottom, I would substitute 'pacifying' for 'transfiguring'. – Have you noticed the splendid example – sometimes even the dialectician recognizes examples! – which van Zeeland has provided for the influence wielded by the 'select organizers'?[19]

And finally to conclude, when can I expect my copy of the Alban Berg piece? – I would also like to hear something from Felizitas about the illustrated French volumes[20] from my library, which I enquired after in September. Are they still in Berlin, or do you have them in London?

Lastly, I must mention that Pollock has imposed the strictest discretion upon me toward the Institute offices and representatives, concerning the arrangement which has been made about my financial affairs.[21] It is obvious that this does not include both of you, but it is necessary for you to know about it anyway. I must also take this opportunity to express once again my heartfelt thanks for everything you have done for me in this business! – I was also delighted to read those words of Max which you passed on to me.

In the last few days, and without much enthusiasm, I have written the friendliest possible review of Grete de Francesco's book.[22] I shall send it on to you when I have the opportunity.

Please do not punish this, my long but now accounted for silence, but write to me very soon and accept my very best wishes for you and Felizitas.

Yours,

Walter

2 November 1937
Boulogne (Seine)
1 rue de Château

1 *you will have learnt . . . from Sohn-Rethel*: Sohn-Rethel had moved from Paris to London at the beginning of October.

2 *the Blum government*: Leon Blum (1872–1950), French politician and writer, leader of the 'Parti Socialiste Française', was the President of the Popular Front government from 1936 to 1937.

3 *the decision from New York*: i.e. the decision to pay Benjamin's monthly grant in dollars instead of francs in future, and to effect the said increase before 1 January 1938.

4 *the Parisian letters on literature*: Benjamin is referring to a series of letters written to Horkheimer over considerable intervals of time in order to keep him and the other participants of the Institute informed about recent developments in the French literary scene; the first of these letters dates from 3 November 1937.

5 *Jean Cocteau's new play*: cf. Jean Cocteau, *Les Chevaliers de la table ronde* [The Knights of the Round Table] (Paris 1937).

6 *The invitation from Felicitas*: Gretel Adorno had expressed the idea in her (unpublished) letter to Benjamin of 29 September.

7 *go and visit Brecht*: Benjamin did not in fact travel to Denmark to see Brecht (see the following letter), but went to San Remo at the end of December.

8 *arranging to have my books transported*: the part of Benjamin's library that he was able to save on leaving Germany was stored with Brecht.

9 *make it to London*: Benjamin did not in fact visit London.

10 *my application for naturalization*: Benjamin's application for naturalization as a French citizen proved unsuccessful.

11 *visits – by Brecht, Lieb and Marcel Brion*: Brecht stayed in Paris during the first half of October to oversee rehearsals for the first performance of his play, *Die Gewehre der Frau Carrar*. – Fritz Lieb (1892–1970), a Swiss theologian who had obtained his post-doctoral degree in Bonn and taught there until November 1933; he lived in Paris between 1934 and 1936, returning in that year to Basel as Extraordinary Professor in Dogmatics and the History of Theology. He was director of the journal *Orient und Occident*, where Benjamin's essay 'Der Erzähler' [The Story-teller] first appeared in October 1936. – Marcel Brion (1895–1984) originally practised as a lawyer before he turned to music, literature and art; he participated in the 'Cahiers du Sud'.

12 *Groethuysen . . . Max has put him in charge of things*: i.e. with respect to the publication of Horkheimer's essays in France.

13 *Alix Guillain*: she was Groethuysen's partner and closely involved with the French publishing house KPF.

14 *Kracauer's work*: i.e. Kracauer's manuscript 'Propaganda and the Masses'.

15 *the 'Thurn Forest'*: the meaning of this remark is unclear; it is possibly a reference to something mentioned in a passage in the Arcades materials

225

(cf. GS V [2], p. 1003): 'Thurn as a georama in the Galerie Colbert', which Sohn-Rethel may have seen when he was with Benjamin, in an album with reproduction illustrations pasted into it (cf. GS 20 [2], p. 1324).

16 *your Night Music*: Benjamin is referring to the work first mentioned in letter 88, Adorno's 'Second Night Music'.

17 *your Mannheim essay . . . the passage about the head of the grand bourgeois household*: cf. GS 20 [1], pp. 41ff.

18 *A couple of suggestions about vocabulary*: now impossible to identify in the absence of the original proof text.

19 *the influence wielded by the 'select organizers'*: cf. the probably slightly altered passage at GS 20 [1], pp. 38ff and GS 10 [1], p. 42. – Paul van Zeeland (1893–1973), Belgian economist and politician, was President of Belgium from 1935 to 1937, as well as Foreign Minister in 1935–6; he was forced to resign in October 1937 in the wake of corruption charges.

20 *the illustrated French volumes*: see letter 90 and the relevant note.

21 *the arrangement . . . about my financial affairs*: from November 1937 Benjamin received a monthly grant of $80 from the Institute of Social Research in New York in order to protect him from the consequences of the devaluation of the French franc; in November he received an additional 1,500 French francs, his previous monthly sum, from Geneva as assistance for his intended change of accommodation.

22 *review of Grete de Francesco's book*: i.e. the book *Die Macht des Charlatans* [The Power of the Charlatan] already mentioned in letter 84; for Benjamin's review, cf. *Zeitschrift für Sozialforschung* 7, issue 1/2 (1938), pp. 296–8; now in GS III, pp. 544–6.

93   BENJAMIN TO THEODOR AND GRETEL WIESENGRUND-ADORNO
     BOULOGNE SUR SEINE, 17.11.1937

Dear Teddie,

The day before yesterday I signed a rent agreement,[1] which may allow me to move into an apartment by the end of the year, but certainly by 15 January at the latest. This has caused a change in my arrangements: a trip to Denmark for the short intervening period would hardly be worthwhile.

But things are not exactly the same as far as making it to London is concerned. At any rate, I have to vacate my present lodgings at the end of this month or the beginning of next; Else H. has announced her imminent return. This would all be much harder to bear if the incredible noise which roars around me here from morning to night

had not seriously affected my capacity for work. I was entirely dependent upon the *Bibliothèque Nationale*, where I have been able to
look through more or less all the Baudelaire literature I need.

What are your arrangements for December? Do let me know as
soon as you can.

I still have not heard a thing from Kracauer.

What is Sohn-Rethel up to?

I have heard from Grete de Francesco to tell me she was very
happy indeed with your letter.[2]

Heartfelt greetings to Felizitas and yourself,

Yours,
Walter

17 November 1937
Boulogne (Seine)
1 rue de Château

1 *I signed a rent agreement*: for the apartment at 10, rue Dombasle,
Benjamin's last place of residence before his flight from Paris.

2 *Grete de Francesco / your letter*: Adorno's (unpublished) letter is dated
10 November 1937.

94   WIESENGRUND-ADORNO TO BENJAMIN
     [LONDON,] 27.11.1937

27 November 1937.

Dear Walter,

The reason I have taken so long in responding is that I could not
conceal from you something I was rather unwilling to communicate
before it had actually attained the very highest degree of probability:
contrary to all expectations, our move to America has now become
an immediate prospect. An arrangement between the Institute and
Princeton University[1] has now transpired which promises immediate collaboration with Max, takes some financial burden off the
Institute, and offers us certain guarantees at the same time. You will
believe me that there were very real and compelling reasons which
encouraged Max to make the proposal and me to accept it. I am very
conscious of what this abandonment of my position in Europe –
in the double sense – will mean. You will know that my thoughts
about you were uppermost in my mind, and it is only to underline
the seriousness of my decision if I add that I must also reckon with
the real possibility of never seeing my mother again if I leave for
America. I think you can imagine how I feel about this. The only

227

partial consolation to me is the prospect that I shall be able to start collaborating with Max on his hopefully crucial work on dialectical materialism,[2] and the increasing difficulties of living here in England, particularly for Gretel, who I am encouraged to hope may finally be able to recover her health in America.

But at the moment everything is still rather in the air. We haven't been able to move into our flat after all and have now halted the process of furniture removal. We are still living in our two rooms, which has proved less than inspiring over this stretch of time. The crucial meeting with the American Consul, the outcome of which is still far from certain as it happens, takes place on 13 December. I don't really think we can expect our departure for America[3] before the beginning of January.

I regard it as a matter of course that we shall see one another before then. But where this will turn out to be, whether in London or Paris, I cannot possibly say at present. In part, at least, this will also depend on the arrangements made in New York. It goes without saying that I shall, therefore, let you know as quickly as possible once the situation is further clarified in any way. In any case, I would like to know whether the arrangement concerning your financial affairs[4] has reached the point where it can now be regarded as definitively settled, and above all whether the sum has been finally agreed upon in dollars. Please do not consider it an indiscretion, but simply as an expression of my concern, a concern which was provoked by a passage in your last major letter, if I ask you exactly how large the sum which has been agreed is. I only pose this question on the condition that it requires no psychological sacrifice on your part to answer it, and on the further condition that Pollock did not impose an *absolute* obligation to silence upon you in this matter, as he certainly did upon me. In that case, however, I would ask you to give me the most detailed instructions you possibly can concerning the further handling of your affairs. Under the present circumstances, I regard it as quite out of the question that there is now even the slightest chance for Sohn-Rethel, Kracauer, the book on mass art, or any of the other related projects. But I believe all the more firmly that I shall now be able to insist on your own case as the really unique one. In this connection, I am also thinking of how we can also bring you over to America as quickly as possible. The substantive necessity that we work together in close physical proximity, a necessity in which I include Max, determines me in this as much as does the conviction that war will be unavoidable in the relatively immediate future. In this connection, the Cagoulard affair[5] and the manifest failure of Halifax's enterprise[6] are simply links in the chain. But it really seems to me that such a catastrophe is the only way out of the entire European predicament, and indeed I am almost tempted to regard this as a solution to the other alternative of a permanent catastrophe. I must say that these considerations seem to me to over-shadow the extremely urgent ones to which you drew attention; namely, with regard to defending the last abandoned European post. In this connection, it might be a source of some ironic consolation to us that the post we have to defend will prove a lost one every-where under all circumstances. Simply reading the issue of *Das neue Tagebuch* in which the unspeakable Schwarzschild denounces Russia,[7] and that of the *Weltbühne*, where an equally unspeakable Herr Georg, but Ernst Bloch[8] as well, undertake a defence of Russia truly worthy of Schwarzschild's original attack, gives an all too vigorous impres-sion of the aporia in which we are entangled. In all seriousness, I can hardly imagine our own relationship to Europe as other than that of Ehrenberg's travel company[9] rummaging its way through her devast-ated cities. And I do not mean by that to express any great optimism about an America where the waves of crisis are obviously gathering pace in a most disturbing manner too. In all seriousness, this cata-strophe, dragged out over decades, is the most perfect nightmare of hell which mankind has ever produced until now. And if I also tell you that my Wagner study is coming on very well, this merely has the significance of that idyll which itself belongs to catastrophe. The preparatory studies are almost complete. The character of my notes is such that writing them up will effectively be a technical matter, in the sense in which the Englishman regards the bagging of his tiger as a technical matter once the original ground has become sufficiently familiar. The figure of the beggar seems to bear more and more upon the heart of the work, and perhaps it is a favourable omen if I tell you that the desire I harboured ten years ago to write the theory behind the verse 'The beggar rushes to the door',[10] seems finally to have been fulfilled. Another dream of mine was also involved here, one I should like to report to you in detail at the next opportunity. Hopefully the work also serves to fulfil something you have long desired: a theory of instrumentation[11] in which the interpretation of the instruments themselves has something decisive to express. In short, I can at least allow myself some optimism in believing that this attempt will find your approval. The fate of the earlier work, the Husserl piece, is still in the dark, but I think that something will actually come of that, too, in one form or another.

Gretel's health is not very good. She is simply not up to coping bodily with the general conditions of life here in England, and with the improvised nature of our existence in particular. The simplest thing would be to gather up our belongings and make for some more agreeable place for the time being; but this does not seem possible either, given the negotiations with the American Consulate, and the difficulties of maintaining telegraphic communication with New York also makes travel more difficult from the technical point of view. All the same, I have not yet entirely given up hope that we might be able to spend a fortnight on the Riviera,[12] and that would certainly mean getting to see you in Paris.

Sohn-Rethel is here, but I am very disappointed since I cannot avoid the impression that he is eagerly trying to rediscover the man who first started on the work in order to disable him completely, and that he is far more interested in spinning things out into the indeterminate future than he is in completing anything within a foreseeable period of time. In addition, the English professor[13] who brought him here and is supposed to be guiding him, is, unfortunately, just as work-shy as Sohn-Rethel himself. At any rate, he has produced nothing whatsoever so far, and belongs in the last analysis more with people like Rix Löwenthal,[14] Haselberg and company than he does with us. The fact that we have no 'heirs' rather fits in with the general catastrophic situation. One of the most amazing pieces I have come across in this connection, incidentally, is an essay by Herr Linfert[15] on the 'Exhibition of Degenerate Art', in which he subjects the enterprise to an ideological critique drawn more or less from the arsenal of our own reflections. My attitude to him and to Sternberger is now completely unambiguous: as far as I am concerned they are both finished. If you have not read this farrago, I can always send it to you. The most repulsive thing about it all is that this stuff excuses itself as a kind of 'disguised opposition'. Cagoulards everywhere.

The Mannheim essay has now been set, along with a large number of changes which I do not care for. I immediately suggested counterproposals of my own, but with what success I do not know.

Let me conclude with the hope that you will soon be able to occupy your new and peaceful quarters for as long as they continue to remain peaceful, while Else, demonic spendthrift that she is, will fall foul of all the infernal horrors of the rue de Rennes and the coming world war. She did not write us a single line during her New York trip, and clearly she did not visit Max either – in my opinion, because she feared that her reception would hardly turn out the way she can now say it surely would, just as long as she doesn't try it out. But perhaps there is also a little shame about the maid's room involved. I have also informed my parents of her extreme largesse, and I think it has had the required effect.

Lots of love from both of us; and write something soon.

In constant friendship as ever,

Yours,

Teddie

230

1 *an arrangement between the Institute and Princeton University*: this arrangement had been facilitated by Paul Lazarsfeld, who had received substantial funding from Princeton University for research into radio, and now wished to see Adorno engaged as musical director of the project. It had been agreed between Lazarsfeld and the Institute that Adorno would commit half his time to the 'Radio Research Project' and half to the *Institute of Social Research*. – The sociologist Paul Lazarsfeld (1901–76) had already gone to America in 1933 and had become professor of sociology at Columbia University in New York.

2 *crucial work on dialectical materialism*: the later work, *Dialectic of Enlightenment*, emerged from a close collaboration between Horkheimer and Adorno, which also involved the intensive discussion of one another's essays.

3 *our departure for America*: the Adornos did not actually leave Europe until the middle of February 1938.

4 *the arrangement concerning your financial affairs*: see letter 92 and the relevant note.

5 *the Cagoulard affair*: Adorno is probably referring to the destruction of the secret right-wing political association by Blum's government.

6 *the failure of Halifax's enterprise*: a reference to Lord Halifax's special visit to Germany in November 1937, undertaken at Neville Chamberlain's request, when Halifax met Hitler at Berchtesgaden.

7 *the issue of Das neue Tagebuch / Schwarzschild denounces Russia*: cf. Leopold Schwarzschild, 'Die Pandorasbüchse', in the journal *Das Neue Tagebuch 5*, issue 46 (13.11.1937), pp. 1089–94.

8 *the Weltbühne / Herr Georg / Ernst Bloch*: cf. Manfred Georg [also: George], 'Der Intellektuelle in der Volksfront', in *Die neue Weltbühne 33*, nr. 46 (11.11.1937), pp. 1449–54 and Ernst Bloch's essay 'Jubiläum der Renegaten', ibid., pp. 1437–43.

9 *Ehrenberg's travel company*: cf. Ilja Ehrenberg's novels *Die ungewöhnlichen Abenteuer des Julio Jurenito und seiner Jünger* [The Remarkable Adventures of Julio Jurenito and his Followers] (Berlin 1923) and *Trust D. E. Die Geschichte der Zerstörung Europas* [Trust D. E. The History of the Destruction of Europe] (Berlin 1925).

10 *the theory behind the verse 'The Beggar rushes to the door'*: cf. chapter IX – entitled 'God and Beggar' – in Adorno's *Versuch über Wagner* [An Essay on Wagner] (now in GS 13, pp. 123–33, and especially 127ff).

11 *a theory of instrumentation*: cf. ibid., chapter V, entitled 'Colours' (GS 13, pp. 68–81).

12 *spend a fortnight on the Riviera*: in the middle of December, Adorno and Gretel went to San Remo for about three months, where they met up with Benjamin.

13 *the English professor*: John Macmurray, Professor of Logic and Metaphysics at the University of London.

14 *Rix Löwenthal*: Adorno is referring to the economist, political scientist and sociologist Richard Löwenthal (1908–91).

15 *an essay by Herr Linfert*: cf. Carl Linfert, 'Rückblick auf "entartete Kunst"' [A Retrospective on 'Degenerate Art'], in the Frankfurter Zeitung of 14.11.1937 (year 82, nr. 581/2), pages 4 and 6. – Carl Linfert (1900–81), journalist and art historian, was correspondent and editor of the *Frankfurter Zeitung* until 1943; after the war he headed the evening programme of 'North-Western German Radio' (later 'Western German Radio').

95   WIESENGRUND-ADORNO TO BENJAMIN
     [LONDON,] 1.12.1937

1 December 1937.

Dear Walter,

Allow me to add a few professional words to Gretel's letter.[1] In the next few days you will probably be receiving a letter from the Engels biographer Gustav Mayer,[2] formerly Extraordinary Professor in Berlin. He had an agreement with Gallimard – recommended through his friend Groethuysen – for a French edition of the Engels book. Groethuysen had promised to find him a translator, and they had been considering one Alexandre[3] for the task. Needless to say, neither the translation nor the edition ever materialized. Mayer has now asked me if I can give him any helpful advice about the question of translation. And I have referred him to you since you are certainly much more intimately informed about these matters than I am. I thought you might be able to interest one of our own friends in the prospect of translation, Klossowski or Etiemble perhaps, provided that neither of them is currently busy with any *urgent* translations for the Institute. If one of them were chosen, you could certainly not avoid informing our dear friend Groethuysen to that effect, given that the plan for the translation and the original recommendation of our two caryatids first came from him; and for my own part, I would like to avoid the impression of anything suddenly boomeranging back on Groethuysen, at least until the question of when Max's essays will

232

appear has finally been settled. I am, therefore, sorry to have to ask you, if indeed you receive Mayer's letter and *only* then, to get in touch with Groethuysen about the matter before you reply to Mayer. But if I am really expecting you to meet Groethuysen again, that requires me at the least to give you a quick picture of the friend whose chances he has managed to sabotage. Mayer is a rather terrifying man, rather like Fuchs, but without those reconciling qualities that spring from the latter's aggressive drives which occasionally turn against the world as it is, something that one can never expect of Mayer. If I tell you that Mayer is friendly not only with Groethuysen, but also the living breathing Fuchs, this will surely produce an image of the most perfect harmony; and you will not deny that we need a character such as this like the dot on the i. And indeed, our relationship to him is one of those fatal necessities. For a number of reasons, which in some cases have a long history behind them, he is consumed with a powerful resentment against the Institute[4] and is wreaking untold damage here. It is extremely important to find some way of appeasing him, especially since he would prove quite insatiable if one became too closely involved with him. For this reason it strikes me as a very good idea if we could find a translator for him and thereby render him obligated to us. That is the background.

I must say that he has expressed an extremely enthusiastic opinion about your essay on Fuchs. But after requiring such self-sacrifice vis-à-vis Groethuysen already, I do not want to inflict more needless suffering upon you.

Hopefully à bientôt in San Remo, heartfelt greetings,

Yours,

Teddie

1 *Gretel's letter*: Gretel wrote to Benjamin on the same date: 'So in all probability we shall be coming to the Villa Verde in San Remo in the second half of December and staying until January . . . Could we not get to meet down there?' (Unpublished letter from Gretel Adorno to Benjamin of 1.12.1937.)

2 *the Engels biographer Gustav Mayer*: Gustav Mayer's *Friedrich Engels. Eine Biographie* first appeared in 1920 in two volumes; a second improved edition was published by Nijhoff in The Hague in 1934.

3 *one Alexandre*: nothing further known.

4 *Mayer / powerful resentment against the Institute*: Gustav Mayer, after a conversation with Felix Weil, had entertained the hope of becoming Director of the *Institute of Social Research*; in fact Carl Grünberg became the first Director.

Dear Teddie,

Really – your letter brought me harsh tidings.

That an equally harsh necessity motivated your own suggestion does nothing to make it sound more agreeable.

Nonetheless, your suggestion does promise to resolve a number of difficulties. But we must also accept that it will only throw up another one in its wake.

But we must on all accounts get together before your departure. It goes without saying that this should involve the three of us.

I have just written to my former wife and will pass the information on to you without delay as soon as it arrives. I hope in any case you will still be able to arrange things so that we have a couple of days to ourselves in Paris. Max would certainly also be delighted if you could get to cast a departing glance at the Continent. I would have loved so much to give you and Felizitas a glimpse of those cracks and joints which shall be my *abri* in future. But I won't be able to move in until 10 January at the earliest. This accounts for my period of probable absence from Paris, which actually corresponds with the period of your own stay.

In short, we will get to see one another in a few days. Therefore, I only mention the following here so that an important passage in your letter should not seem to pass unanswered, however briefly.

When Pollock communicated the decision to me, he also added: 'We would request you to preserve the strictest confidentiality concerning the agreed sum (even with regard to Geneva), since at a time when we are having to make financial cuts everywhere, we do not wish to get involved in arguments about why we are proceeding quite differently in your case.' I cannot possibly imagine that Pollock was thinking about you in this connection. And as far as I am concerned: it would actually impose much greater psychological difficulties upon me if I did *not* feel completely free to express myself openly above all to you and Gretel. I cannot really imagine, as I say, that this is what was meant. For today, let me add another passage from one of Max's letters[1] alongside that of Pollock: 'We have spoken to Fräulein Herzberger here. Perhaps she has now managed to grasp that your financial difficulties are not exactly solved by permitting you to occupy her servant's quarters for a while, and indeed, not even by what we are currently able to do for you.' Max adds: 'However, it is extremely doubtful that she really has.'

The thanks expressed in my last letter should already have revealed that the new arrangement is a very considerable relief compared with the old one. Your letter tells me that you will continue to keep your eyes open for me. If I still need to express the message just how much that means to me, then let Felizitas be the messenger for me.

Please tell her how much I would love to speak to her once again at our leisure. For the rest, I hope that her health has already begun half-way to improve before the trip. Is the mist really still so thick that Sohn-Rethel (as I might put it) cannot find his way from one room to another?

I am very much looking forward to seeing your Wagner piece along with the figure of the beggar. Until we meet soon in the not so distant future then,

Yours,
Walter

4 December 1937
Boulogne (Seine)
1 rue de Château

PS Thanks to your encouraging portrait, Gustav Mayer will receive the best of advice, although I have not heard a word from him as yet.

1 *another passage from one of Max's letters*: this derives from Max Horkheimer's (unpublished) letter to Benjamin of 5 November 1937.

97   WIESENGRUND-ADORNO TO BENJAMIN
     [LONDON,] 1.2.1938

1 February 1938.

Dear Walter,

Lazarsfeld, the man who procured the radio research contract for me, has sent me a memorandum about the project and asked for my express response and attitude to a whole list of radio 'problems'. I shall spare you his memorandum and my letter of reply. On the other hand, my response to his list has expanded into a general *exposé*,[1] like that I produced before concerning jazz, and since Sohn-Riddle[2] was friendly and enthusiastic enough to copy it up for me, I can send it to you today and also ask you to retain the copy. It goes without saying that your opinion on the matter would interest me enormously. If you feel like showing the *exposé* to Kracauer, that is fine by me. I would merely like to add that, for comprehensible reasons, I have only discussed the *one* problem which matters most to me in a rather

235

watered down form, namely, that concerning what happens to music that gets played even though *no one* actually listens to it.[3] The *exposé* essentially discusses this only in relation to background music, but not in relation to music which is not really perceived *at all*, and *that* is what interests me most of all. But I did not want to hasten my committal to the mad house prematurely. As a result, I am not really clear about the effect of the *exposé*. Nevertheless, I must confide to you my view that music which is listened to by no one spells disaster. I have certainly not developed the theoretical basis of this thought as yet, but I rather believe that the relationship between music and time also plays a role here.

Otherwise, I can report that the first chapter of the Wagner book is finished, and that the second will be finished in the next few days. I have rarely taken as much pleasure in any previous work. What is more, I am striving to keep the text as clear of any technical philosophical jargon as I possibly can.

Since I have received no telegram from New York concerning the possibility of a trip to Paris, I must assume that nothing has come of the idea. I am therefore all the more desirous to hear back from you.

Heartfelt best wishes,

Yours,

Teddie

Dear Detlef, thank you for the card[4] and the Frick manuscript.[5] Alfred Sohn has developed a theory[6] of radio and film as socialized organs of perception, which partly complements Frick's ideas; otherwise he is as brilliant and stimulating as ever, but we have naturally seen no results whatsoever from his work. Lots of love as always,

Yours,

Felicitas

1 *a general exposé*: the typescript that survived amongst Adorno's literary remains bears the title 'Questions and Theses'.

2 *Sohn-Riddle*: in Adorno's original German 'Sohn-Rätsel' is a play on the name Sohn-Rethel.

3 *music that gets played even though no one actually listens to it*: for the relevant passage in Adorno's *exposé*, cf. *Briefwechsel Adorno/Sohn-Rethel*, p. 79.

4 *the card*: the card appears not to have survived.

5 *the Frick manuscript*: nothing further known.

6 *Alfred Sohn has developed a theory*: cf. *Briefwechsel Adorno/Sohn-Rethel*, pp. 73–8.

Paris, 11.2.1938
10, rue Dombasle

Dear Teddie,

Many thanks indeed for your news, and for the substantial manuscripts. The 'Wagner'[1] arrived early yesterday.

The radio *exposé*[2] alone would have encouraged me to study the
material, if I had had even a single minute of time to spare. And
although – as you can see – I have entrusted myself rather unusually
to a manifestation of technological progress,[3] I cannot write in the
detail I would have wished.

In short: the radio *exposé* gives me every reason to share Sohn-
Riddle's enthusiasm. In the first place, it is amongst the most illuminating things of yours which I have read. In addition to that, it also
reveals a truly life-enhancing undertone, as though it were gently but
obstinately humming along the words of 'you needn't feel afraid'.[4]
I was uncommonly entertained by your description of the radio
listener's 'attitude' (challenged perhaps by the thought that I have
now finally found my proper place in theory as a 'smoker').[5] But
these passages have not prevented me from appreciating the certainly
more far-reaching ones concerning 'standing' and 'passing' music[6] as
you call it. The whole piece exhibits a fine and transparent eccentri-
city, and if it does get you committed to an *asile d'aliénés*, you have
every right to demand the pavilion next to Paul Klee.

His name instantly suggested itself to me because there has just
been a Klee exhibition here in which some very fine recent works of
his were to be seen. Oil painting is certainly playing a greater role in
his work now than formerly; but I personally still prefer his water-
colours more than anything.

I have been getting about quite a lot during the last few days. It is
not as if everything is already sorted out with my room. For obvious
reasons I have had to entrust myself to the services of a do-it-
yourselfer[7] – a rather nice young man as it happens, a non-Jewish
immigrant who betakes himself to my little room in his spare time in
order to spend it there all the more undisturbed.

I hardly dare openly to express the hope that your departure from
Europe[8] may take longer than expected. But if this should be so, you
must certainly – you and Felizitas – cast a look in my direction.

I have not yet had time to read the first chapter of your Wagner
book properly, but on perusing it I was delighted to come across the
passage where you appeal to my theory of aversion.[9] Are you not

237

intending to read Thomas Mann's essay on Wagner[10] in the next issue of *Mass und Wert*? I hope to do so myself at the first opportunity.

A letter which Max had written to me[11] in December went astray in the post, and I have only now received a copy of it. So I see that the essay for Lion[12] is a real priority.

I met Kracauer and will be passing on your *exposé* on radio at the earliest opportunity. It must be of double, even threefold, interest to him now since he is currently writing a book on film[13] (commissioned by the publishers Allert de Lange). But perhaps you already knew about all that. – I read your review of his book[14] in the last issue of the journal; the review sounded almost elegiac, whereas the book itself only makes one angry.

I found some particularly interesting passages for me in Max's remarks on the nature of critical theory.[15] The conclusion is very fine indeed.

This evening, and not without some apprehension, I shall be going to collect Scholem from the railway station.[16]

Before the busy days ahead of me, I wanted to get this over with. Lots of love to you and Felizitas, and please pass on all my reverential greetings to the High Priest of Economics[17] in his misty stronghold.

As always,

Yours,
Walter

1 *The 'Wagner'*: Adorno had obviously sent Benjamin a typescript copy of the first chapter of his *Essay on Wagner*, the chapter concerned with the social character of the composer and which he had completed on 28 January.

2 *the radio exposé*: the thirteen page typescript copy of Adorno's *exposé* is included in Benjamin's literary remains from his Berlin period.

3 *a manifestation of technological progress*: the letter in question was written on a typewriter.

4 *'you needn't feel afraid'*: a favourite saying of Adorno's; cf. the aphorism with this title in *Minima Moralia* (GS 4, pp. 76ff).

5 *your description of the radio listener's 'attitude' / as a 'smoker'*: the passages in question are to be found on pages 11–13 of Adorno's unpublished typescript; the passage on the 'smoker' (p. 11) reads as follows: 'The gesture of smoking is rather the opposite of that involved in listening to a concert: for it is directed against the aura of the work of art, and it blows smoke in the face of sound. The gesture of smoking indicates a certain turning away from the thing in question, or at least from its power to enchant: the person who smokes is experiencing himself. At the same time, smoking can also serve to concentrate attention. In general, there seems to me to be a close

relationship between smoking and listening to the radio. The smoker isolates himself and makes himself approachable at one and the same time.'

6 *'standing' and 'passing' music*: a passage on page 3 of the *exposé* reads: 'If the film technically transposes the successive images into a single dynamic continuum in an infinitesimal manner, then radio does precisely the opposite as far as music is concerned. The constantly moving tape corresponds to the static screen. And yet, compared with the remorselessly perceived movement of the tape, the music almost seems to stand still. The music is dissociated into "images"; confronted at every moment with the passing of real physical time, it loses all power over the latter and answers for itself. This loss of power over time in an aesthetic semblance which here confronts *temps espace*, is the technical formula for loss of aura, in the sense described in Benjamin's essay on mechanical reproduction.'

7 *a do-it-yourselfer*: nothing further known.

8 *your departure from Europe*: the Adornos actually left Europe for America on the 'Champlain' on 16 February.

9 *my theory of aversion*: cf. the first sentence of Benjamin's piece 'Gloves' from his *One-Way Street*: 'In an aversion to animals, the predominant feeling is fear of being recognized by them through contact' (GS IV [1], p. 90). – For the relevant passage in Adorno's *Essay on Wagner*, cf. GS 13, p. 22.

10 *Thomas Mann's essay on Wagner*: Thomas Mann's lecture on 'Richard Wagner and the Ring of the Nibelung' had appeared in the third issue of the journal *Mass und Wert* (February/January).

11 *a letter which Max had written to me*: Horkheimer's unpublished letter to Benjamin of 17 December 1937.

12 *the essay for Lion*: the piece entitled 'Ein deutsches Institut freier Forschung', first mentioned in letter 90, which Benjamin was intending, at Horkheimer's suggestion, to write for the journal *Mass und Wert*, whose principal editor was Ferdinand Lion (1883–1965).

13 *Kracauer / a book on film*: the book on film, which had been formally agreed between Kracauer and Walter Landauer, the chief financial director of the Allert de Lange Verlag, never materialized.

14 *your review of his book*: see letter 75 and the relevant note.

15 *Max's remarks on the nature of critical theory*: Benjamin is referring to Horkheimer's essay 'Traditional and Critical Theory', already mentioned in letter 83.

16 *to collect Scholem from the railway station*: Scholem describes his visit in his book *Walter Benjamin. Geschichte einer Freundschaft* [W. B. The History of a Friendship] (Frankfurt a.M. 1975), pp. 255–66.

17 *the High Priest of Economics*: Benjamin is referring to Sohn-Rethel (cf. the final paragraph of letter 96).

PRINCETON UNIVERSITY
PRINCETON NEW JERSEY
– –
SCHOOL OF PUBLIC AND INTERNATIONAL AFFAIRS

OFFICE OF RADIO RESEARCH   7 March 1938.
203 ENO HALL

Dear Walter,

These lines are merely to let you know in the rather incredible haste of these first few weeks – which I must place entirely at the disposal of the radio project – that we have indeed travelled and arrived safely, and that we have already taken up provisional residence here in a very pleasant apartment. The radio project has turned out to be something with extraordinary possibilities and a very large potential audience. I am in charge of the entire musical side of things, and effectively of the overall theoretical approach as well, since the official Director who brought me here in the first place, Lazarsfeld, is principally involved in the organizational side of the work.

Today I would merely like to ask you to send me a very brief report, of about two or three typed pages, in your own name, concerning your attempts to develop certain 'listening models'[1] with respect to radio in Germany. I would like to incorporate the material into the archives here and refer to it in my own memorandum, and I certainly do not exclude the possibility that this could also produce some practical results of benefit to you.

As far as my work for the Institute is concerned, all I can say for today is that I have had to postpone the Wagner piece for some weeks due to the considerable amount of extra work on the radio project; further, that Max's essay on Montaigne,[2] very much in line with our own approach, is concerned not so much with a critique of Montaigne as with the changing historical role of scepticism, and is something which I personally regard as extraordinarily successful, and also as an occasion for relevant political observations; that Gretel and I have now got hold of Kracauer's manuscript, although neither of us is expecting great things to come of it. Whether anything here is actually usable or not is still uncertain, but I am quite sure that if one does undertake to salvage any of it, this will only be possible if it is completely demolished first and then pieced together again from the smallest fragments. For the sake of his own socio-psychological insights, Kracauer has entirely missed the significance of the enormous

240

question of advertising, even though this tangibly presents itself in the material he quotes. The theoretical construction involved is arbitrarily tentative, while the material is derived entirely from second-hand sources. – My essay on Mannheim seems to be truly dead and buried, and will only be partially disseminated now in the form of typescripts and page proofs; the Husserl piece, on the other hand, may well appear in some form or other, albeit with substantial cuts. The most serious matter to bear in mind, and this is something I wanted to point out to you in relation to your work on Baudelaire, is that the Institute journal is now being reduced to its original dimensions, which rules out the publication of any works exceeding two and a half sextodecimo sheets.

As we both expected, it has not proved all that difficult getting used to our new situation. It is, *sérieusement*, much more European here than it is in London, and 7th Avenue, which is very close to where we live, rather gently reminds us of boulevard Montparnasse, just as Greenwich Village, where we live, similarly reminds us of Mont St Geneviève. If we had you here with us, we would be as completely happy as anyone possibly could be in a world in which one half is governed by Chamberlain's policy towards Hitler and the other half by Stalin's idea of justice. Letters will reach us most quickly and most reliably at our private apartment: 45 Christopher Street, 11 G, New York City, N.Y. USA. Please do not allow yourself to be disconcerted by the chameleon-like letterhead and write to us as soon as you can, even if we have to reckon with Scholem's arrival and with whatever Cabbalistic signs his stay in Manhattan will have to be interpreted under. Lots of love from both of us,

Your old friend,
Teddie

Dear Detlef:

Not only do I feel much more comfortable here than I did in London, but I am quite convinced that you would too. Perhaps the most surprising thing for me is that everything is not quite as new and advanced as one might actually expect; on the contrary, one is faced everywhere by the contrast between the extremely modern and the downright shabby. One does not have to search for surrealistic things here, for one stumbles across them all the time. In the early evening the high rise blocks are very imposing, but later on, when the offices are all closed and the electric lighting is much reduced, they remind me of badly lit European tenements. And just imagine, there are stars here too, with a steady moon and wonderful sunsets like those of early summer. – E.[3] was here over the weekend; he is extremely well, and I only wonder how long he will continue to bear this relatively quiet life. – You can probably hardly imagine just how much I would love to see you over here. However, I harbour the single fear that you are so at home amongst your Arcades that you will never want to leave the splendid structure, and that it is only when you have finally closed the door on it that any other subject will catch your interest. Please do not laugh at me too much and let us hear from you soon.

Your old friend, from a foreign land,
Felicitas

1 *your attempts to develop 'listening models'*: for Benjamin's 'Hörmodelle' [Listening Models], cf. GS IV [2], pp. 627–720, and the editor's remarks on pp. 1053ff. It is quite possible that the text of the 'Hörmodelle' (ibid., p. 628) originated in early 1938 in response to this request in Adorno's letter.

2 *Max's essay on Montaigne*: cf. Max Horkheimer, 'Montaigne and the Function of Scepticism', in *Zeitschrift für Sozialforschung* 7, issue 1/2 (1938), pp. 1–52; now in Max Horkheimer, *Gesammelte Schriften*, vol. 4, pp. 236–94.

3 *E.*: i.e. Egon Wissing.

100   BENJAMIN TO THEODOR W. AND GRETEL ADORNO
      PARIS, 27.3.1938

27 March 1938
10, rue Dombasle
Paris (I5e)

Dear Teddie,

I was delighted to receive some news, and such good news, from you at last. Neither of us has been exactly spoilt with good news during the recent past.

You will be able to imagine how pleased I was to see that my son has now escaped the wretched situation in Austria. One can hardly bear to think about what is happening now in Vienna unless one is absolutely forced to do so.

Hopefully what I have heard about Krenek[1] is true: that he has more or less completely relinquished his position in Austria and is now in America.

Scholem has been there for some time already, although I have still not received a single line from him, so I have no idea whether he is hiding away in New York or Chicago or some other place. If you have any connections with Jewish circles in New York, you will probably be able to discover his whereabouts fairly easily.

242

You will also realize that recent events are encouraging me to pursue the question of naturalization[2] extremely seriously. As always with such things, one suddenly finds oneself confronted with wholly unforeseen difficulties; at the moment these involve procuring an unbelievable quantity of papers and documents. And these things also consume an enormous amount of time.

Uncertain though my prospects in the undertaking are, now is certainly the right time to follow these matters up – if only to provide an appropriate dossier for the official records of the Ministry of Justice.

Perhaps Max has already told you that I have received the proofs of the Institute essay from *Mass und Wert* – something that was not altogether easy to prise from the rather dangerous saboteur that Lion is.

It is very promising to see that your new work is developing the important perspectives which were intimated in your *exposé*. The way in which Felicitas described where you are living also touched me to the heart. It is a familiar old thought of mine that I wish to be seduced by new cities, and the two of you would seem to be strongly encouraging me in this.

Recently, and quite unexpectedly, I received ten to twenty volumes from the library I left behind in Berlin. I am also anticipating the arrival of the books from Denmark[3] in the near future.

If you, Felizitas, should come across my French books when you are unpacking things, could you have them sent on to me through the Institute as soon as possible?

I have heard tell that many people are now fleeing Prague. I don't know whether it was very wise of Ernst[4] to stay there. But perhaps he will be leaving for Lodz!?

The material on 'Models for Listening' was amongst the manuscripts I had to leave behind in Germany. I have been able to reconstruct the structure of the writings as far as possible from memory. An *exposé*[5] is enclosed.

Please write to me soon and in *great* detail.

Greetings to all our friends and heartfelt wishes to both of you,

Yours,
Walter

PS I pass on two book titles[6] which might be of interest to you in connection with the work on Wagner:

Walter Lange: *Richard Wagners Sippe* [Richard Wagner's Racial Heritage] (Leipzig 1938), Verlag Beck.
Eugen Schmidt: *Richard Wagner wie wir ihn heute sehen* [How we see Richard Wagner today] (Dresden 1938), von Baensch Stiftung.

1 *what I have heard about Krenek*: Krenek, who had long since decided on emigration, arrived in America on 31 August.

2 *the question of naturalization*: see letter 92 and the relevant note.

3 *the books from Denmark*: i.e. the portion of Benjamin's library which he was able to save and was now being looked after by Brecht; on the transportation of Benjamin's books, see letter 109.

4 *Ernst*: i.e. Ernst Bloch.

5 *the material on 'Models for Listening' / An exposé*: Gretel Adorno confirmed the receipt of a letter concerning these pieces in a letter to Benjamin of 10 April 1938.

6 *two book titles*: Benjamin made a slight error in giving the name of the second author; the full details are: Walter Lange, *Richard Wagners Sippe. Vom Urahn zum Enkel* (Leipzig 1938) and Eugen Schmitz, *Richard Wagner, wie wir ihn heute sehen* (Dresden 1937), Verlag Heimatwerk Sachsen (Schriftenreihe Grosse Sachsen, Diener des Reiches. 2).

101 ADORNO TO BENJAMIN
     [NEW YORK,] 8.4.1938

8 April 38.

Dear Walter, is this card[1] louche enough for you? What do you think about the idea that we may soon become blood relations[2] with one another? Lots of love from your not so distant Teddie.

1 *this card*: the postcard in question showed three photographs of the Entrance, the 'Main Dining Room' and the 'Bar and Cocktail Lounge' of the restaurant 'Gaston à la bonne soupe French Restaurant, 44 West 55th. Street, N.Y.C.'

2 *blood relations*: Egon Wissing, Benjamin's nephew, and Liselotte Karplus, Gretel Adorno's sister, were intending to get married.

102 BENJAMIN TO THEODOR W. AND GRETEL ADORNO
     PARIS, 16.4.1938

10, rue Dombasle
Paris, XVe
16.4.1938

Dear Teddie,
    Your restaurant postcard for Easter arrived here yesterday.
    I have to tell you that the first I knew of the relationship, to which you allude as if it were something generally known, was precisely

244

through this allusion. Thus it is that we, you and I, are now about to start nodding at one another like little leaves on the family tree; and just as we have already managed to communicate fairly well in the airy language of zephyrs, so too we shall, with God's help, bring something forth from the storms that threaten.

I was particularly pleased to see Egon flanked by two helpers who are not nearly as flighty as those at K.'s disposal, but just as cunning, and of whom it could be said that they are more or less constantly aware of what is going on in the 'Castle'. Be sure to let him know my emphatic view of the matter, for it hoists aloft a very long cable of congratulations.

When I think about it, it was only the new title you mention which occasioned your substantial letter. For I have not heard anything in detail from you since my last letter. I make an exception here for the Wagner material, of which I now have the first four chapters. These contain an abundance of appealing and in part extremely important themes from my point of view. But of course, I shall have to have the whole thing in front of me so I can study it properly, before you can really expect any rational response from me. As you know, the subject matter itself will pose some problems for me in this respect, unfortunately something which is only magnified by the state of the copy you sent me. It is very faint and extremely difficult to read. I hope you will be able to send me a better copy as soon as you can spare one.

I was particularly struck by your remarks about the 'accompanying' character of Wagner's music.[1] I was also extremely taken with your observations about Wagner's musical language[2] in comparison with Schubert's word-setting in 'Forest and Cave' – a quotation from Faust that can certainly be invoked in this connection! I hardly need to add that the conclusions you draw from the allegorical dimension of Wagner's idea of the 'Leitmotiv' [Leading Theme][3] were particularly significant for me. – I look forward to the moment when I shall be able to wander my way through the whole text, carefully seeking out the thoughts I can also regard as my own.

– –

And here I must also say a word to you, dear Felizitas, to wish you all the best for Easter and all Easter things; also to thank you for the lines you sent me on 1 April, which gave me a lot of pleasure. Your willingness to copy out my essay on Mechanical Reproduction is quite invaluable to me. I accept your offer with the greatest delight. As soon as I find the time to look through the manuscript once again, you will receive it from me. It really looks as though your intervention here has raised a lucky star over my opuscula. For only yesterday I managed to get Levy-Ginsberg to take away the manuscript of 'A Berlin Childhood'[4] with him, and there is now the prospect of recovering the Rowohlt copies[5] which he appropriated from you.

It is certainly not hard for me to admit that Elisabeth[6] is indeed an extremely charming and remarkable creature. Unfortunately, she was not here long before she floated away – perhaps she will soon come floating back.

The following piece of news may serve to build a bridge from my little note here to the resumption of our interrupted correspondence.

– –

Dolf Sternberger has just brought out his 'Panorama – Nineteenth Century Views'[7] (published by Goverts, i.e. Claassens, in Hamburg). The title itself is an admission of attempted plagiarism at my expense, and, indeed, the only successful example of it as far as the fundamental concept of the book is concerned. For the concept of the 'Arcades' has here been forced through the filter not once but twice. What has managed to survive the passage through Sternberger's brain (filter 1) has also had to make its further passage through the *The National Writers Association* (filter 2). It will not be difficult for you to imagine the end result of this process. Perhaps the programmatic formulation to be found in the 'Aphoristic Preface' will provide you with some assistance: 'deeds and circumstances, freedom and coercion, matter and spirit, innocence and guilt, cannot really be separated out from one another in that historical past with whose immutable manifestations, however fragmentary and incomplete they may be, we find ourselves confronted. For all these things have always been hopelessly interwoven with one another ... It is a question of the contingency of history itself, as it has revealed and preserved itself in the contingent choice of quotations, in the contingent and unruly confusion of its different features, which manage nonetheless to assume the form of inscription.'

The unbelievably impoverished conceptual apparatus which Sternberger employs has been pieced together from things he has purloined from Bloch, from you, and from me. Particularly barefaced is the use of the concept of allegory, as found on page three. A couple of wretched excursions on the subject of sympathy only prove to me that he has also been poking around in my work on the Elective Affinities.

Working under the eyes of the National Writers' Association, he of course didn't dare refer to any French, i.e. essential, sources. And if you consider that it is Bölsche, Haeckel, Marlitt and the like to whom the supposedly conceptual apparatus is applied, you will be able to form an accurate idea of what would otherwise seem utterly incredible when you actually have it before you in black and white.

That this young man should have made his first contribution to literature with the Munich report on Hitler's speech[8] against degenerate art, before approaching his recent masterpiece, is hardly surprising in the context.

I imagine you will want to get hold of a copy. Perhaps you could also discuss with Max whether or not I might be able to review it – or in simple German to denounce it – publicly.

I am now thoroughly occupied with a schematic articulation of the 'Baudelaire', and I have sent Max a short report about it. After I have spent so long piling up books on books, excerpts on excerpts, I am now ready to compose a series of reflections[9] which will furnish the foundation for an entirely transparent structure. For dialectical rigour, I should like this piece to be the equal of my work on the Elective Affinities.

In conclusion, an accumulated pile of mixed post.

But first of all a few requests. One to Felizitas, to send me the illustrated French books as soon as she can, and preferably insured, and a repeated one to you, to send your Kierkegaard. It would also be equally important for me to hear something from you about any of your potentially frequent meetings with Scholem in the meantime. – I spoke to Jean Wahl recently, and just on his way back from seeing Bergson. The latter is already imagining the Chinese at the gates of Paris – and this while the Japanese were still winning the war. Wahl also told me that Bergson held the railways responsible for everything. (It is worth asking the further question what we will be able to get out of Jean Wahl when he is eighty years old.) – Grete de Francesco has passed through Paris. I only managed to speak to her on the telephone. She is extremely depressed about things. Her parents, along with some considerable assets, have got caught in the Austrian trap.

I hope to receive some very detailed news from you soon, and in the meantime all my greetings to you, Felizitas and the general circle,

Yours,

Walter

1 *the 'accompanying' character of Wagner's music*: cf. GS 13, pp. 57 and 118.

2 *your observations about Wagner's musical language*: cf. ibid., pp. 56ff.

3 *the allegorical dimension of Wagner's idea of the 'Leitmotiv'*: cf. ibid., pp. 43ff.

4 *Levy-Ginsberg . . . the manuscript of 'A Berlin Childhood'*: Arnold Levy had taken away the last typescript copy of 'A Berlin Childhood' in order to have it transcribed, as Benjamin's letter to Gretel Adorno of 1 September 1935 makes clear (for a substantial excerpt from this letter, cf. GS V [2], p. 1141).

5 *recovering the Rowohlt copies*: see letter 15.

6 *Elisabeth*: i.e. Elisabeth Wiener, a friend of Gretel's about whom the latter had made enquiries in her unpublished letter to Benjamin of 1 April.

7 *Sternberger / 'Panorama – Nineteenth Century Views'*: cf. Dolf Sternberger, *Panorama order Ansichten vom 19. Jahhrundert* (Hamburg 1938).

8 *the Munich report on Hiltler's speech*: cf. Dolf Sternberger's 'A Temple of Art. Adolf Hitler opens the "House of German Art" ', in *Frankfurter Zeitung*, 19.7.1938 (year 81, nr. 362), pp. 1ff, and on p. 3 of the same issue his article: 'A City in Celebration. Festivities at the Opening of "The House of German Art" '.

9 *the 'Baudelaire' / a series of reflections*: most probably the materials published in facsimile with an accompanying transcription in GS VII [2], pp. 744–63.

103 ADORNO TO BENJAMIN
     [NEW YORK,] 4.5.1938

PRINCETON UNIVERSITY
PRINCETON NEW JERSEY
– –
SCHOOL OF PUBLIC AND INTERNATIONAL AFFAIRS

OFFICE OF RADIO RESEARCH   4 March 1938.
203 ENO HALL

Dear Walter:

The Wagner is finished and Lazarsfeld is now in Columbia, Ohio: hence I get to write to you at last.

But first about Scholem. You may find this hard to believe, but the first time we got to meet him was at the Tillichs, together with Goldstein[1] and his new wife. Not exactly the best atmosphere in which to be introduced to the Sohar; and especially since Frau Tillich's relationship to the Kabbala seems to resemble that of a terrified teen-ager to pornography. The antinomian Maggid was extremely reserved towards me at first, and clearly regarded me as some sort of danger-ous arch-seducer: I had the strange feeling of finding myself identified with Brecht. Needless to say, nothing of the kind was actually said, and Scholem contrived to sustain the fiction, with considerable brash grace, that he knew nothing at all about me except that a book of mine had been published by the blessed Siebeck.[2] Nevertheless, I somehow succeeded in breaking the spell and he began to show some kind of trust in me, something which I think will continue to grow.

248

We have spent a couple of evenings together, as the ringing in your ears has presumably already told you by now; once on our own, in a discussion which touched in part upon our own last conversation in San Remo concerning theology, and in part upon my Husserl piece, which Scholem read with great care, as if it were some intelligence test. We spent the second evening in the company of Max, and Scholem, who was in great form, regaled us in detail with the most astonishing things in connection with Sabbatian and Frankist mysticism; a number of which, however, sounded so clearly reminiscent of some of Rosenberg's notions about 'the people', that Max was seriously concerned about the prospect of more of this kind actually appearing in print. It is not altogether easy for me to convey my own impression of Scholem. This is indeed a classic case of the conflict between duty and inclination. My personal inclination comes into play most strongly when he makes himself the mouthpiece of the theological moment of your, and perhaps I might also say of my own, philosophy; and it will hardly have escaped you that a number of his arguments against simply abandoning the theological moment, and above all his argument that in truth this moment is no more eliminated by the method of your work than it is by mine, corresponds with my own excursions on the subject in San Remo; and not to mention that philosopher's stone, and rock of offence, currently living in Denmark.[3] But my sense of duty also immediately asserts itself here and compels me to admit that your own comparison with the sheet of blotting paper,[4] your own intention to mobilize the power of theological experience anonymously within the realm of the profane, seems to me utterly and decisively superior to all of Scholem's attempts to salvage the theological moment. Thus I insisted on maintaining the general line of approach agreed between us at San Remo, that is, while I certainly conceded to him the presence of this 'alien body', I simultaneously affirmed the necessity of its intrusion. Part of the problem here is the particular form which theology has now assumed for Scholem himself. For one thing, this attempted salvation of theology is a strangely linear and romantic one: when he emphasizes, for example, the opposition between the 'content' and its genesis, and accuses Marxism of simply concerning itself with the latter and ignoring the content as such, I am very strongly reminded of Kracauer or even Theodor Haecker. But when one takes a closer look at the things which he himself presents – and for my own part I was unable to separate the contents of his mysticism from the very historical fate as he described it himself – then their most essential characteristic seems to be the fact that they 'explode'. He himself insists upon a sort of radioactive decay which drives us on from mysticism, and indeed equally in all of its monadically conceived historical shapes and forms, towards enlightenment. It strikes me as an expression of the most profound irony that the very conception of mysticism which he urges presents itself from the perspective of the philosophy of history precisely as that same incursion into the profane with which he reproaches both of us. The narratives he describes, if not his thoughts themselves, actually provide a rigorous justification for the very changes in your own thought which offend him the most. – The spiritual energy and power of the man is enormous, and he certainly belongs amongst those very few individuals with whom it is still worthwhile discussing such serious matters. But it is rather strange how this power sometimes abandons him at a stretch and allows prejudice and the most banal observations to prevail uncontested instead. This is also true for his style of historical interpretation, when he explains the 'explosions' of Jewish mysticism in exclusively internal theological terms, and then precisely for that reason violently repudiates the social connections which would otherwise ineluctably force themselves upon one's attention. It is as if a lifeboat has just been released with enormous care; but the art then principally consists in swamping it with water and getting it to capsize. For my part, I share your view that it would be best for the whole ship to sink with all hands on board, and then at least some of the freight could be saved, even without the crew. Nonetheless, I am quite fascinated by the man, and Felicitas likewise, and I think there is some real contact between us, which on occasion assumes the form of a certain trust – rather like that which might develop between an Ichthyosaurus and a Brontosaurus meeting for coffee, or even better, if Leviathan should decide to drop in on Behemoth. In a word, one is still amongst one's own. Perhaps I should also add that Scholem is obviously bound to you emotionally to a quite remarkable degree, and at least initially regards anyone else who crops up in this connection, whether it is Bloch, Brecht or whoever, as one of the enemy. As far as I myself am concerned, I feel that he has been mollified somewhat; I cannot speak for how he stands toward Max. For his part, Max reacted very positively, and I should like to believe that the meeting, which took place incidentally in a New York bar, also proved valuable in so far as it gave Max a fresh perspective on certain things with regard to you from before his time. On the other hand, Scholem obstinately refuses to become involved with the Institute and even turned down our invitation for him to come and give a lecture there – this is presumably connected with the fact that he knew Löwenthal and Fromm during their Zionist period.[5]

Here is the rest of my Wagner; unfortunately, I do not have a better copy to offer at the moment. My plans for the immediate future are still uncertain. Max and I are considering a first substantial collaborative venture together; there are two ideas[6] in prospect, but I am too superstitious to discuss the matter as yet. My major report on the radio research,[7] in effect a small book, has also been completed in the meantime, and it has also been decided that the results of my work on music and radio[8] should appear as an independent and probably substantial volume with Princeton University Press, and that means prominently too. In this connection I am also thinking of a shorter piece in German[9] on the regression of listening and the fetish character in music, as a kind of counterpart to my essay on jazz. Whether I can begin work on this soon is a question of the time available to me: I still have to extract a suitable complex of material from the Wagner book for journal publication (I am considering chapters five to seven), the question of publishing my work on Husserl now that he has died has become topical again, and in addition, I have also been given the task of turning Kracauer's substantial piece on propaganda,[10] 170 typed pages of it, into an essay of appropriate length for journal publication. You do not have to envy me this work, and as a totality Kracauer's product is much as you will imagine it to be. Nonetheless, I feel there is enough usable material here for the piece to be salvaged; an opinion which I am apparently so unique in sharing that I do not know if it will lead to a positive result in the end. All this in the strictest confidence, of course.

I am very pleased to hear from Pollock that things are going well with you and the Baudelaire work, and I am waiting expectantly for further news. As far as Sternberger is concerned, I have encouraged acquisition of the book, and I would certainly have nothing against such a denunciation. I would merely point out to you that, according to my latest and extremly reliable information, Sternberger's position at the newspaper has now become untenable anyway, and I am not sure whether one should anticipate the world spirit in this connection.

What we can expect to hear one day from an eighty-year-old Jean Wahl is already abundantly revealed by his 745-page book on Kierkegaard.[11] It is a solid scholarly work, but also an indescribably tedious one. Nothing more than a lot of interpretation, exposition and existential bridge-building, with special chapters on Kierkegaard and Jaspers and Kierkegaard and Heidegger; there is no attempt to develop a critique or a theoretical elucidation of the philosophy of existence, but simply the desire to fortify the latter with a kind of 'standard work' or textbook. I have the task of reviewing the work twice: in an American journal and in our own. I cannot possibly force myself to express any great show of friendship. I would, therefore, be grateful, if you could let me know how you think we should proceed tactically with regard to Wahl. Incidentally, I do believe that my David is just as unattractive to him as his Goliath is to me.

As far as the Museum of Modern Arts is concerned, you should really establish contact with Schapiro,[12] who is extremely familiar with your writings and in general is a well-informed and intellectually imaginative man – if not always discriminating, as when he tried to convince us once that your essay on mechanical reproduction was quite compatible with the methods of logical positivism. I tell you this merely in order to inform you that amongst the avant-garde here, the trees are no more toweringly impressive than they are amongst the Parisians. But the material resources of such circles here may be rather greater, and the idea of bringing you over through some *combine* between Schapiro and the Institute certainly does not strike me as altogether utopian. However, that is just my own private opinion; for some very good reasons, and with your own agreement, I have not yet discussed the whole matter with Max. Politically speaking, Schapiro is an active Trotskyist. Here is his address: Prof. Meyer Schapiro, 279 West 4th Street, New York, N. Y. (he reads German fluently). In this connection, I would also like to point out that your security in Paris has hardly increased in the light of recent events. The fact that it will not come to war, according to our theory, does nothing to make the prospect less dangerous if the theory should prove false.

I have seen Eisler quite a lot, and on one occasion we had a lengthy conversation. He is extremely friendly and approachable, presumably on account of the Institute or the radio project; his latest pose in relation to me is that of an old weather-beaten materialist politico, whose fatherly function lies in protecting the young and inexperienced idealist like me from the illusions of the age, and all by communicating his newest insights that politics must also learn to reckon with human beings as they are, that the workers too are no angels etc. I listened with not a little patience to his feeble defence of the Moscow trials, and with considerable disgust to the joke he cracked about the murder of Bukharin. He claims to have known the latter in Moscow, telling me that Bukharin's conscience was already so bad that he could not even look him, Eisler, honestly in the eyes. I am not inventing all this. Incidentally, I have learned a good deal from reading Trotsky's book *La Révolution trahie*,[13] and despite your aversion against getting involved in this whole matter, I think you should take a look at it some time.

Things are continuing to go well for Gretel and me, and through our window, while I was dictating this letter, we could see the Normandie leaving on its return voyage to France.

Lots of love from both of us,

Your old friend,
Teddie

Please forgive your Felicitas a rather cheeky question: is Scholem himself a Frankist, and does he actually believe everything he says?

Lots of love,

your Felicitas

1 *Goldstein*: Adorno is referring to the psychiatrist and neurologist Kurt Goldstein (1878–1965), who was an acquaintance of his and Benjamin's from their time in Frankfurt.

2 *a book of mine . . . published by the blessed Siebeck*: Adorno's book *Kierkegaard* had appeared in January 1933 with the publishing house of J. C. B. Mohr (Siebeck).

3 *that philosopher's stone, and rock of offence, . . . in Denmark*: an allusion to Brecht's influence upon Benjamin.

4 *your own comparison with the sheet of blotting paper*: cf. GS V [1], p. 588: 'My thought relates to theology just as a piece of blotting paper relates to ink. It absorbs the latter completely. But if we were solely concerned with the blotting paper, then there would be nothing written left for us to read.'

5 *Löwenthal and Fromm / their Zionist period*: during the 1920s, Löwenthal and Fromm had both worked at the Jewish Teaching Institute (Das jüdische Lehrhaus) in Frankfurt a.M.

6 *a first substantial collaborative venture / two ideas*: see letter 104, following.

7 *My major report on the radio research*: Adorno is probably referring to the unpublished 170-page typescript with the title 'Music in Radio'.

8 *the results of my work on music and radio*: the book Adorno had planned under the title 'Current of Music', which was to have included his studies on radio, never materialized.

9 *a shorter piece in German*: cf. Adorno's essay, completed in the late summer of 1938, 'On the Fetish Character of Music and the Regression of Listening', which appeared in *Zeitschrift für Sozialforschung* 7, issue 3 (1938), pp. 321–55; now in GS 14, pp. 14–50.

10 *Kracauer's substantial piece on propaganda*: on 5 March 1938, Adorno had recommended in an unpublished report (a typescript copy of which survives amongst his literary remains) on the first part of Kracauer's work 'Totalitarian Propaganda in Germany and Italy', that the piece should be reduced to the dimensions of a journal article and then published in the *Zeitschrift für Sozialforschung*: 'Since the positive parts of the work are permeated by theoretical improvization and marked by naiveties, and since, even if the first thirty to forty pages are cut entirely, the work far exceeds the appropriate length for the journal, I would suggest that it be examined for its usable parts, that these be noted down under suitable subtitles and detached from the context Kracauer has provided for them whenever the said context appears arbitrary. On the other hand, Kracauer's arrangement

of the material would have to be preserved where usable. It would then be possible to produce a new journal article of two sextodecimos at most. I would be prepared to undertake this task myself' (p. 3). – When Kracauer received Adorno's edited and condensed version of his work, he decided against its publication.

11 *Jean Wahl / his book on Kierkegaard*: cf. Jean Wahl, *Études Kierkegaardiennes* (Paris 1938); for Adorno's review of the book, cf. *Zeitschrift für Sozialforschung* 8, issue 1/2 (1939/40), pp. 232ff; now in GS 20 [1], pp. 232ff. – There is no trace of a further review in an American journal.

12 *Schapiro*: Meyer Schapiro (born 1904), an American art historian of Lithuanian origin, who had lived in the USA since 1907; he taught at Columbia University in New York.

13 *Trotsky's book La Révolution trahie*: cf. Leon Trotsky, *La Révolution trahie. Qu'est-ce-qu'est l'U.R.S.S et où va-t-elle?* (Paris 1936), translated from the Russian by Victor Serge.

104 ADORNO TO BENJAMIN
[NEW YORK,] 8.6.1938

8 June 1938.

Dear Walter:

I haven't heard anything from you in a long while, and I am writing now with a request, and a rather obvious one: namely, for you to finish the Baudelaire soon enough for inclusion in the next issue of the journal, that is, to make sure it is here by the first half of September. The reason is this: if the issue materializes as we are currently hoping, it will consist of an essay by Grossmann on Marx's real innovations in economics, namely, his conception of exchange-value and use-value, your piece on Baudelaire, and my piece on Husserl[1] – this in a shortened and heavily revised form, which attempts above all to avoid a certain myopic proximity to Husserl's texts and to articulate the argument sufficiently independently of Husserl so that the overall critical intention is clearly expressed. This revision is the last thing which I am now expecting to accomplish before the holidays. If the three pieces actually did appear together in this single issue, we would have produced something to be proud of. However, there is still the awkward question of requisite length to be considered. I am determined that I shall not exceed two sextodecimos, and a length of two and a half sextodecimos at most would also really be the only means of securing publication of the Baudelaire piece in the next issue. *Dira necessitas.*[2] I am sure I hardly have to explain to you just how particularly grateful I should be if you could fulfil this

254

request of mine. I think I can probably say that the problems which the revision of the Husserl piece have given me are not much more humanly bearable than those which might be occasioned by your attempt to limit the size and the schedule of the Baudelaire piece.

As for the rest, my literary plans with Max are now beginning to assume a very concrete shape. It has already been virtually decided that we shall collaborate in writing a major essay on the new, open form of dialectic. We are both consumed with enthusiasm for the idea, and if it proves as remotely successful as we hope it will, then I believe it will also represent your own theoretical interests in a way which should certainly give you some satisfaction. The essay in question will contribute its part to our substantial projected materialist logic. The latter belongs to our current plans for future publications, as well as an entertaining book on the critique of sociology,[3] in which my Mannheim piece will celebrate a happy resurrection under application to even broader subjects. All of this in the strictest confidence for the present. Max is travelling west and will not be back here until September.

In the meantime I have managed to produce what I take to be a publishable essay from Kracauer's manuscript by reducing his own 170 pages, even while making numerous additions and further explanatory comments, to 30 pages of typescript. Amongst other things, there is now a chapter on the 'Führer' which I think is rather successful, as indeed the whole thing now generally appears. Apart from the Hitler quotations, not a word of Kracauer's original really remains. He still has no idea of what is in store for him, and I must ask you to exercise discretion here as well.

Like Solvejg for Peer Gynt, I am waiting to hear your response to my Wagner piece.

And one more thing. On behalf of a certain organization for immigrants, I had to write a report on a piece entitled 'Optimism' by one Herr Greid,[4] who regards himself as a Marxist but is just a fool. The report was framed accordingly. With my permission it was then made available to Herr Greid, who has now written me an indescribably appalling letter.[5] All this would be of absolutely no consequence, of course, if the letter had not explicitly referred to Greid's relationship to Brecht, and then gone on to claim that Greid has never heard any of his acquaintances say anything whatsoever about me or my Marxist credentials. That is particularly irritating, and I would be especially grateful to you if you could ignore the matter, at least as long as it does not cause you any great inconvenience to do so. Mille grazie.

Lots of love from both of us,

Your old friend,
Teddie

I have just heard from Max that he has also written to you today[6] and in much the same sense as I have. However, we actually wrote our letters without either of us knowing about the other.

1 *the next issue / an essay by Grossmann / your piece on Baudelaire / my piece on Husserl*: no issue containing these pieces together ever materialized.

2 *Dira necessitas*: cf. Horace, *Odes* III, 24, 6.

3 *an entertaining book on the critique of sociology*: the book actually remained unwritten.

4 *a report / piece entitled 'Optimism' / Herr Greid*: Adorno wrote the report about the piece in question in January 1938, for the 'American Guild for German Cultural Freedom'. – Hermann Greid (1892–1975), an actor and director, had emigrated to Sweden where he also collaborated with Brecht.

5 *an indescribably appalling letter*: the letter does not survive amongst Adorno's literary remains.

6 *Max has also written to you today*: the copy of the letter which survives amongst Horkheimer's literary remains is actually dated 7 July 1938. The unpublished letter also contained a 'certificat de travail' which Benjamin required for the naturalization proceedings and had requested in his own letter to Horkheimer of 28 May (cf. GS VI, p. 775): 'Nous certifions que Monsieur Walter Benjamin a travaillé à partir du mois de juillet 1934 jusqu'à maintenant pour l'Institut de Recherches Sociales, Paris, 45, rue d'Ulm, en qualité de collaborateur à la revue de cet Institut, et que depuis cette date jusqu'à ce jour, il a toujours résidé en France.' (After the typescript copy in the Max Horkheimer Archive.)

105 BENJAMIN TO THEODOR W. AND GRETEL ADORNO
     PARIS, 19.6.1938

19.6.1938
10, rue Dombasle
Paris, XV

Dear Teddie,
   The time has come, and I set myself to write the letter about your 'Wagner'; I shall plunge *in medias res*, on the assumption that you are less urgently concerned to learn about what has delayed my letter than you are about what it has to say concerning the matter itself.
   I have now studied this material enough to begin to feel a little at home in it. I only wish you could have made this study as easy for *me* as it will prove to be for other people; *rebus sic stantibus* I have often

gently sighed to myself: an excerpt is no pleasure to a lover of manuscripts, and not particularly conducive to careful study either.

The matter in question – to come directly to the point without beating about the bush – is one of enormous richness and the most astonishing perspicacity. The unfavourable conditions which I necessarily bring to your essay, as one so unfamiliar with the field itself, is also an excellent touchstone for judging it. I would never have believed it possible for me to grasp the piece even on a first reading, with some feeling already for the detailed technical discussions, and with an even clearer perspective on the other parts. How much this testifies to the successful composition of the work goes without saying.

As far as I can see, you have never written anything with quite the same pregnant physiognomy as this piece. Your portrait of Wagner is totally convincing from head to toe. The way in which you have captured the interplay of gesture and attitude in the man is masterly.

I cannot attempt here, as I sometimes have before, to give detailed examples of those things which struck me as particularly effective in terms of insight and formulation. (Amongst the most convincing I would simply name in passing: the inner connection between Wotan and the figure of the beggar,[1] the element of 'German Socialism' in Wagner's attitudes,[2] the political illumination you bring to the Ring motif,[3] the observation about King Mark[4] as the original father of the League of Nations, an observation which struck me as vividly as one of the famous caricatures in the *Evening News*.)

As far as the central issue is concerned, I was particularly fascinated by the emphatic way in which you brought out that specific 'formlessness'[5] which clearly permeates Wagner's work. The expression 'accompanying music'[6] – does it actually originate with you? – is a real find. Similarly illuminating for me was your reference to the shifting contours of the figures, the way in which Wotan and Siegfried, for example, sometimes seem to pass over into one another. In short, I have no doubt whatsoever that the individual elements of your critique of Wagner all derive from an overall conception which owes its strength and plausibility to the authentic historical signature of your own powers of reflection.

And yet the question which first began to hover spiritually over our exchanges after a certain conversation on the terrace in Ospedaletti,[7] has not yet been interred for good. Perhaps you will allow me to evoke the memory of this question with a question of my own: was it always part of your very earliest *experiences* with Wagner to feel completely at home in it as far as your explicit *insight* was concerned? I would like to imagine some grassy plot and someone quite familiar with it from playing on the spot since early childhood;

and standing there one day, he suddenly and unexpectedly finds that it has now become the allotted place for a pistol duel to which he has been challenged by a personal enemy. The kind of tensions such a situation would surely produce also seem to persist throughout your Wagner book. Should it not be precisely these tensions which place the prospect of successful 'salvation' into question here? – and that is exactly what our former conversation turned upon. You have brought out the motifs in which such salvation might announce itself with both clarity and care. The finest formulation in the work, that of the golden nothing and the silver wait-a-while,[8] hovers even now before my mind. It is certainly not the precision of your material-ist deciphering of Wagner which threatens to rob such passages of resonance. But they do not seem to possess the full measure of their possible resonance. Why not? Am I wrong to reply: because they have not been sung at the very cradle of their conception? A work like your 'Wagner' hardly lacks for grottoes or ravines from which the relevant motifs might echo back again. And why do they fail to do so? And all those fine passages where such motifs do suggest their presence (like that remarkable one where you cite the lines: 'The spring's fair goddess from the hill drew near'),[9] why are they as conspicuous for their rarity as they are for their beauty?

If I attempt to formulate the matter briefly, I would have to say: the fundamental conception behind your Wagner, which God knows is quite a powerful one, is essentially polemical. I would not be sur-prised if that were the only one appropriate for us, the only one which would permit us, like you, to draw on all the resources of our wealth. And all your vigorous technical musical analyses, and indeed especially these, also seem to me to find their proper place within the same conception. A polemical engagement with Wagner by no means has to exclude illumination of the progressive elements in his work, as you yourself show, and especially if these cannot simply be separ-ated from the regressive ones like the sheep from the goats.

But yet – and here, dear Teddie, you must allow me to surprise you in body and soul with your own favourite image from Indian Joe about unearthing the hatchet and provoking a fight – it seems to me that any such salvation, undertaken from the perspective of the philosophy of history, is incompatible with one undertaken from a critical perspective that is focused upon progress and regress. Or more precisely – is compatible only in those philosophical connec-tions in which we have ourselves occasionally discussed the question of 'progress' *sub vocem*. The unconditional use of concepts like those of the progressive and the regressive, concepts whose justification I would be the last to deny in the central sections of your work, makes the idea of an attempted 'salvation' of Wagner utterly problematic (a salvation upon which, once again, I would be the last person to insist at the present time – and especially after reading the devastating analyses contained in this work).

I hardly imagine you will wish to contradict me if I say that the philosophical project of such salvation requires a form of writing which – somewhat clumsily expressed because I do not know how to put it any better – has a particular affinity with musical form itself. Salvation is a cyclical form, polemic a progressive one. The ten chapters of your Wagner study appear to me to represent a progression rather than a cycle. And this is the context in which your socio-critical and technical analyses find their sovereign expression. But it is also the context which seems to compromise those other long-standing and highly significant elements in your theory of music – of opera as consolation, of music as protest[10] – which reifies the motif of eternity in its functional connection with phantasmagoria[11] and therefore ignores its affinity with the idea of happiness.

All of this, as I said before, already began to emerge as a question in one of our last conversations.[12] And I do not imagine that you are any less at home in what I have been saying here than I am. Perhaps such a redemption of Wagner might have created a space precisely for one of your earliest themes – that of *décadence* and the Trakl quotation[13] of which you are so fond. For the decisive element in such salvation – am I not right? – is never simply something progressive; it can resemble the regressive as much as it resembles the ultimate goal, which is what Kraus calls the origin.[14]

The difficulties involved in my 'Baudelaire' are perhaps precisely the inverse of yours. There is so little room here for polemic even on the surface level, and certainly not in the matter itself, there is so little here that is simply obsolete or disreputable that the form which salvation takes with this object could itself become a problem. I hope to be clearer in my own mind about this some time soon.

But now to your letters and my silence. I have in front of me the letters of 10 April (when Felizitas wrote to me), of 4 May and 8 June. I would feel even more embarrassed if I did not assume that you have not heard something about me indirectly in the meantime, since I did write a substantial letter to Max[15] and a very detailed one to Scholem.[16] At the same time, and as I was intending finally to provide you both with a copy of 'A Berlin Childhood', I suddenly found myself confronted once again with this text and started making some considerable revisions to it. You will find several examples of this in the last issue of the journal *Mass und Wert*.[17]

To tell the truth, even this catalogue of hindrances is incomplete. I was also afflicted for six weeks with the most terrible chronic migraine. Finally I decided upon a proper tour around the doctors;

at first some kind of malarial recidivism was suspected, although the relevant signs of this were absent. Then, just as I had subjected myself to a thoroughgoing eye examination, the symptoms suddenly disappeared altogether. It was about time, too, for I was feeling quite exhausted by then. Obviously all of this has hardly helped the progress of my work; I shall make an enormous effort to catch up when I am in Denmark. I set off the day after tomorrow.

The various diplomatic representations required for my naturalization have recently begun to multiply. I have given Max all the details[18] in my last letter of 28 May. I am almost certain in assuming that he received the letter[19] before his departure to the western states. He will therefore have been able to inform Pollock of my request for a certificate, which is required in connection with the naturalization procedure, before he left. In case this assumption should prove mistaken, I now enclose a copy of the relevant passage from my letter to Max and ask you to pass it on to Pollock if necessary. He is very well informed about my intentions. The formal process involved here is incredibly tedious; the *earlier* I could receive the certificate the better.

In return for your consignment of the newspaper literary sections,[20] I am sending you both, as printed matter, a prose piece by Claudel[21] which recently appeared in *Figaro*. A fine demonstration of the impressive vision and the unparalleled ability of this terrifying man.

In addition I have a little tip – this will strike you both as comical – for New York. At the moment they are showing a retrospective exhibition of American art here. Thanks to the latter, I have become acquainted with ten to twenty rather primitive pictures by unknown artists of the period between 1800 and 1840. I have never seen pictures quite like this before, which would certainly have made a great impression on me if I had. Those that are not already in the possession of Mrs John Rockefeller junior, mostly come from the 'American Folk Art Gallery'. You really must not miss the chance of seeing them once they are back in place there. – While we are touching on American matters: do you know the work of Melville? Some significant works of his have been appearing over here.

A few words about my own recent literary activities. You will probably have learnt something about this already from Scholem, and especially about my work on Brod's biography of Kafka.[22] I have used this as an opportunity to compose some notes of my own about Kafka,[23] and which take a different point of departure from my earlier essay. In this connection I have returned with great interest to study Teddie's letter on Kafka of 17 December 1934. The letter was just as convincing as Haselberg's Kafka essay,[24] which I also came across amongst my papers, was superficial. – I have been reading Ronsard for the first time and have found there my motto for the

'Baudelaire'.[25] I have also been looking at a translation of Priestley's 'Benighted'.[26] This book provided the basis for a most remarkable film called 'The Old Dark House'. If you ever get the chance to catch the film again, be sure to do so.

And, dear Teddie, I read your account of Leviathan's visit to Behemoth[27] with all due pleasure, and will always remember it with all due respect. But I feel myself rather at a loss for an answer when confronted with Felizitas' question about whether Scholem is a Frankist or not. If I say no, which I feel entitled to do, that will not really help her very much. You must remember that you made Scholem's acquaintance while he was on a kind of special tour. That alone – and not to mention anything else perhaps – means that your chances of getting anything out of him are a hundred times greater than mine. I am still hoping that I shall be able to arrange another meeting with him[28] in Paris, but I am not sure about this yet.

Bloch is still in Prague; he is preparing to move to America.[29] He published a very fine article on Brecht in the journal 'Weltbühne', and a quite appalling one on Bukharin's final words.[30] In this connection I should tell you that bits of news, like the one[31] you gave me about Eisler and Bukharin, are always extremely welcome.

Else Herzberger's American trip has not done anything for me. Since then, I have not managed to have more than a couple of telephone conversations with her, the principal content of which involved constant reference to the losses she has suffered. As you can imagine, I am rather disappointed by this, but I really do not see much space for manœuvre here now.

From amongst your own projects, I am of course especially interested to hear about your work on a new form of dialectic. But presumably your work on 'Music in Radio'[32] will take precedence at the moment?

If I should encounter Greid, about whom you spoke in your letter, I shall behave as you suggest. Fortunately, your letter hardly leads me to consider this a very likely prospect. Unless perhaps he is going to be in Denmark?

And the Sternberger piece[33] will also have to have a rigid deadline? – Anyway, I have already said plenty for today and will close now with heartfelt greetings as ever,

Yours,

Walter

1 *the inner connection between Wotan and the figure of the beggar*: in chapter IX of Adorno's *Essay on Wagner*; cf. GS 13, pp. 127ff.

2 *the element of 'German Socialism' in Wagner's attitudes*: cf. ibid., pp. 126ff.

3 *the political illumination you bring to the Ring motif*: in chapter IX of the *Essay on Wagner* (cf. GS 13, pp. 134–42; cf. also pp. 111–14).

4 *the observation about King Mark*: cf. Adorno, 'Fragmente über Wagner', in *Zeitschrift für Sozialforschung* 8, issue 1/2 (1939/40), pp. 1–48; the relevant quotation is found on page 40: 'Mark is the original father of the League of Nations.' In the *Essay on Wagner* this reads: 'Mark is the original father of appeasement'. (GS 13, p. 137).

5 *that specific 'formlessness'*: cf. GS 13, pp. 38–40.

6 *The expression 'accompanying music'*: cf. ibid., p. 118 – the expression did not in fact originate with Adorno.

7 *a certain conversation on the terrace in Ospedaletti*: during Gretel and Theodor Adorno's stay in San Remo over the New Year 1937/38; see also letter 23, where Adorno mentions the place, and the relevant note. (Ospedaletti Ligure lies a few kilometres to the west of San Remo.)

8 *the golden nothing and the silver wait-a-while*: the sentence in question, which originally stood in chapter X of the manuscript, was deleted by Adorno before the publication of the 'Fragments on Wagner': 'The silver wait-a-while belongs to the golden nothing' (*Theodor W. Adorno Archiv*, Ts. 2927).

9 *'The spring's fair goddess from the hill drew near'*: cf. Richard Wagner, 'Tannhäuser und der Sängerkrieg auf Wartburg', Act 1, Scene 3; Adorno quotes the line in chapter VI of the *Essay on Wagner* (GS 13, p. 88).

10 *old and highly significant elements in your theory of music / opera as consolation / music as protest*: 'The true idea of opera, that of consolation, which once caused the very gates of Hades to open, has now been lost' (ibid., p. 118). In the version which Benjamin most probably had before him, Adorno says: 'For all its expressive force, a moment of soullessness still clings essentially to the musical execution: the original power of opera, the idea of consolation, is quite lost in Wagner' (*Theodor W. Adorno Archiv*, Ts. 2897ff). Also compare the conclusion of chapter X, the last of the book: 'Whoever could really snatch this precious metal from the roaring waves of Wagner's orchestra, for them a different sound would then vouchsafe that consolation which the music obstinately withholds for all its rapture and its phantasmagoria. In so far as such music does express the anxious fears of helpless human beings, it might also then, however feebly and distortedly, invoke the spectacle of help, and promise once again just what the immemorial and protesting claim of music has always promised: a life that can be lived without anxiety' (GS 13, p. 145).

11 *the motif of eternity in its functional connection with phantasmagoria*: cf. GS 13, p. 84.

12 *in one of our last conversations*: at San Remo during the New Year of 1937/38 .

13 *one of your earliest themes – that of décadence and the Trakl quotation*: in the summer of 1936 Adorno was planning to write an essay on 'Decadence' for the *Zeitschrift für Sozialforschung*; in this connection he noted down the line: 'A motto for the piece on decadence: "Wie scheint doch alles

Werdende so krank" [How everything that moves seems struck with sickness]. Georg Trakl.' ('Grünes Buch', p. 38.) – The line is found in the first strophe of Trakl's poem 'Heiterer Frühling'.

14 *the ultimate goal, which is what Kraus calls the origin*: cf. Karl Kraus, *Worte in Versen* I (Leipzig 1916), p. 69 ('Der sterbende Mensch', verse 40).

15 *a substantial letter to Max*: Benjamin's letter to Horkheimer of 28.5.1938; for an excerpt from the letter, cf. GS I [3], p. 1076.

16 *a very detailed one to Scholem*: for Benjamin's two letters to Scholem written on 12.6.1938, cf. *Briefwechsel Scholem*, pp. 266–75.

17 *'A Berlin Childhood' / some considerable revisions / Mass und Wert*: cf. Benjamin's final version of the work in GS VII [1], pp. 385–433, and the annotations in GS II [2], pp. 691–9; seven pieces from the book appeared in the next rather than the last issue of the journal *Mass und Wert*; cf. *Mass und Wert* 1, issue 6 (July/August 1938), pp. 857–67; on these pieces, cf. GS IV [2], p. 972.

18 *my naturalization / I have given Max all the details*: in Benjamin's letter of 28 May; for the relevant passage concerning naturalization, cf. GS VI, p. 775.

19 *Max / assuming that he received the letter*: Max Horkheimer confirmed the arrival of Benjamin's letter with his reply of 7 June (see the relevant note to letter 104) before leaving New York for a considerable period.

20 *your consignment of the newspaper literary sections*: it is no longer possible to identify the particular editions of the literary section of the *Frankfurter Zeitung* in question.

21 *a prose piece by Claudel*: probably the essay published by Paul Claudel (1868–1955) in the newspaper *Le Figaro* on 26.3.1938 and entitled 'Le poison wagnérien'; for the essay, cf. P. Claudel, *Oeuvres en prose*. Préface par Gaetan Picon, édition établie et annotée par Jacques Petit et Charles Galpérine (Paris 1965), pp. 367–72 (Bibliothèque de la Pléiade. 79).

22 *my work on Brod's biography of Kafka*: cf. Max Brod, *Franz Kafka. Eine Biographie (Erinnerungen und Dokumente)* (Prague 1937). It was on Scholem's initiative (cf. *Briefwechsel Scholem*, p. 264), that Benjamin had formulated his critique of Brod's book in his letter to Scholem of 12.6.1938 (ibid., pp. 266–73); Benjamin attempted without success to get the section of his letter dealing with Brod published as a review in the journal *Mass und Wert* (cf. GS III, pp. 526–9 and pp. 686–91).

23 *some notes of my own about Kafka*: cf. *Briefwechsel Scholem*, pp. 269–73.

24 *Haselberg's Kafka essay*: in the summer of 1935, Peter von Haselberg had sent Benjamin some 'Notes on Kafka', which had been written for the cultural section of the *Frankfurter Zeitung*, although it was not published there.

25 *Ronsard / my motto for the 'Baudelaire'*: the French poet Pierre de Ronsard (1524–85); the motto for Benjamin's unfinished book 'Charles Baudelaire. Ein Lyriker im Zeitalter des Hochkapitalismus' is found at the head of Convolute 'J' amongst the materials for the Arcades (cf. GS V [1], p. 301).

26 *Priestley's 'Benighted'*: the novel by J. B. Priestley (1894–1984) had first appeared in 1927; the American edition was entitled *The Old Dark House*; the eponymous film by James Whale, which appeared under the German title of 'Das Haus des Grauens', dates from 1932.

27 *your account of Leviathan's visit to Behemoth*: see letter 103.

28 *arrange another meeting with him*: Benjamin and Scholem did not in fact get to meet one another again in Paris since Benjamin stayed in Denmark with Brecht until October 1938.

29 *Bloch / preparing to move to America*: Bloch came to New York with his family in the middle of July 1938.

30 *a fine article on Brecht and a quite appalling one on Bukharin's final words*: cf. Ernst Bloch, 'Ein Leninist der Schaubühne' [A Leninist of the Stage], in the journal *Die neue Weltbühne* 34 (1938), pp. 624–7 (nr. 20 of 19.5.1938), and also his essay 'Bukharins Schlusswort', in *Die neue Weltbühne* 34 (1938), pp. 558–63 (nr. 18 of 5.5.1938).

31 *bits of news, like the one . . .*: see letter 103.

32 *'Music in Radio'*: see letter 103 and the relevant note.

33 *the Sternberger piece*: Benjamin had obviously understood Adorno's remarks in letter 103 to mean that Benjamin's suggested review of Sternberger might be rather inopportune. Although, in fact, Benjamin was commissioned to write the review, it only appeared posthumously (cf. GS III, pp. 572–9 and pp. 700–2).

106 THEODOR W. AND GRETEL ADORNO TO BENJAMIN
     BAR HARBOR, MAINE, 2.8.1938

From 15 August: Bar Harbor Maine,
290 Riverside Drive, 13 D   2 August 1938
New York, N.Y.

Dear Walter,
  First of all let me thank you from the heart for your letter of 19 July and its critique of my Wagner piece. I would also like to apologise right away for the poor quality of the copy. Unfortunately, it is only the original which is any more easily readable, but since I

have been inserting constant alterations and improvements to the text, I would not like to part with it yet.

As far as your critical remarks are concerned, I am uncommonly delighted by your positive response. As far as the more negative side is concerned, I am forced to respond rather laconically, if only because I cannot help agreeing with you. The reason I do so, however, is necessarily slightly different from the one you suggested. I believe it is simply due to the fact that I have never had the kind of experiences which you, and Max likewise, feel are lacking in the work. Wagner never really belonged amongst the stars above in my childhood,[1] and even today I could not invoke his aura any more effectively than I have already attempted in certain passages, like the one which refers to Robert Reinick.[2] As a somewhat attenuating circumstance, I would still like to point out that I did not relate the idea of 'saving' Wagner solely and unconditionally to the progressive features of his work, but rather attempted everywhere to emphasize the entanglement of the progressive and the regressive moments. I think that if you examine the final chapter very carefully you will be willing to concede me that. And perhaps it is also indicative of this fact that the work possesses more of a cyclical form in your own sense than you are ready to credit. The motifs of the final chapter are precisely attuned to those of the first. [Added alongside the paragraph in Adorno's hand:] Please forgive these problems with the typewriter![3] [and then in English:] I am *so* sorry!

The fate of the work[4] is still undecided. At first the difficulties of shortening it struck me as so enormous that I dropped the idea and undertook the substantial revision and shortening of my Husserl essay[5] instead. I am extremely pleased with the results of my labours here, and I would like to think that they will also please you, though without being too pleasant in general. This new version will definitely be ready by 10 September, and I am also definitely hoping to see it published in the next issue of the journal. I should therefore be all the more delighted if your 'Baudelaire' could also be ready by then. This concern is one of the reasons why I turned to the Husserl piece and postponed any further work on the Wagner. Baudelaire and Wagner in a single issue does not strike me as a particularly felicitous idea.

As far as American conditions generally are concerned, we have found an exceptionally pleasant location here: on an island resembling something between southern France, Rügen and Cronberg. Egon and Lotte[6] were here for a week, and their motor car has proved as beneficial for our topographical opportunities as their presence has been for our human ones. – Otherwise I am busy reading Hegel's *Logic* again, a truly astonishing work, which speaks to me today in

265

every one of its parts. You will find this fact reflected in my Husserl piece. Apart from that I am reading Hindemith's utterly repulsive work,[7] *Unterweisung im Tonsatz* [The Craft of Composition], something that I would dearly love to settle my accounts with – either in the Institute journal or perhaps in '23'. And while we are talking of repulsive things, Caillois has just published an essay called 'L'Aridité'[8] in the journal 'Mesures', in which he plays the strong-minded man on the one hand, while enthusing about the regulation of thought on the other, without it being made very clear who or what is to do the regulating. Nonetheless, it is naturally still clear enough. And yet the first page of the essay, with a theory of beauty applied to the Alpine landscape, is another sign of his quite extraordinary gifts. There are very few human beings about whom one can feel such regret as one does with him. In the same issue Bataille[9] rails against the Lord God once again. If only it had some effect.

We would both be very pleased to get hold of a copy of the Berlin Childhood[10] in the near future. We have not yet seen the issue of '*Mass und Wert*', and it would be very kind if you could possibly have one sent on to me. I hope you have now fully recovered from your attack of migraine. I informed Pollock immediately about the naturalization issue and hope that it all works out.

I shall be going along to see the American paintings you mentioned in the company of Schapiro, who has also promised to initiate me into these things somewhat. He is a most remarkable man. If I were in your position, I would not hesitate at all to make contact with him, quite independently of Leyda.[11] It is probably only shyness which has prevented him from writing to you already. You can gather how intensely he has engaged with your interests from the question he once put to me: how does your critique of the auratic dimension relate to the auratic character of your own writings? If anyone deserves an honorary copy of your One-Way Street it is surely Schapiro. I would also mention in passing that he has a particular interest in Grandville.

A real contact has begun to develop with Scholem, and his relationship to the Institute has entered a more friendly stage as well. On the last evening we spent together, he read out your extraordinary letter on Kafka[12] and spoke about his special plan of getting you to write something on Kafka. The idea filled me with enthusiasm and caught Löwenthal's interest as well. I am quite sure that you would be able to publish a major essay on Kafka in the Institute journal. The only difficulty here is that Scholem and presumably you yourself are thinking in terms of a *book*, and book publications inevitably face all the usual and familiar difficulties. Today I am simply throwing the ball in your direction in the hope that you will catch it. A devastating critique of Brod's book would be extremely welcome in

266

the journal. I would also say, in order to prevent any misunderstandings, that I would have absolutely no objection to a similar review of Herr Sternberger, since he now seems to be sitting prettier than ever. In the meantime he has set about writing[13] an appreciation of Dacqué. And the *Frankfurter Zeitung* has recently started writing Baudelaire as Beaudelaire, *ne ulla virtus pereat*.

Bloch has now arrived. And possibly aboard a ship with eight sails. At any rate, he is busy challenging our entire century arm in arm with Eisler. Unless, that is, the people's lectures[14] of the latter become so unbearable to him that he finally deserts the red flag that was. But even then his chances with the Institute would hardly be that promising. Max was just as enraged about his essay on Bukharin[15] as we both were. It is inevitable precisely with people like Bloch that they find themselves in knots once they start to get clever. Nevertheless, when Eisler tells me that Bloch is now so much better than he was, so much clearer and no longer so mystical, my heart still beats for the Indian, even if I lend credence to Scholem's claim that the principal German source of Indian-Jewish mysticism is the Bubu of Montsalvat.[16]

I recommended the Hotel Littré to Scholem and consequently I can just imagine both of you sitting in the Versailles,[17] which means I envy you, him and the Versailles alike. Spare a drop of grenadine in my memory and write something soon,

Your old friend,
Teddie

Dear Detlef,

My letter is particularly badly typed today because it was so windy out in the garden – please forgive me. We shall be here for another ten days or so, and then I return to New York, which will probably still be as hot as a greenhouse, in order to see to our new apartment: 3 rooms on the 13th floor with a view of the river. Although the furnishings have not been specially chosen for the place – it is old stuff from Frankfurt and Berlin, which reduces the considerable customs duty – I hope that we will be able to make it nice at least for us and a few friends, if not for larger groups. Although we still have no special guarantees from the Institute on this for the moment, I am certainly expecting to see you here for the date of the World Exhibition. Then I shall be able to show you around the city, or perhaps even drive you there myself. (Though New York presents a major problem for cars: one usually cannot find a parking place, on Sundays it is so overcrowded everywhere that you can't move, the tax and insurance is very high – but in fact I rather like being chauffeured around in smart cars anyway.)

Lotte and E. have not got married yet, and they would prefer to wait until the employment question is sorted out. E.'s time at Mass. Memorial Hospital is almost over, and he will probably have to take a degree here before he finds a new job. He will certainly be writing to you with all the details himself. Apart from a single greeting, I have not heard a word from them since they left Bar Harbor on the 20th, but we shall be travelling back ourselves via Boston anyway. And as to my own reservations about E: if I am totally honest, I liked him better under morphine; and despite all his merits, these days I cannot bear his company for long; we shall have to talk about this properly again some time, when you have got to know Lottchen and seen what he is like at the moment. Lots of love and a kiss, as in the good old days,

Yours ever,

Felizitas

1 *Wagner never really belonged amongst the stars above in my childhood*: Adorno only began to study Wagner after his own studies with Berg and with the explicit encouragement of the latter, as one of Adorno's letters to Berg reveals: 'I am seriously engaged with investigating the reception of Wagner's music (and nobody in the world but you could ever have brought me to do so!).' (Unpublished letter of Adorno to Alban Berg of 23.11.1925.)

2 *passages, like the one which refers to Robert Reinick*: cf. GS 13, pp. 141ff.

3 *problems with the typewriter*: the carbon paper had slipped while Adorno typed on the back of the page, so that the text on the reverse side also appeared back to front between some of the lines on the first side.

4 *The fate of the work*: chapters I, VI, IX and X were published under the title 'Fragments on Wagner', together with short paraphrase summaries of the omitted chapters, in the *Zeitschrift für Sozialforschung* 8, issue 1/2 (1939), pp. 1–48.

5 *revision and shortening of my Husserl essay*: Adorno is referring to the essay 'Zur Philosophie Husserls'; see letter 72 and the relevant note.

6 *Egon and Lotte*: i.e. Egon Wissing and Lotte Karplus. In his letter to Gretel Karplus of 20 July, Benjamin had asked whether the marriage between Egon Wissing and Liselotte Karplus had already taken place or was about to transpire (cf. *Briefe*, p. 769).

7 *Hindemith's work*: cf. Paul Hindemith, *Unterweisung im Tonsatz. Theoretischer Teil* (Mainz 1937); Adorno's review of the book for the issue of the *Zeitschrift für Sozialforschung* planned for the autumn of 1939, failed to appear, like the entire issue, because of the outbreak of war. In 1968 Adorno incorporated it as section IV into 'Ad vocem Hindemith. Eine Dokumentation' (cf. GS 17, pp. 229–35).

8 *Caillois / 'L'Aridité'*: the essay appeared in 'Mesures. Cahiers trimestriels', 15.4.1938, nr. 2, Paris: Librairie José Corti, pp. 7–12; for Benjamin's pseudonymous review, which formed part of a discussion of several other books, cf. *Zeitschrift für Sozialforschung* 7, issue 3 (1938), pp. 463ff; now in GS III, pp. 549ff.

9 *In the same issue Bataille*: see letter 108 and the relevant note.

10 *a copy of the Berlin Childhood*: Benjamin did not send the manuscript of 'A Berlin Childhood Around 1900' to the Adornos until April 1940; cf. GS IV [2], p. 968.

11 *Leyda*: see letter 84 and the relevant note.

12 *your extraordinary letter on Kafka*: i.e. Benjamin's letter to Scholem of 12 June 1938; cf. *Briefwechsel Scholem*, pp. 266–73.

13 *Herr Sternberger has set about writing*: cf. Dolf Sternberger, 'Verwandlung. Edgar Dacqué zum 60. Geburtstag', in the *Frankfurter Zeitung* of 8.7.1938 (year 82, nr. 342/43), p. 10.

14 *Eisler / the people's lectures*: an allusion to Eisler's activities as teacher of composition at the New School for Social Research in New York.

15 *his essay on Bukharin*: see letter 105 and the relevant note.

16 *the Bubu of Montsalvat*: presumably an allusion to Martin Buber, made up from the title of Charles-Louis Philippe's novel *Bubu du Montparnasse* and the mountain of Montsalvat from Wagner's 'Parsifal'.

17 *in the Versailles*: Adorno is referring to the 'Café de Versailles', which was situated in the Rue de Rennes opposite the station of Montparnasse.

107   THEODOR W. AND GRETEL ADORNO TO BENJAMIN WRITTEN
      ON A LETTER FROM MEYER SCHAPIRO TO ADORNO
      [BAR HARBOR, MAINE, C.12.8.1938]

South Londonderry, Vt.
August 10, 1938

My dear Wiesengrund-Adorno,
   I have just returned from a two-weeks visit to the city. Everyone was away, but the libraries were always crowded. I had hoped to find you in town – though I am glad you didn't have to suffer the terrible heat and humidity . . .
   I took the liberty to recommend you to the Brooklyn Institute,[1] without finding out first whether you cared to lecture. By some odd confusion, the letter was first sent to the Rhode Island Museum, because the people at the NY Museum of Modern Art mistook your name for that of A. Dorner (over the telephone! you see what machine reception does to sound and especially to nuances in names). I also recommended Krenek for the lecture on modern music.[2] But since we couldn't reach him or find out when he would be in New

269

York, and whether he spoke English well enough, we had to give up the idea. I liked his book very much, except for the social interpretation and the pathos.

Will Bloch remain in New York until October? I should be sorry if I missed him. I will probably return to the city in the middle of September. Perhaps you might make an auto trip through New England during the next month and stop here for a day or two with Bloch. Sidney Hook[3] is not far away, and among our neighbours are Ernest Nagel[4] (who teaches philosophy at Columbia) and Selig Hecht[5] (the biophysicist who works on colorvision). I have read a part of the controversy in *Das Wort* on Expressionism,[6] and although I agree with Bloch in much that he says, it seems to me the whole controversy masks other issues, of a political nature (evident in the attitude of Mann and in Lukács' astonishing retraction of his old work on dialectics).

I do not know of an essay by Stevenson on Gas Light.[7] If it is Robert Louis Stevenson that Benjamin has in mind, I can refer him to a sweet little poem in a Child's Garden of Verses called the Lamplighter. The collected works of RLS are easy enough to find; perhaps they contain an essay on Gas Light. You probably know the story about RLS, that as a student excited by ideas of adventure and mystery, he used to go about the streets at night with a lamp under his cloak . . . Benjamin probably knows that in the 70s there were critics who attributed Impressionism to the influence of gas-light! and that Baudelaire discussed the influence of gas-light on taste (see his *Curiosités Esthétiques*).

Do you by any chance know of Germans in New York who need the services of a competent English translator? I have a friend who for years has made first-rate translations from the German and French (he also translates Spanish) for Simon and Shuster and now works for the Oxford Univ. Press. He is an able literary man himself and could also revise manuscripts for grammar and style. My friend is in great need at the moment. Is it possible that the Institute could employ him? He has experience with social and economic literature, history, biography and novels, also natural science; but not technical works of philosophy.

Best regards to both of you,

Cordially,
Meyer Schapiro

Dear Walter,

I am sending you this letter, partly because of the information it contains about gaslight, but also because it expresses something about the sender – namely Meyer Schapiro – which might perhaps encourage

270

you to write to him. You would also be doing me a great favour thereby, since I am always mindful of the importance of building on your own prospects in America. And S. is really at home in the same cultural climate as we are. His address until September is:

> Prof. M. Schapiro
> South Londonderry (Vt.)
> USA

We are leaving for New York tomorrow to move into our own apartment. I have also written a polemical piece on Sibelius[8] and three analyses of famous Salon pieces.[9]
Lots of love, your old friend Teddie

Schapiro reads and speaks German very well.
In the meantime there is also a new manuscript by Sohn-Rethel[10] in which I am presented as the Prince of Hell.

Dear Detlef,
I hope to be able to send you a copy of the 'Diary of a Seducer' along with your books. Is Elisabeth Hauptmann[11] in New York, and if so what is her address? One other thing: is Brecht familiar with Butler's 'Erewhon'?[12] There are some remarkable things in it, like the claim that one should never think through an idea to its conclusion or that one only gets punished for being impecunious. Simply these greetings for today. Lots and lots of love as always, yours, Felicitas.

[Dating: the hand-written lines by Theodor and Gretel Adorno are inscribed on the letter from Meyer Schapiro, which is dated 10 August; since the return trip from Maine to New York took place on Friday, 13 August, and Meyer Schapiro's letter will have arrived on the 11th at the earliest, and probably on the 12th, then the 12th or possibly 13th of August – the day of their trip – is the most likely date for the Adornos' letter.]

1 *the Brooklyn Institute*: Adorno spoke at the Brooklyn Institute of Arts and Sciences in January 1939 as part of a series of lectures arranged by Shapiro on 'Aesthetic Aspects of Radio'.

2 *Krenek for the lecture on modern music*: Meyer Schapiro, whom Adorno had presented with Krenek's book *Über Neue Musik*, had attempted without success to get Krenek invited to give a lecture at the Brooklyn Institute (cf. *Briefwechsel Adorno/Krenek*, p. 130).

3 *Sidney Hook*: American philosopher, born in New York in 1902.

271

4 *Ernest Nagel*: the American philosopher Ernest Nagel (1901–85) had taught at Columbia University in New York since 1931.

5 *Selig Hecht*: from Adorno's correspondence nothing further is known about the biologist who also taught at Columbia University.

6 *the controversy in Das Wort on Expressionism*: cf. *Die Expression-ismusdebatte. Materialen zu einer marxistischen Realismuskonzeption*, ed. Hans-Jürgen Schmitt (Frankfurt a.M. 1973).

7 *an essay by Stevenson on Gas Light*: in his letter to Gretel Adorno of 20.7.1938, Benjamin had asked if she could obtain this essay for him, which he required for his Baudelaire essay (cf. *Briefe*, p. 771). – For the reference to Stevenson in the *flâneur* chapter of 'Das Paris des Second Empire bei Baudelaire', cf. GS I [2], p. 553.

8 *a polemical piece on Sibelius*: published as a review of B. de Törne's book *Sibelius. A Close Up* (London 1937) in the *Zeitschrift für Sozialforschung* 7, issue 3 (1938), pp. 460–3; Adorno later incorporated the piece into his collection *Impromptus* under the title 'Glosse über Sibelius' [Some Remarks on Sibelius] (cf. GS 17, pp. 247–52).

9 *three analyses of famous Salon pieces*: these analyses, collected in Adorno's typescript under the title 'Steckbriefe' – 'Ave Maria von Gounod', 'Prélude cis-moll von Rachmaninoff' and 'Humoresque von Dvorak' – were later incorporated into the first part of Adorno's 'Musikalische Warenanalysen' (cf. GS 16, pp. 284–8).

10 *a new manuscript by Sohn-Rethel*: the typescript which Sohn-Rethel sent to Adorno with his letter of 8 July, comprised the first two chapters of an unpublished manuscript with the title 'Kritische Liquidierung des philo-sophischen Idealismus. Eine Untersuchung zur Methode des Geschichtsmater-ialismus' [A Critical Exposure of Philosophical Idealism. An Investigation into the Method of Historical Materialism]; cf. *Briefwechsel Adorno/Sohn-Rethel*, pp. 87–93).

11 *Elisabeth Hauptmann*: the writer Elisabeth Hauptmann (1897–1973) collaborated with Brecht on many plays after 1923, and later became Liter-ary Manager of the Berlin Ensemble and an editor of Brecht's writings.

12 *'Erewhon'*: the novel *Erewhon, or, Over the Range* (1872/1901) by Samuel Butler the Younger (1835–1902).

108 BENJAMIN TO THEODOR W. AND GRETEL ADORNO
SKOVSBOSTRAND, 28.8.1938

Dear Friends,

Instead of something fresh and green, here is something in dotted black and white for your new place! – there are certain orchids which produce a similar effect.

I was absolutely delighted to receive the recent letters from you both. It would be lovely if Felizitas, who always likes to underestimate the significance of her letters for me, would write me a longer one before long. It would be one of the very few things for which I would be prepared to interrupt my work!

I shall remain entirely laconic today – but you should infer from this nothing but the fact that I must jealously guard every single minute of my time. And the enclosed copy[1] of the principal passages of a letter which is just going off to Pollock by the same post, will tell you why. The reason for writing it was the circumstance that an extremely detailed letter, which I sent to Max on 3 August concerning the current state of my work on the 'Baudelaire',[2] seems to have got lost in the post.

I am very strongly tempted to tell you both about the Baudelaire piece – not so much indeed about the second part, which I am about to broach, but about the first and third parts of the work. These two parts provide the armature for the whole: the first presents the character of allegory in Baudelaire as a problem, while the third presents the social resolution of the problem. Indeed it is this task, apart from the difficult period of serious migraine in Paris, which has caused me to fall behind with the work somewhat: under all circumstances I felt I had to have the substantial totality of the thing clearly before my eyes in all its aspects before I could even begin to write a line. I have now accomplished this purpose with a large number of notes and materials[3] which I have produced during the first two months of my stay here.

The other side of the coin, so to speak, is that all this pressure has also affected the composition of the second part. And perhaps I myself did not really suspect the full magnitude of the task involved: as it is I can hardly imagine the final shape of this second part being properly contained within natural limits at all!

In addition to this, I also have to move lodgings. The noise of children has made the house in which I have been staying quite useless for my work. I will be exchanging this house for another one that is inhabited by a man with mental illness. Perhaps Felizitas will remember the strongly idiosyncratic feelings which I have always entertained towards such people! – In truth there is hardly any chance of finding appropriate accommodation here.

Many thanks for Schapiro's letter. I will write to him once the Baudelaire is done with. I feel I will be able to communicate very freely with people like him; and recently this has rarely been the case with me.

In that sense I would ask you all the more warmly to thank him on my behalf. The relevant essay by Stevenson is indeed included in the complete edition of his works and I have already managed to get hold of it from there. His observation about the Impressionists was extremely interesting and quite new to me.

I was pleased to read Teddie's remarks about Caillois. In this regard you should compare a passage in my letter to Max[4] of 28 May this year. Under certain circumstances Max wanted to publish this and several other passages[5] of my letter. The letter that has gone astray explained that I would be perfectly happy about the idea. I would be grateful if you could communicate the same to him on his return. (The only part I did not want to see published was the passage on Bataille,[6] and I explained my reasons to him.)

I have not forgotten about the Berlin Childhood, or about the Brecht poems.[7] While that is all too late to include in this letter, I enclose a photograph of Brecht's house[8] from just in front of the garden gate; it was taken by his son.[9] I am sure you will be able to find a suitable place for it where it is no more obvious to the eye than the works of the original himself have always been.

Do not forget to give my greetings to Bloch, and please accept my own heartfelt and elegiac greetings from a part of the world that seems to be falling apart,

Yours,
Walter

28 August 1938
Skovsbostrand per
Svendborg c/o Brecht

PS After careful consideration, I must say something else about the title of the second part[10] as suggested in the accompanying letter excerpt. Last night I attempted to develop, in a preliminary version, the most precise possible concept of the overall range of the second part. The attempt clearly revealed that this part too will significantly exceed the length which I have been allowed as far as the next issue of the journal is concerned. It is quite possible, therefore, that I shall have to limit myself here to the two fundamental sections of the second part – namely, the theory of flânerie and the theory of modernity. The title of the actual manuscript[11] may well differ accordingly from that suggested in my letter to Pollock.

It might interest Teddie to learn – if he is not already aware of the fact – that Löwith refers to his 'Kierkegaard'[12] at a significant juncture of his book 'Nietzsches Philosophie der ewigen Wiederkunft des Gleichen' [Nietzsche's Philosophy of the Eternal Return of the Same] (Berlin 1935).

1 *the enclosed copy*: for the draft version of Benjamin's letter to Friedrich Pollock of 28 August 1938, cf. GS I [3], pp. 1085–7.

2 *an extremely detailed letter ... on the 'Baudelaire'*: Benjamin's letter to Horkheimer did not actually go astray as he had feared; cf. GS I [3], pp. 1082–4.

3 *a large number of notes and materials*: Benjamin is probably referring to the fragments, or a substantial part of them, on 'Central Park'; cf. GS I [2], pp. 655–90.

4 *compare a passage in my letter to Max*: in the letter Benjamin writes: 'I hear that you have obtained the April issue of "Mesures" directly. I have borrowed a copy myself. The principal essay by Caillois only confirms to a considerable degree the justified concerns which Wiesengrund has already expressed about 'The Praying Mantis'. This *dialectique de servitude volontaire* rather uncannily illuminates those involved trains of thought where we come across a Rastignac who has more to do with Goebbels' clique than the house of Nucingen. In this essay the very real gifts of Caillois have found an object which cannot but reveal them in the form of insolence. It is repulsive to behold how the characteristic and historically conditioned features of the contemporary bourgeois, which you have elucidated in your anthropology of the type, are simply subsumed, through a metaphysical hypostasization of the same, under an elegantly fashioned 'remarque' glossing the present age. The concentrated strokes of the whole design bear all the marks of pathological cruelty. It provides the indispensable foundation for revealing the "higher sense" of the characteristic praxis of monopoly capitalism, which would "far rather expend its means upon destruction than it would upon utility or happiness" (p. 9). When Caillois says: "on travaille à la libération des êtres qu'on désire asservir et qu'on souhaite ne voir obéissants qu'envers soi" (p. 12), he has simply characterized Fascist practice itself. – It is sad to see such a broad and muddy stream as this fed by such an elevated source.' (Unpublished letter from Benjamin to Horkheimer of 28.5.1938).

5 *to publish this and several other passages*: the New York editors of the Institute's journal slightly adapted Benjamin's report on current French literature contained in his letter to Horkheimer and published a selection of his remarks under the anagram J. E. Mabinn in the *Zeitschrift für Sozialforschung* 7, issue 3 (1938), pp. 463–6; the selection included the following reviews by Benjamin: Roger Caillois, 'L'aridité', from 'Mesures', 15ᵉ Avril 1938, nr. 2, pp. 7–12; Julien Benda, *Un régulier dans le siècle* (Paris 1937); Georges Bernanos, *Les grands cimetières sous la lune* (Paris 1938); G. Fessard, *La main tendue? Le dialogue catholique-communiste est-il possible?* (Paris 1937). (Cf. GS III, pp. 549–52 and pp. 695ff.)

6 *the passage on Bataille*: 'Georges Bataille, who offers us a rather more innocuous interpretation of the Place de la Concorde in the same issue [sc. of *Mesures*], is a librarian at the Bibliothèque Nationale. I see him quite frequently in connection with my work there. You will probably have formed a distinctive impression of him, I imagine, from reading his "Acephale". In the said essay he has simply collected his idées fixes in a more or less comical fashion as a kind of pictorial broadsheet illustrating the various stages of a

"secret history of humanity" through different views of the Place de la Concorde. This secret history is dominated by the struggle between the monarchic, static, and here that means Egyptian, principle, and the anarchic, dynamic, actually destructive and liberating process of time, a struggle which Bataille sees expressed now in the image of an infinite and precipitous ruin, now in that of an explosion. Bataille and Caillois between them have founded a "Collège de sociologie sacrée", where they openly proselytize amongst young people on behalf of their own secret society – a society whose secret mysteries seem essentially to consist in what the two original founders effectively have in common' (Benjamin to Horkheimer, 28.5.1938). – Benjamin mentions the reason why he would not like to see this passage in print in his letter to Horkheimer of 3 August 1938: 'Your idea of publishing a fragment of my letter of 28 May this year in the Institute journal is [. . .] of course a doubly welcome one. But quite apart from that, I am particularly pleased that you are finding these kinds of report useful. [. . .] As far as this particular report on the literary scene is concerned . . . I would ask you to omit the second paragraph, beginning "Georges Bataille . . ." The overall drift of the argument will not be adversely affected in any way. And in this way my own relationship with Georges Bataille will not be adversely affected either, something I would like to maintain, both because of his assistance at the Bibliothèque Nationale, and because of my plans for naturalization. – The fragment would not escape his attention since the Institute journal is openly displayed in the reading room where he often works; and he is hardly the kind of person to react serenely to its contents.'

7 *the Brecht poems*: in a letter to Benjamin of 3 August 1938 (excerpted in GS I [3], pp. 1084ff), Gretel Adorno had asked for a copy of Brecht's 'pornographic poems', which she may have learnt about from Benjamin himself. – A selection of these poems was first published in 1982; cf. Bertolt Brecht, *Gedichte über die Liebe*. Ausgewählt von Werner Hecht (Frankfurt a.M. 1982).

8 *a photograph of Brecht's house*: the photograph in question is reproduced at the beginnning of volume 2 of the 1966 German edition of Benjamin's letters.

9 *his son*: i.e. Stefan Brecht.

10 *the title of the second part*: in the draft version of Benjamin's letter to Pollock, the title given is: 'The second empire in the poetry of Baudelaire' (cf. GS I [3], p. 1086).

11 *the title of the manuscript*: the essay is entitled: 'The Paris of the Second Empire in Baudelaire'.

12 *Teddie / that Löwith refers to his 'Kierkegaard'*: cf. Karl Löwith, *Nietzsches Philosophie der ewigen Wiederkunft des Gleichen* [Nietzsche's Philosophy of the Eternal Return of the Same] (Berlin 1935), p. 166 (n. 30).

Dear Teddie,

Only eight days ago I was putting the finishing touches to the second part of the Baudelaire[1] piece; two days later the European situation suffered its provisional dénouement.[2] I have been under enormous stress during the last few weeks through the collision of historical events and editorial deadlines. Hence my delay in sending you these lines.

Yesterday I was busy organizing the several hundred books which I have here ready for shipment to Paris. I am increasingly coming to feel, however, that this destination will have to become another stepping stone for me and the books. I do not know how long it will still physically be possible to breathe this European air; it is already spiritually impossible to do so after the events of past weeks. It is not easy for me to accept that this is the case; but there is simply no avoiding it any longer.

This much has now become indisputably clear: Russia has permitted the amputation of its European extremity. As far as Hitler's pledge is concerned, namely, that his territorial claims in Europe have now been met and that his colonial ones could never prove an occasion for war, I can only interpret this to mean that any such colonial territorial claims will therefore turn out to be Mussolini's occasion for war. I expect that Tunisia, inhabited as it is by a large number, if not an actual majority, of Italians, will soon provide the next subject for 'negotiation'.

You can easily imagine how worried I have been over the last few weeks about my wife and above all about Stefan. At the moment I do not have to fear the worst, although that is only something I have known for a very short time. Stefan is now in England; my wife will attempt to transfer her business[3] over to someone else without incurring too many losses. In order to gain some time, she will try and relinquish the business purely formally for the time being.

I spent ten days in Copenhagen in order to prepare the Baudelaire manuscript for publication. The city was enjoying the most magnificent Indian summer imaginable. But on this occasion I was unable to see more of the place – which I am especially fond of – than is visible en route from my desk to the radio set in the 'salon'. Autumn is now setting in, accompanied by the most tremendous rain storms. If nothing unexpected turns up, I shall be back a week this coming Saturday. The easier and more relaxed my contact with Brecht has been over the summer, the less I have worried this time about leaving him behind. I think I am justified in seeing our communication, which was much less problematic this time than I am used to, as an indication of his own increasing sense of isolation. I do not entirely wish to exclude the more obvious explanation of the situation – that this isolation has diminished the pleasure he often used to take in the more provocative tactics during our conversations; a more genuine explanation, however, lies in recognizing this growing isolation as a consequence of that loyalty to what we have in common. Given the conditions under which he is living at the moment, he will find himself directly challenged by this isolation during a Svendborg winter.

I have seen almost nothing of Brecht's new piece 'Caesar',[4] since I found it impossible to do any reading while I was engaged on my own work.

I assume you will already have read the second section of the Baudelaire piece by the time this letter arrives. I felt I was racing against the war, and, despite choking anxiety, I nonetheless experienced a great sense of triumph when I finally wrapped up the *'flâneur'*, after almost fifteen years in gestation and just before the end of the world (the fragility of a manuscript!).

Max will certainly have informed you about my comments concerning the relationship between the Baudelaire piece and the Arcades plan, something which I explained to him in detail in a covering letter.[5] As I formulated the matter to him, the decisive thing is that a Baudelaire essay that did not deny its responsibility to the issues addressed in the Arcades, could only be written as part of a Baudelaire *book*. What you already know about the book from our discussions in San Remo[6] will permit you per contrarium a fairly precise idea of the function of the now completed second section. You will have noticed that the various critical motifs – the new and the immutable, fashion, the eternal return, the stars, Art Nouveau – are all of them mentioned, but not one of them fully discussed. It is precisely the task of the third part to demonstrate the obvious convergence of these basic ideas with the plan of the Arcades.

I have not heard very much from you directly since you moved into your new apartment.[7] I hope to hear from you at length once you have been able to read the Baudelaire manuscript. Please do let me know at the same time how your radio project[8] is progressing and the way in which you are approaching it. For I still know nothing about this.

Many thanks for the book on aeronauts:[9] it is currently resting amongst the other contents of your parcel in boxes ready for shipping. I am looking forward to reading it in Paris. Please pass on my heartfelt thanks to Felizitas for the parcel. I shall write to her[10] from Paris, at the latest. – You will be receiving the Kierkegaard book,[11] for which many thanks, along with the book by Löwith,[12] through Madame Favez.[13] I got hold of the latter since I need to consult it for the third part of the Baudelaire piece.[14] Please send it back to me once you are finished with it.

Felizitas was asking about Elisabeth Wiener,[15] but I have heard nothing from her. What is even more important for me is that I have also not heard a word from Scholem[16] since his departure from America. He seems put out that he was unable to find me in Paris. But for me everything has to take the back seat with respect to my work. I could never have got through it without imposing strict seclusion upon myself. Have you had any communication from him?

I am eagerly waiting to hear what you have to tell me about Ernst Bloch.[17] En attendant, I glance every now and then at the town plan of New York, which Brecht's son Stefan has mounted on the wall, and stroll up and down the lengthy street on the Hudson where your house is situated.

Most sincere regards.

Yours,
Walter

4 October 1938
Skovsbostrand
per Svendborg

1 *the second part of the Baudelaire*: the manuscript of 'The Paris of the Second Empire in Baudelaire', which contains the three chapters entitled 'Bohemianism', 'The *Flâneur*' and 'Modernity'; cf. GS I [2], pp. 511–604.

2 *the European situation suffered its provisional dénouement*: an allusion to the Munich agreement of 29 September and the first entry of German troops into the Sudeten region of Czechoslovakia.

3 *my wife will attempt to transfer her business*: i.e. to sell her share in the guest house 'Villa Verde' in San Remo. Dora and Stefan Benjamin fled to London from San Remo at the beginning of 1939.

4 *Brecht's new piece 'Caesar'*: Benjamin has spoken of this novel, 'The Affairs of Herr Julius Caesar', which was destined to remain a fragment, in his letter to Gretel Adorno of 20 July: 'On the other hand, I greatly appreciate Brecht's intention to respect the isolation which I require [. . .] But this has allowed me to concentrate on my own work to such an extent that I have not even read his new novel, which is already half finished' (*Briefe*, p. 770).

5 *in detail in a covering letter*: Benjamin's letter to Horkheimer of 28 September 1938 (*Briefe*, pp. 772–6).

6 *our discussions in San Remo*: See letter 105 and the relevant note.

7 *your new apartment*: since the middle of August, the Adornos had been living at the address '290 Riverside Drive, 13 D, New York' with 'a magnificent view over the Hudson' (unpublished letter from Gretel Adorno to Benjamin of 24.8.1938); see Benjamin's allusion below.

8 *radio project*: see letter 99 and the relevant note.

9 *the book on aeronauts*: a hitherto unidentified work.

10 *I shall write to her*: see the letter of 1 November 1938 (*Briefe*, pp. 780–2).

11 *the Kierkegaard book*: see letters 57, 102 and 108.

12 *the book by Löwith*: i.e. the work mentioned in the previous letter.

13 *Madame Favez*: Juliane Favez, the Secretary of the Geneva division of the Institute of Social Research.

14 *the third part of the Baudelaire piece*: i.e. the planned third part of the projected book on Baudelaire, none of which was ever actually written.

15 *Elisabeth Wiener*: in an unpublished letter of 12 September, Gretel Adorno had asked after her friend; see letter 102 and the relevant note.

16 *I have also not heard a word from Scholem*: cf. *Briefwechsel Scholem*, p. 280; Scholem's reply to Benjamin's reminder followed on 8.11.1938 (cf. ibid., pp. 281–7).

17 *what you have to tell me about Ernst Bloch*: see letter 105 and the relevant note; for Adorno's report, see letter 110.

110   ADORNO TO BENJAMIN
      [NEW YORK,] 10.11.1938

10 November 1938.

Dear Walter,
   The tardiness of my letter levels a menacing charge against myself and all of us. But perhaps this accusation already contains the grains of a defence. For it should be obvious that a full month's delay in responding to your Baudelaire piece cannot be due to negligence.
   The reasons are entirely objective in nature. They involve the attitude of all of us to your manuscript,[1] and, considering my special interest in the question of the Arcades study, I think I can say without immodesty, in particular my own attitude. I had been looking forward to the arrival of the Baudelaire manuscript with the greatest eagerness and literally devoured the piece. I am filled with admiration for the fact that you were actually able to complete it by the appointed time, and it is this admiration which makes it all the harder for me to speak about what has come between my passionate expectations and the text itself.
   Your idea of providing a model for the Arcades study with the Baudelaire piece was something I took extremely seriously, and I approached the satanic scene much as Faust approached the

280

phantasmagoria of the Brocken when he expected many a riddle to be solved at last. May I be excused for having had to give myself the same reply as Mephistopheles, that 'many a riddle poses itself anew'? Can you understand that reading the treatise, one of whose chapters is entitled 'The Flâneur' and another 'Modernity', produced a certain feeling of disappointment in me?

The basic reason for this disappointment is that those parts of the study with which I am familiar[2] do not constitute a model for the Arcades project so much as a prelude to the latter. Motifs are assembled but they are not elaborated. In your covering letter to Max you presented this as your express intention, and I am well aware of the ascetic discipline you have imposed on yourself by omitting everywhere the conclusive theoretical answers to the questions involved, and indeed only reveal these questions to the already initiated. But I wonder whether such asceticism can be sustained in the face of such a subject and in a context which makes such powerful inner demands. As a close reader of your works, I realize that there is certainly no shortage of precedents for this procedure in your writings. In this connection I recall your essays on Proust and Surrealism[3] which appeared in 'Die literarische Welt' [The Literary World]. But can you apply the same method to the complex plan of the Arcades? Panorama and 'traces', the *flâneur* and the arcades, modernity and the ever-same, all this *without* theoretical interpretation – can such 'material' as this patiently await interpretation without being consumed in its own aura? And if the pragmatic context of these topics is isolated, does not this itself conspire in an almost demonic fashion against the possibility of its own interpretation? During our unforgettable conversations in Königstein,[4] you once said that every idea in the Arcades had to be actually wrested from the realm where madness reigns.[5] I wonder whether these ideas need to be as immured behind impenetrable layers of material as your ascetic discipline demands. In the present text the arcades are introduced[6] with a reference to the narrowness of the *trottoirs* which impede the *flâneur*'s progress along the streets. It seems to me that this pragmatic introduction prejudices the objectivity of phantasmagoria – something that I so stubbornly insisted upon even at the time of our Hornberg correspondence[7] – as much as the approach of the first chapter reduces phantasmagoria to characteristic types of behaviour in the literary *bohème*. You need not fear that I would suggest that phantasmagoria should simply survive in your text in unmediated form, or that the study itself should assume a phantasmagorical character. But the liquidation of phantasmagoria can only be accomplished in a truly profound manner if they are treated as an objective historico-philosophical category rather than as a 'vision' on the part of social characters. It is precisely at this point that your own conception differs from all other approaches to the nineteenth century. But the redemption of your postulate cannot be postponed to the *Kalendas Graecas*, or 'prepared for' through a more innocuous presentation of the issues in question. This is my objection. If in the third part, to employ the old formulation, prehistory *in* the nineteenth century is to take the place of the prehistory *of* the nineteenth century – most clearly in the Péguy quotation about Victor Hugo[8] – then this is merely another expression of the same problem.

But it seems to me that my objection certainly concerns more than the questionable procedure of 'abstention' with regard to a subject matter which the ascetic refusal of interpretation only serves to transport into a realm quite opposed to asceticism: a realm where history and magic oscillate. On the contrary, I see a close connection between those places where your essay falls behind its own a priori and its relationship to dialectical materialism – and here I am speaking not merely for myself, but also for Max, with whom I have discussed this question in great detail. Let me express myself in as simple and Hegelian manner as possible. Unless I am very much mistaken, your dialectic is lacking in one thing: mediation. You show a prevailing tendency to relate the pragmatic contents of Baudelaire's work directly and immediately to adjacent features in the social history, and wherever possible, the economic features, of the time. I am thinking, for example, of the passage about the duty on wine[9] (I, p. 23), of certain remarks about the barricades,[10] or especially of the aforementioned passage on the arcades (II, p. 2), which strikes me as particularly problematic since this is where the transition from a general theoretical discussion of physiologies to the 'concrete' representation of the *flâneur* is especially precarious.

I am struck by a feeling of artificiality whenever you substitute metaphorical expressions for categorical ones. A case in point is the passage about the transformation of the city into an *intérieur*[11] for the *flâneur*, where one of the most powerful ideas in your study seems to be presented in terms of a mere as-if. There is a very close connection between these materialist excursions – in which one never quite loses the apprehension one feels for a shivering swimmer who plunges into cold water – and the appeal to concrete modes of behaviour like that of the *flâneur*, or the subsequent passage about the relationship between seeing and hearing in the city, which not entirely by accident also employs a quotation from Simmel.[12] All of this makes me rather uncomfortable. You need not fear that I am about to mount my old hobby-horse. I am content merely to offer it a lump of sugar in passing, and for the rest I shall attempt to supply the theoretical reason for my aversion to this particular kind of concreteness

282

and its behaviouristic overtones. The reason is that I regard it as methodologically inappropriate to give conspicuous individual features from the realm of the superstructure a 'materialist' turn by relating them immediately, and perhaps even causally, to certain corresponding features of the substructure. The materialist determination of cultural traits is only possible if it is mediated through the *total social process*.

Even though Baudelaire's wine poems may have been occasioned by the wine duty or the town gates, the recurrence of these motifs in his œuvre can only be explained by the overall social and economic tendencies of the age – that is, in keeping with your formulation of the problem *sensu strictissimo*, through analysis of the commodity form in Baudelaire's epoch. No one is more aware of the problems involved here than I am; the phantasmagoria chapter of my book on Wagner[13] has certainly not succeeded in resolving them yet. Your Arcades study in its definitive form will not be able to avoid the same obligation. The direct inference from the duty on wine to L'Ame du vin imputes to phenomena precisely the kind of spontaneity, tangibility and density which they have lost under capitalism. This sort of immediate – and I would almost say again 'anthropological' – materialism harbours a profoundly romantic element, and the more abruptly and crudely you confront the Baudelairean world of forms with the harsh necessities of life, the more clearly I detect it. The 'mediation' which I miss and find obscured by materialistic-historiographical evocation, is simply the theory which your study has omitted. But the omission of theory affects the empirical material itself. On the one hand, this omission lends the material a deceptively epic character, and on the other it deprives the phenomena, which are experienced merely subjectively, of their real historico-philosophical weight. To express this another way: the theological motif of calling things by their names tends to switch into the wide-eyed presentation of mere facts. If one wanted to put it rather drastically, one could say that your study is located at the crossroads of magic and positivism. This spot is bewitched. Only theory could break this spell – your own resolute and salutarily speculative theory. It is simply the claim of this theory that I bring against you here.

Forgive me if this also brings me to a subject that is bound to be of particular concern to me since my experience with the study on Wagner. I am referring to the 'ragpicker'. It seems to me that his role as the figure of the lower limits of poverty[14] is hardly captured by the way in which the evocative term is actually used in your study. It conveys nothing of the dog-like cringing; nothing of the sack slung over the back; nothing of the voice which, for instance, still provides much of the sombre background for the entire opera in Charpentier's

283

Louise;[15] nothing of that meteoric train of jeering children behind the old man. If I may venture into the domain of the Arcades once again: the figure of the ragpicker should have provided the occasion for theoretically decoding the inner connection of cloaca and catacombs. I wonder if I am actually exaggerating in assuming that your failure to do so is related to the fact that the capitalist function of the ragpicker – namely, to subject even rubbish to exchange-value – is not articulated. At this point the asceticism of your study takes on features which would prove worthy of Savonarola. For the reappearance of the ragpicker in the Baudelaire quotation[16] in the third section almost tangibly addresses this question. What it must have cost you, not to take it up!

I think this brings me to the heart of the matter. The impression which your entire study conveys – and not only to me with my Arcades orthodoxy – is that you have here done violence upon yourself. Your solidarity with the Institute, which pleases no one more than myself, has led you to pay the kind of tributes to Marxism which are appropriate neither to Marxism nor to yourself. Not appropriate to Marxism because the mediation through the entire social process is missing, and because of a superstitious tendency to attribute to mere material enumeration a power of illumination which really belongs to theoretical construction alone rather than to purely pragmatic allusions. Not appropriate to your own individual nature because you have denied yourself your boldest and most fruitful ideas through a kind of pre-censorship in accordance with materialist categories (which by no means correspond to Marxist ones), even if this is only in terms of the aforementioned postponement. I speak not only for myself, unqualified as I am, but also for Horkheimer and the others when I say that we are all convinced that it would not only benefit 'your' production if you could elaborate your ideas without recourse to such considerations (in San Remo you raised counter-objections to this charge, and I am taking them very seriously), but that it would also prove most beneficial to the cause of dialectical materialism and the theoretical interests represented by the Institute, if you surrendered to your own specific insights and conclusions without combining them with other ingredients, which you obviously find so distasteful to swallow that I cannot expect anything good to come of it. God knows, there is only one truth, and if your powers of intelligence can seize this one truth through categories which may seem apocryphal to you given your conception of materialism, then you will capture more of this one truth than you will ever do by employing conceptual tools that merely resist your grip at every turn. After all, there is more of this one truth in Nietzsche's Genealogy of Morals than there is in Bukharin's ABC of Communism.[17] I believe the position I have

284

expressed here cannot be accused of laxity and eclecticism. Your study of Goethe's Elective Affinities and the book on the Baroque are better Marxism than your wine tax and your deduction of phantasmagoria from the practices of the feuilletonists. You may be confident that we are prepared to make your most extreme theoretical experiments our own. But we are equally confident on our part that you will actually carry out these experiments. Gretel once jokingly remarked[18] that you dwell in the cavernous depths of your Arcades and that you shrink from completing the study because you are afraid of leaving what you have built. We would exhort you to offer us some access to the Holy of Holies. I am sure you do not have to worry either about the stability of the structure or its profanation.

As regards the fate of your study, a rather strange situation has arisen in which I have had to act rather like the singer of the song: 'It's done to the sound of a muffled drum'.[19] Publication in the current issue of the journal proved impossible because the weeks spent in discussing your study would have caused intolerable delays in our printing deadlines. There was a plan to print the second chapter *in extenso* and part of the third. Leo Löwenthal in particular strongly urged this course. But I am quite set against the idea – not indeed for editorial reasons, but for your own sake and the sake of Baudelaire. This study does not represent you as this, of all your writings, must represent you. But since I am of the firm and unshakeable conviction that it will be quite possible for you to produce a Baudelaire manuscript of undiminished impact, I would earnestly entreat you to forgo publication of the present version and to compose that other version. Whether the latter would then have to possess a new formal structure, or could essentially be identical with the still unwritten final part of your book on Baudelaire, I am not in a position to say. You alone would be able to decide on that. I should like to make it clear that this is a request on my part and does not represent an editorial decision or rejection.

I still have to explain why it is I who have written to you rather than Max, who is the responsible addressee of the manuscript. His time is currently claimed by enormous commitments connected with his intended move to Scarsdale. He wishes to free himself of all administrative work in order to dedicate his undivided energies to the book on dialectic[20] over the next few years. This means that he must 'shake off' all his ongoing obligations. I have not seen him myself for two weeks. He asked me, as a kind of 'sponsor' of the Baudelaire work, to write to you instead. His request corresponded with my own intention.

I shall report on my own work in detail in the next letter. The publication of the Husserl book has been postponed again. Immediately on his return in the middle of September, Max asked me to pursue my long intended project instead, and compose the essay 'On the Fetish Character of Music and the Regression of Listening'.[21] I completed the manuscript just three days before your own arrived. It has now gone to press and I have given Brill instructions to send you the galley proofs, along with those of my polemical piece on Sibelius. The work certainly bears the marks of haste in composition; but perhaps that is not entirely a bad thing. I am particularly eager to hear your response to the theory that today exchange-value itself is being consumed.[22] The tension between this theory and your own concerning the buyer's empathy with the soul of the commodity,[23] could prove to be a very fruitful one. Incidentally, I think I can add the hope that the far more innocuous character of my piece will allow you to read it more gently than I was permitted to do with yours.

We have seen Ernst Bloch a few times. The impression was uncommonly negative. The transformation of the corrupted 'Volksfront' mentality into a kind of industrious stupidity can be studied more clearly in him than any other German I know. Things got heated on two occasions, though not to any real effect. We go and see him under the motto: 'the finest place on earth I have, that is the grassy mound upon my parents' grave'.[24]

But let me close with some epilegomena to the Baudelaire material. First a stanza from the second Mazeppa poem by Victor Hugo[25] (the man who is supposed to see all these things is Mazeppa, strapped to the back of his horse):

> Les six lunes d'Herschel, l'anneau du vieux Saturne,
> Le pôle, arrondissant une aurore nocturne
>   Sur son front boréal,
> Il voit tout; et pour lui ton vol, que rien ne lasse,
> De ce monde sans borne à chaque instant déplace
>   L'horizon idéal.
> [The six moons of Herschel, old Saturn's ring,
> the pole, curving its nocturnal dawn
>   on its northern extremity,
> he sees everything; and for him your unflagging flight
> constantly moves the ideal horizon of this
>   limitless world.]

– Also: the tendency towards unqualified statements which you observe, citing Balzac and the description of the employees in *The Man of the Crowd*,[26] also applies, astonishingly enough, to de Sade.[27] One of the first tormentors of Justine, a banker, is described as follows: 'Monsieur Dubourg, gros, court, et insolent commes tous les

286

financiers' [short, fat and rude, like all businessmen]. The motif of the unknown beloved appears in rudimentary form in Hebbel's poem 'To an Unknown Woman',[28] which contains these memorable lines: 'Und kann ich Form Dir und Gestalt nicht geben, / So reisst auch keine Form Dich in die Gruft' [And though I cannot give you shape or form, no form will ever take you to the grave]. – And finally, a few sentences from the *Herbst-Blumine* of Jean Paul,[29] which is a real find: 'A single sun was granted to the day, a thousand to the night, and the aether's endless blue seems as if it is sinking down towards us in drizzling light. How many street lamps shimmer up and down along the Milky Way! These are lit, too, even if it is summer or the moon is shining. The night, meanwhile, adorns itself not merely with that cloak of stars which the ancients imagined it was wearing, and which I shall more tastefully call its *religious* vestments rather than its ducal robes, but pushes its adornment much further, imitating the ladies of Spain. And like them, when they replace the jewels in their head-dress with glow worms in the darkness, the night studs the lower reaches of its cloak, where there are no glittering stars, with similar tiny creatures which the children often steal off with.' The following sentences from a very different piece[30] in the same collection seem to me to belong in the same context: 'And more of the same; for I noticed not only that Italy was like a moon-lit Eden to us poor people of the drift-ice, because day and night we there encountered the living fulfilment of that adolescent dream of nights spent wandering about and singing, but I was also driven to ask why people here merely walked around and sang in the streets at night like peevish night-watchmen, instead of assembling in whole evening-star and morning-star parties and roaming in a colourful troop (for everyone was in love) through the most magnificent leafy woods and the brightly moon-lit flowery fields, adding a few phrases on the flute to the joyful prevailing harmony, to this double-ended extension of the brief night by sunrise and sunset plus the added dawn and dusk.' The idea that the longing which draws one to Italy is a longing for a country where one does not need to sleep is profoundly related to the later image of the roofed-over city. But the light which rests equally on the two images is surely none other than the light of the gas-lamp, with which Jean Paul was not acquainted.

Tout entier,

Yours,

Teddie

---

1 *the attitude of all of us to your manuscript*: the plural refers to the members of the editorial board of the *Zeitschrift für Sozialforschung*, and particularly to Horkheimer and Löwenthal.

2 *those parts of the manuscript with which I am familiar*: the typescript which Adorno had before him figured as the second part of a projected three-part book on Baudelaire; only preliminary studies for the remaining parts remain cf. GS VII [2], pp. 735–70.

3 *your essays on Proust and Surrealism*: Benjamin's essay 'Zum Bilde Prousts' [On the Image of Proust] had appeared in three instalments – on 21.6, 28.6, and 5.7.1929 – in the weekly journal 'Die literarische Welt'; for the essay on Surrealism see letter 41 and the relevant note.

4 *our unforgettable conversations in Königstein*: see letter 7 and the relevant note.

5 *wrested from the realm where madness reigns*: see letter 39 and the relevant note.

6 *in the present text the arcades are introduced*: cf. GS I [2], pp. 538f.

7 *at the time of our Hornberg correspondence*: see letter 39.

8 *the Péguy quotation about Victor Hugo*: cf. GS I [2], p. 587.

9 *the passage about the duty on wine*: cf. ibid., pp. 519f.

10 *certain remarks about the barricades*: cf. ibid., pp. 516f.

11 *the transformation of the city into an intérieur*: cf. ibid., pp. 538f.

12 *a quotation from Simmel*: cf. ibid., pp. 539f.

13 *the phantasmagoria chapter of my book on Wagner*: cf. GS 13, pp. 82–91.

14 *the 'ragpicker' / the figure of the lower limits of poverty*: cf. GS I [2], pp. 520f.

15 *Charpentier's Louise*: the opera 'Louise' by Gustave Charpentier (1860–1956), pupil of Jules Massenet, dates from 1900.

16 *the reappearance of the ragpicker in the Baudelaire quotation*: cf. GS I [2], pp. 582f.

17 *Bukharin's ABC of Communism*: cf. Nikolai Bukharin and E. Preobrazhensky, *Das ABC des Kommunismus. Populäre Erläuterung des Programms der Kommunistischen Partei Russlands (Bolschewicki)* (Hamburg 1921).

18 *Gretel once jokingly remarked*: see Gretel Adorno's remarks in letter 99.

19 *'It's done to the sound of a muffled drum'*: the line comes from Adelbert Chamisso's 'Song of the Soldier' (1832).

20 *the book on dialectic*: see letter 94 and the relevant note.

21 *'On the Fetish Character of Music and the Regression of Listening'*: see letter 103 and the relevant note.

22 *the theory that exchange-value itself is being consumed*: cf. GS 14, pp. 25f.

23 *the buyer's empathy with the soul of the commodity*: cf. GS I [2], p. 558.

24 *'the finest place on earth I have ...'*: these lines come from the poem 'Before my Parents' Grave' (1874) by Marie Eichenberg.

25 *a stanza from the second Mazeppa poem by Victor Hugo*: cf. Victor Hugo, *Œuvres complètes. Édition définitive d'après les manuscrits originaux, Poésie II: Les orientales. Les feuilles d'automne* (Paris 1880), p. 184.

26 *the description of the employees in The Man of the Crowd*: cf GS I [2], p. 541.

27 *Sade*: for the quotation from de Sade's novel, cf. *Histoire de Justine ou les malheurs de la Vertu. Par le Marquis de Sade.* Tome premier, en Hollande 1797, p. 13.

28 *Hebbel / 'To an Unknown Woman'*: cf. Friedrich Hebbel, *Sämtliche Werke. Historisch-kritische Ausgabe*, edited by Richard Maria Werner, vol. 6: Demetrius – Gedichte I und II (Berlin Steglitz undated), p. 207.

29 *a few sentences from the Herbst-Blumine of Jean Paul*: cf. Jean Paul, *Sämtliche Werke*, edited by Norbert Miller, Part 2: Jugendwerke und Vermischte Schriften, vol. 3: Vermischte Schriften II (Munich 1978), p. 280.

30 *the following sentences from a very different piece*: ibid., p. 119.

111   BENJAMIN TO ADORNO
      PARIS, 9.12.1938

Paris, 9–12–38
10, rue Dombasle, XVe

Dear Teddie,
    You will not have been particularly surprised to notice that it has taken me some time to draft my reply to your letter of 10 November. Although the long delay in the arrival of your own letter led me to suspect something of its contents, it still came as quite a blow to me. In addition, I wanted to await the arrival of the galley proofs you promised me,[1] and they did not come until 6 December. The time I gained in this way gave me the opportunity to weigh your critique as carefully as I was able. I am far from considering the critique as unfruitful, let alone incomprehensible. I shall try to respond to it with regard to fundamentals.
    I shall be guided by a comment which appears on the first page of your letter. You write: 'Panorama, and "traces", the *flâneur* and the arcades, modernity and the ever-same, all this without theoretical interpretation – can this "material" patiently await interpretation?'

289

The understandable impatience with which you searched through the manuscript for a definite 'signalement' has, it seems to me, led you astray in some important respects. In particular, you were bound to arrive at a disappointing view of the third section[2] once it had escaped your attention that nowhere is modernity cited as the ever-same – and this important key concept is not actually exploited in the completed portion of the study.

Since the sentence quoted above offers something like a compendium of your objections, I should like to go through it word for word. First you mention the panorama. My text refers to it in passing. And in point of fact, the panoramic view is not appropriate in the context of Baudelaire's œuvre. Since the passage in question is not destined to find anything corresponding to it in either the first or the third part,[3] it might perhaps be best to omit it. The second item on your list is 'traces'. In my covering letter I pointed out that the philosophical foundations of the book cannot be grasped from the perspective of the second part. If a concept like the trace was to receive a penetrating interpretation, then it had to be introduced directly and straightforwardly at the empirical level. This could be done in a more convincing form. Actually, the first thing I did on my return here was to trace a very important passage in Poe, which touches upon my construction of the detective story out of the obliteration or ossification of the traces of the individual in the big-city crowd. But the treatment of traces in the second part must remain on this level, precisely if it is to receive a sudden illumination in the decisive contexts later on. This illumination is intended. The concept of the trace is defined and determined philosophically in opposition to the concept of the aura.

The next thing in the statement I am examining is the *flâneur*. Although I am well aware of the deep inner concern which underlines your material and your personal objections, your erroneous approach here makes me feel as though the ground were giving way beneath me. Thank God there is one firm and reliable branch for me to cling to in this regard. And that is your reference elsewhere to the fruitful tension between your theory concerning the consumption of exchange-value and my own theory about empathy with the soul of the commodity. I, too, regard this as a theory in the strictest sense of the word, and my discussion of the *flâneur* culminates in this. This is the place, and indeed the only place in this part, where the theory comes into its own in *undistorted* fashion. It breaks like a single ray of light into an artificially darkened chamber. But this ray, broken down prismatically, suffices to give an idea of the nature of the light whose focus lies in the third part of the book. That is why this theory of the *flâneur*, and I shall discuss the possibilities for improvement in certain respects below, essentially redeems the picture of the *flâneur* that I have had in mind for many years.

I proceed to the next term, the arcades. I feel even less inclined to say anything more about it since the abyssal *bonhomie* of its use can hardly have escaped you. Why question the term? Unless I am very much deceived, the arcade is not destined to enter the context of the Baudelaire in any but this playful form. It appears here like the picture of a rocky spring on a drinking cup. That is why the invaluable passage from Jean Paul to which you referred me will have no place in the Baudelaire. Finally, with regard to 'modernity': as my text makes clear, this is Baudelaire's own term. The section that bears this title could not go beyond the limits imposed on the word in Baudelaire's usage. But you will remember from San Remo that these limits are by no means definitive. The philosophical reconnaissance of modernity is assigned to the third part, where it is initiated with the concept of Art Nouveau and concluded with the dialectic of the new and the ever-same.

Recalling our discussions in San Remo, I should like to proceed to the passage in your letter where you do the same. If I refused there, in the interests of my own writing, to pursue an esoteric intellectual path for myself, and to pass on to other matters beyond the interest of dialectical materialism and the Institute, there was more at stake than solidarity with the Institute or simple fidelity to dialectical materialism, namely, a solidarity with the experiences which we have all shared during the last fifteen years. Here, too, it is therefore a question of my most personal interests as a writer. I will not deny that these may occasionally do some violence to my original interests. There is an antagonism here of which I would not wish to be relieved even in my dreams. And overcoming this antagonism constitutes the problem of my study, and that is a problem of construction. I believe that speculation can only begin its inevitably audacious flight with some prospect of success if, instead of donning the waxen wings of estericism, it seeks its source of strength in construction alone. It is the needs of construction which dictated that the second part of my book should consist primarily of philological material. What is involved here is less a case of 'ascetic discipline' than a methodological precaution. Incidentally, this philological part was the only one which could be completed independently – a circumstance which I also had to bear in mind.

When you speak of a 'wide-eyed presentation of mere facts' you are characterizing the proper philological attitude. This attitude was required not merely for the results it brings, but had to be solidly embedded in the construction for its own sake as well. It is true that the indifference between magic and positivism, as you so aptly put it, should be liquidated. In other words, the philological interpretation of the author should be preserved and overcome in the Hegelian manner by the dialectical materialist. Philology consists in an examination of texts which proceeds by details and thus magically fixates the reader on it. What Faust took home with him in black and white, and Grimm's fascination with little things,[4] are closely related to one another. What they have in common is that magical element whose exorcism falls to philosophy, here to the final part. You write in your Kierkegaard that 'astonishment'[5] reveals 'the profoundest insight into the relationship between dialectics, myth and image'. I might feel tempted to invoke this passage here. But instead I propose an amendment to it (as I am also intending to do with the related definition of the dialectical image on a later occasion). I think one should say that astonishment is an outstanding *object* of such an insight. The appearance of closed facticity which attaches to philological investigation and places the investigator under its spell, dissolves precisely to the degree in which the object is construed from a historical perspective. The base lines of this construction converge in our own historical experience. In this way the object constitutes itself as a monad. And in the monad everything that formerly lay mythically petrified within the given text comes alive. Therefore, it strikes me as a misjudgement of the issue when you identify 'a direct inference from the wine duty to L'Ame du Vin'. This conjunction was established quite legitimately in the philological context – just as we would also have to do in interpreting an ancient classical author. It lends the poem that specific gravity which it properly assumes in any genuine reading – something that has not frequently been practised in the case of Baudelaire. Only when the poem has come into its own in this way can the work be touched, or even shaken, by the act of interpretation. The latter would concentrate not on questions of taxation but on the significance of intoxication [Rausch] for Baudelaire.

If you consider my other writings, you will find that a critique of the philological attitude is an old concern of mine – and is essentially identical with that of myth. Yet in each case it is the critique which provokes the philological effort itself. To use the language of my work on the Elective Affinities, it demands the exposure of that material content in which the truth-content can be historically deciphered. I can understand how this aspect of the question was less significant in your mind. But this is equally true for some of the other important interpretations. I am not thinking merely of the interpretations of the poems here – *A une passante* – or of the prose pieces – *The Man of the Crowd* – but above all of my exploratory analysis of the concept of modernity [Modernität], where I was especially concerned to remain within philological bounds.

Let me note in passing that the Péguy quotation to which you object as an evocation of prehistory in the nineteenth century, had its proper place in preparing to advance the insight that the interpretation of Baudelaire has no need to appeal to any chthonian elements whatsoever (in the *exposé* of the Arcades I was still attempting something of the kind). That is why I believe that the catacomb and the cloaca have no role to play in the interpretation here. Charpentier's opera, on the other hand, strikes me as particularly promising, and I shall follow up the suggestion as soon as I have the opportunity. The figure of the ragpicker is infernal in origin. It will reappear in the third part, in contrast with the chthonian figure of the beggar in Hugo.

I had been worrying for some time about the much-delayed arrival of your letter, as you can imagine, when I chanced across a chapter in Regius[6] just before hearing from you. Under the title of 'Waiting' it reads as follows: 'Most people wait for a letter every morning. That no letter arrives, or if it does only contains a rejection of some kind, generally holds true for those who are sad already.' When I came across this passage I already felt sad enough to take it as a hint or presentiment of your own letter. If after all there was something encouraging in its content for me – for I say nothing about the unchanged perspective it expresses – then it is the fact that your objections, however closely they may be shared by other friends, should not be interpreted as a repudiation.

Permit me to add some frank words here. It would prove rather detrimental to the 'Baudelaire' if no part of this text, which is indeed the product of a creative effort that is incomparable with that involved in any of my earlier literary efforts, were to appear in your journal. For one thing, the printed form allows the author a certain detachment from his work, something that is of incomparable value. And then, if it appeared in printed form, the text could become a subject of discussion, and no matter how inadequate the discussion partners may be over here, this would compensate me somewhat for the isolation in which I am working. To my mind, the focal point of such a publication should be the theory of the *flâneur*, which I regard as an integral part of the Baudelaire study. That does not mean I am speaking of an unaltered text here. The critique of the concept of the masses, a phenomenon highlighted by the modern metropolis, should be given a much more central position than it occupies in the present version. This critique, which I begin to develop in the passages on Hugo,[7] would have to be filled out with the interpretation of important literary documents. I regard the section on *The Man of the Crowd*[8] as a model here. The euphemistic interpretation of the masses – namely, the physiognomic one – could be illustrated by means of an analysis of the story by E. T. A. Hoffmann[9] that is mentioned in the text. I shall have to develop a more detailed clarification as far as Hugo is concerned. The decisive point is the theoretical progress that is registered in all these views of the masses. The climax of it is indicated in the text, but it is not brought out strongly enough. Hugo rather than Baudelaire lies at the end of it all. More than any other writer, it was Hugo who anticipated the contemporary experience of the masses. The demagogue in him is an element of his genius.

You will see from this that certain points of your critique do strike me as convincing. But I am afraid that an *outright* correction in the spirit indicated above would be extremely problematic. The lack of theoretical transparency to which you rightly allude is by no means a *necessary* consequence of the philological procedure I have principally adopted in this section. I am more inclined to see it as a consequence of the fact that this philological procedure has not been expressly specified as such. This apparent deficiency may be traced in part to the rather bold attempt to write the second half of the book before the first. Only in this way could the appearance have arisen that phantasmagoria are described rather than integrated into the construction of the text. – The aforementioned emendations will only benefit the second part when the latter is properly anchored in every respect within the overall context of the book. My first task, therefore, will be to re-examine the construction of the whole.

With regard to the sadness alluded to earlier, there were, apart from the already mentioned presentiment, a number of good reasons for it. For one thing, there is the situation of the Jews in Germany, from which none of us can dissociate ourselves. In addition to this my sister has been gravely ill.[10] At the age of 37 she has been found to be suffering from a form of hereditary arteriosclerosis. She is almost incapable of movement and therefore also scarcely employable for anything. (At the moment she still has modest funds.) The prognosis for someone of her age is almost hopeless. Quite apart from all this, it is not always possible to live here without anxiety either. Naturally, I am doing my best to speed along the process of naturalization. But unfortunately the necessary steps not only cost me a good deal of time, but some money as well – thus at present the horizon looks rather clouded in this direction too.

The enclosed fragment of a letter to Max[11] of 17 November 1938 and the accompanying message from Brill, concern a matter which could wreck the naturalization appeal. You will therefore appreciate its significance. May I ask you to take the matter in hand yourself and request Max without delay, and preferably by telegram, to authorize Brill to publish my review in the next issue of the journal under the pseudonym of HANS FELLNER rather than under my own name.

This brings me to your recent work and thus to the sunnier part of my letter. The subject matter of your work touches upon my own in two respects, both of which you have indicated yourself. Firstly, in those parts which relate certain characteristics of the contemporary acoustic perception of jazz to the optical perception of film[12] as I have described it. *Ex improviso*, I cannot decide whether the different distribution of light and shade in our respective approaches is due to theoretical divergences or not. Perhaps it is only a case of apparent differences between two perspectives, which are in fact equally adequately directed upon different objects. I do not mean to suggest that acoustic and optical perception are equally susceptible to revolutionary transformation. This may explain the fact that the prospect of a quite different way of listening,[13] with which you conclude your essay, is not immediately clear, at least to someone like me, for whom Mahler is not a completely intelligible experience.

In my own essay[14] I attempted to articulate the positive moments as clearly as you have articulated the negative ones. I can therefore see that your study is strong precisely in places where mine was weak. Your analysis of the psychological types produced by the industry,[15] and your presentation of the way in which they are produced, seems particularly felicitous. If I had devoted more attention to this aspect of the matter, my own study would have gained something in historical plasticity. I see more and more clearly that the launching of the sound film must be regarded as an operation of the film industry designed to break the revolutionary primacy of the silent film, which had produced reactions that were difficult to control and hence dangerous politically. An analysis of the sound film would constitute a critique of contemporary art, which would provide a dialectical mediation between your views and mine.

What I liked most of all about the conclusion of your essay is the reservation it expresses concerning the concept of progress.[16] For the time being you ground this reservation rather casually and by reference to the history of the term. I would dearly like to penetrate to its root and origins[17] as such. But I do not underestimate the difficulties involved here.

Finally, I come to your question concerning the relationship between the views developed in your essay and those presented in my section on the *flâneur*. Empathy with the commodity presents itself to self-introspection or inner experience as empathy with inorganic matter: next to Baudelaire, my principal witness here is Flaubert with his 'Tentation'. Basically, however, empathy with the commodity is probably empathy with exchange-value itself. And in fact, one can hardly imagine the 'consumption' of exchange-value as anything else but an empathy with it. You write:[18] 'The consumer really worships the money which he has spent on a ticket for a Toscanini concert.' Empathy with exchange-value can turn guns into articles of consumption more attractive than butter. When in popular parlance someone is said to be 'loaded to the tune of five million', then the entire national community also feels itself loaded with millions more; and it empathizes with those millions. If I put it this way I can perhaps begin to approach the image of the gun which underlies the behaviour in question. I am thinking about what is behind the game of chance. A gambler directly empathizes with the sums which he bets against the bank or an opponent. Games of chance, in the form of speculation on the Stock Exchange, paved the way for this empathy with exchange-value rather like the way in which the World Fairs[19] did. (The latter represented schools where the masses, forced away from consumption, learned how to empathize with exchange-value.)

There is one particularly important issue which I should like to reserve for a subsequent letter, or perhaps a conversation. What is the significance of the fact that music and lyric poetry can become comic?[20] I can hardly imagine that this is an entirely negative phenomenon. Or do you see a positive element in the 'decline of sacred reconciliation'?[21] I confess that I can't quite see my way here. Perhaps you will take the opportunity to return to this question some time?

In any case, I would ask you to write soon. Please ask Felizitas, when she gets the chance, to send me the fairy-tales of Hauff[22] which I treasure on account of Sonderland's illustrations. I shall be writing to her sometime soon, but I would also like to hear from her too.

With heartfelt greetings as ever,

Yours,

Walter

1 *the galley proofs you promised me*: those of Adorno's essay on 'The Fetish Character in Music and the Regression of Listening'.

2 *the third section*: which carries the title 'The Modern Age'.

3 *in either the first or the third part*: Benjamin is speaking here of the parts of his planned book on Baudelaire, and not of the three *sections* of the essay under discussion.

4 *Grimm's fascination with little things*: Benjamin was probably thinking of Jacob Grimm's remark, which he had already quoted in his commentary on Grimm's letter to Dahlmann in *Germans*: 'The task was to explore the word-hoard, to interpret and to explain it, for all collecting without understanding leaves us empty, a German etymology that has not asserted its independence is incapable of producing anything, and anyone who thinks that the precise study of inscription is a little thing will never be able to love and recognize what is great in language' (GS IV [1], p. 217).

5 *your Kierkegaard* / *'astonishment'*: cf. GS 2, p. 80.

6 *a chapter in Regius*: i.e. in Max Horkheimer's *Dämmerung* [Twilight], which had appeared under the literary pseudonym of Heinrich Regius (see letter 25 and the relevant note); for his passage on 'Waiting', cf. Horkheimer, *Gesammelte Schriften*, vol. 2, p. 450.

7 *the passages on Hugo*: cf. GS I [2], pp. 562–9.

8 *the section on The Man of the Crowd*: cf. ibid., pp. 550ff.

9 *the story by E.T.A. Hoffmann*: the story in question, *Des Vetters Eckfenster*, is mentioned in Benjamin's chapter on 'The *Flâneur*'.

10 *my sister has been gravely ill*: for Dora Benjamin (1901–46), cf. the *Benjamin-Katalog*, pp. 21ff.

11 *The enclosed fragment of a letter to Max*: the whole paragraph of the letter reads as follows: 'On the other hand, my current intentions [i.e. Benjamin's resumption of his attempt to acquire French naturalization] encourage me to return to my review of Caillois, the proofs of which I have in front of me. Only a few days ago I was fortunate enough to discover that Caillois is on very friendly and indeed confidential terms with Roland de Renéville. And up until now this Renéville has been dealing with my application in his capacity as secretary at the "Bureau des Naturalisations du Garde du Sceaux". He could exercise a positive or, as the case may be, extremely negative effect upon my application once it has proceeded from the "Préfecture" to the Ministry of Justice. Under these circumstances, my naturalization could actually be jeopardized if the review of *Aridité* should appear under my own name. For this reason, I would strongly ask you to have the reviews of Benda and Caillois appear under the name of HANS FELLNER' (GS III, p. 695).

12 *certain characteristics of the . . . acoustic perception of jazz* / *the optical perception of film*: cf. GS 14, pp. 37ff.

13 *a quite different way of listening*: cf. ibid., p. 49.

14 *In my own essay*: the essay entitled 'The Work of Art in the Age of Mechanical Reproduction'.

15 *Your analysis of the psychological types produced by the industry*: cf. GS 14, pp. 41–4.

16 *the reservation . . . concerning the concept of progress*: ibid., p. 50.

17 *progress* / *the history of the term* / *penetrate to its roots and origins*: cf. the collection of manuscripts marked N (on the Arcades project): 'Epistemological issues, the theory of progress' (GS V [I], pp. 570–611). – Also compare Benjamin's letter to Horkheimer of 24 January 1939: 'I have been delving into Turgot and one or two other theoreticians in order to trace the history of the concept of progress. I am currently examining the entire structure of the Baudelaire from the epistemological angle and have reported back to Teddie about my revisions in my last letter. The question of the

concept of history, and of the role played by the idea of progress, has thus become very important to me. The destruction of the concept of the cultural continuum, which was postulated in my essay on Fuchs, must produce certain epistemological consequences, one of the most crucial of which for me seems to concern the limits which circumscribe the application of the concept of progress in history' (GS I [3], p. 1225).

18 *You write*: for the relevant sentence in Adorno's essay, cf. GS 14, pp. 24ff.

19 *Games of chance / speculation on the Stock Exchange / empathy with exchange-value / the World Fairs*: cf. GS I [3], pp. 1173ff.

20 *that music and lyric poetry can become comic*: cf. GS 14, pp. 48ff.

21 *the 'decline of sacred reconciliation'*: cf. ibid., p. 49.

22 *the fairy-tales of Hauff*: in her letter to Benjamin of 12 September, Gretel Adorno had written: 'I hope your books have safely arrived by now; on looking through the stuff I also came across Hauff's "Fairy-Tales" and "Madame Bovary", both of which I imagine must be yours.' (Unpublished letter from Gretel Adorno to Walter Benjamin of 12.9.1938.) – The edition in question was: *Märchen. Von Wilhelm Hauff. Mit 6 Radierungen von Johann Baptist Sonderland*, 8th edition (Stuttgart 1853).

112   ADORNO TO BENJAMIN
      [NEW YORK,] 1.2.1939

1 February 1939.

Dear Walter,

This time my delay in writing has nothing to do with theoretical questions. It is explained by the most recent events in Germany.[1] I do not know whether you are aware how closely my parents have become involved in all the turmoil. We did succeed in getting my father out of prison, but he suffered further injury to his already bad eye during the pogrom; his offices were destroyed, and a short time afterwards he was deprived of all legal control over his property. My mother, who is now 73 years old, also found herself in custody for two days. Just as both of them were beginning to recover from their terrible experience, my father was afflicted by serious pulmonary inflammation. He seems to have survived the worst of the illness, but this will now keep him in Germany for weeks, perhaps even months, although we have succeeded in the meantime, with the help of American friends, in securing an entry visa to Cuba for both my parents.[2] But it hardly needs saying that we are still extremely concerned as long as they have to remain in that appalling country, and that our attempts to assist them have absorbed all my attention for several weeks now.

There can no longer be any doubt that another European crisis is now approaching, and this time I am by no means so sure as I was last autumn that it will not end in war. I still believe that even this time there is every chance that the Germans will get everything they want, even if they still do not know exactly what they want. Although I am more convinced than ever that Germany is not in any position to wage war, the decisive point seems to me that the English ruling class cannot risk anything that could result in a loss of prestige for Hitler since they are so fearful of what might follow afterwards. France has finally lost all sense of initiative – otherwise it would be quite impossible to explain the events in Spain.[3] The French will certainly have to pay the price for this, and they will soon be experiencing a similar fate to Czechoslovakia, and it is still not even clear whether France will remain an English sphere of influence or become a German one instead, through the indigenous progress of fascism in the country. In short, the prospect of peace is hardly less disturbing than that of war – and as I said, the latter itself no longer seems as impossible as it did in the autumn; on the one hand, because this time the German demands conflict directly with the interests of the British Empire, something which the capitalists themselves will find it very difficult to ignore, however reluctantly, and also because perception of the internal situation in Germany itself could well provoke a resistance that would unwittingly transform an act of bluff into something much graver. I am simply communicating this possibility to you as my own personal opinion; at the Institute they still continue to believe in peace at almost any price, although Max is also of the opinion that the price would be the establishment of the new order throughout Europe. I would not want to cause you any panic in this matter, but I also feel it would be quite irresponsible of me not to tell you how I view the situation.

As far as the Baudelaire is concerned: if I understand you correctly, you are essentially proposing that we should publish, with certain alterations, the second part of the manuscript we have before us (with the general title of 'The Flâneur'), and indeed in a form which has been significantly modified in response to the theoretical interests which I have already articulated. We are all agreed in principle with this proposal, with the single condition that the section does not really exceed its present length. If some expansion is required in certain places, we could perhaps make certain cuts in other parts of the manuscript which might be difficult to develop properly within the limits of such an essay anyway (I am thinking in particular of the final part).

Perhaps it would be advisable if I make a number of further re-marks on details of your text that could show what sort of altera-tions I had in mind. It is the first sentence of the chapter[4] in particular which seems to me to court the danger of subjectivising the phantas-magoria, and a number of very carefully considered remarks about the character of the latter from the perspective of the philosophy of history would certainly be extremely helpful here. The transition from the physiologies to the *habitus* of the *flâneur*[5] (p. 2) does not appear entirely convincing, for one reason because the metaphorical charac-ter of this 'botanizing along the asphalt' does not seem to correspond entirely with the real claim which the categories of the philosophy of history at work in your text necessarily imply; but also for the reason that the rather technological reference to the narrowness of the *trottoir* as an explanation of the arcades does not seem to accomplish what you have here expressly set out to do. I am inclined to think that one cannot ignore the specific interests which motivated the householders to unite in supporting the construction of the arcades. This point also coincides precisely with that about introducing the category of the arcades objectively rather than simply as 'a mode of behaviour' pecu-liar to the promenading *littérateur*. The conclusion of the paragraph on the arcades[6] (the middle of p. 3) also courts the very strong dan-gers involved in metaphor here: the comparison with the gambler seems to resist precise identification rather than to assist it. The mean-ing of the introductory sentence of the next section ('not appropri-ate') is not entirely clear to me. Is it not the case that the physiologies in question are *all too* 'appropriate'? I have already expressed my reservations about the ensuing deduction in the context of your quota-tion from Simmel.[7] Once again you end up at one point by making the immediate reactions of human beings – in this case their anxiety in the face of something visible but inaudible – unconditionally re-sponsible for phenomena which can only be understood in terms of mediation through society. If you find the idea of grounding the physiological in the diversionary tendencies of human reactions much too general – something I can certainly understand – it could perhaps be concretized by reference to the fact that in this phase human beings themselves acquire the appearance of a commodified object of attention, something which the physiologies then explicitly present. Perhaps this could also be introduced in the context of fashion as an idea of all-round visibility. I cannot help feeling here that your invaluable Arcades project requires much more cunningly fashioned instruments than quotations from Simmel can provide. As far as the concluding and very remarkable quotation from Foucaud[8] is con-cerned (pp. 4f), I would merely like to say that the context in which it is cited could easily give the impression that you are simply making

300

a mockery of it; whereas I actually think that this could provide a good opportunity for wresting the grain of truth from the whole fraudulence of the thing, namely, the correct observation of the proletarian's distaste for the 'restorative cure' and for the bourgeois notion of 'nature' as a mere complement to exploitation. As far as the next paragraph is concerned (p. 5),[9] I would simply like to emphasize my idiosyncratic dislike for the idea of the authentically empirical, and here I am quite certain you will agree with me. I only have to imagine Kracauer's endorsement of the expression to feel quite sure that you should definitely place it on the index of forbidden terms.

As for the following part, from the Balzac quotation on page 5 through to page 10,[10] I would like to share a few ideas which I have developed through reading your own work, some de Sade, and recently Balzac once again. But I should also stress in advance that the deepest problem arising in connection with the idea of a type – namely, the thought that human beings of a certain type actually become identical with one another in the context of phantasmagoria – has certainly been broached in this regard, but by no means properly resolved. Yet my general sense of direction suggests that here, with Poe's description of the humbler employees for example, we find the real point of contact between your present essay and the innermost intentions of the Arcades project. – I would start from your critique of the antithesis Lukács sets up[11] between Balzac and Don Quixote. Balzac himself is very much a Don Quixote type. His generalizations reveal a tendency to transfigure capitalist alienation into 'sense', rather like the manner in which Don Quixote responds to the barber's placard. Balzac's fondness for unqualified statements[12] is grounded in this. It originates from anxiety in the face of the sameness of bourgeois dress. When he says, for example, that one can recognize a genius on the street at a single glance, this is an attempt to reassure himself of immediacy, despite the uniformity of dress, through the adventure of surmise. But this adventure, and this Balzacian transfiguration of the world of things, is also intimately connected with the gesture of the prospective buyer. Just as the latter beholds the goods displayed in the shop window, separated from him only by the glass, weighing them up to see whether they are worth the price, whether they really are what they appear to be, this is also how Balzac relates to human beings, investigating their market-value and simultaneously tearing off the mask which bourgeois standardization has imposed upon them. The 'speculative' moment is common to both procedures. The age of financial speculation permits the kind of fluctuations in price which can turn the acquisition of these goods in the window either into an intoxicating gain or into a case of downright deception for the buyer, and it is the same for those who

301

interpret the physiologies. The risk factor which Balzac's unqualified claims take on board is the same as that which the stock market speculator also accepts. It is by no means accidental, therefore, when Balzac makes the kind of unqualified statements specifically about financial speculators that I also find in de Sade.[13] A masked ball in Balzac and a bull market at the Stock Exchange may well have been very similar to one another in his time. This thesis about the literally quixotic element could probably be mediated through reference to Daumier; for his types, as you yourself observed in your essay on Fuchs, did indeed closely resemble Balzac's figures, just as Don Quixote also assumes a central place amongst the motifs of his oil paintings. It seems to me extremely plausible to suggest that these pictorial 'types' in Daumier are immediately connected with Balzac's unqualified statements, indeed, I am almost tempted to argue that they are the very same. The Daumier caricature is a speculative venture very like those spontaneous identifications which Balzac permits himself to make. They represent an attempt to shatter the external appearance of uniformity physiognomically. The physiognomic perspective which immeasurably highlights the distinctive detail in contrast to the uniform, has no other meaning than to salvage the particular in the universal. Daumier has to indulge in caricature, to present us with 'types', in order to reveal the sartorial world of the ever-same speculatively, to show it to be just as strange as the early world of the emergent bourgeois once appeared to Don Quixote. In this connection, the concept of the type is especially important, since the image of the universal must also be maintained within the image of the particular, with his hugely exaggerated nose or protruding shoulders, and it is much the same with Balzac, who is tempted, when he is describing Nucingen, to display his eccentricities as characteristic of the species of banker as such. This seems implicitly to suggest the idea that the type is not merely intended to distinguish the individual from the uniform, but also to render the masses themselves commensurable with the speculator's gaze, in so far as the categories applicable to the masses, organized as they are into types, can be regarded almost as if they were so many natural species or varieties. I would even say that there is an equivalent expression of this tendency in Poe, in that thought which produced the story of the gold bug,[14] which was, incidentally, the only great commercial success which Poe ever enjoyed in his lifetime, namely, in the thought that any secret code of writing, however complex it might be, can always be deciphered. In this connection, the secret script is obviously an image of the masses, and its written characters would coincide exactly with the 'types' in Balzac and Daumier. It is almost superfluous to point out how closely this idea, and that of the crowd as a secret script, corresponds to the

302

allegorical intentions of Baudelaire. And indeed, Poe actually kept his promise to decipher any secret script he ever encountered. One could not properly say the same of Baudelaire or of Balzac, and perhaps this itself might contribute something to your theory about why Poe alone composed detective stories,[15] while Baudelaire did not. The concept of human beings as ciphers also plays a certain role in Kierkegaard, and it might well be worth considering his concept of the 'spy'[16] in this regard.

I was particularly delighted with page 8, and it is surely one of the most promising indications of your work that the passage you quote from the publisher's brochure,[17] and especially the conclusion, reads as though it were simply your own interpretation. At this point the relationship between material content and truth content has really become an utterly transparent one. – The way in which you combine the elements from Poe with those from Valéry[18] (p. 9), uninterpreted as it is, sounds a little abrupt in the German. At the top of page 10, I do not find the contrast you draw between Baudelaire and the detective story[19] by reference to 'the structure of the instincts' entirely convincing. I am quite sure that the attempt to articulate this contrast in objective categories would indeed prove extraordinarily fruitful. I regard the passage on the 'passer-by', and particularly that on 'footsteps',[20] as especially successful. And the conclusion on page 13,[21] immediately before your discussion of The Man of the Crowd, is brilliant.

What I would like to say about all this is already contained in my remarks about the 'type'. I should merely like to add, with reference to page 14,[22] that coffee houses certainly existed in Berlin in the nineteenth century, but not in London. And that there are no coffee houses there now, either, any more than there are in America (Poe himself had never been to London).

The interpretation of the uniformity of types could probably best be introduced on page 17, where you discuss the exaggeration of uniformity,[23] that is, this exaggeration itself and its relationship to caricature would then constitute the object of interpretation. The description of Senefelder's lithographs[24] (page 18) is remarkably fine, but this also requires interpretation. Of course, I was particularly taken with the passage on 'reflex behaviour'[25] (page 19), which was completely unknown to me when I wrote my piece on the fetish character of music. Since this is a theme of considerable importance from the perspective of politics and the philosophy of history alike, here would certainly be a good place for a glimpse of the way in which the ornamental ostentation of fascism penetrates right into the torture chambers of the concentration camp, just as the opening of the detective story always already harbours the figure of its end.

(In this connection: to my mind there are few things as symptomatic as the fact that Barcelona presented us with the same spectacle we witnessed a year ago in Vienna: the masses who now rejoiced in the fascist conquerors were the very same which had rejoiced in the opponents of the fascists only the day before.)

As for the rest, I do not really wish to go into the details: in the case of the theory of commodification, I am rather an interested party and hardly feel qualified to make any further suggestions. But it does still seem to me that the concept of empathy with inorganic matter does not provide the decisive resources. Of course, one is treading on extremely delicate ground here, particularly as far as the journal is concerned, since a kind of absolute Marxist competence is rightly postulated for every claim that is made. I have now reformulated my own position concerning the substitution of exchange-value, with enormous effort and the assistance of Max, as compared with its rather more audacious version in the first draft, and if the physical distance between us has ever proved a significant disturbing factor, then it is the case with your theory concerning the soul of the commodity. I would merely ask here that you once again pay particularly careful attention to this theory and compare it with the chapter on commodity fetishism in the first volume.[26] Otherwise, the conclusion of the first and the beginning of the second paragraph on page 21[27] might create some 'troubles'. Concerning the Baudelaire quotation in the text (page 22),[28] I would merely say that the concept of the 'imprévu' is the central concept of Berlioz's musical aesthetic (and one which dominates the whole school of Berlioz and especially Richard Strauss). I can hardly regard the Engels quotation (page 23)[29] as that much of a *trouvaille*, and if we are thinking of cuts, then this passage could well be the first to go. (Löwenthal has already suggested cutting the first half of the quotation, and for my part I would gladly see the whole thing disappear.) As far as the passage about labour power as a commodity[30] is concerned (page 24), what I said above still holds: be careful! I am not entirely happy about the characterization of Baudelaire in terms of the petit bourgeois class. And in general it strikes me that the paragraph about the crowd does not possess the same concentrated power as what precedes it, and that the whole paragraph could benefit from receiving something from your treasure chest of materials. In the last section before Hugo[31] (page 25), I would simply express a mild doubt whether one can really ascribe Brecht's extraordinary stanza to Shelley.[32] Directness and bluntness hardly seem to be his typical characteristics. In any case, one would have to go and compare it with the original.

I am not really sure what to say about the conclusion (from page 26).[33] I hope you will not be angry with me if I suggest that, in spite of repeated and attentive reading, the whole section on Hugo struck me as lacking in proper plasticity, as if it had not yet found its appropriate place in the overall construction. I have no doubt that there are some extraordinarily important motifs here. But when I suggested earlier that certain motifs would be difficult to develop satisfactorily within the context of the essay, I was thinking principally of this part on Hugo. The material could certainly go into a text where the image of the mass provided the central category. If we should decide to publish the second chapter with certain alterations, then the philosophy of history focused on the image of the mass would no longer be thematically so central as to require the excursus on Hugo. The simple reflection that a limited essay on Baudelaire does not demand a relatively substantial discussion of another author is also something to be borne in mind. My proposal, therefore, would be to develop the passages already mentioned, to strengthen the section on the crowd in such a way that it will provide a powerful conclusion, and to save the section on Hugo either for the book on Baudelaire or the Arcades.

Just a few words on what you said about my essay on fetishism. I agree with you entirely that the somewhat different angle of the problem as presented in cinema and jazz results essentially from the material elements in each case, and one must not forget that film involves an effectively new material altogether, whereas jazz does not. I am all too aware of the weakness of the work. And this consists, to put it crudely, in the tendency to indulge in Jeremiads and polemics. You are absolutely right that lamenting the conditions of the present is quite fruitless, although I would also add that the perspective of the philosophy of history currently prohibits any attempt at 'salvation' anyway. The only possible question we must pose now, so it seems to me, is *an experimental one*: what will become of human beings and their capacity for aesthetic perception when they are fully exposed to the conditions of monopoly capitalism? But when I composed the essay, I was not yet psychologically capable of posing the question in such diabolical and behaviouristic terms. The piece must be seen essentially as an expression of my experiences here in America, which may well inspire me one day to grapple with something that we have both rightly felt was previously missing in our writings on mass art and monopoly capitalism.[34] I agree with your view on sound film, and something very similar can also be observed in jazz itself, although I believe it has more to do with objectively developing tendencies than it does with the intrigues of business interests. As far as the advance of the comic dimension in music is concerned: I do indeed see something entirely positive in this, just as I do in the 'disintegration of the feeling of sacred reconciliation', and I am sure that my work nowhere corresponds more powerfully with your own essay on mechanical reproduction than it does here. If that remained less than obvious in the text, I would look upon it as a serious deficiency. As far as the decisive theoretical issue is concerned, namely, the relationship between aesthetic perception and the commodity character, I would ask you to be patient for a while longer.

Please forgive the abstruse dimensions of this letter; at least it may do something to compensate for its tardy arrival.

Lots of love from both of us. We are looking out over the Hudson and are astonished to behold the ice fragments moving down river.

Yours ever,
Teddie

I would just like to add a couple of short observations, one of which I owe to Schapiro. It concerns Villiers de l'Isle Adam,[35] a rather amazing representative of the nineteenth century, who is, incidentally, also responsible for Péladan.[36] I would wager that you will find very rich pickings here if you look.

The other thing is much more immediate, and also much more remote. Have you ever dedicated much time to Auguste Comte, especially his later period and his idea of a 'Religion of Humanity'?[37] I have been reading an American book (by one Hawkins)[38] on the history of (Comtean) positivism in America between 1853 and 1861. It is the most remarkable thing I have set eyes on in a long time. Poe was obviously influenced by Comte, and the scientific challenge to poetry may well derive from the same source. What is the relationship between Comte and Saint-Simonism, and that of Baudelaire to both of them? Amongst other things, Comte wished to incorporate an element of 'fetishism' into his religion of humanity. If you are interested, I can have Hawkins' book sent to you. Above all it contains the correspondence between Comte and his American disciple Edger, who turned, with clearly reactionary political motivations, to Comte's authoritarian-positivistic religion of humanity after deserting the cause of Fourier. The whole thing exactly as if we had predicted it ourselves!

Cordially yours!

1 *the most recent events in Germany*: Adorno is thinking of the pogroms which took place after 9 November 1938.

2 *an entry visa to Cuba for both my parents*: Adorno's parents arrived in Cuba early in 1939.

3 *the events in Spain*: the Catalan capital of Barcelona had fallen into the hands of General Franco's forces in January 1939, and the supporters of the Spanish Republic were forced to flee in large numbers over the Pyrenees to

France; at the same time, the French government had opened negotiations with fascist Spain concerning diplomatic recognition of the Franco regime and decided on 30 January to prevent able-bodied men from crossing the border.

4 *The first sentence of the chapter*: cf. GS I [2], p. 537.

5 *The transition from the physiologies to the habitus of the flâneur*: cf. ibid., p. 538.

6 *The conclusion of the paragraph on the arcades*: cf. ibid., p. 539.

7 *my reservations . . . in the context of your quotation from Simmel*: see letter 110 and the relevant note.

8 *very remarkable quotation from Foucaud*: cf. GS I [2], pp. 540ff.

9 *the next paragraph . . . (page 5)*: cf. ibid., p. 541.

10 *from the Balzac quotation on page 5 through to page 10*: cf. ibid., pp. 541–5.

11 *the antithesis Lukács sets up*: cf. Georg Lukács, *Die Theorie des Romans. Ein geschichtsphilosophischer Versuch über die Formen der grossen Epik* [Theory of the Novel] (Berlin 1920), pp. 100–13.

12 *Balzac's fondness for unqualified statements*: cf. GS I [2], p. 541.

13 *unqualified statement / I also find in de Sade*: see letter 110 and the relevant note.

14 *Poe / the gold bug*: Edgar Allan Poe's eponymous story.

15 *your theory about why Poe alone composed detective stories*: cf. GS I [2], p. 545.

16 *Kierkegaard / his concept of the 'spy'*: cf. GS 2, pp. 20ff.

17 *the passage you quote from the publisher's brochure*: cf. GS I [2], p. 544.

18 *the way in which you combine the elements from Poe with those from Valéry*: cf. ibid., p. 545.

19 *the contrast you draw between Baudelaire and the detective story*: cf. ibid.

20 *the passage on the 'passer-by', and particularly that on 'footsteps'*: cf. ibid., pp. 547ff and pp. 546ff.

21 *the conclusion on page 13*: cf. ibid., p. 550.

22 *with reference to page 14*: cf. ibid., p. 551.

23 *where you discuss the exaggeration of uniformity*: cf. ibid., p. 554.

24 *the description of Senefelder's lithographs*: cf. ibid., p. 555.

25 *the passage on 'reflex behaviour'*: cf. ibid., p. 556.

26 *the chapter on commodity fetishism in the first volume*: Adorno is referring to the chapter in the first volume of Marx's *Capital*.

27 *on page 21*: cf. GS I [2], p. 559.

28 *Concerning the Baudelaire quotation . . . (page 22)*: cf. ibid., p. 559.

29 *the Engels quotation (page 23)*: cf. ibid., p. 560.

30 *the passage about labour power as a commodity*: cf. ibid., p. 561.

31 *the last section before Hugo*: cf. ibid., p. 562.

32 *whether one can really ascribe Brecht's extraordinary stanza to Shelley*: cf. ibid., p. 562; in fact Brecht's translation does follow the English of Shelley's original very closely: 'Hell is a city much like London – / A populous and a smoky city, / There are all sorts of people undone, / And there is little or no fun done; / Small justice shown, and still less pity.'

33 *the conclusion (from page 26)*: cf. ibid., pp. 562–9.

34 *in our writings on mass art and monopoly capitalism*: see letter 83 and the relevant note.

35 *Villiers de l'Isle Adam*: Jean-Marie Mathias Philippe Auguste, Comte de Villiers de l'Isle-Adam (1839–89), became famous principally through his *Contes cruels* and his novel, *L'Eve future*.

36 *Péladan*: Joséphin Péladan (1859–1919), French writer and author of the 21 volumes of the cycle of novels entitled *La Décadence Latine. Ethopée*.

37 *Comte . . . a 'Religion of Humanity'*: Auguste Comte (1798–1857) developed and presented his 'religion de l'humanité' in his *Catéchisme positiviste* of 1852.

38 *an American book (by one Hawkins)*: cf. Richard Laurin Hawkins, *Positivism in the United States 1853–1861* (Cambridge, Mass. 1938), and Adorno's review of the book, which was not published during his lifetime (GS 20 [1], pp. 242ff).

113   BENJAMIN TO ADORNO
      PARIS, 23.2.1939

23.2.39
10, rue Dombasle
Paris XVe

Dear Teddie,

on est philologue ou on ne l'est pas. After I had studied your last letter, my first impulse was to return to my important bundle of papers containing your comments on the Arcades.[1] Reading these letters again, some of which go back quite some way, was a great encouragement. I recognized once again how the original foundations have not been eroded or damaged. Above all, however, your earlier comments also helped to illuminate your last letter, and especially the reflections it contained on the question of the 'type'.

'All hunters look alike.' This is what you said on 5 June 1935, in the course of a reference to Maupassant. This leads right to the heart of a matter which I shall be able to articulate properly as soon as I know what the editorial board of the journal are essentially expecting of a treatise on the *flâneur*. You have given the most felicitous interpretation of the letter I wrote to this effect. Without relinquishing the place this chapter will have to occupy in the book on Baudelaire – and now that the more obvious sociological materials have been successfully identified – I can really devote myself to defining the *flâneur* within the overall context of the Arcades in my usual monographic form. I would give the following indications about how this is to be accomplished.

The self-same [Gleichheit] is a category of cognition; strictly speaking, it has no place in soberly straightforward perception. Perception that is straightforward in the strictest sense of the word, free of all pre-judgement, could only ever encounter the 'similar', even in the most extreme case. However, the kind of pre-judgement that as a rule innocuously accompanies our perception, can become provocative in exceptional cases. It can openly reveal the percipient as one who is *not* so sober after all. This is the case with Don Quixote, for example, when the chivalric romances have gone to his head. However various the situations which he encounters, he invariably perceives the same thing in all of them – namely, the adventure that is simply waiting for the itinerant knight to come along. With respect to Daumier: you are quite right in suggesting that he paints his own mirror image when he paints Quixote. Daumier is also constantly stumbling upon the same thing: in the heads of all those politicians, ministers and lawyers he perceives the same – the commonness and mediocrity of the bourgeois class. And one thing above all is important here: this hallucination of sameness (one that is shattered by caricature only to be instantly restored: since the further removed a grotesque nose may be from the empirical norm, the more emphatically the nose per se will reveal the typical aspect of all human beings with noses), this hallucination is essentially a comic matter in Daumier and in Cervantes. In Don Quixote, the reader's laughter salvages the honour of the bourgeois world, in contrast to which the chivalric world presents itself as something uniform and simplistic. But Daumier's laughter is directed against the bourgeoisie; he sees through the 'equality' it flaunts: namely, as the same tenuous égalité that was vaunted

309

in Louis Philippe's sobriquet. By means of laughter, Cervantes and Daumier both dispel a sameness and equality which they firmly recognize as a historically generated illusion. Equality makes a quite different appearance in Poe, not to mention in Baudelaire. But while the possibility of a kind of comic exorcism still flashes up in 'The Man of the Crowd', there is nothing of the sort in Baudelaire. He artificially came to the aid of the historical hallucination of equality which had insinuated itself along with a commodity economy. And the tropes in which hashish finds expression in his work can be deciphered in this context.

The commodity economy arms that phantasmagoria of sameness which simultaneously reveals itself, as an attribute of intoxication, to be the central image of illusion. 'Once you've had this potion down you, you will see in every woman Helen.'[2] The price makes the commodity equal and identical to all those other commodities which could be purchased for the same price. The commodity – and this is the essential place where Sommer's text must be corrected – insinuates itself, not only and not merely with the buyer, but above all with its own price. And it is precisely in this respect that the *flâneur* accommodates himself to the commodity; he imitates it utterly; and since there is no economic demand, and therefore no market price, for him, he makes himself thoroughly at home in the world of saleable objects. In this, he even outdoes the whore; he takes the abstract concept of the whore for a stroll, so to speak. It is only in the final incarnation of the *flâneur* that this concept is totally fulfilled: as the man with a sandwich board[3] over his head.

From the perspective of my study of Baudelaire,[4] the revised construct will look like this: I shall do justice to the definition of *flânerie* as a state of intoxication and its consequent relationship to the kind of experiences Baudelaire produced through recourse to drugs. The concept of the ever-same [des Immergleichen] will already be introduced in the second part as ever-same *appearance* [Erscheinung], but its definitive configuration as the self-same *event* [Geschehen] will be largely reserved for the third part.

You can see how much I owe to your suggestive remarks concerning the 'type'. When I have gone beyond them, I have always done so very much in the spirit of the original concept of the Arcades itself. And in this connection Balzac rather drifts away from me, as it were. He now retains a merely anecdotal significance, since he brings out neither the comical nor the horrible aspects of the 'type'. (For the novel, I think Kafka was the first person to combine these two aspects successfully – in his work Balzac's types have firmly taken up residence in the sphere of illusion: they have now become all those 'aides', 'officials', 'villagers', and 'lawyers', with whom K. finds himself confronted as the only individual human being, as an atypical being for all his typical averageness.)

Secondly, I would also like to respond briefly to your expressed desire to see the arcades introduced as more than simply a milieu for the *flâneur*. I can certainly repay your trust in my personal archive, and will give voice to those remarkable reveries that helped in mid-century to construct the city of Paris as a complex of glassy galleries, of winter gardens, as it were. The name of the Berlin cabaret – I shall try and discover where it originated – gives some impression of what life in this dream city may well have been like. – Thus the chapter on the *flâneur* will be much more like the chapter which earlier appeared in the physiognomic cycle, where it was surrounded by the studies on the collector, the forger and the gambler.

I do not wish to deal with your comments on particular passages in any detail today. I certainly understood, for example, the one you made about the Foucaud quotation. But I cannot agree, amongst other things, with your doubts concerning Baudelaire's social status as a petit bourgeois. Baudelaire lived on a small income derived from some land he owned in Neuilly, and he had to share this with a stepbrother. His father was a *petit maître* who enjoyed a sinecure as curator of the Luxembourg Gardens during the Restoration period. The decisive thing is that all throughout his life Baudelaire was cut off from all acquaintance with the world of finance or that of the upper middle classes.

You cast a disparaging glance at Simmel – is it not time he was recognized as one of the forefathers of cultural bolshevism? (I do not say this in defence of my quotation, which I should not like to lose, although I think I placed undue stress on it in the present context.) I have been reading his 'Philosophy of Money' recently. It is certainly no accident that it is dedicated to Reinhold and Sabine Lepsius;[5] and certainly no accident that it hails from the time when Simmel was permitted to 'approach' George and his circle. There is, nonetheless, a great deal of interest to be found in the book, as long as one is prepared to ignore the basic idea behind it.

The observations on the philosophy of absolute concentration[6] in the last issue of the journal were a particular pleasure to read. Feeling homesick for Germany has its problematic aspects; and homesickness for the Weimar Republic (and what else would this philosophy be?) is simply appalling. The allusions to France in the text strike much the same tune as my own most personal experiences and reflections. In the last report on literature which I sent to Max,[7] I had a good opportunity to go into this. Here is a *fait divers* that will give you some idea of which way the wind is blowing: the local party newspaper has recently been available to residents at the Littré. I came

311

across it when I went to see Kolisch. I listened to his quartet giving a concert and spent a pleasant hour with him before his departure. Once again I found his lady companion to be an uncommonly winning personality. On the same occasion, by the way, I saw Soma Morgenstern, who managed to escape Vienna at the very last minute.

If you could spare it, I would very much like to have a look at the book by Hawkins. It would certainly be tempting to explore the possible relationship between Poe and Comte. As far as I am aware there is no real relationship between Baudelaire and the latter, any more than there is one between Baudelaire and Saint-Simon. But Comte, on the other hand, was, in his twenties, a *disciple attitré* of Saint-Simon for a time. Amongst other things, he adopted the speculations on the role of the mother developed by the Saint-Simonians, but gave them a positivist twist, coming out with the claim that nature will eventually succeed in producing a self-fertilizing female being in the form of the *vierge-mère*. You may be interested to know that Comte was just as quick to surrender in the coup d'état of 2 September as the Parisian aesthetes were. But at least he had already compensated for this in his 'Religion of Humanity', which included an anniversary celebration dedicated to the solemn condemnation of Napoleon I.

And while we are talking about books: you have already drawn my attention to Maupassant's 'La nuit, un cauchemar'.[8] I have looked through twelve volumes of his stories without being able to locate it. Could you let me know a little more about the matter? Another no less urgent request: could you please send me a copy of your Kierkegaard if you have one to spare. I would also be very grateful if you could lend me 'The Theory of the Novel'.

I was very sad to learn, as I also did from Kolisch, what your parents have been through. I hope they have managed to put all this behind them by now.

I also confirm the receipt of the Hauff book with the greatest of gratitude. I shall be writing to Felizitas next week.

Heartfelt regards to both of you,

Yours,

Walter

1 *my important bundle of papers . . . your comments on the Arcades*: see letters 31, 33 and 39 in particular.

2 '*Once you've had this potion down you, you will see in every woman Helen*': cf. Johann Wolfgang von Goethe, *Faust*. Part 1, lines 2603ff.

3 *the flâneur / the man with a sandwich board*: cf. GS V [1], pp. 562 and 565.

4 *From the perspective of my study of Baudelaire*: Benjamin is referring here to his projected book on Baudelaire.

5 *Reinhold and Sabine Lepsius*: two painters married to one another and members of Stefan George's circle.

6 *observations on the philosophy of absolute concentration*: cf. Max Horkheimer, 'Die Philosophie der absoluten Konzentration', in *Zeitschrift für Sozialforschung* 7, issue 3 (1938), pp. 376–87; now in Horkheimer, *Gesammelte Schriften*, vol. 4, pp. 295–307. – The essay is a critique of the book *Der Neuhumanismus als politische Philosophie* (1938) by Siegfried Marck.

7 *the last report on literature which I sent to Max*: Benjamin's (unpublished) letter to Horkheimer is dated 24 January 1939.

8 *you have already drawn my attention to Maupassant's 'La nuit, un cauchemar'*: see letter 39.

114 THEODOR W. AND GRETEL ADORNO TO BENJAMIN
[NEW YORK,] 15.7.1939

15 July 1939.

My dear Walter,
  On this your birthday, Max has actually given us the finest gift we could wish for: the prospect that you will soon be joining us[1] here, and the hardly less encouraging one that the Baudelaire[2] will soon be in our hands as well. We can hardly express just how happy we feel: for the first time we have adopted the customs of the place and performed a proper Indian dance ourselves, and Max is just as happy as we are about it. For today, just something in great haste concerning our plans: I only received the French *exposé* of the *Tableaux Parisiens*[3] yesterday, and I shall be writing to you in response once I have been able to study it at leisure.
  Firstly, as far as the Baudelaire is concerned, the prospect of publishing it[4] in the first issue of the journal this year (a double issue) would be the ideal fulfilment of a dream. For apart from the Baudelaire piece, this issue will also contain an extremely important essay by Max[5] which I have intensively collaborated on myself – the piece is provisionally entitled 'Europe and the Jews', but it essentially presents the first outline of a theory of fascism. In addition, it will contain four chapters from my study of Wagner[6] (namely, chapters I, VI, IX and X linked together with short connecting passages). If the issue

313

does appear in this form, then it will really approach what I wish for the journal, and I think I can also safely say the same for Max.

On the question of visiting here: we would suggest that you plan for some time around the end of September or the beginning of October. And this for the following reasons. In the first place, the academic year will be in full swing again by then. We are hoping that you will be able to come and defend the principal ideas of the Arcades project here at an official gathering of the Institute, and the more important people we can get to attend the better. There may also be a possibility of arranging a lecture for you on some aspect of aesthetic theory in the philosophy department at Columbia University. Only a few months ago I spoke there myself about the inevitable Husserl material,[7] and with considerable success. – Furthermore: Meyer Schapiro will almost certainly not be appearing in Paris before 25 August. We all ascribe the greatest importance to your meeting him,[8] and not merely because he has an extremely close relationship to the substance of our own work, or because he is as capable of providing fertile suggestions for us as we are to him. The decisive thing is, rather, that we see in him the most important means either of effectively getting you settled over here or of procuring an American research proposal for you in France. I am absolutely convinced that you should be able to spend at least four weeks with him. Simultaneously with this letter to you, I am writing to him in London on your behalf. You are well aware of his strong Trotskyist sympathies: it might be advisable to exercise some caution in selecting people for him to meet, in so far as problems can easily arise where individuals committed to a particular political line are concerned.

Max informs me that under certain circumstances you might have to prove you have some financial resources at your disposal before you can obtain an entry visa, and he asks me to tell you that the Institute would confirm this if necessary; you should realize, however, that this is essentially only a formality. If I understand Max correctly, you would bear the travel costs yourself, but you would be a guest of the Institute while you are in New York.

We shall probably be spending August in Bar Harbor like last year, and would be delighted to hear something from you before we go. – I read the George–Hofmannsthal correspondence[9] with enormous interest and am thinking of writing a substantial review of the book.

Please forgive my haste – perhaps the prospect of imminent reunion will make up a little for this.

Lots of love from both of us,

Your old friend,
Teddie

314

Dear Detlef,

I am quite overcome with joy and spend my whole time wondering where I should begin in showing you all the attractions of New York in order to make you feel at home in barbarous foreign lands. Just imagine that we will be able to see one another again two and a half months from now. I have never waited with such expectation at the pier. Lots and lots of love, a pleasant summer and a most enjoyable time with Schapiro.

Yours as ever,
    Felizitas

1 *the prospect that you will soon be joining us*: in a letter of 24 July, Benjamin had informed Horkheimer that the American Consulate had no objections to his receiving an entry visa for the United States. – Benjamin's planned visit to New York was to have concerned the theoretical discussion of his work and the further possibility of his moving to the United States.

2 *the Baudelaire*: Benjamin had informed Horkheimer by telegram that the manuscript entitled 'Some Motifs in Baudelaire' would be ready by the end of July.

3 *the French exposé of the Tableaux Parisiens*: i.e. Benjamin's 'Notes sur les Tableaux parisiens de Baudelaire', which were delivered as a lecture in Pontigny in May 1939 (cf. GS I [2], pp. 740–8).

4 *the Baudelaire ... the prospect of publishing it*: the essay 'Über einige Motive bei Baudelaire' appeared in the *Zeitschrift für Sozialforschung* 8, issue 1/2 (1939), pp. 50–89; cf. GS I [2], pp. 605–3.

5 *an extremely important essay by Max*: Horkheimer's essay 'Die Juden und Europa' appeared in the said double issue of the Institute journal (pp. 115–36); now in Horkheimer, *Gesammelte Schriften*, vol. 4, pp. 308–31.

6 *four chapters from my study of Wagner*: the four chapters opened the double issue of the Institute journal under the title 'Fragmente über Wagner' (pp. 1–148).

7 *the philosophy department at Columbia University / the inevitable Husserl material*: Adorno presented his lecture on 'Husserl and the Problem of Idealism' in May 1939; for the text, cf. GS 20 [1], pp. 119–34.

8 *Meyer Schapiro / your meeting him*: Benjamin wrote to Gretel Adorno at the end of September 1939: 'Schapiro est rentré, je suppose. Nous avons passé une soirée pleine d'agréments' [Schapiro is back by now, I suppose. We spent an entire evening agreeing with one another] (*Benjamin-Katalog*, p. 296).

9 *the George–Hofmannsthal correspondence*: cf. *Briefwechsel zwischen George und Hofmannsthal* (Berlin 1938). – Instead of writing *a substantial review*, Adorno actually wrote a substantial essay entitled 'George und

Hofmannsthal. Zum Briefwechsel: 1891–1942', which first appeared in the mimeograph volume published in Benjamin's memory by the Institute of Social Research in 1942, *Walter Benjamin zum Gedächtnis*; cf. GS 10 [1], pp. 195–237.

115 BENJAMIN TO THEODOR W. AND GRETEL ADORNO
PARIS, 6.8.1939

Paris XVe
10, rue Dombasle
6 August 1939.

Dear Teddie,

I think you are currently on holiday with Felizitas. These lines will probably reach you with some delay, which will give the Baudelaire manuscript, sent off to Max a week ago, a little time to catch up with them.

As for the rest, I hope you will not be too angry with me if these lines resemble an index of headings more than they do a letter. After a week's rigorous solitary confinement, indispensable if I was to complete the Baudelaire chapter, and subjected to a spell of appalling weather, I am feeling unusually exhausted. But that will not prevent me from telling you and Felizitas how much I too am looking forward to the prospect of seeing one other again. (I must not completely lose sight of the fact that there are still difficulties to be overcome before this prospect becomes a reality. I have written to Morgenroth about the sale of my Klee painting;[1] if you see him, don't forget to ask him about it.)

Although my new Baudelaire chapter can hardly be considered a real 'revision' of a chapter you are already familiar with, I think you will nonetheless be able to see in it the influence of our earlier correspondence about last summer's 'Baudelaire'. Above all, I did not have to be told twice how gladly you would be willing to trade the panoramic overview of the material content for a more precise articulation of its basic theoretical structure. And how prepared you are to absolve the precipitous ascents that are required to obtain a clear perspective on those parts of the structure which have already been erected higher up.

As far as the aforementioned list of headings is concerned, it is essentially an index to the numerous and many-layered motifs which have been omitted from the new chapter (in comparison with last summer's chapter on the *flâneur*). These motifs are naturally not to be eliminated from the total complex of the Baudelaire book, and I am intending to supply them with detailed interpretative commentary in their proper place.

The motifs of the arcade itself, of noctambulism, of the *feuilleton*, and the theoretical introduction of the concept of phantasmagoria, are reserved for the first section of the second part. The motifs of the trace, of the type, of empathy with the soul of the commodity, are destined for the third section. The present middle section of the second part will only present the complete figure of the *flâneur* when it is combined with its first and third sections.

I have taken account of your reservations about the quotations from Simmel and Engels as expressed in your letter of 2 February, although I have not actually dropped them. This time I have indicated what was so important to me about the Engels quotation. Your objection to the Simmel quotation struck me as well-grounded from the outset. In the text as it now stands, it has assumed a changed role and a less emphatic function.

I am delighted at the prospect of seeing it printed in the next issue of the journal. I have written to Max to tell him how much I have striven to keep the essay free of any fragmentary elements and thereby to stay within the prescribed limitations of space. I would be very happy if no drastic changes were to be made to the text (*pour tout dire*: no cuts).

I will permit my Christian Baudelaire to be borne aloft to heaven by Jewish angels alone. But arrangements are already in hand to let him fall during the last third moment of Ascension, as if by accident, just before his final entrance into glory.

In conclusion, my dear Teddie, I must thank you for inviting my Jochmann[2] piece to participate in the impending jubilee issue of the journal.

All best wishes to you and Felizitas for an enjoyable holiday and a pleasant return home,

Yours,
Walter

And a special word of thanks, dear Felizitas, for the book by Dreyfus[3] and the lines which announced and accompanied its arrival. I am often thinking of you both.

1 *the sale of my Klee painting*: in order to meet the travel costs of his planned trip to New York, Benjamin had been considering selling the Klee painting he owned, 'Angelus Novus', to the arts patron Ernest Morgenroth, who had already left for America; Benjamin was well-acquainted with his son Ernest Gustave Morgenroth (later known as Stephan Lackner). The transaction never transpired.

2 *my Jochmann piece*: the essay entitled 'Rückschritte der Poesie', and first mentioned in letter 75, for which Benjamin had written the 'Introduction'.

3 *the book by Dreyfus*: Gretel Adorno had responded to Benjamin's request (*Briefe*, p. 823) and sent him the book *De Monsieur Thiers à Marcel Proust* (Paris 1939) by Robert Dreyfus.

116 GRETEL AND THEODOR W. ADORNO TO BENJAMIN
   [NEW YORK,] 21.11.1939

21 November 1939.

My dear Detlef:
    just this moment we got the news[1] that you are back in Paris. I cannot tell you how glad we are, to know you are safe. – In the meantime I got your second letter[2] with the marvellous dream in it, many many thanks. – If you would do me the great favour as to send me a copy of your Kraus,[3] I would be very grateful. As to my health I did not feel so very well and had to go to a new physician Dr Brenheim, an Endocrinologist, as E[4] thought that my fits of migraine could be connected with the 'Hypophyse' the functions of which I am not so sure about. But only after three or four months I shall know, if he will be able to help me. Otherwise I have to resign and to consider myself an old suffering woman. We hope to hear very soon from you
    love
        Felicitas

I am very happy that you are at home again – happier than I could tell you! And my enthusiasm about the Baudelaire increases steadily! I made the German abstract[5] and the English translation – please, check the French translation of this resume which does not yet satisfy me. Good luck and à bientôt!
                                        Yours ever
                                            Teddie

[Both of the above letters were written in English]

1 *just this moment we got the news*: the news about Benjamin's release from the internment camp in Nevers and his return to Paris.

2 *your second letter*: cf. *Briefe*, pp. 828–31.

3 *your Kraus*: see letter 26 and the relevant note.

4 *E*: Egon Wissing.

318

5 *the German abstract*: German language essays in the *Zeitschrift für Sozialforschung* were accompanied by a résumé in English and French; Adorno had obviously composed a résumé in German first and then had it translated into English.

117   ADORNO TO BENJAMIN
      [NEW YORK,] 29.2.1940

29 February 1940.

My dear Walter:
   The fact that I have taken such a long time to write to you[1] is easily explained. I really felt an almost insuperable embarrassment about having written to you in a foreign language. Unjust though this may be as far as the empirical character is concerned, there is nevertheless some justice in it as far as the intelligible character is concerned, and I hope and trust that you will forgive me.
   It is my greatest hope that you will be able to do so in person here in New York. The affidavit supplied by Miss Razovsky[2] is a considerable boon, and of course Max completely agrees that you should refer to your relations with the Institute prior to 1933 – for your current involvement is already quite obvious from all the documents. Please keep us constantly informed about developments. I would also advise you in any event to write to Schapiro[3] in the matter immediately, and particularly in relation to the fact that he is already setting up some courses or other for you here in order to improve your financial circumstances. If he is successful, I think that this can only promote the whole development in the most favourable manner, and such courses would certainly not have to claim more than a very small proportion of your time.
   You are aware of the enthusiasm with which I read your Baudelaire, and not one of the various telegraphic or otherwise abbreviated responses which you have received about it is exaggerated in the least. That is as true for Max as it is for me. I believe it is hardly an exaggeration to describe this work as the most perfect thing you have done since the book on Baroque drama and the work on Kraus. If I have sometimes had a nagging conscience about my own insistent carping in the matter, I can say it has now transformed itself into a rather vain feeling of pride, and it is you who are responsible for that – however dialectical the relation between our respective productions remains. It is really difficult to single out anything in particular, since every moment of the work is so equally close to the centre and the construction is so successfully accomplished. The theory of the

gambler[4] is, if you will permit the metaphor, the first ripe fruit to fall from the totem pole of the Arcades. I hardly have to tell you what a *trouvaille* the section on the aureole[5] represents. Let me just make one or two remarks. Your theory of forgetting and the theory of 'shock'[6] touches very closely indeed upon my musical writings, especially in relation to the perception involved in hit songs: a connection which can hardly have been present to your mind and therefore delights me all the more as a kind of independent confirmation. Here I am thinking of the passage on forgetting, remembering and advertising[7] in my essay on fetishism, page 342. I felt very similarly about the contrast you draw between reflex behaviour and experience [Erfahrung].[8] Indeed, I can say that, since I have been here in America, all of my reflections on materialist anthropology have come to centre upon the concept of the 'reflex character', and here again our intentions coincide intimately with one another: indeed, one could describe your Baudelaire as the primal history of the reflex character. I originally had the feeling that you didn't really like my own piece on fetishism, the only one of my German texts which deals with aspects of these issues, either because it seems to provoke the misunderstanding that its aim was to 'save' culture or, and this is closely connected with that, because the construction of the piece was not entirely successful. If you would be kind enough to look at the piece again in the light of these considerations, and if in your eyes it were then to fall apart into those fragments which it ought to, perhaps you would be able to reconcile yourself with some of its aspects. Please forgive the rather selfish character of my response to your Baudelaire, but it is certainly not a reflex response, and I feel it is almost a confirmation of the objective truth of such a text if it seems to touch the utterly peculiar interest of its every reader.

Any criticisms I have to make about the Baudelaire are largely insignificant. But I will mention a few things here simply so that I don't forget them later. The appropriation of Freud's theory of memory as a defence mechanism against certain stimuli, and the way in which you apply it to Proust and Baudelaire,[9] does not seem entirely transparent to me. This enormously complex problem involves the question concerning the unconscious nature of the fundamental impression, which certainly has to be assumed if the latter belongs to the *mémoire involontaire* rather than to the sphere of consciousness. But can we really speak of an 'unconscious impression' in this way? Was the moment when Proust tasted the madeleine, the moment which provoked his *mémoire involontaire*, actually unconscious? It seems to me that a dialectical element has dropped out of the theory here, and that is the element of forgetting itself. In a certain sense 'forgetting' is the foundation for both these things, for the sphere of experience [Erfahrung] or *mémoire involontaire*, and for the reflex character of a sudden act of recall that already presupposes the forgetting. Whether an individual human being is capable of having such experiences depends in the last instance upon how that person forgets. You allude to this question in a footnote,[10] where you point out that Freud makes no explicit distinction between recall [Erinnerung] and memory [Gedächtnis] (and I take this to be a criticism). Is it not the case that the real task here is to bring the entire opposition between sensory experience [Erlebnis] and experience proper [Erfahrung] into relation with a dialectical theory of forgetting? Or one could equally say, into relation with a theory of reification. For all reification is a forgetting: objects become purely thing-like the moment they are retained for us without the continued presence of their other aspects: when something of them has been forgotten. This raises the question as to how far this forgetting is one that is capable of shaping experience, which I would almost call epic forgetting, and how far it is a reflex forgetting. I do not wish to suggest an answer to this question today, but merely to pose it as precisely as possible. – And this because I also believe that the fundamental distinction made in your essay will only acquire its universal social potential in connection with this question of reification. In this regard, I hardly need to add that there is absolutely no question for us of merely repeating Hegel's verdict upon reification here, but rather of formulating a proper critique of reification, i.e. of unfolding the contradictory moments that are involved in such forgetting; or one could also say, of formulating a distinction between good and bad reification. Certain passages in your edited anthology of letters, like the introduction to the letter from Kant's brother,[11] would seem very much to point in this direction. You can see that I am attempting here to draw a connecting thread between the Jochmann piece and the Baudelaire essay.

The other matter concerns your chapter on the aura.[12] I am convinced that our own best thoughts are invariably those that we cannot entirely think through.[13] In this sense the concept of the aura still seems to me to be incompletely 'thought out'. One can argue about whether, indeed, it should be fully thought out as such. Yet I would still like to point out one aspect of your approach which also touches upon another piece, and this time my study of Wagner, and especially its unpublished fifth chapter. In the Baudelaire essay you write:[14] 'To experience the aura of a phenomenon is to lend it the ability to look back in turn.' With the concept of 'lending' here, this differs from your earlier formulation.[15] But is this concept not an indication of that moment upon which I grounded the construction of phantasmagoria in my Wagner study, namely, the moment of human *labour*?[16]

321

Is not the aura invariably a trace of a forgotten human moment in the thing, and is it not directly connected, precisely by virtue of this forgetting, with what you call 'experience'? One might even go so far as to regard the experiential ground which underlies the speculations of idealist thought as an attempt to retain this trace – and to retain it precisely in those things which have now become alien. Perhaps idealist philosophy as a whole, for all the splendour of its dramatic appearance, is nothing but one of those 'occasions' which you have developed in so exemplary a fashion in your Baudelaire.

In the meantime you will have received the manuscript of my essay on the correspondence between George and Hofmannsthal. I have never been quite so eager to hear your response as I am with this work – to which I have perhaps dedicated a quite inordinate amount of effort. I would merely like to say that I have here attempted, for the first time, to disencumber myself of all terminological ballast, of everything that you, *à propos* of Sohn-Rethel, have called 'the language of the pimp'. Let us hope that, as a result, I have not merely opened up a little tobacco shop instead, which is what often happens with academics in their retirement. The association here leads me to Maupassant and thus to my question whether you have ever read his story on the night, and if so, what impression it made upon you.

I am now finally free of the Radio Project, for which I eventually produced three texts,[17] including a very substantial one, at the end of last year (one of these discusses the constitutive transforming effect of radio upon symphonic form in terms of a rigorous technical analysis. I would very much like you to read this some time). This new freedom has given me enormous encouragement: apart from the George material, I have written a substantial review of Rickert's posthumously published book;[18] assembled a number of technical analyses of musical 'hits'[19] together with some theoretical observations to form a properly composed text; and written, first in German and subsequently in English, a lecture on Kierkegaard's Religious Discourses,[20] in which I pursue certain themes and directions of my Kierkegaard book with reference to new material that was not discussed in the earlier study. About a week ago I made my début on American radio:[21] I introduced a concert of modern music in which Kolisch and Steuermann were involved. You can see that I have not exactly been idle. But this is all simply a prelude to the collaboration I am planning with Max. I am particularly pleased that you like his essay on the Jews.[22] It is more than empty words if I concede to you that in the presence of your Baudelaire and his Jews, my Wagner no longer entirely looks like the pinnacle of achievement. But I can only say with Max: 'Attendons patiemment la réorganisation des tramways'.

322

In reply to your letter of 17 January:[23] I was extremely concerned to hear that your health is still not fully recovered. In the meantime, Gretel has an encouraging practical suggestion to make to you in this connection. Thanks to the treatment she has been receiving, she is really feeling much better at the moment, and this time we are hoping this is more than the usual success encountered at the beginning of such treatment. – The question as to whether it would be better for you to start on the Gide or to conclude the Baudelaire[24] is really rather difficult for me to answer à distance. From the technical point of view of producing the journal, the Gide would be the more practical option, as long as it involves no external difficulties. The best thing of all would be to discuss the matter explicitly with Max. – I would be particularly delighted if you were able to produce an essay on the New Melusine.[25] This is undoubtedly one of the most crucial junctures of our work, and the question concerning the character of the water-spirit in relation to the concepts of phantasmagoria and miniaturism would produce a truly astrological constellation of thoughts.

In the meantime my parents have arrived here and are spending the winter months in Florida. – May I conclude with a request? You write that Soma Morgenstern is likely to come over here soon, and report that you see him from time to time. In earlier years he was not particularly friendly towards Gretel, for reasons which cast little positive light upon him, and even less upon his wife, although I do not know whether she is still together with him now or not. Ernst Bloch has hinted that he is also saying idiotic and unfriendly things about me, and in such a risible context (Soma is supposed to have suggested that my theories concerning Kafka are all derived from him and that I have openly published nothing on the subject) that I can hardly take it very seriously – and especially since Ernst in particular must be considered a rather dubious and universally disreputable source in such matters. But as far as Gretel is concerned, the situation is such that I do not relish the thought of meeting Soma unless I can be quite sure that he will treat Gretel very differently in future. It would really be very helpful if, the next time you chance to meet, and without referring to any difficulties in the past, you could say something about Gretel to Soma – who always liked to display an extremely unattractive *orgueil de toute gueuserie* as far as she was concerned. I think this would be to everyone's advantage. In general Soma certainly has many very appealing qualities, but unfortunately he also reveals a wretched tendency to mediocrity even in his own regard. I would very much like to know what you feel about him – as a writer as well as a person. He has never shown me his novel,[26] but reputable sources have only ever said bad things about it and disreputable ones only ever good things. The differences here surely lie much deeper than the mere irritation sometimes expressed between correspondents. In any case, I would certainly be sincerely grateful for your opinion in the case of Soma. Let me conclude with the wish that your English lessons[27] will prove to be 'a tremendous success'.

Entirely yours as ever,
Teddie

1 *such a long time to write to you*: Adorno's last letter to Benjamin is dated 21 November 1939.

2 *The affidavit supplied by Miss Razovsky*: through the good offices of Cecilia Razovsky (1886–1968), who worked with the 'National Refugee Service', Benjamin received an affidavit from Mr Milton Starr of Nashville, Tennessee, in January 1940.

3 *I would advise you . . . to write to Schapiro*: there is no knowledge of any letter from Benjamin to Schapiro.

4 *The theory of the gambler*: cf. GS I [2], pp. 632–7.

5 *the section on the aureole*: cf. ibid., pp. 651ff.

6 *Your theory of forgetting and the theory of 'shock'*: cf. ibid., pp. 612–15.

7 *the passage on forgetting, remembering and advertising*: for the passage from Adorno's essay 'On the Fetish Character in Music and the Regression of Listening', cf. GS 14, pp. 35ff.

8 *the contrast you draw between reflex behaviour and experience*: cf. GS I [2], pp. 532ff.

9 *theory of memory as a defence mechanism / the way in which you apply it to Proust and Baudelaire*: cf. ibid., pp. 612–15.

10 *You allude to this question in a footnote*: cf. ibid., p. 612.

11 *your edited anthology of letters / the introduction to the letter from Kant's brother*: for Benjamin's 'Introduction' to the book *Deutsche Menschen* [Germans], see letter 61 and the relevant note, and GS IV [1], pp. 151ff.

12 *your chapter on the aura*: cf. GS I [2], pp. 644–50.

13 *I am convinced that our own best thoughts are invariably those we cannot entirely think through*: cf. Adorno's aphorism in *Minima Moralia*: 'Only those thoughts are true which do not understand themselves' (GS 4, p. 214).

14 *In the Baudelaire essay you write*: cf. GS I [2], pp. 646ff.

15 *this differs from your earlier formulation*: cf., for example, GS II [1], pp. 378ff. and GS I [2], pp. 477–80.

16 *the construction of phantasmagoria in my Wagner / the moment of human labour*: cf. GS 13, pp. 80ff.

17 *the Radio Project / three texts*: Adorno is probably referring to the following studies: 'The Radio Voice' (unpublished); 'Analytic Study of the NBC Music Appreciation Hour' – which eventually became the chapter entitled 'Die gewürdigte Music' [Music Appreciated] in Adorno's book *Der getreue Korrepetitor* (cf. GS 15, pp. 163–7); and 'The Radio Symphony' (cf. Adorno, 'The Radio Symphony. An Experiment in Theory', in *Radio Research 1941*, edited by Paul Lazarsfeld and Frank N. Stanton (New York 1941), pp. 110–39).

18 *a review of Rickert's posthumously published book*: Adorno's review of Heinrich Rickert's *Unmittelbarkeit und Sinndeutung. Aufsätze zur Ausgestaltung des Systems* [Immediacy and Interpretation. Essays towards an Articulation of the System] appeared in English in *Studies in Philosophy and Social Science* 9 (1941), pp. 479–82; for the German version, cf. GS 20 [1], pp. 224–50.

19 *a number of technical analyses of musical 'hits'*: Adorno is referring to the pieces 'Especially for you', 'In an eighteenth century drawing room', and 'Penny Serenade', which were collected in manuscript under the title 'Neue Schlageranalysen' and published later as the second part of Adorno's 'Musikalische Warenanalysen' (GS 16, pp. 289–94).

20 *a lecture on Kierkegaard's Religious Discourses*: the lecture which Adorno gave on 23 February 1940 at Columbia University, appeared in English under the title 'Kierkegaard's Doctrine of Love' in the *Zeitschrift für Sozialforschung*, which had now been renamed *Studies in Philosophy and Social Science*, 8, issue 3 (1939), pp. 413–29; for the German version, 'Kierkegaards Lehre der Liebe', cf. GS 2, pp. 217–36.

21 *my début on American radio*: on 22 February 1940, Adorno himself introduced a radio broadcast of a concert involving Eduard Steuermann and the Kolisch Quartet and featuring compositions by Schönberg, Zemlinsky, Eisler and Krenek (cf. GS 18, pp. 576–80).

22 *his essay on the Jews*: see letter 114 and the relevant note.

23 *your letter of 17 January*: for this letter of Benjamin's to Gretel Adorno, cf. *Briefe*, pp. 841–5.

24 *to start on the Gide or to conclude the Baudelaire*: Benjamin had informed Horkheimer of his plan to write a comparative study on Rousseau's 'Confessions' and Gide's 'Journal', but had also expressed his great desire to finish the book on Baudelaire; cf. GS I [3], pp. 1127–30 and 1133–5.

25 *an essay on the New Melusine*: Benjamin had long considered writing something on the tale from Goethe's novel *Wilhelm Meisters Wanderjahre*, but the plan was never realized.

26 *Soma Morgenstern / his novel*: i.e. *Der Sohn des verlorenen Sohnes* [The Son of the Prodigal Son] (Berlin 1935).

27 *your English lessons*: In his letter to Gretel Adorno of 17 January, Benjamin had written: 'Mes leçons anglaises vont commencer la semaine prochaine' (*Briefe*, p. 845).

Paris 15, d. 7. V. 40
10, rue Dombasle.

My dear Teddie,

Thank you for your letter of 29 February. Unfortunately, we shall just have to get used to this kind of delay intervening between your letters and my replies for the time being. And in addition, as you can easily see for yourself, this letter[1] was not constructed in a day any more than Rome itself.

I was (and am) of course delighted by your attitude to my 'Baudelaire'. You may know that the telegram[2] which you, Felizitas and Max had sent actually only reached me at the camp, and you can easily imagine the significance it possessed for my psychological constitution during those months.

I have re-read the passages on regressive listening to which you referred me and can certainly recognize the correspondence of approach between our respective investigations. There is no better example for the methodical destruction of experience than when the popular lyric is set to the melody.[3] (This clearly reveals that the individual prides himself on treating the contents of potential experience in the same way that the political administration treats the elements of potential sociality.) There is no reason to conceal from you the fact that the roots of my 'theory of experience' can be traced back to a childhood memory. My parents would go on walks with us, as a matter of course, wherever we spent the summer months. There would always be two or three of us children together. But it is my brother[4] I am thinking of here. After we had visited one or other of the obligatory places of interest around Freudenstadt, Wengen or Schreiberhau, my brother used to say, 'Now we can say we've been there'. This remark imprinted itself unforgettably on my mind. (Incidentally, I would be rather surprised if your impressions of my own reaction to your essay[5] on the fetish character in music were really correct. Are you not perhaps confusing this with my reaction to the essay on jazz? I certainly expressed certain reservations about the latter.[6] But I agreed unreservedly with the former. And indeed, I have been thinking about it a lot recently, especially in regard to the comments you make there, in relation to Mahler, about 'musical progress'.)[7]

There can be no doubt that the concept of forgetting which you introduce into the discussion of the aura is of great significance. I shall bear in mind the possibility of distinguishing between epic and reflex forgetting. But please do not regard it as evasion if I do not pursue the question further here. I vividly remembered the passage in the fifth chapter of your Wagner[8] study to which you draw my attention. But even if the question of the aura does in fact involve a 'forgotten human moment', this is still not necessarily the moment of human labour. The tree and the shrub which offer themselves to us are not made by human hands. There must therefore be something human in the things themselves, something that is *not* originated by labour. But I do not wish to go any further here. It seems obvious to me that I shall not be able to avoid confronting the question you raise as my work proceeds (and whether already with the work immediately following on from the 'Baudelaire' I am not sure). In that case, my first task will be to go back and consult the *locus classicus* of the theory of forgetting, which is represented for me, as you well know, by 'Der Blonde Eckbert'.[9]

But in order to grant full significance to the phenomenon of forgetting, I do not think it is really necessary to contest the concept of *mémoire involontaire*. The original childhood experience of tasting the madeleine, which one day came back *involontairement* to Proust, was indeed unconscious. It was certainly not the first bite of his first madeleine that returned. ('Trying' something is a conscious act.) But tasting surely becomes unconscious to the degree that the taste itself becomes more familiar. The adult experience of 'tasting something again' is then, naturally, a conscious one.

Since you asked about Maupassant's 'La nuit':[10] I have read this important piece extremely carefully. There is a fragment of my 'Baudelaire' which deals with it, and you will certainly get to see it some day. (*En attendant*, I am gratefully returning to you, via the Paris office, the volume you loaned me.)

As far as the choice between Gide and Baudelaire is concerned, Max has kindly left me entirely free to decide.[11] And I have opted for the Baudelaire. This is the subject which stubbornly continues to present itself to me as the most pressing; and my most urgent task is to do full justice to its demands. I cannot conceal from you the fact that I have not yet been able to dedicate myself to it with the same intensity I could have wished. One of the principal reasons for this is my work on the 'Theses',[12] some of which you will be receiving from me during the next few days. For their part, they do indeed present a certain stage of my reflections in continuation of the 'Baudelaire'. In the coming days I am expecting to begin a period of hopefully uninterrupted work,[13] when I can dedicate myself to this continuation.

But now to the George–Hofmannsthal correspondence. One cannot have everything after all. Now when I find myself in a position to respond to you in an area where I feel completely at home, I cannot even fulfil the modest wish of knowing the book in question from direct experience. Since I certainly do not enjoy this firsthand experience in the field of music, you should not take my judgement of your essay[14] too categorically. Be that as it may, it is, as far as I can see, the best thing you have ever written. I shall make a number of detailed comments in what follows. But I would like to say right away that the crucial strength of the essay lies in your uncommonly assured, striking and original outline of the historical context: the spark which leaps between Mach and Jens Peter Jacobsen[15] lends the same plasticity to the historical landscape that sudden lightning from a gloomy sky bestows upon the natural landscape.

From your account it looks very much as if George's image is impressed rather more sharply on this correspondence than is that of Hofmannsthal. After all, the struggle of the one to acquire a literary position with respect to the other was one of the driving forces behind this exchange of letters, and it was George who was, and continued to remain, the aggressive one here. And whereas, in a certain sense, I find a comprehensive portrait of George in your essay, a good deal still remains in the background as far as Hofmannsthal is concerned. It is very clear from some of the passages that you would be quite capable of illuminating certain aspects of this background. Your remark about the actor,[16] and even more so that about the child in Hofmannsthal, which culminates in that wonderful quotation from 'Ariadne',[17] which creates a tremendous effect by virtue of the way you work it into the text – all of this leads right to the heart of the matter. I would have loved to hear your views about all those echoes from the world of childhood which are expressed, and so forlornly, in George's 'Lied des Zwergen' [Song of the Dwarf][18] or in his poem 'Entführung' [Abduction].[19]

But there is one side of Hofmannsthal, and one which is very dear to me, that you leave untouched. I can hardly think the suggestions I would like to make about this here (and perhaps not for the first time?) will really say anything new. If that is the case, then it is not clear that my suggestions will prove particularly illuminating to you after all. Despite the rather fragmentary nature of my formulations, I shall communicate them all the same. There are essentially two texts which, if taken together, are capable of revealing what I want to say. You refer to one of them yourself, when you cite Hofmannsthal's Lord Chandos letter.[20] And here I am thinking of the following passage:[21] 'I cannot say how often this Crassus and his moray eel comes to mind as a mirror-image of myself, tossed up over the abyss of the centuries . . . Crassus . . ., shedding tears over his moray. And I feel compelled to contemplate this figure, whose absurdity and contemptibility in the midst of a Senate that rules the entire world and deliberates upon the most elevated of matters is strikingly obvious, and compelled to do so by something unnameable that seems utterly foolish to me the moment I attempt to express it in words.' (The same motif recurs in *Der Turm* [The Tower]:[22] with the insides of a slaughtered pig which the Prince was forced to look upon when he was a child.) As for the rest, the second passage I spoke of is also to be found in *Der Turm*:[23] namely, the conversation between Julian and the physician. Julian, the man who lacks nothing but a tiny effort of will, nothing but a single moment of commitment, to enjoy the highest experience imaginable,[24] is a self-portrait of Hofmannsthal. Julian betrays the Prince: Hofmannsthal turned his back upon the task which emerges in his Lord Chandos letter. His 'loss of speech' was a kind of punishment for this. Perhaps the language which escaped Hofmannsthal was the very language which was given to Kafka at around the same time. For Kafka took on the task which Hofmannsthal had failed morally, and therefore also poetically, to fulfil. (The highly suspect and feebly supported theory of sacrifice[25] to which you refer bears all the traces of this failure.)

I believe that, throughout his entire life, Hofmannsthal looked upon his own talents the way that Christ would have looked upon his Kingdom if he had been forced to establish it with Satan's assistance. His unusual versatility goes hand in hand, so it seems to me, with the awareness of having betrayed what was best in himself. That is why no familiarity with the rabble was ever able to frighten him.

Nevertheless, I really do not think it is appropriate, in ascribing Carossa[26] to a 'school' of which Hofmannsthal was supposedly the leader, to speak of German writers towing the official political line[27] *under the sign of this school,* i.e. of Hofmannsthal himself. Hofmannsthal died in 1929. If in no other way, he has at least purchased through his death a *non liquet* in the charge you bring against him. I feel that you should reconsider this passage, and am almost tempted to request you to do so.

You are quite right to bring up Proust.[28] I have been thinking about his work a great deal myself recently. And once again, my thoughts seem to correspond closely with your own here. You speak felicitously about the experience of 'that's not it at all'[29] – that experience when time turns into something we have lost. And it seems to me that Proust was able to find a deeply hidden (but not, therefore, necessarily an unconscious) model for this fundamental experience: namely, the experience of 'that is not it' with regard to the assimilation of French Jews. You will remember the famous passage in *Sodome et Gomorrhe*[30] in which the complicity of sexual inverts is compared with the constellation governing the way the Jews behave amongst

329

one another. The very fact that Proust was only half Jewish allowed him insight into the highly precarious structure of assimilation; an insight which was then externally confirmed by the Dreyfus affair.

As far as George is concerned, there will surely be nothing written on him, even at some historical distance, that will brook comparison with your essay. I have absolutely no reservations about it in this respect; and I am not ashamed to admit that I was very pleasantly surprised by this. However difficult it seems these days to regard George as anything other than the poet whose 'Stern des Bundes' [Star of the League] anticipated and helped to choreograph the Saint Vitus' Dance that is now sweeping over ravaged German soil – this was hardly something to be expected of you. Yet you have accomplished this unseasonable and thankless task, that of 'saving' George, as decisively as it could be done, and as tactfully as it had to be done. In recognizing the moment of defiance as the poetical and political source of strength in George,[31] you have succeeded in illuminating the most important aspects, both interpretatively (the significance of translation for him)[32] and critically (his monopolistic ambitions and his rejection of the market).[33] Your work is all of a piece where everything is equally convincing, and there are some passages which even on their own would prove that the effort you have expended on this text, however great it may have been, was not wasted. I am thinking, for example, of your excellent comment on the 'Gentleman',[34] and of all those resonant quotations like 'for now the hour is late'.[35] Your work has rendered conceivable what was previously quite inconceivable, something which could well initiate a renewal of interest in George: namely, an anthology of his poetry. Some of them sound better in your text than they do where you originally found them.

There is one important point that I do not want to forget here, and something we should (and I think could) come to an agreement about. It concerns what you discuss under the rubric of 'bearing' [Haltung].[36] I think the comparison with smoking doesn't really do justice to the matter. It could mislead people into thinking that someone's 'bearing' is always something that is consciously 'adopted' or 'put on display'. But it can certainly be encountered in an unconscious form that is nonetheless a kind of 'bearing'. I imagine you probably see things the same way, since you also understand gracefulness in terms of this concept, although it is rarely something that is consciously displayed by anyone. (As far as gracefulness is concerned, I am speaking only of children, even though I would not want to treat a natural phenomenon in an unacceptably abstract fashion by separating it from the society in which it appears. The gracefulness of children does exist, and it exists primarily as a kind of corrective to society; it is one of those 'hints' we are vouchsafed of 'a happiness as yet undisciplined'.[37] A strong attachment to childlike innocence, something of which one might well accuse Hofmannsthal in an ungenerous moment (that innocence which allowed him to enjoy the Salten's feuilleton literature[38] almost as much as my book on Baroque drama), does not justify us in simply abandoning what is genuinely attractive in such attachment.) I could try and suggest something of the reservations which I feel about your remarks on bearing in the narrower sense by borrowing from your own text here. And precisely from the passage where you allude to my Baudelaire essay with the finely expressed observation[39] that the lonely individual is a dictator for everyone who is equally lonely. I do not think it is too bold to claim that we encounter someone's 'bearing' when the essential loneliness of an individual properly manifests itself to us. That loneliness which, far from representing the site of all the individual's richness, could well represent instead the site of the individual's historically conditioned emptiness, of the persona as the individual's sorry fate. I understand and fully share all your reservations where bearing and posture explicitly represent a richness on display (and this is indeed how it was understood by George). But there is also an imprescriptible bearing that is expressive of emptiness (as with aspects of the later Baudelaire). In short: bearing, as I understand it, differs as much from what you are denouncing as a branded skin differs from a tattooed one.

The last two pages of your essay (pages 52–3) struck me like a table of birthday gifts upon which the passage on 'happiness as yet undisciplined' represented the very light of life. The work also resembles something of a birthday table in other respects as well; the thoughts expressed here were quite as free of terminological tags as personal gifts are free of price-tags.

In conclusion, I shall adopt your admirable habit of submitting suggestions by way of marginalia. 'Even now the final train is leaving for the mountains'[40] is a sentence that is just as much at home in the Schwabing atmosphere as Kubin's imaginary city of 'Pearl'.[41] 'Pearl' is itself the city which contains the 'temple' within whose damp-infested walls the 'Seventh Ring' is still preserved.

Your allusion to Kraus[42] might have acquired more weight had you referred to his critique of George's translation of the Shakespeare sonnets,[43] especially since you explicitly touch upon the question of translation.

George's appreciative judgement of Hofmannsthal[44] repeats down to the last detail Hugo's famous judgement of Baudelaire:[45] 'Vous avez créé un frisson nouveau.' When George speaks of the granitic-Germanic element in Hofmannsthal,[46] he might well have been thinking of a passage from Hölderlin's letter to Böhlendorf of 4 December 1801 in terms of tone and subject matter.

331

It might also be worth asking oneself in passing whether this correspondence may not have been influenced by that between Schiller and Goethe – a correspondence which, documenting as it did the friendship of two princes amongst poets, contributed so much to the deterioration of the upper air which plays around the peaks in Germany.

In response to your remark that 'The noble is noble by virtue of the ignoble'[47] – Victor Hugo's splendid comment: 'L'ignorant est le pain que mange le savant'[48] [The ignorant are bread for the wise].

The medallions you fashioned for Carossa and Borchardt[49] are very finely cast, and I was delighted, as you can imagine, by the inscription *lucus a non lucendo*[50] which you dedicated to the symbolist movement. The analysis of Rimbaud's 'Voyelles',[51] with which you substantiate the device, also strikes me as entirely convincing. The combination of technicism and esotericism, which you identify so early on, has vividly manifested itself in a political regime that has established mediaeval and quasi-religious institutions for its pilots.

In conclusion: I was very pleased to see the role which Jacobsen plays in your essay.[52] Some very early themes of yours are clearly revealed here. The effect of the name itself is now inseparably bound up with your own reflections, like a boy with burning cheeks who comes storming out of the woods while we are strolling along a cool avenue.

You ask about my English lessons. By the time I received the address of the teacher which Felizitas[53] sent to me, I had already begun my studies with someone else. I fear that my progress, which is not exactly barn-storming, far exceeds my ability to use what I have learned in actual speech. I, too, originally felt that Miss Razovsky's affidavit was, as you say, a 'substantial boon'. But unfortunately I have had to change my opinion. All the information I have received about the current practice of the American Consulate here (from whom I have still heard nothing) only confirms that the processing of standard applications takes a very long time. Now it transpires that my own application, without the slightest intervention on my part, has unfortunately become a 'standard' one, and that because of the arrival of the affidavit. Otherwise it would have been possible for me to apply for a visitor's visa, like that only recently approved for the writer Hermann Kesten,[54] for example. (He will be appearing in New York very soon, where he will get in touch with Max.)

Kesten is also acquainted with Soma Morgenstern. Unfortunately, as things have turned out, I have not actually seen the latter for many weeks. What you describe as his 'tendency towards mediocrity even towards himself' seems to have complicated his contact with me to such a degree that it would have required the greatest initiative on my part to maintain it. And I lack this initiative. If we should meet up again, however, I shall certainly remember your request.

But to return to the question of the visa: in addition to a letter of appointment, some proof of having held an official teaching position has also been made a condition for receiving a *non quota* visa (and that is the only kind that would allow me to come over soon). And as far as this regulation is concerned, they have recently been laying great stress upon precisely *that* section which explicitly requires proof of teaching activity *within the last two years* before the visa can be granted. That has significantly increased my hesitation about writing to Schapiro at the moment. I would rather not turn to him before I really know how to make the very best use of his interest in me. But that will only be the case once the date of my arrival in America has become more definite, either by some acceleration of the immigration process itself or by some easing of the regulations governing the distribution of *non quota* visas. As things stand right now, I am afraid that these regulations, even with an official letter of appointment, will work against me. But of course, I would be willing to write to Schapiro without further reservations, if you think that he could help me in finding an appointment.

Can I bother you with an administrative (or more than administrative) question? Why is the Institute journal proving so difficult over several of my reviews? I am principally thinking of the reviews of Sternberger and Hönigswald'[55] since I have not received the proofs for either of them.

The NRF publishing house has just brought out a new book on Baudelaire by Georges Blin[56] – a young man from the Ecole Normale. I found it neither helpful nor interesting, and I feel that this itself says something. I have no inclination to review the piece.

Do you know Faulkner? For I would very much like to hear what you think of his work. At the moment I am reading his *Lumière d'août* [Light in August].[57]

Your letter arrived here without much delay. I think you can write to me in German, and should therefore write more often, too. For my part, writing letters in German is now necessarily rather the exception. – Please include the Rickert review in your next letter. I am myself a pupil of Rickert (as you are a pupil of Cornelius) and I am particularly looking forward to seeing the text.

With heartfelt greetings

Yours as ever,
Walter Benjamin

1 *as you can easily see for yourself, this letter*: Benjamin's typewritten letter runs to fifteen pages and was transcribed with great care in someone else's

hand; it also contains Benjamin's detailed remarks on questions raised in Adorno's last letter and on the latter's essay on the George–Hofmannsthal correspondence.

2 *the telegram*: this has not survived.

3 *There is no better example . . . than when the popular lyric is set to the melody*: cf. GS 14, p. 37.

4 *my brother*: for Georg Benjamin (1895–1942), cf. the *Benjamin-Katalog*, pp. 22–4.

5 *your impression of my reaction to your essay*: see letter 117.

6 *the essay on jazz / certain reservations about the latter*: Benjamin had formulated these criticisms during a conversation with Adorno in Paris in October 1936; the effect of these reservations can partly be seen in the 'Supplementary Materials' which Adorno subsequently composed in Oxford.

7 *the comments you make . . . about 'musical progress'*: cf. GS 14, p. 50.

8 *the passage in the fifth chapter of your Wagner*: cf. letter 117 and the relevant note.

9 *'Der Blonde Eckbert'*: the story by Ludwig Tieck, which Benjamin held in particularly high regard.

10 *Maupassant's 'La nuit'*: cf. GS V [2], p. 707.

11 *Max has kindly left me entirely free to decide*: Benjamin is referring here to Horkheimer's letter of 22.12.1939, part of which reads: 'Vous vous imaginez bien comme, nous autres, nous tremblons que maintenant vous pourrez rétablir votre santé et poursuivre vos travaux. / Quant aux derniers, c'est l'idée d'une étude comparée des 'Confessions' et du 'Journal', qui nous a enthousiasmée. Consentirez-vous vraiment à vous dévouer à un tel article avant de retourner au Baudelaire? Si oui, c'est notre Revue qui aurait à s'en féliciter' (GS I [3], pp. 1127ff).

12 *my work on the 'Theses'*: cf. Benjamin, 'On the Concept of History', first published in the mimeograph volume *Walter Benjamin zum Gedächtnis* [In Memory of Walter Benjamin] in 1942; now in GS I [2], pp. 691–704.

13 *to begin a period of hopefully uninterrupted work*: this did not transpire; although Benjamin was able to escape the renewed threat of internment through the efforts of Henri Hoppenot (cf. *Benjamin-Katalog*, pp. 298–300), he was forced to flee Paris for Lourdes as the German troops approached.

14 *my judgement of your essay*: Benjamin is referring to Adorno's essay 'On the Fetish Character in Music and the Regression of Listening'.

15 *the spark which leaps between Mach and Jens Peter Jacobsen*: cf. GS 10 [1], pp. 198ff.

16 *Your remark about the actor*: cf. GS 10 [1], pp. 210–13.

17 *that wonderful quotation from 'Ariadne'*: cf. ibid., p. 213.

18 *George's 'Lied des Zwergen'*: cf. Stefan George, *Die Bücher der Hirten- und der Preisgedichte, der Sagen und Sänge und der hängenden Gärten*, in *Gesamt-Ausgabe der Werke*, vol. 3 (Berlin 1930), pp. 79–81.

19 *his poem 'Entführung'*: cf. Stefan George, *Das Jahr der Seele*, ibid., vol. 4 (Berlin 1928), p. 64.

20 *you cite Hofmannsthal's Lord Chandos letter*: cf. GS 10 [1], pp. 212ff. (n. 16).

21 *Lord Chandos letter / the following passage*: cf. Hugo von Hofmannsthal, *Gesammelte Werke*, vol. 2 (Berlin 1924), pp. 175–88; the passage in question is found on p. 187.

22 *the same motif recurs in 'The Tower'*: cf. Hugo von Hofmannsthal, *Der Turm. Ein Trauerspiel*, 2nd revised edition (Berlin 1927), pp. 60ff; for Benjamin's two reviews of the play, cf. GS III, pp. 29–33 and pp. 98–101.

23 *the second passage I spoke of*: cf. ibid., pp. 26–9.

24 *the man who lacks nothing but a tiny effort of will . . . to enjoy the highest experience imaginable*: Benjamin is here quoting directly from his 1926 review of 'The Tower' (cf. GS III, p. 32).

25 *theory of sacrifice*: cf. GS 10 [1], pp. 233ff.

26 *Carossa*: the poet and physician Hans Carossa (1878–1956) had shown some temporary sympathy for the cultural policies of the National Socialists. For the relevant passage in Adorno's essay, cf. GS 10 [1], p. 206.

27 *German writers towing the official political line*: in his original manuscript, Adorno began the next paragraph after the passage on Carossa as follows: 'The George School did not show itself quite so willing to follow the official line'; Adorno later altered this, presumably in response to Benjamin's request that *you should reconsider this passage*, to read: 'The George School, with rather less worldliness, revealed a greater resistance.' (GS 10 [1], p. 206.

28 *You are quite right to bring up Proust*: cf. GS 10 [1], p. 204.

29 *'that's not it at all'*: cf. ibid., p. 204.

30 *the famous passage in Sodome et Gomorrhe*: cf. Marcel Proust, *A la recherche du temps perdu*. Texte établi et présenté par Pierre Clarac et André Ferré, vol. 2 (Paris 1954), Bibliothèque de la Pléiade. 101, pp. 614–18.

31 *the moment of defiance as the poetical and political source of strength in George*: cf. GS 10 [1], pp. 216 and 236.

32 *the significance of translation for him*: cf. ibid., p. 236, n. 27.

33 *his monopolistic ambitions and his rejection of the market*: cf. ibid., pp. 220–2.

34 *comment on the 'Gentleman'*: cf. ibid., p. 207.

35 *'for now the hour is late'*: cf. ibid., p. 216.

36 *the rubric of 'bearing'*: cf. ibid., pp. 200–4.

37 *a happiness as yet undisciplined*: an allusion to a passage in the essay which was later deleted by Adorno: 'The social contract announces the termination of happiness. There are indeed others who exercise a critique of society. But they remain faithful to society's own image of happiness: that of a healthy, well-organized and rationally arranged life. Disciplined happiness presupposes class society, presupposes a world 'où l'action n'est pas la sœur du rêve' (*Theodor W. Adorno Archiv*, Ts. 23218).

38 *Salten's feuilleton literature*: writings by the Austrian story-teller, dramatist and essayist Felix Salten (1869–1947).

39 *the finely expressed observation*: cf. GS 10 [1], pp. 220ff, n. 21.

40 *'Even now the final train is leaving for the mountains'*: Benjamin may have derived this quotation, from George's dream narrative 'Zeit-Ende' (cf. Stefan George, *Tage und Taten*, op. cit., p. 30), from a reference in Adorno's manuscript; it is also possible that Benjamin is quoting from memory since George wrote simply 'mountain' in the original text. – For the passage in Adorno's essay which alludes to the railway image in George's narrative, cf. GS 10 [1], p. 207.

41 *Kubin's imaginary city of 'Pearl'*: cf. Alfred Kubin, *Die andere Zeit* (Munich 1909).

42 *Your allusion to Kraus*: the passage, which was later deleted by Adorno, runs as follows: 'Karl Kraus had attacked the inflated journalistic German of those who liked to describe a couple pretentiously as "offiziös" rather than "offiziell" engaged. As a neutral realm, George's Café has something of the same tone. In that verse from George's "Hanging Gardens": "within the splendid realm of other rulers", it is actually sublated into the sphere of lyric poetry' (*Theodor W. Adorno Archiv*, Ts. 23202).

43 *his critique of George's translation of the Shakespeare sonnets*: cf. Karl Kraus, 'Sakrileg an George oder Sühne an Shakespeare', in the journal *Die Fackel*, December 1932 (year 34, nr. 885–7), pp. 45–64.

44 *George's appreciative judgement of Hofmannsthal*: 'You can hardly compose a single strophe which fails to enrich us with a new quickening of sensation, and even a new kind of feeling' – *Briefwechsel zwischen George und Hofmannsthal* (Berlin, undated), p. 85; for Adorno's use of the quotation in his essay, cf. GS 10 [1], p. 195.

45 *Victor Hugo's famous judgement of Baudelaire*: Hugo's words – 'Vous créez un frisson nouveau' [You are creating a new kind of feeling] – are to be found in his letter to Baudelaire of 6 October 1869 and express his reaction to the two poems which Baudelaire had dedicated to him, 'Les Sept Vieillards' and 'Les Petites Vieilles'. – For Benjamin's source here, cf. GS V [2], p. 911.

46 *When George speaks of the granitic-Germanic element in Hofmannsthal*: cf. GS 10 [1], p. 214.

47 *'The noble is noble by virtue of the ignoble'*: the original remark, found in GS 10 [1], p. 201, reads: 'The noble itself is noble by virtue of the ignoble.'

48 *'L'ignorant est le pain que mange le savant'*: the source of this remark has not as yet been identified.

49 *The medallions you fashioned for Carossa and Borchardt*: cf. GS 10 [1], pp. 206 and 210ff. (n. 12).

50 *the inscription lucus a non lucendo*: cf. ibid., p. 231.

51 *analysis of Rimbaud's 'Voyelles'*: cf. ibid., pp. 196–8.

52 *the role which Jacobsen plays in your essay*: cf. ibid., pp. 198 and 212.

53 *my English lessons / the address of the teacher from Felizitas*: with a view to his planned trip to the United States, Benjamin had started to learn English at the end of January 1940; Gretel Adorno had passed on a recommendation (now lost) from her own English teacher in her (unpublished) letter to Benjamin of 20.1.1940: 'As to your English lessons I talked to my English teacher and got the enclosed answer; perhaps it is of some help for you.' Who actually gave Benjamin his English lessons remains unknown.

54 *the writer Hermann Kesten*: the writer Hermann Kesten, born in 1900, had emigrated to The Netherlands in 1933, where he headed the German language division of the publishers Allert de Lange; he was later able to escape from French internment and flee to New York in 1940.

55 *my reviews / that of Sternberger / that of Hönigswald*: Benjamin's reviews of Richard Hönigswald's *Philosophie und Sprache* (Basel 1937) and Sternberger's *Panorama oder Ansichten vom 19. Jahrhundert* did not actually appear in the *Zeitschrift für Sozialforschung* and remained unpublished during his lifetime; for these reviews, cf. GS III, pp. 564–9 and pp. 572–9.

56 *a book on Baudelaire by Georges Blin*: cf. Georges Blin, *Baudelaire*. Préface de Jacques Crépet (Paris 1939).

57 *Lumière d'août*: cf. the French translation of William Faulkner's *Light in August*: *Lumière d'août*. Traduction et introduction de Maurice E. Coindreau (Paris 1935).

119 ADORNO TO BENJAMIN
NEW YORK, 16.7.1940

T. W. Adorno   16 July 1940.
429 West 117th Street
New York City
Air-Mail

My dear Walter:

Today is your birthday[1] and I want to convey to you our most cordial congratulations. I do not need to express my good wishes for you and ourselves as well. You may be assured that whatever can be done as far as we are concerned to realize these wishes, certainly will be done.

Max has left for a journey to gather information about academic conditions in the west. As he will be away from New York for several months he has asked me to look after your problems. We do everything possible to hurry your immigration into this country. You will possibly get a notice directly from the consulate in Marseille. I am not certain which kind of visa the American Consulate may offer you since there is a choice between the following three possibilities: a quota visa because you registered for it, a non-quota visa because you have been a member of our Institute for many years, or even a visitors visa. We advise you to accept whichever visa will be offered you first.

However, we do not confine ourselves to the attempt to bring you into the USA but are also trying other ways. One of them is the attempt to 'lend' you as a guest lecturer to Havana University. This plan, however, is too far from materializing as to be reckoned with as an immediate chance. The San Domingo plan[2] does not appear to be workable at present. Of course, it will always be good to remain in closest touch with Madame Favez who is most cooperative and has an excellent judgement about the situation.

I am going to stay here for the summer, mainly in order to be able to attend to your interests. Gretel, is staying too, she is very worried and in a very bad state of health but sends you her love and all her best wishes for your birthday. Max has asked me before leaving once again to assure you of his friendship and unchanging solidarity.

We are in constant touch with him with regard to your problems. Fritz[3] is staying here and sends you his kindest regards.

I am happy about every word I get from you but, of course, I understand very well that you are not in the mood for long letters.

PS It would be very important for us to have your *curriculum vitae*[4] with a list of your publications. Will you, therefore, please let us have both as quickly as possible.

[Yours ever
Teddie]

[The above letter was written by Adorno in English and is here reproduced unchanged.]

1 *Today is your birthday*: the date, which is wrongly given in the copy of the letter – July 16, 1940 – was probably corrected in the original letter itself

since Benjamin wrote in his reply: 'I was delighted to receive your letter of 15 July for a number of reasons.'

2 *The San Domingo plan*: at the beginning of July, the members of the Institute of Social Research, and especially Max Horkheimer and Friedrich Pollock, had arranged an immigration visa to San Domingo for Benjamin in order to facilitate his escape from Europe. – The precise reasons why the plan no longer seemed viable are unknown.

3 *Fritz*: i.e. Friedrich Pollock.

4 *your curriculum vitae*: cf. GS VI, pp. 225–8.

120   BENJAMIN TO ADORNO
        LOURDES, 2.8.1940

My dear Teddie,
  I was delighted to receive your letter of 15 July for a number of reasons – for one, because you kindly remembered my birthday; and for another, because of the great understanding which spoke from your words. No, it really is not that easy for me to write letters. I spoke to Felizitas about the enormous uncertainty in which I find myself concerning my writings (although I fear rather less for the notes and papers connected with the Arcades project[1] than I do for the other materials). But as you know, things currently look no better for me personally than they do for my works. The circumstances that suddenly befell me in September[2] could easily be repeated at any time, but now with a wholly different prospect. In the last few months, I have seen a good number of people who have not so much simply drifted out of their steady bourgeois existence as *plunged headlong* from it almost overnight; thus every reassurance provides an inner succour that is less problematic than the external support. And in this sense I was profoundly grateful to receive the document[3] addressed 'à ceux qu'il appartient'. I can easily imagine that the letterhead,[4] which was a delightful surprise, could significantly reinforce the possible effect of the document.
  The complete uncertainty about what the next day, even the next hour, may bring has dominated my life for weeks now. I am condemned to read every newspaper (they now come out on a single sheet here) as if it were a summons served on me in particular, to hear the voice of fateful tidings in every radio broadcast. My attempt to reach Marseilles, in order to put my case at the Consulate there, was a wasted effort. For some time now it has been impossible for foreign nationals to obtain a permit for a change of residence. Thus I

remain dependent on what all of you are doing for me from abroad. In particular, the prospect of hearing something from the Consulate in Marseilles renewed my hopes somewhat. A letter from the Consulate there would probably get me permission to go down to Marseilles. (I am actually still unable to decide whether I should make contact with any Consulates in the occupied territories. A letter which I sent to Bordeaux before the German occupation, received a fairly cordial but noncommittal answer: the required documents were still in Paris.)

I have heard something about your negotiations with Havana and your efforts concerning San Domingo. I am quite sure you are doing everything humanly possible, and indeed 'more than humanly possible' as Felizitas puts it, to help me. My great fear is that we have much less time at our disposal than we imagined. And although I would not have contemplated the possibility a fortnight ago, new information received has moved me to ask Mme Favez, with the intervention of Carl Burckhardt, if she could possibly obtain permission for me to visit Switzerland on a temporary basis. I realize there is much to be said against trying this escape route, but there is one very powerful argument in its favour: and that is time. If only this way out were possible! – I have written a letter to Burckhardt[5] for help.

You will be getting my *curriculum vitae* via Geneva – which is also how I shall probably be sending these lines. I have incorporated the bibliography of my writings into the biographical information because I don't have the resources here to organize the material more precisely. (All in all it comes to approximately 450 items.) If a bibliography in the narrower sense is still required, the Institute's official prospectus[6] contains one you could use. I cannot provide you with a better one at present.

It is a great comfort for me to know that you remain 'reachable' in New York, and constantly watchful, in the deepest sense, for me. Mr Merril Moore[7] lives in Boston at 384 Commonwealth Avenue. Mrs W. Bryher,[8] the publisher of *Life and Letters Today* has often mentioned me to him. He probably has a good idea of my situation and the will to do something to help. I think it might be worthwhile for you to get in touch with him.

For the rest, you can be sure that I have learned to value the efforts which Mrs Favez is making on my behalf and her general reliability very much indeed.

I am very sorry to hear that Felizitas' condition remains so unstable and that she will be unable to profit from a relaxing holiday break this time. Please give her my heartfelt regards.

Could you also pass on my sincere thanks and kindest regards to Herr Pollock.

Lots of love from your

Walter Benjamin

2 August 1940
Lourdes
8 rue Notre Dame

PS Please forgive the painfully complete signature: it is officially required.

1 *the notes and papers connected with the Arcades project*: Benjamin had handed these over to Georges Bataille, who concealed them in the *Bibliothèque Nationale*; cf. GS I [2], p. 759.

2 *The circumstances that suddenly befell me in September*: Benjamin is referring here to his internment, first outside Paris and subsequently at Nevers; cf. *Benjamin-Katalog*, pp. 291–7.

3 *the document*: i.e. officially confirming Benjamin's association with the Institute.

4 *the letterhead*: the document in question appeared on the official headed paper of *The Institute of Social Research*, on which the name Walter Benjamin was also printed. In response to Hannah Arendt's attacks on Adorno and the Institute in her essay 'Walter Benjamin' (cf. *Merkur* 238–40), Friedrich Pollock later wrote to Hans Paeschke, the editor of *Merkur*, as follows: 'In view of the rather scholastic philological precision which informs the polemic against Adorno, I can certainly inform you that documentary confirmation of Benjamin's position in the Institute is available. I possess some official headed letter-paper from the Institute in New York which lists, under the head of "Research Staff", the two directors first, and then the names of the "members" of the Institute in alphabetical order. The list commences with the names: 'Theodor W. Adorno, Walter Benjamin . . .' (*Merkur* 22, issue 6 (June 1968), p. 576).

5 *a letter to Burckhardt*: for Benjamin's letter of 25 July 1940, cf. *Benjamin-Katalog*, p. 305.

6 *bibliography / the Institute's official prospectus*: cf. *International Institute of Social Research. A Report on its History, Aims and Activities 1933–1938* (New York: Columbia University Press 1938), p. 27.

7 *Mr Merril Moore*: nothing further known has come down to us.

8 *Mrs Bryher*: the writer and patron of the arts Winifred Ellermann Bryher (died 1983) – she had legalized the pseudonym of 'Bryher' – had married the American poet Robert McAlmon in 1921; she had probably made Benjamin's acquaintance through Adrienne Monnier; Benjamin mentioned her in a letter to Horkheimer in December 1939, saying that she 'me suit dans mes travaux depuis assez longtemps, et s'était, elle aussi, beaucoup inquiétée de mon

internement' [she has been following my works closely for a long time, and she too had become extremely concerned about my internment] (*Briefe*, p. 838).

121 BENJAMIN TO HENNY GURLAND [AND ADORNO?]
[PORT BOU, 25.9.1940]

Dans une situation sans issue, je n'ai d'autre choix que d'en finir. C'est dans un petit village dans les Pyrénées où personne ne me connait ma vie va s'achever.

Je vous prie de transmettre mes pensées à mon ami Adorno et de lui expliquer la situation où je me suis vu placé. Il ne me reste assez de temps pour écrire toutes ces lettres que j'eusse voulu écrire.

[In a situation with no escape,[1] I have no other choice but to finish it all. It is in a tiny village in the Pyrenees, where no one knows me, that my life must come to its end.

I would ask you to pass on my thoughts to my friend Adorno and to explain to him the situation in which I have now found myself. I no longer have enough time to write all those letters I would dearly have written.]

1 *In a situation with no escape*: just before 15 August 1940, Benjamin had arrived in Marseilles where the affidavit which had been arranged by Max Horkheimer was waiting for him. On 23 September, Benjamin had left Marseilles together with Henny Gurland and her son in the direction of the Spanish border. He was forced to cross the border illegally because he lacked the required French exit visa. (For an account of the flight across the Pyrenees to Port Bou, cf. *Benjamin-Katalog*, p. 311.) – 'The result: the threatened deportation of the refugees back to France, which would have been equivalent to handing them over to the Germans' (ibid.) is what Benjamin meant by the 'situation without escape'. Having decided to take his own life, Benjamin wrote these lines to Adorno and Henny Gurland. The text survives only in Henny Gurland's hand amongst Adorno's literary remains (cf. GS V [2], pp. 1201ff).

Editor's Afterword

~∞~

Henri Lonitz

A large number of the surviving letters of Walter Benjamin and Theodor Wiesengrund-Adorno, a correspondence presented here in its entirety for the first time, are not exactly unknown as far as their content is concerned: in the selection of Benjamin's correspondence which he co-edited with Gershom Scholem in 1966, Adorno included eleven letters from Benjamin to himself and two of his own letters to Benjamin; in 1970 Rolf Tiedemann published excerpts from a series of Adorno's letters to Benjamin dating from the 1930s on issues related to Benjamin's major writings of the period. A revised and expanded edition of that volume – Theodor W. Adorno, *Über Walter Benjamin. Aufsätze, Artikel, Briefe* (edited and annotated by Rolf Tiedemann, Frankfurt a.M. 1990) – was able to include a few more letters. The editors of Walter Benjamin's *Gesammelte Schriften* – Rolf Tiedemann and Hermann Schweppenhäuser – finally published excerpts from both Adorno's and Benjamin's letters in the apparatus to their edition. This served to document not only the genesis and development of Benjamin's work, but also to reveal the intensity of the discussions which transpired between the correspondents.

'All reification is a forgetting: objects become purely thing-like the moment they are retained for us without the continued presence of their other aspects: when something of them has been forgotten.' If we consider this observation from Adorno's letter to Benjamin of 29 February 1940, we could hardly find a better way of revealing the decisive difference between the discussions which developed in the critical theory of the 1930s and the way in which the results of these discussions are summarized and presented in the secondary literature

343

of today. The mutual critique which Adorno and Benjamin exercised upon each other's works during their years of emigration is worlds away from the congealed form in which these crucial works have been first dissected and then clumsily recombined, received, interpreted and 'transmitted' by those who have come afterwards. A considerable portion of the correspondence is directly concerned with Benjamin's 'Arcades Project', destined to remain a fragment, which had attempted to decipher the nineteenth century in terms of a philosophy of history, and with Benjamin's 'part-payment' in advance, as it were, the essay on Baudelaire (and it is from a letter discussing this work that the above quotation from Adorno is taken). But the letters in general, and especially those exchanged between Benjamin and Adorno during the years of emigration after 1934, also turn upon the appropriate theoretical presentation of a fundamental experience of bourgeois culture that was irrevocably beginning to disappear with the phenomenon of fascism – a loss and a forgetting that was not at all like the liberating emancipation of a traveller who sees the goal of his journey immediately before his very eyes.

But if these letters are directly concerned with sustaining the spiritual resources that are indispensable to these emigrants, they are equally directly concerned with all of the empirical ballast involved as well, with the material conditions of life, with the actual opportunities for publishing their own work in a cultural environment which was largely unfavourable to their radical critique of the increasingly fragile social preconditions of bourgeois intellectual life. The correspondence reveals the enormous significance of the practical and cultural solidarity which Benjamin and Adorno shared with one another during the period of their intellectual isolation – the one an alien body amongst the French literary élite who, with one or two admirable exceptions, in spite of all the diplomatic overtures which Benjamin was sometimes capable of making, were not remotely interested in furthering the cause of his work. The other, forced at Merton College in Oxford, 'to lead the life of a mediaeval student in cap and gown', as Adorno puts it in one of his letters to Benjamin, maintaining a vital outlook which a conventional middle-of-the-road wisdom would easily interpret as one of ruthless critique. This ruthlessness with regard to the essential questions – and the authors regarded every one of their individual works as a contribution to a shared project of theoretical importance – expressed precisely that solidarity of criticism which is equally and simultaneously a form of intellectual self-criticism. That republic of the learned, which had lost its place in the established academic world, lived on in those who were forced to relinquish all academic security and to renounce all conventions external to the fundamental issues. Adorno described the way in which this primacy of the substantive issues left its empirical mark upon the individual subject in 1965: 'The individual ruthlesslessly asserted the primacy of spirit both in relation to himself and in his relation to others, and instead of immediacy itself, this primacy became the immediate issue.' Even if this remark was specifically fashioned with regard to Benjamin, it holds equally well of its author. And it is just this 'ruthlessness' which allowed Benjamin, whom Adorno once described as a 'great and passionate letter writer', and Adorno himself, to compose letters which must rank amongst the most significant ones which have come down to us from this century of barbarism.

Benjamin's earliest surviving letter to Adorno of 2 July 1928, with which this correspondence begins, is a reply to a lost letter from Adorno. It already reveals the degree to which the correspondence itself represents a continuation of the discussions they had been having together since 1923, first in Frankfurt and subsequently in Berlin. It is unquestionably a great loss, and this not merely from the perspective of the correspondence, that all of Adorno's letters to Benjamin prior to the beginning of 1930 are now lost: they were left behind in Benjamin's last Berlin apartment in the Regentenstrasse when he was forced to leave Germany in March 1933. The original Adorno letters from 1934–40 belong predominantly to the portion of Benjamin's literary remains formerly held in East Berlin, as part of the *Literaturarchive der Akademie der Künste* of the former German Democratic Republic. Some of the letters form part of the Benjamin papers belonging to the Bibliothèque Nationale in Paris. These are letters which Benjamin had kept separate from the rest of the correspondence on account of their extensive theoretical character; before his flight from Paris, Benjamin gave these and various other papers to Georges Bataille, who hid them in the national library where he worked. These letters were only discovered in 1981. The original Benjamin letters, which Adorno preserved, were found amongst his literary remains and now belong to the *Theodor W. Adorno Archive* in Frankfurt am Main. In the cases where one of Benjamin's original letters has been lost or was perhaps deliberately destroyed by the recipient for reasons of security (see letter 20), it was occasionally possible, with typewritten letters, to consult surviving carbon copies.

The surviving letters and postcards of this correspondence have been printed in their entirety, without deletions or abbreviations, in chronological sequence. Any additions made by Gretel Adorno to Adorno's cards and letters to Benjamin have been included and printed in smaller type. In one particular case, a letter to Adorno from a third party – namely, the American art historian Meyer Schapiro – has been incorporated into the correspondence because it responds directly to certain questions Benjamin had addressed to Adorno, and because Adorno himself had sent it on to Benjamin with some relevant explanatory remarks of his own.

The annotations to the letters are intended to elucidate the personal names or particular circumstances which are either directly mentioned or alluded to in the letters. Copious reference has also been made to individuals, developments and events which could be usefully illuminated by citation of other relevant correspondence as yet unpublished: that of Adorno with Siegfried Kracauer and Max Horkheimer, as well as that of Benjamin with Gretel Adorno and with Max Horkheimer. When the theoretical and literary works of the two correspondents are mentioned in detail in the letters, which sometimes assume the character of textual commentaries, then the annotations generally provide the reader not only with the relevant bibliographical information about the works in question, but also with appropriate references to the standard German editions of the collected writings of both authors.

Textual Notes and
Source References

~∞~

The following symbols have been adopted for the textual notes and source references:

O	Original
Ms	Manuscript
Ts	Typescript
Tsc	Carbon Copy
PS	Postscript
Sc	Setting Copy
Fp	First published
Pp	Part published

1 BENJAMIN TO WIESENGRUND-ADORNO: BERLIN, 2.7.1928
SOURCE: O: Ms, 1 p.; Theodor W. Adorno Archiv, Frankfurt a.M.

2 BENJAMIN TO WIESENGRUND-ADORNO: BERLIN, 1.9.1928
SOURCE: O: Ms, 1 p.; Theodor W. Adorno Archiv, Frankfurt a.M.

3 BENJAMIN TO WIESENGRUND-ADORNO: BERLIN, 29.3.1930
SOURCE: O: Ms, 1 p.; Theodor W. Adorno Archiv, Frankfurt a.M.

4 BENJAMIN TO WIESENGRUND-ADORNO: BERLIN, 10.11.1930
SOURCE: O: Ms, 1 p.; Theodor W. Adorno Archiv, Frankfurt a.M.

5 BENJAMIN TO WIESENGRUND-ADORNO: BERLIN, 17.7.1931
SOURCE: O: Ms, 3 pp.; Theodor W. Adorno Archiv, Frankfurt a.M.

6 BENJAMIN TO WIESENGRUND-ADORNO: [BERLIN,] 25.7.1931
SOURCE: O: Ms, 1 p.; Theodor W. Adorno Archiv, Frankfurt a.M.

7 BENJAMIN TO WIESENGRUND-ADORNO: BERLIN, 31.3.1932
SOURCE: O: Ms, 2 pp.; Theodor W. Adorno Archiv, Frankfurt a.M.

8 BENJAMIN TO WIESENGRUND-ADORNO: POVEROMO, 3.9.1932
SOURCE: O: Ms, 2 pp.; Theodor W. Adorno Archiv, Frankfurt a.M. – Fp: *Briefe*, 557–9.

9 BENJAMIN TO WIESENGRUND-ADORNO: [ADDRESS OF SENDER NOT INDICATED,] 10.11.1932
SOURCE: O: Ms, 1 p.; Theodor W. Adorno Archiv, Frankfurt a.M.

10 BENJAMIN TO WIESENGRUND-ADORNO: BERLIN, 1.12.1932
SOURCE: O: Ms, 1 p.; Theodor W. Adorno Archiv, Frankfurt a.M. Pp: *Benjamin-Katalog*, 189.

11 BENJAMIN TO WIESENGRUND-ADORNO: BERLIN, 14.1.1933
SOURCE: O: Ts with handwritten corrections, 1 p.; Theodor W. Adorno Archiv, Frankfurt a.M.

12 BENJAMIN TO WIESENGRUND-ADORNO: PARIS, 29.1.1934
SOURCE: O: Ms, 2 pp.; Theodor W. Adorno Archiv, Frankfurt a.M. – Fp: Adorno, *Der Schatz des Indianer-Joe*. Singspiel nach Mark Twain, edited with an afterword by Rolf Tiedemann, Frankfurt a.M. 1979, 122f.

13 WIESENGRUND-ADORNO TO BENJAMIN: BERLIN, 4.3.1934
SOURCE: O: Ts with handwritten corrections, 2 pp.; Literaturarchive der Akademie der Künste, Berlin. – Sc: copy. – T. Adorno, *Der Schatz des Indianer-Joe*, 123f.

14 BENJAMIN TO WIESENGRUND-ADORNO: PARIS, 9.3.1934
SOURCE: O: Ms, 2 pp.; Theodor W. Adorno Archiv, Frankfurt a.M. – Pp: Adorno, *Der Schatz des Indianer-Joe*, 124f; GS V [2], 1100.

15 WIESENGRUND-ADORNO TO BENJAMIN: BERLIN, 13.3.1934
SOURCE: O: Ts with handwritten corrections, 2 pp.; Literaturarchive der Akademie der Künste, Berlin. Sc: copy. – Pp: GS V [2], 1101f.

16 BENJAMIN TO WIESENGRUND-ADORNO: PARIS, 18.3.1934
SOURCE: O: Ms, 4 pp.; Theodor W. Adorno Archiv, Frankfurt a.M. – Pp: GS V [2], 1102f.

17 WIESENGRUND-ADORNO TO BENJAMIN: BERLIN, 5.4.1934
SOURCE: O: Ts with handwritten corrections and PS, 2 pp.; Literaturarchive der Akademie der Künste, Berlin. – Sc: copy.

18 BENJAMIN TO WIESENGRUND-ADORNO: PARIS, 9.4.1934
SOURCE: O: Ms, 3 pp.; Theodor W. Adorno Archiv, Frankfurt a.M. – Pp: GS V [2], 1103f.

19 WIESENGRUND-ADORNO TO BENJAMIN: FRANKFURT A.M.,
13.4.1934
SOURCE: O: Ms, 2 pp.; Literaturarchive der Akademie der Künste, Berlin. Sc: copy.

20 WIESENGRUND-ADORNO TO BENJAMIN:
BROOKLYN (WEST DRAYTON), 21.4.1934
SOURCE: O: Ts with printed letter-head and handwritten corrections, 3 pp.; Literaturarchive der Akademie der Künste, Berlin. – Sc: copy.

21 BENJAMIN TO WIESENGRUND-ADORNO: PARIS, 28.4.1934
SOURCE: O: Tsc, 2 pp.; Literaturarchive der Akademie der Künste, Berlin. – Sc: copy.

22 BENJAMIN TO WIESENGRUND-ADORNO: PARIS, 24.5.1934
SOURCE: O: Ms, 2 pp.; Theodor W. Adorno Archiv, Frankfurt a.M.

23 WIESENGRUND-ADORNO TO BENJAMIN: OXFORD, 6.11.1934
SOURCE: O: Ts with handwritten corrections, 2 pp.; Literaturarchive der Akademie der Künste, Berlin. Sc: copy. – Pp: GS V [2], 1105–7.

24 BENJAMIN TO WIESENGRUND-ADORNO: SAN REMO, 30.11.1934
SOURCE: O: Ms of final page (the rest lost); Theodor W. Adorno Archiv, Frankfurt a.M.

25 WIESENGRUND-ADORNO TO BENJAMIN: OXFORD, 5.12.1934
SOURCE: O: Ts with printed letter-head and handwritten corrections, 4 pp.;
Literaturarchive der Akademie der Künste, Berlin. – Sc: copy. Pp: GS V [2],
1107–9.

26 WIESENGRUND-ADORNO TO BENJAMIN: BERLIN, 16.12.1934
SOURCE: O: Ms, postcard with additions by Gretel Karplus and Egon Wissing;
Literaturarchive der Akademie der Künste, Berlin. – Sc: copy. Fp: Adorno,
Über Walter Benjamin, 2nd ed., 107.

27 WIESENGRUND-ADORNO TO BENJAMIN: BERLIN, 17.12.1934
SOURCE: O: Ts with handwritten corrections, 2 pp.; Theodor W. Adorno
Archiv, Frankfurt a.M. – Pp: Adorno, *Über Walter Benjamin*, 1st ed., 103–
10; 2nd ed., 108–14.

Textual Details: p. 67: *This relationship ... prolegomenon of scripture*:
marked twice with a question mark in Benjamin's hand in the right hand
margin of the letter. – p. 69: **and this ... other contexts as well*: a handwritten addition along the left hand side of the second page.

28 BENJAMIN TO WIESENGRUND-ADORNO: SAN REMO, 7.1.1935
SOURCE: O: Ms, 3 pp.; Theodor W. Adorno Archiv, Frankfurt a.M. Fp:
Briefe, 638–41.

29 BENJAMIN TO WIESENGRUND-ADORNO:
MONACO-CONDAMINE [EARLY APRIL 1935]
SOURCE: O: Ms, 3 pp.; Theodor W. Adorno Archiv, Frankfurt a.M. – Pp:
GS II [3], 1320f.

30 BENJAMIN TO WIESENGRUND-ADORNO: PARIS, 1.5.1935
SOURCE: O: Ms, 2 pp.; Theodor W. Adorno Archiv, Frankfurt a.M. – Pp:
GS V [2], 1111f.

31 WIESENGRUND-ADORNO TO BENJAMIN: OXFORD, 20.5.1935
SOURCE: O: Ts with handwritten corrections, 4 pp.; Bibliothèque Nationale,
Paris. – Sc: copy. – Pp: GS VII [2], 854–7.

32 BENJAMIN TO WIESENGRUND-ADORNO: PARIS, 31.5.1935
SOURCE: O: Ms, 4 pp.; Theodor W. Adorno Archiv, Frankfurt a.M. – Pp:
Briefe, 662–6.

33 WIESENGRUND-ADORNO TO BENJAMIN: OXFORD, 5.6.1935
SOURCE: O: Ms with printed letter-head, 4 pp.; Bibliothèque Nationale, Paris. – Sc: copy. – Fp: Adorno, *Über Walter Benjamin*, 2nd ed., 120–3.

34 WIESENGRUND-ADORNO TO BENJAMIN: OXFORD, 8.6.1935
SOURCE: O: Ms with printed letter-head, 4 pp.; Literaturarchive der Akademie der Künste, Berlin. – Sc: copy. – Pp: GS II [3], 1322; GS V [2], 119f.

Textual Details: p. 96: *the new one you are currently preparing*: marked by Benjamin with a + in the left margin; p. 96: *Please be sure ... telephone number*: marked by Benjamin with an X in the left hand margin; p. 96: *Perhaps it would be advisable ... exposé I have already seen* : marked by Benjamin with an X in the left hand margin.

35 BENJAMIN TO WIESENGRUND-ADORNO: PARIS, 10.6.1935
SOURCE: O: Ms, 4 pp.; Theodor W. Adorno Archiv, Frankfurt a.M. – Pp: GS V [2], 1120–2.

36 BENJAMIN TO WIESENGRUND-ADORNO: PARIS, 19.6.1935
SOURCE: O: Ms, 2 pp.; Theodor W. Adorno Archiv, Frankfurt a.M. – Pp: GS V [2], 1122f.

37 BENJAMIN TO WIESENGRUND-ADORNO: PARIS, 5.7.1935
SOURCE: O: Ms, 1 p.; Theodor W. Adorno Archiv, Frankfurt a.M.
Textual Details: Adorno wrote 'answered' on the right hand bottom of the page.

38 WIESENGRUND-ADORNO TO BENJAMIN: [FRANKFURT A.M., 12.7.1935]
SOURCE: O: Ms on the reverse side of a printed thank you card with the text: 'We would like to communicate our sincere thanks for the many heartfelt demonstrations of sympathy which we have received during the illness and upon the passing of our beloved AGATHE CALVELLI ADORNO. Frankfurt a.M., 12 July 1935. The bereaved.' – Literaturarchive der Akademie der Künste, Berlin. – Sc: copy.

39 WIESENGRUND-ADORNO AND GRETEL KARPLUS TO
BENJAMIN: HORNBERG, 2–4 AND 5.8.1935
SOURCE: O: Ts/Ms with handwritten addition by Gretel Karplus and added emphases and marginalia by Benjamin, 5 pp.; Bibliothèque Nationale, Paris. Sc: copy. – Pp: *Briefe*, 671–83.

Textual Details: p. 106: *Hic et nunc . . . Tragic Drama*: double marked by Benjamin in the left hand margin; p. 107: *the very perfection of the commodity character . . . phantasmagoria*: double marked by Benjamin in the left hand margin; p. 108: *It seems to me . . . examples of 'regression' in themselves*: marginalium by Benjamin: 'And the significance of this in relation to exchange-value?'; p. 108: *A restoration of theology . . . motifs*: double marked by Benjamin in the left hand margin; p. 109: *The division into chapters . . . and so forth?*: double marked by Benjamin in the left hand margin; p. 109: *every epoch dreams . . . catastrophes*: double marked by Benjamin in the left hand margin; p. 109: *intérieur section of the book on Kierkegaard*: underlined by Benjamin; pp. 109–10: *intérieur section . . . social products*: marked by Benjamin with a ! and a circled x in the left hand margin; p. 110: *as models, dialectical images are not social products*: underlined by Benjamin; p. 110: *My objection . . . the means of production*: marginalium by Benjamin: 'The positive perspective upon the machine through the medium of Fourier: social organization is its equivalent'; p. 110: *concept of second nature*: underlined by Benjamin and marked by a ? and a circled x in the left hand margin; p. 110: *for the share . . . productive force* : marked by Benjamin in the left hand margin and supplied with a question mark and a circled x; pp. 110–11: *Page 12 was a mene tekel . . . sober reflection*: marginalium by Benjamin: 'Culture as the apotheosis of history; the "meaning" of history as the core of this apotheosis'; p. 111: *the conception of the commodity fetish . . . man who discovered it*: marginalium by Benjamin: 'fetish character, "alienation", writings on Marx and Hegel'; p. 111: *'changeant'*: double marked by Benjamin below and in the left hand margin; pp. 111–12: *I believe that the commodity category . . . remnants and debris*: marginalium by Benjamin: 'On the concept of commodity in monopoly capitalism: how is the division of labour, developed to an extreme, projected into the demands of consumption?'; p. 112: *The passage about the 'office' . . . other kinds of material)*: marginalium by Benjamin: 'The bureau: an office which has lost its self-contained enclosed character'; p. 112: *Mallarmé's interiors*: underlined by Benjamin and marked with a circled x in the left hand margin; p. 112: *In the place of interiority . . . period around 1910*: marginalium by Benjamin: 'This sexuality appears as a schema of *youth* and belongs to interiority'; p. 112: *let me also draw your attention . . . published works*: double marked by Benjamin in the left hand margin; p. 113: *I would also like to draw your attention . . . cornerstone*: double marked by Benjamin in the left hand margin; p. 113: *the 'Interior' chapter of my Kierkegaard book*: underlined by Benjamin and marked with a circled x in the margin; p. 114: *The fine dialectical conception . . . interpreted beforehand*: double marked by Benjamin in the left hand margin; pp. 114–15: *5 August 1935 . . . meanings into the oldest*: handwritten PS; p. 114: *to reconcile*: underlined by Benjamin; p. 115: *still present* [unvergangene]: not an absolutely reliable reading; in his excerpt of this passage for the Arcades,

Benjamin read 'primordially past' [urvergangene] here (cf. GS V [1], 582); p. 115: *Dialectical images . . . the oldest*: double marked by Benjamin in the left hand margin.

40 BENJAMIN TO GRETEL KARPLUS AND WIESENGRUND-
ADORNO: [PARIS, 16.8.1935]
SOURCE: O: Ms, of which only the first page has survived amongst Adorno's literary remains; the lost part of the original letter is based upon a transcript by Gretel Adorno. Theodor W. Adorno Archiv, Frankfurt a.M. – Fp: *Briefe*, 685–8.

Textual Details: pp. 118–19: *And the somewhat dilatory character . . . the act of waking*: only survives in Gretel Adorno's transcript.

41 BENJAMIN TO WIESENGRUND-ADORNO: PARIS, 27.12.1935
SOURCE: O: Ms, 2 pp.; Theodor W. Adorno Archiv, Frankfurt a.M.

42 WIESENGRUND-ADORNO TO BENJAMIN: [FRANKFURT A.M.,]
29.12.1935
SOURCE: O: Ts with handwritten corrections, 1 p.; Literaturarchive der Akademie der Künste, Berlin. – Sc: copy.

43 BENJAMIN TO WIESENGRUND-ADORNO: [PARIS,] 3.1.1936
SOURCE: O: Ms, 2 pp.; Theodor W. Adorno Archiv, Frankfurt a.M.

44 WIESENGRUND-ADORNO TO BENJAMIN: LONDON, 29.1.1936
SOURCE: O: Ms, postcard; Literaturarchive der Akademie der Künste, Berlin. Sc: copy.

45 BENJAMIN TO WIESENGRUND-ADORNO: PARIS, 7.2.1936
SOURCE: O: Ms, 2 pp.; Theodor W. Adorno Archiv, Frankfurt a.M. – Pp: GS V [2], 1152f.

46 BENJAMIN TO WIESENGRUND-ADORNO: PARIS, 27.2.1936
SOURCE: O: Ts, 2 pp.; Theodor W. Adorno Archiv, Frankfurt a.M. – Fp: *Briefe*, 708f.

47 WIESENGRUND-ADORNO TO BENJAMIN: LONDON, 18.3.1936
SOURCE: O: Ts with handwritten corrections and PS; also later corrections, reformulations and square brackets supplied by Adorno in pencil when he

examined the text for publication amongst his selected letters; 6 pp.; Theodor W. Adorno Archiv, Frankfurt a.M. – Fp: Adorno, *Über Walter Benjamin*, 1st ed., 126–34; 2nd ed., 143–50.

Textual Details: p. 128: *counter-revolutionary*: in a later variant Adorno writes here 'reactionary'; p. 129: *At this point . . . consigned to hell*: placed in square brackets by Adorno in pencil; p. 130: *Les extrèmes me touchent*: later footnoted by Adorno as 'Quotation from André Gide'; pp. 132–3: *I am leaving for Germany . . . State and Revolution*: placed in square brackets by Adorno in pencil; p. 133: *I should also like . . . your book on the Baroque*: the handwritten PS placed in square brackets by Adorno in pencil.

48 BENJAMIN TO WIESENGRUND-ADORNO: [PARIS, SOME TIME LATER THAN 18.3.1936]
SOURCE: O: Ms, 2 pp.; Theodor W. Adorno Archiv, Frankfurt a.M.

49 WIESENGRUND-ADORNO TO BENJAMIN: OXFORD, 28.5.1936
SOURCE: O: Ts with handwritten corrections and PS; also marginalia by Benjamin in the left hand margin; 2 pp.; Literaturarchive der Akademie der Künste, Berlin. – Sc: copy.

Textual Details: p. 135: *I would be extremely interested . . . my essay on jazz*: marginalium by Benjamin: 'Combine an answer to the letter on film with my response to the piece on jazz. Take another look at the letter on film (amongst my notes?)'; p. 135: *acquainted with your work*: marginalium by Benjamin: 'point out the gaps in my own: inadequate critique of the capitalist basis of film production'; p. 135: *offprint . . . typescript*: marginalium by Benjamin: 'the text on jazz'; p. 135: *they will also touch upon your own interests*: marginalium by Benjamin: 'the analyses of Berg'; p. 135: *an essay on Mahler*: marginalium by Benjamin: 'Essay on Mahler'; p. 136: *precise formulation . . . domain of logic*: marginalium by Benjamin: 'social critique of logic'; p. 136: *introduction to your book on Baroque drama*: marginalium by Benjamin: 'relation to the book on drama'; p. 136: *essay on Baudelaire*: marginalium by Benjamin: 'Baudelaire: a collaborative essay'; p. 136: *I would also be quite prepared . . . in principle*: marginalium by Benjamin: 'Social theory of neo-romanticism: Fourier? Prou[d]hon? Hello? Flaubert?'; p. 136: *the idea of translation*: marginalium by Benjamin: 'idea of translation'; p. 136: *essays on materialism*: marginalium by Benjamin: 'Horkheimer's essays'; p. 136: *When I shall make it to Paris*: marginalium by Benjamin: 'best to come at the end of July. But the piece on Baudelaire longer term (the Fuchs literary report)'; p. 136: *the French version of your piece*: marginalium by Benjamin: 'Paralipomena'; p. 137: *Please write back soon . . . Wiesengrund*: handwritten PS; p. 137: *film of the Midsummer Night's Dream*: marginalium by Benjamin: 'Midsummer Night's Dream'.

50 WIESENGRUND-ADORNO TO BENJAMIN: OXFORD, 2.6.1936
SOURCE: O: Ms, postcard with printed letter-head, 2 sides; Literaturarchiv der Akademie der Künste, Berlin. – Sc: copy.

51 BENJAMIN TO WIESENGRUND-ADORNO: PARIS, 4.6.1936
SOURCE: O: Ms, 4 pp.; Theodor W. Adorno Archiv, Frankfurt a.M.

52 WIESENGRUND-ADORNO TO BENJAMIN: OXFORD, 16.6.1936
SOURCE: O: Ms with printed letter-head, 2 pp.; Literaturarchiv der Akademie der Künste, Berlin. – Sc: copy.

Textual Details: p. 141: *'He who quickly gives, gives twice as much'*: preceded by a word or fragment of a word, apparently crossed out, that is no longer legible. On the second page of the letter, back and front, Benjamin drafted a reply to the letter as follows [deletions and corrections omitted]: 'There is probably not much more to be hoped for. [par.] I have now asked Levy-Ginsburg to arrange a meeting between her and myself as soon as possible. [par.] . . . I cannot deny that all these matters make it seem doubly important for you to come. [par.] Yesterday I had a long conversation with . . . Groethuysen in which the business was largely clarified. Before a beginning is made with the translation, we shall have to deal with specific questions raised by the fact that the volume is being planned with French readers in mind. [par.] The work will basically be done by the beginning of July. [par.] . . . The order of the essays ch. . . . Problem . . . of the introduction [par.] I assume this is more important than the detailed questions of the translation, which should only be dealt with once the actual production volume is settled. I also think . . . that your participation in the production, from Max's point of view as well, . . . is more important than . . .' [Draft breaks off at this point.]

53 BENJAMIN TO WIESENGRUND-ADORNO: PARIS, 20.6.1936
SOURCE: O: Ts with handwritten PS, 3 pp.; Theodor W. Adorno Archiv, Frankfurt a.M.

Textual Details: p. 143: *PS . . . title of the book*: it is not absolutely certain that the PS, which is written on a separate sheet, belongs here.

54 BENJAMIN TO WIESENGRUND-ADORNO: PARIS, 30.6.1936
SOURCE: O: Tsc, 2 pp.; Literaturarchive der Akademie der Künste, Berlin.
– Sc: copy.

55 WIESENGRUND-ADORNO TO BENJAMIN: BERLIN, 6.9.1936
SOURCE: O: Ts/Ms, 2 pp.; Bibliothèque Nationale, Paris. – Sc: copy. Pp:
GS VII [2], 864; Adorno, *Über Walter Benjamin*, 2nd ed., 152–4.

Textual Details: p. 145: *This visit . . . most appropriate*: placed in brackets
by Benjamin.

56 BENJAMIN TO WIESENGRUND-ADORNO: SAN REMO, 27.9.1936
SOURCE: O: Ms, 2 pp.; Theodor W. Adorno Archiv, Frankfurt a.M.

57 WIESENGRUND-ADORNO TO BENJAMIN: OXFORD, 15.10.1936
SOURCE: O: Ms with printed letter-head, 4 pp.; Literaturarchive der Akademie
der Künste, Berlin. – Sc: copy.

Textual Details: the following names and words are all underlined by
Benjamin: p. 150: *Mahler . . . Worth . . . Noack . . . Kierkegaard . . . Hölderlin
. . . Valéry . . . Kaufmann . . . naturalization . . . military service*; p. 151:
uncomfortable . . . Max . . . Kracauer . . . Goldbeck.

58 WIESENGRUND-ADORNO TO BENJAMIN: OXFORD, 18.10.1936
SOURCE: O: Ms, postcard bearing the Coat of Arms of Merton College,
Oxford, 2 pp.; Literaturarchive der Akademie der Künste. Sc: copy.

59 BENJAMIN TO WIESENGRUND-ADORNO: PARIS, 19.10.1936
SOURCE: O: Ts, 2 pp.; Theodor W. Adorno Archiv, Frankfurt a.M.

60 BENJAMIN TO WIESENGRUND-ADORNO: PARIS, 26.10.1936
SOURCE: O: Ms, 2 pp.; Theodor W. Adorno Archiv, Frankfurt a.M.

61 BENJAMIN TO WIESENGRUND-ADORNO: PARIS, 5.11.1936
SOURCE: O: Ts, 2 pp.; Theodor W. Adorno Archiv, Frankfurt a.M.

62 WIESENGRUND-ADORNO TO BENJAMIN: OXFORD, 7.11.1936
SOURCE: O: Ts with handwritten corrections, 2 pp.; Literaturarchive der
Akademie der Künste, Berlin. – Sc: copy.

63 WIESENGRUND-ADORNO TO BENJAMIN: OXFORD, 28.11.1936
SOURCE: O: Ts with handwritten PS, 1 p.; Literaturarchive der Akademie der Künste, Berlin. – Sc: copy.

64 BENJAMIN TO WIESENGRUND-ADORNO: SAN REMO, 2.12.1936
SOURCE: O: Ms, 3 pp.; Theodor W. Adorno Archiv, Frankfurt a.M. – Pp: GS V [2], 1156.

65 BENJAMIN TO WIESENGRUND-ADORNO: PARIS, 29.1.1937
SOURCE: O: Ms, 2 pp.; Theodor W. Adorno Archiv, Frankfurt a.M. – Pp: GS II [3], 1328.

66 WIESENGRUND-ADORNO TO BENJAMIN: OXFORD, 17.2.1937
SOURCE: O: Ts with handwritten corrections, 1 p.; Literaturarchive der Akademie der Künste, Berlin. – Sc: copy. – Pp: GS II [3], 1328.

67 BENJAMIN TO WIESENGRUND-ADORNO: PARIS, 1.3.1937
SOURCE: O: MS, 4 pp.; Theodor W. Adorno Archiv, Frankfurt a.M. – Pp: GS II [3], 1329f; GS V [2], 1156f.

68 BENJAMIN TO WIESENGRUND-ADORNO: [PARIS,] 16.3.1937
SOURCE: O: Ts, 3 pp.; Literaturarchive der Akademie der Künste, Berlin. Sc: copy.

69 GRETEL KARPLUS AND WIESENGRUND-ADORNO TO BENJAMIN: WÜRZBURG, 31.3.1937
SOURCE: O: Ms, picture postcard of the *Haus zum Falken* at Würzburg; Literaturarchive der Akademie der Künste, Berlin. – Sc: copy. – Pp: GS II [3], 1341.

70 BENJAMIN TO WIESENGRUND-ADORNO: [PARIS,] 13.4.1937
SOURCE: O: Ms, 2 pp.; Theodor W. Adorno Archiv, Frankfurt a.M.

71 WIESENGRUND-ADORNO TO BENJAMIN: FRANKFURT A.M., 15.4.1937
SOURCE: O: Ms, postcard; Literaturarchive der Akademie der Künste, Berlin. Sc: copy.

72 WIESENGRUND-ADORNO TO BENJAMIN: OXFORD, 20.4.1937
SOURCE: O: Ts, 2 pp.; Literaturarchive der Akademie der Künste, Berlin. – Sc: copy.

73 BENJAMIN TO WIESENGRUND-ADORNO: PARIS, 23.4.1937
SOURCE: O: Ms, 3 pp.; Theodor W. Adorno Archiv, Frankfurt a.M. – Pp: GS I [3], 1067; GS II [3], 1342.

74 WIESENGRUND-ADORNO TO BENJAMIN: OXFORD, 25.4.1937
SOURCE: O: Ts with handwritten corrections; very faded ink in places; with jottings in Benjamin's hand; 2 pp.; Literaturarchive der Akademie der Künste, Berlin. – Sc: copy. – Pp: GS II [3], 1344.

Textual Details: at the foot of the second page, added in Benjamin's hand: 'Kracauer / Marcuse / Material situation / Jazz'.

75 BENJAMIN TO WIESENGRUND-ADORNO: PARIS, 1.5.1937
SOURCE: O: Ms, 2 pp.; Theodor W. Adorno Archiv, Frankfurt a.M. – Pp: GS I [3], 1068.

Textual details: a handwritten draft of the opening of this letter has also survived: 'Dear Teddy, / Above all I sincerely hope you are successful with the two-year visa. That way we shall certainly get to see one another before you leave for America! / I must begin these lines with an apology as far as the handwritten copy of your essay on jazz. I hope you have not been anxious about it; it is going off recorded delivery with this very post.'

76 WIESENGRUND-ADORNO TO BENJAMIN: OXFORD, 4.5.1937
SOURCE: O: Ms, postcard with printed letter-head, 2 pp.; Literaturarchive der Akademie der Künste, Berlin. – Sc: copy.

77 BENJAMIN TO WIESENGRUND-ADORNO: PARIS, 9.5.1937
SOURCE: O: Ms, 5 pp.; Theodor W. Adorno Archiv, Frankfurt a.M. – Pp: GS VII [2], 868.

78 WIESENGRUND-ADORNO TO BENJAMIN: OXFORD, 12.5.1937
SOURCE: O: Ts with handwritten corrections, 2 pp.; Literaturarchive der Akademie der Künste, Berlin. – Sc: copy. – Pp: GS I [3], 1068f.

79 WIESENGRUND-ADORNO TO BENJAMIN: OXFORD, 13.5.1937
SOURCE: O: Ts with handwritten corrections and PS, 1 p.; Bibliothèque Nationale, Paris. – Sc: copy. – Pp: GS VII [2], 869.

80 BENJAMIN TO WIESENGRUND-ADORNO: [PARIS,] 17.5.1937
SOURCE: O: Ms, 2 p.; Theodor W. Adorno Archiv, Frankfurt a.M. – Pp: GS I [3], 1069f.

81 BENJAMIN TO WIESENGRUND-ADORNO: PARIS, 15.6.1937
SOURCE: O: Ms, 2 pp.; Theodor W. Adorno Archiv, Frankfurt a.M. – Pp: GS II [3], 1346f.

82 WIESENGRUND-ADORNO TO BENJAMIN: NEW YORK, 17.6.1937
SOURCE: O: Ms with printed letter-head, 1 p.; Literaturarchive der Akademie der Künste, Berlin. – Sc: copy. – Pp: GS II [3], 1347.

83 WIESENGRUND-ADORNO TO BENJAMIN: ABOARD THE 'NORMANDIE', 2.7.1937
SOURCE: O: Ms with printed letter-head, 4 pp.; Literaturarchive der Akademie der Künste, Berlin. – Sc: copy. – Pp: GS I [3], 1070; GS II [3], 1347.

Textual Details: marginalium by Benjamin on the top left hand corner: 'Albemarle Court Hotel / 18 Leinster Gardens, London W2'.

84 BENJAMIN TO WIESENGRUND-ADORNO: SAN REMO, 10.7.1937
SOURCE: O: Ms, 4 pp.; Theodor W. Adorno Archiv, Frankfurt a.M. – Pp: GS I [3], 1070; GS II [3], 1348f.

85 BENJAMIN TO WIESENGRUND-ADORNO: [SAN REMO, C. MID JULY 1937]
SOURCE: O: Ms, 2 pp.; Theodor W. Adorno Archiv, Frankfurt a.M.

86 BENJAMIN TO WIESENGRUND-ADORNO: SAN REMO, 21.8.1937
SOURCE: O: Ms, 4 pp.; Theodor W. Adorno Archiv, Frankfurt a.M.

87 THEODOR AND GRETEL WIESENGRUND-ADORNO TO BENJAMIN: LONDON, 13.9.1937
SOURCE: O: Ts with printed letter-head and a handwritten addition by Gretel Adorno, 4 pp.; Literaturarchive der Akademie der Künste, Berlin. – Sc: copy. – Pp: GS I [3], 1070; GS II [3], 1349f.

88 WIESENGRUND-ADORNO TO BENJAMIN: LONDON, 22.9.1937
SOURCE: O: Ts with handwritten corrections and PS, small amount of text missing on the final page due to tearing, 3 pp.; Literaturarchive der Akademie der Künste, Berlin. – Sc: copy.

89 BENJAMIN TO THEODOR AND GRETEL WIESENGRUND-ADORNO:
PARIS, 23.9.1937
SOURCE: O: Ms, 5 pp.; Theodor W. Adorno Archiv, Frankfurt a.M. Pp:
GS II [3], 1350f.

90 BENJAMIN TO THEODOR AND GRETEL WIESENGRUND-ADORNO:
BOULOGNE SUR SEINE, 2.10.1937
SOURCE: O: Tsc, 2 pp.; Literaturarchive der Akademie der Künste, Berlin.
Sc: copy.

91 WIESENGRUND-ADORNO TO BENJAMIN: [LONDON,] 22.10.1937
SOURCE: O: Ts, 1 p.; Literaturarchive der Akademie der Künste, Berlin.
Sc: copy.

92 BENJAMIN TO WIESENGRUND-ADORNO: BOULOGNE SUR
SEINE, 2.11.1937
SOURCE: O: Ms, 6 pp.; Theodor W. Adorno Archiv, Frankfurt a.M. Pp:
GS II [3], 1352f.

93 BENJAMIN TO THEODOR AND GRETEL WIESENGRUND-ADORNO:
BOULOGNE SUR SEINE, 17.11.1937
SOURCE: O: Ms, 2 pp.; Theodor W. Adorno Archiv, Frankfurt a.M. Pp:
GS I [3], 1071; GS II [3], 1353.

94 WIESENGRUND-ADORNO TO BENJAMIN: [LONDON,] 27.11.1937
SOURCE: O: Ts with handwritten corrections, 4 pp.; Literaturarchive der
Akademie der Künste, Berlin. Sc: copy.

95 WIESENGRUND-ADORNO TO BENJAMIN: [LONDON,] 1.12.1937
SOURCE: O: Ts with handwritten corrections, 2 pp.; Literaturarchive der
Akademie der Künste, Berlin. Sc: copy.

96 BENJAMIN TO WIESENGRUND-ADORNO: BOULOGNE SUR
SEINE, 4.12.1937
SOURCE: O: Ms, 4 pp.; Theodor W. Adorno Archiv, Frankfurt a.M.

97 WIESENGRUND-ADORNO TO BENJAMIN: [LONDON,] 1.2.1938
SOURCE: O: Ts with handwritten addition by Gretel Adorno, 1 p.; Literaturarchive der Akademie der Künste, Berlin. Sc: copy.

98 BENJAMIN TO WIESENGRUND-ADORNO: PARIS, 11.2.1938
SOURCE: O: Ts with handwritten corrections, 2 pp.; Theodor W. Adorno Archiv, Frankfurt a.M.

99 THEODOR W. AND GRETEL ADORNO TO BENJAMIN:
[NEW YORK,] 7.3.1938
SOURCE: O: Ts with printed letter-head and handwritten corrections, 3 pp.; Literaturarchive der Akademie der Künste, Berlin. Sc: copy.

100 BENJAMIN TO THEODOR W. AND GRETEL ADORNO:
PARIS, 27.3.1938
SOURCE: O: Ts with handwritten corrections, 2 pp.; Theodor W. Adorno Archiv, Frankfurt a.M.

101 ADORNO TO BENJAMIN: [NEW YORK,] 8.4.1938
SOURCE: O: Ms, picture postcard: 'Gaston à la bonne soupe / typical Cafe & Restaurant as in Paris / Parisian atmosphere – Real French Cuisine / large assortment of Choice imported Wines / Aperitifs and Liquers. Private Dining Room / for Banquets and Weddings', with additional contributions by Gretel Adorno, Lotte Karplus and Egon Wissing; Literaturarchive der Akademie der Künste, Berlin. Sc: copy.
Contribution of Egon Wissing: 'Nothing is as good here as at Dagorno [?] – but the enchanting social life naturally compensates somewhat. Au revoir, Yours E, – (an answer to the letters will follow).'
Contribution of Lotte Karplus: 'Heartfelt Greetings, Yours, Lotte Karplus.'
Contribution of Gretel Adorno: 'Dear Detlef, what did you think of Elisabeth [Wiener]? Don't we* have good taste? Affectionately Felizitas.'
[Added in Egon Wissing's hand]: '*who are we?'

102 BENJAMIN TO THEODOR W. AND GRETEL ADORNO:
PARIS, 16.4.1938
SOURCE: O: Ts with handwritten corrections, 4 pp.; Theodor W. Adorno Archiv, Frankfurt a.M. Pp: GS I [3], 1075 and GS V [2], 1164f.

103 ADORNO TO BENJAMIN: [NEW YORK,] 4.5.1938
SOURCE: O: Ts with handwritten corrections and a handwritten addition by Gretel Adorno, together with underlinings by Benjamin, 6 pp.; Literaturarchive der Akademie der Künste, Berlin. Sc: copy. Pp: GS I [3], 1075.

Textual Details: in the top right hand margin of the first page in Benjamin's hand: 'Caillois: Praying Mantis'. The following words and phrases are

361

underlined by Benjamin: p. 248: *Scholem*; p. 250: *Leviathan dropping in on Behemoth . . . involved with the Institute . . . two ideas . . .* ; p. 251: *music and radio . . . Princeton University . . . chapters five to seven . . . the Baudelaire work . . . Sternberger . . . proceed tactically with regard to Wahl*; p. 252: *Professor Meyer Schapiro . . . 279 West 4th Street . . . Eisler.*

104 ADORNO TO BENJAMIN: [NEW YORK,] 8.6.1938
SOURCE: O: Ts with handwritten corrections and PS, 2 pp.; Literaturarchive der Akademie der Künste, Berlin. Sc: copy. Pp: GS I [3], 1077.

Textual Details: on the top right hand margin in Benjamin's hand: '45 Christopher / Street 11 G.'

105 BENJAMIN TO THEODOR W. AND GRETEL ADORNO:
PARIS, 19.6.1938
SOURCE: O: Ts with handwritten corrections, 7 pp.; Theodor W. Adorno Archiv, Frankfurt a.M. Pp: GS I [3], 1077.

106 THEODOR W. AND GRETEL ADORNO TO BENJAMIN:
BAR HARBOR, MAINE, 2.8.1938
SOURCE: O: Ts with handwritten corrections and an addition by Gretel Adorno, 4 pp.; Literaturarchive der Künste, Berlin. Pp: GS I [3], 1082.

107 THEODOR W. AND GRETEL ADORNO TO BENJAMIN,
WRITTEN ON A LETTER TO ADORNO FROM MEYER SCHAPIRO
AND PASSED ON BY THE RECIPIENT: [BAR HARBOR, MAINE,
C.12.8.1938.]
SOURCE: P: Ts/Ms, 2 pp.; Literaturarchive der Akademie der Künste, Berlin. Sc: copy. Pp: GS I [3], 1085.

Textual Details: p. 271: *Schapiro reads . . . Hell*: added by Adorno in the left hand margin of the second page.

108 BENJAMIN TO THEODOR W. AND GRETEL ADORNO:
SKOVSBOSTRAND, 28.8.1938
SOURCE: O: Ms, 5 pp.; Theodor W. Adorno Archiv, Frankfurt a.M. Pp: GS I [3], 1087.

109 BENJAMIN TO ADORNO: SKOVSBOSTRAND, 4.10.1938
SOURCE: O: Ms, 6 pp.; Theodor W. Adorno Archiv, Frankfurt a.M. Fp: *Briefe*, 776–9.

110 ADORNO TO BENJAMIN: [NEW YORK,] 10.11.1938
SOURCE: O: Ts with handwritten corrections, 6 pp.; Bibliothèque Nationale,
Paris. Sc: copy. Pp: *Briefe*, 782–90.

Textual Details: p. 287: *and night . . . flowery fields*: double marked by
Benjamin in the left hand margin.

111 BENJAMIN TO ADORNO: PARIS, 9.12.1938
SOURCE: O: Ts with handwritten corrections, 8 pp.; Theodor W. Adorno
Archiv, Frankfurt a.M. Pp: *Briefe*, 790–9.

112 ADORNO TO BENJAMIN: [NEW YORK,] 1.2.1939
SOURCE: O: Ts/Ms, 9 pp.; Bibliothèque Nationale, Paris. Sc: copy. Pp: Adorno,
Über Walter Benjamin, 1st ed., 147–56; 2nd ed., 165–73.

113 BENJAMIN TO ADORNO: PARIS, 23.2.1939
SOURCE: O: Ts with handwritten corrections, 6 pp.; Theodor W. Adorno
Archiv, Frankfurt a.M. Pp: *Briefe*, 805–9.

114 THEODOR W. AND GRETEL ADORNO TO BENJAMIN:
[NEW YORK,] 15.7.1939
SOURCE: O: Ts with handwritten corrections, 2 pp.; Literaturarchive der
Akademie der Künste, Berlin. Sc: copy.

115 BENJAMIN TO THEODOR W. AND GRETEL ADORNO:
PARIS, 6.8.1939
SOURCE: O: Ts with handwritten corrections and PS, 3 pp.; Theodor W.
Adorno Archiv, Frankfurt a.M. Fp: *Briefe*, 823–5.

116 GRETEL AND THEODOR W. ADORNO TO BENJAMIN:
[NEW YORK,] 21.11.1939
SOURCE: O: Ms, postcard, 2 pp.; Literaturarchive der Akademie der Künste,
Berlin. Sc: copy. Pp: GS I [3], 1127.

117 ADORNO TO BENJAMIN: [NEW YORK,] 29.2.1940
SOURCE: O: Ts with handwritten corrections, together with marginalia and
underlinings in Benjamin's hand, 4 pp.; Literaturarchive der Akademie der
Künste, Berlin. Sc: copy. Pp: Adorno, *Über Walter Benjamin*, 1st ed., 157–
61; 2nd ed., 174–7.

Textual Details: p. 319: *improve . . . I think*: heavily underlined marginalium by Benjamin in the left hand margin: 'Consulate'; p. 320: *Indeed I can say . . . reflex character*: underlined marginalium by Benjamin: 'Fetish character'; the following words and phrases underlined by Benjamin: p. 320: *piece on fetishism . . . didn't really appeal to you . . . madeleine . . .* ; p. 321: *a distinction between good and bad reification . . . introduction to the letter from Kant's brother . . . Is not the aura inevitably a trace of a forgotten human moment in the thing? . . .* ; p. 322: *Maupassant . . . Radio Project . . . Rickert's posthumously published book . . . Kierkegaard's Religious Discourses . . .* ; p. 323: *Morgenstern*; p. 324: *English lessons.*

118 BENJAMIN TO ADORNO: PARIS, 7.5.1940
SOURCE: O: Ts with handwritten corrections, 15 pp.; Theodor W. Adorno Archiv, Frankfurt a.M. Pp: *Briefe*, 848–57.

119 ADORNO TO BENJAMIN: NEW YORK, 16.7.1940
SOURCE: O: Tsc, 1 p.; Theodor W. Adorno Archiv, Frankfurt a.M. Fp: *Benjamin-Katalog*, 306.

120 BENJAMIN TO ADORNO: LOURDES, 2.8.1940
SOURCE: O: Ms, 4 pp.; Theodor W. Adorno Archiv, Frankfurt a.M. Fp: *Die Neunzehn. Texte und Informationen*, 1964, 9–11.

121 BENJAMIN TO HENNY GURLAND [AND ADORNO?]: [PORT BOU, 25.9.1940]
SOURCE: O: Ms Henny Gurland, 1 p.; Theodor W. Adorno Archiv, Frankfurt a.M. Fp: GS V [2], 1203.

Bibliographical Index

~∞~

The following index of the writings of Adorno and Benjamin refers directly to the text of the correspondence itself, whereas the general index of names also refers to the editor's annotations. Page references in brackets indicate disguised or less-than-obvious mention of works. The list of Adorno's writings also includes the fragmentary version of his projected 'Theory of Musical Reproduction' and the hitherto unpublished book project entitled 'Current of Music'; the list of Benjamin's writings includes references, under the title of 'The Arcades', to the various notes and manuscripts relevant to this project.

1 Adorno's Works and Writings

The Actuality of Philosophy
[ET: 'The Actuality of Philosophy' [*Die Aktualität der Philosophie*], *Telos* 31 (1977), pp. 120–30] (8–9), (12)

Analyses of the Musical Commodity [*Musikalische Warenanalysen*]. *See* New Analyses of Popular Songs

Analytical Study of the NBC Music Appreciation Hour [Current of Music] (251), (322)

Beethoven's Late Style [*Spätstil Beethovens*] 38, 159, 220, 223

Ludwig van Beethoven: Six Bagatelles for Piano, op. 126 [*Ludwig van Beethoven: Sechs Bagatellen für Klavier, op. 126*] 38

The Berg Monograph: Alban Berg. With Berg's Writings and Contributions by Theodor W. Adorno and Ernst Krenek, edited by Willi Reich.
[ET: T. W. Adorno: *Alban Berg: Master of the Smallest Link* [*Alban Berg. Mit Bergs eigenen Schriften und Beiträgen von Theodor Wiegengrund-Adorno und Ernst Krenek*], trans. Julian Brand and Christopher Hailey (Cambridge:

Kierkegaard. Construction of the Aesthetic
[ET: T. W. Adorno: *Kierkegaard: Construction of the Aesthetic* [*Kierkegaard. Konstruktion des Ästhetischen*], trans. Robert Hullot-Kentor (Cambridge, Mass.: MIT Press, 1993)]   (7), 19, 20–1, 22, 24, 26, 47, 50, 51, 67, 68, 84, 92, 106, 109, 111, 113, 150, 247, (248), 274, 278, 292, 312, 322

On Kierkegaard's Doctrine of Love
[Published in English: *see* 'On Kierkegaard's Doctrine of Love' [*Kierkegaards Lehre von der Liebe*], in *Studies in Philosophy and Social Science* 8, issue 3 (1939), pp. 413–29]   322

Kracauer, Siegfried: Jacques Offenbach und das Paris seiner Zeit (Review)   209, 238

Krenek: On the New Music [*Krenek, Ernst, Über neue Musik*] (Review)   (181), 209

On the Lulu Sumphony (*Zur Lulu-Symphonie*] (Berg)   (125–6)

'Mannheim piece'. *See* The New Value-Free Sociology

Marginalia on Mahler [*Marginalien zu Mahler*]   135, 140, 150, 160

The Metacritique of Epistemology. Studies on Husserl and the Phenomenological Antinomies
[ET: T. W. Adorno: *Against Epistemology* [*Zur Metakritik der Erkenntnistheorie. Studien über Husserl und die phänomenologischen Antinomien*], trans. Willis Domingo (Oxford: Blackwell, 1982)]   55, (63), 78, (83), (85), (91), 100, (102), (123), (127), (135–6), (140), (147), (150), (162), (167), (174), (176), (181), (183), (210)

Motifs III [*Motive III*]   (4–5)

Music in Radio [Current of Music]   (240), (251), 261

The Natural History of the Theatre [*Naturgeschichte des Theaters*]   15

A Note on Sameness [*Notiz über Gleichmacherei*]   (71)

A Note on Travellers' Tickets [*Notiz über Fahrscheinmodelle*]   71, 75

New Analyses of Popular Songs [*Neue Schlageranalysen*]   (271), (322)

New Tempi [*Neue Tempi*]   38

The New Value-Free Sociology
[ET of revised version: 'The Sociology of Knowledge and Its Consciousness' [*Neue wertfreie Soziologie*], in T. W. Adorno: *Prisms*, trans. Samuel and Shierry Weber (Cambridge, Mass.: MIT Press, 1981), pp. 35–49]   55, 59, 162, 166–7, 168–9, (170), 177, 208, 213, 220, 224, 230, 241, 255

Night Music [*Nachtmusik*]   38

On the Use of Loan Words [*Über den Gelorauch von Fremdwörtern*]   38, 46

2 Walter Benjamin's Works and Writings

On Some Themes in Baudelaire
[ET: 'Some Motifs in Baudelaire' [*Über einige Motive bei Baudelaire*], in Walter Benjamin, *Illuminations*, pp. 157–202; translation reprinted in Walter Benjamin, *Charles Baudelaire*, pp. 107–54]   309, 311, 313, 316–17, 318, 319–22, 326, 331

Unpacking My Library. On Collecting.
[ET: 'Unpacking My Library' [*Ich packe meine Bibliothek aus. Eine Rede über das Sammeln*], in Walter Benjamin, *Illuminations*, pp. 59–67]   (12–13)

What is Epic Theatre?
[ET: 'What is Epic Theatre' [*Was ist das epische Theatre?*], in Walter Benjamin, *Illuminations*, pp. 149–56]   49, 51

The Wild Otter (A Berlin Childhood) [*Der Fischatter (Berliner Kindheit)*] (43)

The Work of Art in the Age of Mechanical Reproduction
[ET: 'The Work of Art in the Age of Mechanical Reproduction' [*Das Kunstwerk im Zeitalter seiner technischen Reproduzier barkeit*], in Walter Benjamin, *Illuminations*, pp. 219–53]   (122), (123–4), (125), (127–33), (135), (136–7), (139–40), (144), 147, (154), 213, 218, 245, 252, (266), (295), (305)

Name Index

~∞~

Notes: (1) Page references in roman type relate to the text itself (including preliminaries and Afterword), those in italic to notes. As in the bibliographical index, those page references in brackets indicate disguised reference to a person (through a book title, allusion, etc.). (2) ä is interfiled with ae, ö with oe, ü with ue. Thus, for example, Schoen, Johanna is followed by Schönberg, Arnold; Buck-Morss, Susan is followed by Büchner, Georg.

Compiled by Timothy Penton